IF
DATA PARROTS WHISPER VITAL INFORMATION

THEN

THE PECKING ORDER WILL CHANGE

IF
CAN'T
AALTO
TRUST

THEN
THEY WANT RELATIONSHIP TECHNOLOGIES

Getting On! pages 40 - 57

IF

COMPANIES ARE GOING TO FACE UP TO INCREASING COMPLEXITY

-Free to do as you like, you randomly decide that page 7 will be the same as page 4, and page 8 the same as page 9,

Then:

Pierre Bismuth. If/Then January 1999. Page 7

KINDERGARTEN

ALS/DAN

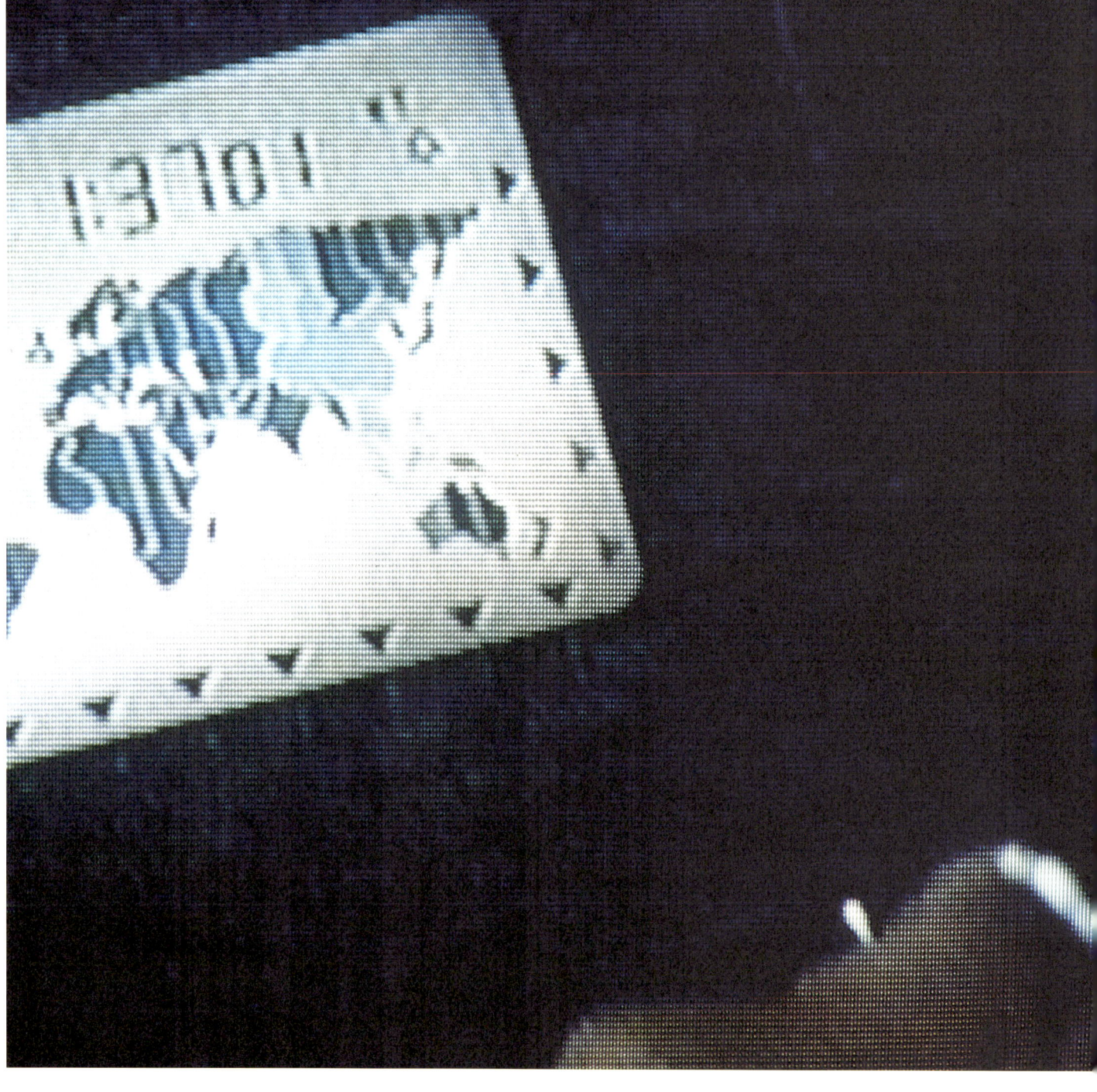

A few years ago, in the pioneer days of 'Silicon Alley', a group of New York new media designers and critics gathered regularly to discuss this emerging field. The Digital Algonquin, as we called it, met both face-to-face and online; postings to *thelist@avsi.com* were lively and contentious. In an early thread about our diverse educational backgrounds, one participant made mention of 'if/then conditionals' in the course of a riff about his Montessori schooling.

For some reason, 'if/then' lit up my screen: here was the title for a journal! We did indeed talk of starting one, but the pressures of the burgeoning new media industry left little time for reflection and the Digital Algonquin gradually dissipated, leaving lasting friendships but, until now, no publication.

It has taken a while and a change of continents to realise *If/Then*, which is published from the Netherlands Design Institute in Amsterdam. This 'think-and-do tank' has investigated 'the design implications of new media' during its five years of existence, under its 'Connectivity' theme.

The main business of the Netherlands Design Institute is to test ideas about the kinds of design that might be desirable and necessary in diverse social, economic and technological conditions. The Institute also looks at how design practice is being transformed by these evolving circumstances.

A knowledge-gathering forum, we think of *If/Then* as a 'yearbook of the near future' that asks 'if/then' questions about the impact of new technologies on contemporary culture, and vice versa. *If/Then* looks at notions of 'new' media in a longer historical time-frame than just 'since the advent of the World Wide Web'.

This issue divides into four sections. The first examines the European Union's i^3 program, which involves over 100 organisations in projects to develop 'intelligent information interfaces' to improve the lives of ordinary people, rather than simply those of globe-trotting symbolic analysts.

The second section covers the Netherlands Design Institute's 1998 *Getting On!* seminars, which examined the everyday outposts of the 'Information Revolution' — the efflorescence of interfaces from the body to the city. The third addresses various recent Dutch design and new media initiatives.

The fourth section is devoted to Play, complementing the Netherlands Design Institute's fifth *Doors of Perception* conference, held in November 1998, which asked such questions as: How can we design play into tomorrow's learning? Is there a role for play in business? What kinds of play are emerging from hybrids of 'old' and 'new' media?

With essays by *Doors* speakers and many others, plus several specially-commissioned visual portfolios, this issue of *If/Then* covers many topics: board games and playground rites; streetplay and toy emporia; the earliest keyboard instruments and the latest LEGO; computer games set in outer space, and a dance performance inspired by *Tomb Raider* heroine Lara Croft. Here are a baseball game played with a deck of cards, a football game played with two balls, and a discussion about *Solitaire* as an addiction. The only doll featured is an electronically-controlled 'infant simulator' — part of the recent wave of inanimate devices (post-Tamagotchi) whose digital souls call forth our caring instincts. Just how different *is* a Baby Think It Over doll from a Palm Pilot? Several themes recur: the educational play-value of building blocks, whether wooden, plastic or digital; the virtues of the manual; and keyboard skills, musical as well as electronic.

If/Then is about many scales of communication and their design: from a thousand-seater conference to a campfire discussion, from an interview to a conversation muttered over mobile phones.

This journal has been hugely enriched by the contributions of its art directors, Mevis and Van Deursen, not just in terms of its layout, but also by their suggestions for specific subjects. Without Julia van Mourik, my assistant editor, who joined me in July 1998, *If/Then* would not have progressed beyond the wish-list which it constituted at that time. To all three, I say: *Dank je wel.*

This journal is dedicated with gratitude in memory of my mentor and beloved friend, Steven J. Groák, 1944-1998, who (as usual) understood what this project was about before I did, and encouraged me to stick with it.

Janet Abrams
Editor

| 13 | **If/Then
Introduction**
Janet Abrams | 14
15 | **European Union's i³
Map**
LUST
Introduction
John Thackara | 25
26
27
28
33
34
35
36 | **European Union's i³
Amusement
Campiello
Comris
Presence
Populate
Persona
eRena
Maypole**
Andrea Moed | 38 | **European Union's i³
Europe's Virtual
Media Lab**
Andrea Moed |

| 40
42 | **Getting On!
1 furNETure**
public access to the
Internet
Ineke Schwartz | 47 | **Getting On!
2 DataButlers**
portable digital
assistants
Nico Macdonald | 51

54 | **Getting On!
3 Bread/Circuits**
smartcards, ATMs
and *Microwave Banks*
Jules Marshall
From Touch to Hold
Sarah Woods at the
NCR Knowledge Lab
J.J. King | 58 | **Knowledge Maps
Knowledge Maps**
knowledge
managers meet
interaction designers
Marek Kohn |

| | **Knowledge Maps**
66 **Perspecta**
68 **Dynamic Diagrams**
70 **i/o360/Rare Medium**
Marek Kohn
72 **Meaningful Space**
Yuri Engelhardt | 75

83 | **No Image
No Message**
Martijn Sandberg
Tracks
Max Bruinsma | 84 | **P/reviews
Melting Media**
Exploding Cinema
1999 International
Film Festival
Rotterdam
Femke Wolting | 86 | **P/reviews
Anatomy Lessons**
Shu Lea Cheang's
Brandon in New York
and Amsterdam
Dick van Dijk
Peter Hall |

| 90 | **P/reviews
Strange Enough
Already**
*Do Normal: Recent
Dutch Design*
Max Kisman | 96 | **P/reviews
Holland's Virtual
Platform**
Real Progress in
Dutch Media Culture
Cathy Brickwood | 100 | **Audition**
Sharon Lockhart | 112 | **Play
The Rules of the
Game**
Boardgames
Eric Zimmerman |

| 118 | **Play
Pauline Thinks It
Over**
babysitting an
'infant simulator'
Pauline Bax | 124 | **Play
Games Children
Play**
Iona Opie: *doyenne*
of playground rites
and rituals
Matilda Blyth | 132 | **Play
Discovery in Digital
Craft**
Malcolm McCullough | 140 | **Play
Photo Play**
Helen Levitt's eye on
children's street play
Susan Delson |

152	Huts Johannes Schwartz	160	**Play** **Web Word War** Craighead & Thomson's *Trigger Happy* J.J. King	162	**Play** **Toy Storeys** Toys'R'Us vs Store of Knowledge J.C. Herz	170	**Play** **Bricks with Brains** the making of the new LEGO Janet Abrams
176	**Play** **Ideologists at Play** Abbatt Toys: an education in wood Hannah Ford	180	**Play** **Lara Joins the Corps** what computer games can teach modern dance Paul Groot	186	**Play** **Action Baseball** Paul Auster	196	**Play** **Demi Dubbel** a Dutch wired classroom adventure Pauline Bax
198	**Play** **Why the Computer Revolution Hasn't Happened Yet** Alan Kay	206	**Play** **Remote/Involved** computer games vs the Space Race Alex Wilkie Noortje Marres **timeline design** Maureen Mooren Daniël van der Velden	218	**A Few Free Years** videogames at the Vienna Secession Jason Rhoades	220	IF PIERRE BISMUTH THEN JEREMY MILLAR
222	**Play** **Toys Were Us** Pieter Bruegel's *Kinderspelen* 1560 Michiel Schwarz	226	**Union Rave** Andreas Gursky	228	**Play** **Three Mouseketeers** IJsfontein design a TV/Internet game Ine Poppe	233 245	**A User's Guide** Uri Tzaig Danny Goldberg **Other Victories** Janet Abrams
252	**Play** **Long Lake III** toys vs tools a roundtable discussion	217	**Play** **Finger on the Button** Bas Ording's interface design Ine Poppe	7 8 31 32 63 64 97 98 185 186	Pierre Bismuth	260 264	**Go/To** **biographies and resources colophon**

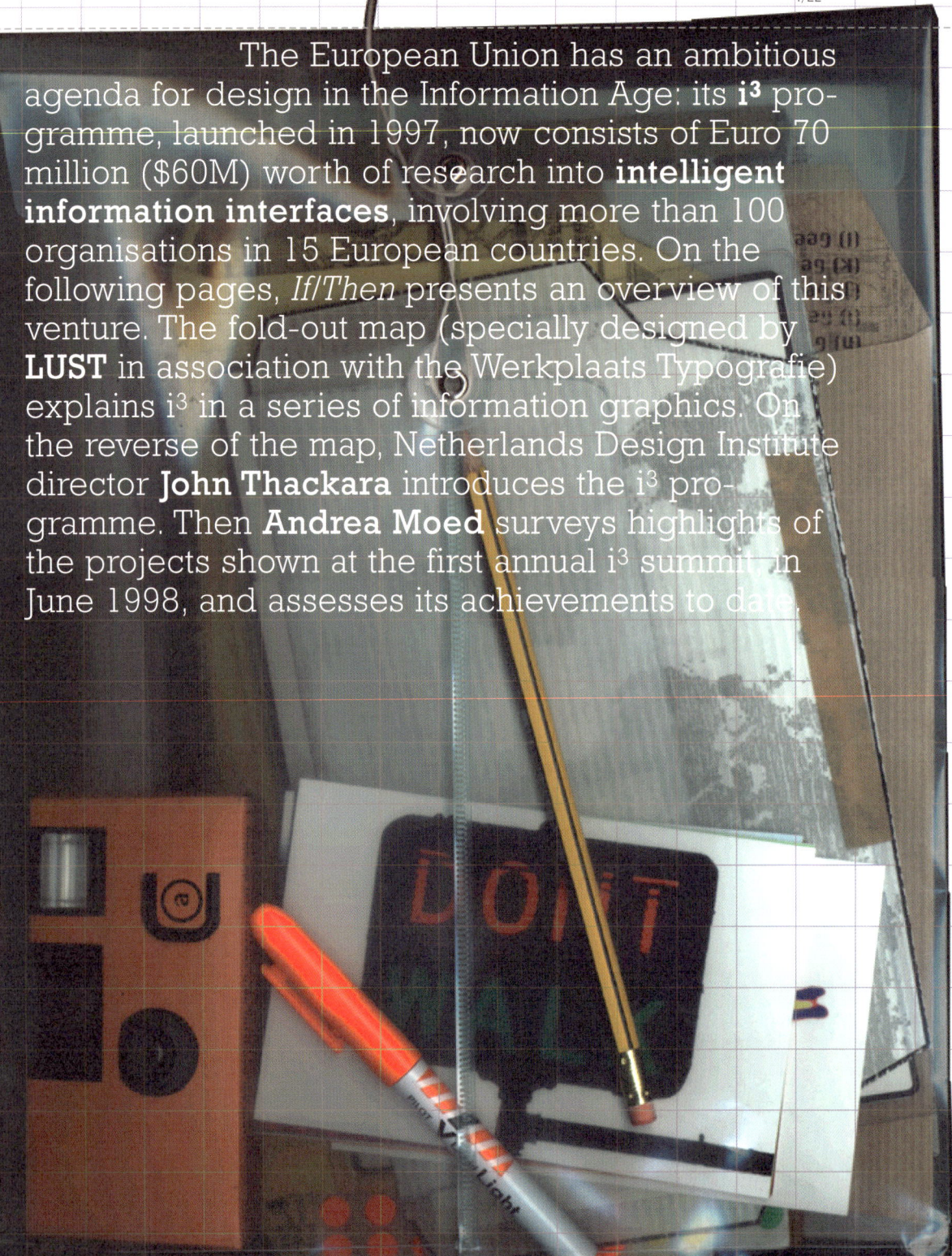

The European Union has an ambitious agenda for design in the Information Age: its **i³** programme, launched in 1997, now consists of Euro 70 million ($60M) worth of research into **intelligent information interfaces**, involving more than 100 organisations in 15 European countries. On the following pages, *If/Then* presents an overview of this venture. The fold-out map (specially designed by **LUST** in association with the Werkplaats Typografie) explains i³ in a series of information graphics. On the reverse of the map, Netherlands Design Institute director **John Thackara** introduces the i³ programme. Then **Andrea Moed** surveys highlights of the projects shown at the first annual i³ summit, in June 1998, and assesses its achievements to date.

A PACKET OF **PRESENCE** 'CULTURAL PROBES'

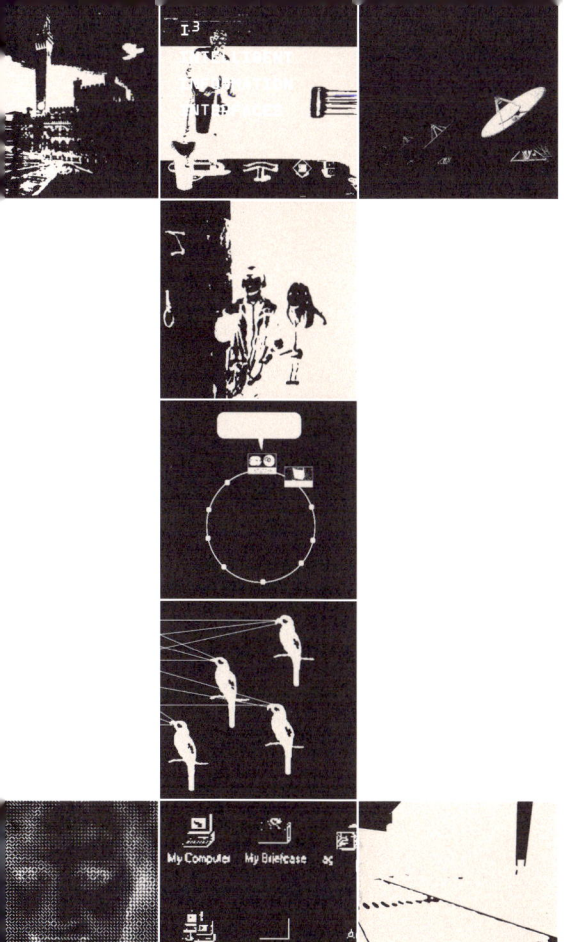
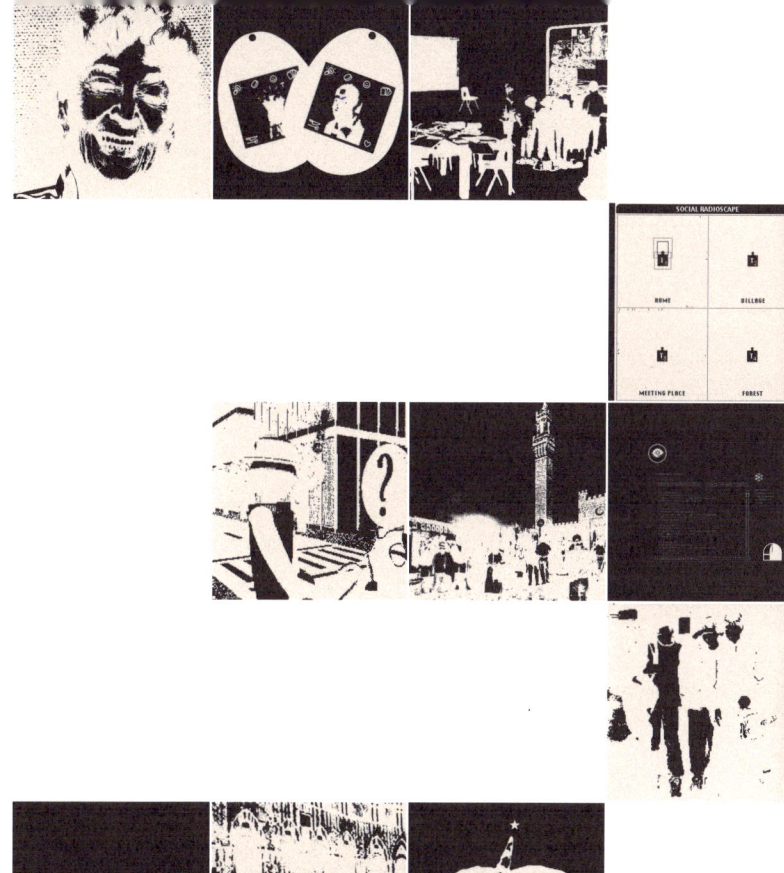

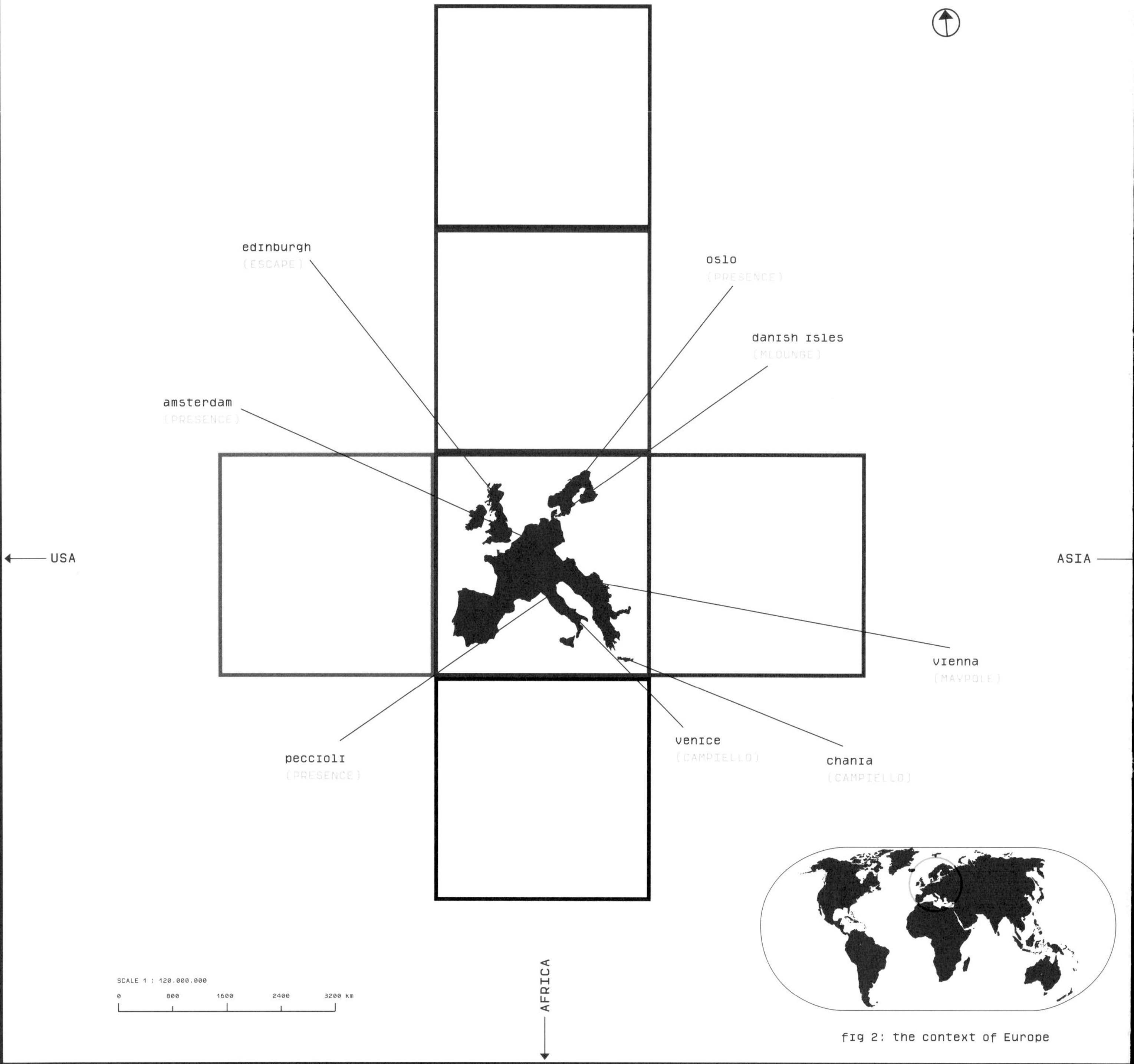

edinburgh
(ESCAPE)

oslo
(PRESENCE)

danish isles
(MLOUNGE)

amsterdam
(PRESENCE)

← USA

ASIA →

vienna
(MAYPOLE)

peccioli
(PRESENCE)

venice
(CAMPIELLO)

chania
(CAMPIELLO)

SCALE 1 : 120.000.000
0   800   1600   2400   3200 km

↓ AFRICA

fig 2: the context of Europe

fig 1: I³ geography showing physical sites of project case-studies

fig 3: fig 1 as a cube, seen from the left

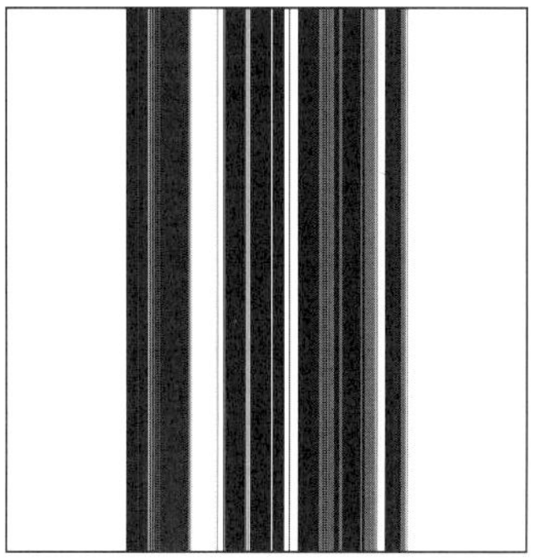

fig 4: fig 1 as a cube, seen from above

fig 5: fig 1 as a cube, seen from the right

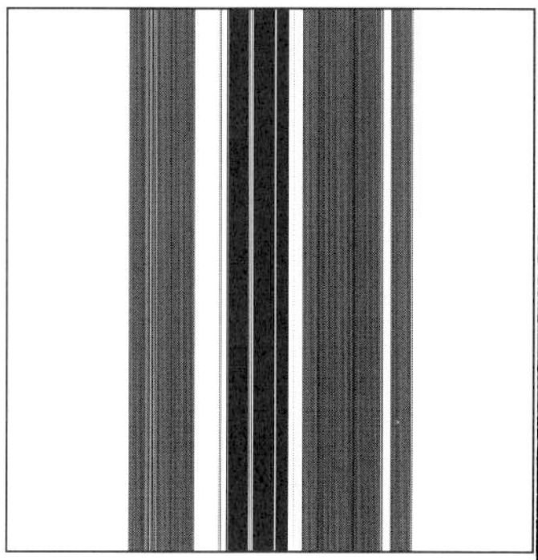

fig 6: fig 1 as a cube, seen from the bottom

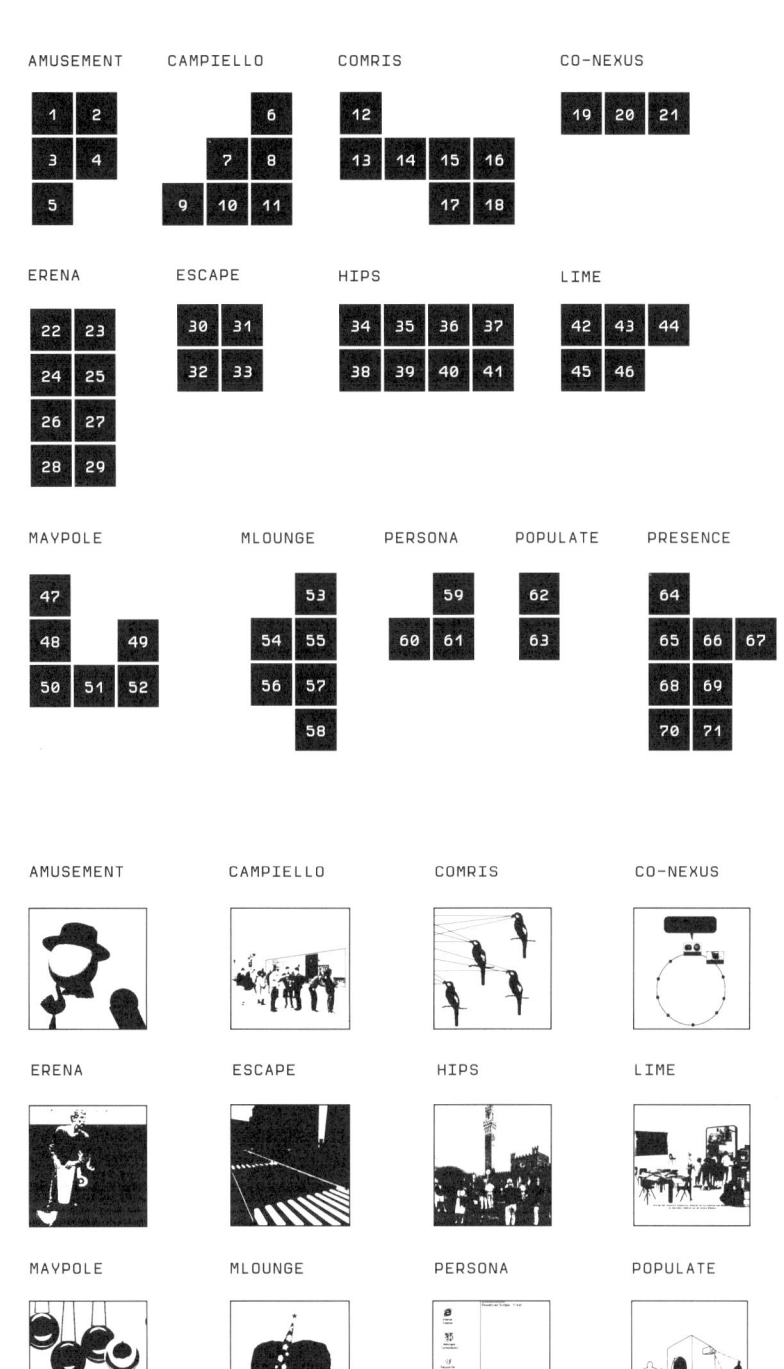

fig 12 [above]: i³ project consortia   fig 13 [below]: sample design proposals

CONNECTIONS OF INSTITUTIONS

AMUSEMENT
01. Universidad Politecnica de Madrid
02. Instituto Europeo de Transferencia de Tecnología (IETT) (Madrid)
03. Roma Ricerche (Rome)
04. Skydata (Rome)
05. Telecom-Bretagne (Brest)

CAMPIELLO
06. University of Milan
07. Domus Academy (Milan)
08. FORTHnet - Hellenic Telecommunications & Telematics Application Company
09. Municipality of Chania
10. Technical University of Crete (Chania)
11. Xerox Research Centre Europe (Meylan, France)

COMRIS
12. Vrije Universiteit, Brussels
13. GMD - Forschungszentrum Informationstechnik GmbH (Sankt Augustin)
14. Institut d'Investigació en Intelligència Artificial (IIIA - CSIC) (Blanes Catalonia)
15. IPO - Center for Research on User-System Interaction
16. Starlab - Riverland Research (Zaventem, Belgium)
17. The University of Reading
18. Universität Dortmund

CO-NEXUS
19. Public Library of Turnhout (Belgium)
20. ACS-Interactive Media Research & Projects (Amsterdam)
21. Linc vzw (Leuven)

ERENA
22. Royal Institute of Technology (KTH) (Stockholm)
23. British Telecom Laboratories (Ipswich)
24. Ecole Polytechnique Federale de Lausanne (EPFL)
25. GMD - Forschungszentrum Informationstechnik GmbH (Sankt Augustin)
26. Illuminations Ltd (London)
27. University of Geneva
28. University of Nottingham
29. ZKM Zentrum für Kunst und Medientechnologie (Karlsruhe)

ESCAPE
30. Lancaster University (UK)
31. Swedish Institute of Computer Science (SICS) (Stockholm)
32. The Victoria University of Manchester
33. ZKM Zentrum für Kunst und Medientechnologie (Karlsruhe)

HIPS
34. Università degli Studi di Siena
35. Alcatel Italia (Florence)
36. Cara Broadbent & Jegher Associes (Paris)
37. GMD -Forschungszentrum Informationstechnik GmbH

I³: FROM SCIENCE FICTION

With a current budget of €70 million/ $60 million, the European Union's I³ program involves more than 100 industrial, technological, design and academic organisations based all round Europe. John Thackara introduces this major long-term research venture, whose thirteen consortium projects aim to develop new paradigms for 'Intelligent Information Interfaces' that meet real social needs.

In thermodynamics when a system becomes disengaged from its context and runs out of energy, the condition is called entropy.

Entropy afflicts a lot of design 'research' today. Even though the world is changing in profound and exciting ways, a generation of young designers is missing out on meaningful interaction with industry and society. Too many design schools and professional organisations are more interested in protecting professional turf than in exploring new challenges in the world at large.

The industrial research situation is not much better. Some $160 billion is spent each year on research and development by companies and governments in industrialised countries — but less than five per cent, by some estimates, ends up as a product or service that someone can buy. The reason is the same as for design: research is disengaged from its context. The majority of industrial research and development (r&d) is driven by a frantic scampering after technological Holy Grails — not by an exploration of changing social needs.

PEOPLE ARE SOCIAL

This is where I³ comes in. I³, which stands for Intelligent Information Interfaces, seeks new ways to enhance communication and information exchange among people in their everyday lives. I³ is a next-generation research and innovation programme, funded by the Long-Term Research division of ESPRIT, the European Commission's telematics programme, and by European industry. Launched in Autumn 1997, I³ consisted by the beginning of 1999 of seventy million Euros ($60m) of research involving 300 researchers, and more than 100 organisations, in 15 European countries. This unique network includes big telecommunication companies, small manufacturing enterprises, national universities, media centres and design research organisations. (The Netherlands Design Institute is managing two I³ projects, PRESENCE, and MAYPOLE)

NEW TOOLS, NEW MARKETS

What, you may ask, do they all do? In short, I³ develops scenarios and pilot projects for new services in travel, education, entertainment, news and information, health care, social interaction, and trade — all of them markets being transformed by information technology. From play and learning in childhood, through new forms of work as adults, to self-help in old-age, tremendous opportunities are opening up for new forms of technologically-enhanced communication and community. The role of I³ is to help companies and other organisations exploit these opportunities — and to develop new innovation techniques so they can continue to do so.

I³ projects are currently grouped in three clusters:
CONNECTED COMMUNITY
INHABITED INFORMATION SPACES
EXPERIMENTAL SCHOOL ENVIRONMENTS

CONNECTED COMMUNITY projects explore the situated use of information by communities of ordinary people; future service and technologies to enhance social interaction; devices to help children and adults stay in contact.

INHABITED INFORMATION SPACES projects examine new ways to embody information, and support virtual communities; new ways of managing access to online resources; new forms of interactive television; new forms of community participation.

EXPERIMENTAL SCHOOL ENVIRONMENTS investigates learning environments of the future for four to eight-year-old children, and their teachers and parents; visualisation of ecological processes; sound and gesture interfaces. (ESE projects are not indicated on this map, since they were only launched in 1998) >>

CONTACTS

ESPRIT, LONG TERM RESEARCH
contact: Jakub Wejchert
<Jakub.Wejchert@dg3.cec.be>
Av des Nerviens 105 6/42
B 1040 Brussels, Belgium
phone: +32 2 2968032
fax: +32 2 2968397
http://www.cordis.lu/esprit

I³ NET COORDINATION SITE
contact: Niels Ole Bernsen
<nob@mip.ou.dk>
The Maersk Mc-Kinney Moller
Institute for Production
Technology, Odense University
Science Park 10
5230 Odense M, Denmark
phone: +45 65 573544
fax: +45 63 157224
http://www.mip.ou.dk
Secretary Merete Bertelsen
phone: +45 65 573551

AMUSEMENT
contact: Javier Segovia
<fsegovia@fi.upm.es>
Facultad de Informatica, Dept.
Lenguajes y Sistemas
Informaticos e Ingenieria del
Software
Campus de Montegancedo,
Boadilla del Monte
E-28660 Madrid, Spain
phone: +34 91 3367402
fax: +34 91 3367412
http://asterix.fi.upm.es/~amuse/amusement

CAMPIELLO
contact: Alessandra Agostini
<agostini@dsi.unimi.it>
Dept. of Computer Science,
Laboratory of Cooperation
Technologies, Via Comelico 39
I-20135 Milan, Italy
phone: +39 2 55006313
fax: +39 2 55006276
http://www.dsi.unimi.it/~campiello

COMRIS
contact: Walter Van de Velde
<wvdv@starlab.net>
Starlab - Riverland Research
Research Laboratories
Excelsiorlaan 42
B-1930 Zaventem, Belgium
phone: +32 2 7215454
fax: +32 2 7215380
http://www.starlab.net

CO-NEXUS
contact: Luc Mertens
<bibliotheek@turnhout.be>
Warandestraat 42
B-2300 Turnhout, Belgium
phone: +32 14 419494
fax: +32 14 420821
http://www.conexus.org

ERENA
contact: Yngve Sundblad
<yngve@nada.kth.se>
Numerical Analysis and Computing
Science (NADA), Valhallavägen 79
S-10044 Stockholm, Sweden
phone: +46 8 7907147
fax: +46 8 7900930
http://www.nada.kth.se/erena

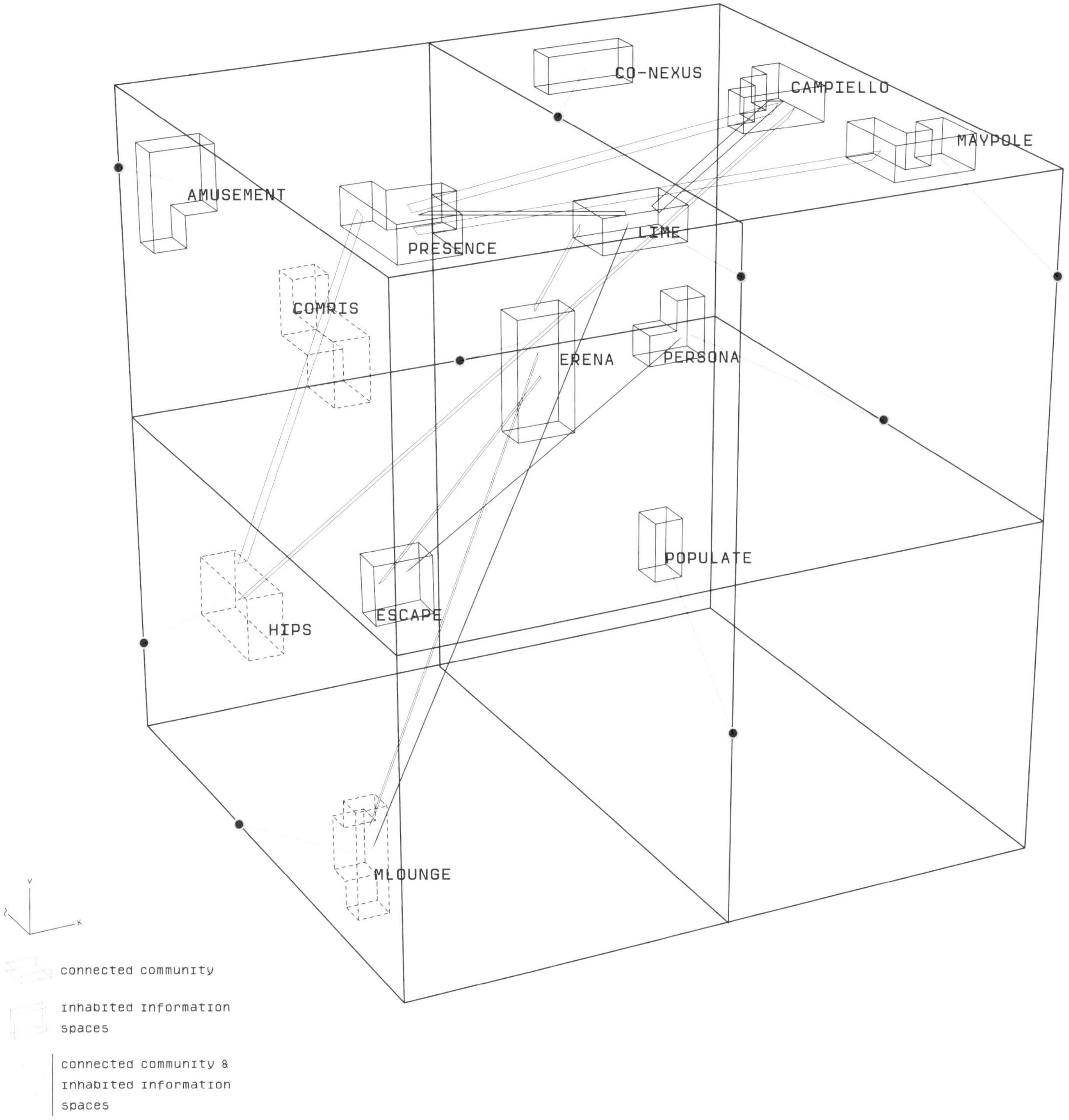

connected community

inhabited information
spaces

connected community &
inhabited information
spaces

fig 7: I³ projects showing connections

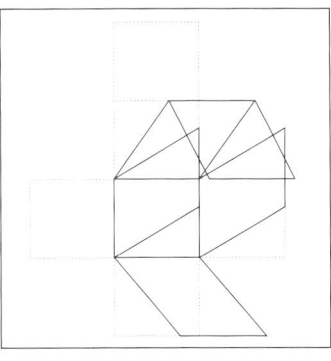

fig 8: fig 1 in motion to a cube

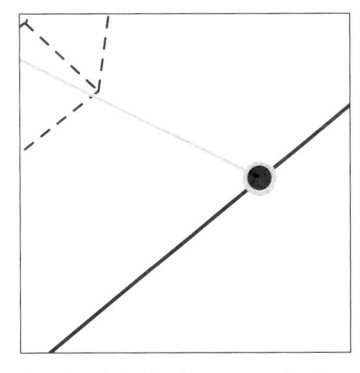

fig 9: detail showing virtual
site of project case study

fig 10: connections between
project consortia

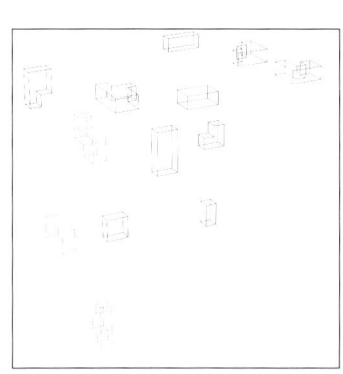

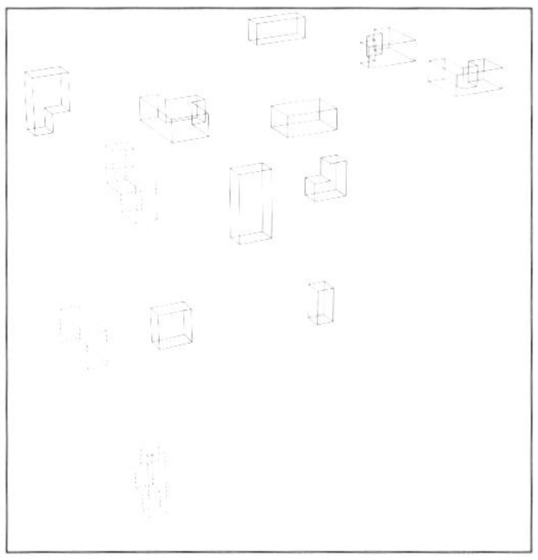

fig 11: project consortia

TO SOCIAL FICTION

>> NEW INTERACTION PARADIGMS

I³ projects move beyond conventional thinking on interaction design exhibited in today's consumer electronic products and personal computers. Among the novel interaction scenarios for devices and media already emerging from I³ projects are:

- new forms of social communication in homes, museums, streets, cafés, cars, schools
- broadcast television linked to interactive local content
- new sensorial tools for children to tell stories and share experiences
- wireless devices to connect children and parents
- wearable agents
- interest-based physical navigation devices
- public information systems around the city
- techniques to map and visualise information flows in a community
- interfaces for specific users — elderly, children, computer novices
- avatar-inhabited television
- way-finding, exploration and social interaction within information spaces
- new forms of social interaction such as collective memories, oral/digital storytelling

REAL-TIME, REAL WORLD

Industrial members of I³ are encouraged to see their consortium as an extension of their in-house research and development — and so far, the response from companies taking part has been very positive. The reason: in I³, know-'how' is given as much emphasis as know-'what'— and the network emphasizes rapid uptake of ideas, concepts and innovation processes. The thinking is that ideas should be exploited as close to real-time as possible — not, as in traditional academic research, at the end of an endlessly long publishing process. (Academic papers can take three years to see the light of day; in I³, three months to publication is the normal time horizon).

Finding unexpected new partners has proved to be an extra benefit for companies in I³, prompting the founders of I³ to consider broadening the range and mix of companies involved. During 1999, a new entity will be created for research and marketing managers in large corporations; visionaries developing new business concepts and alliances; entrepreneurs from dynamic small enterprises; and modernising managers from the public sector. These new industrial members will be offered rapid access to I³ research results, and to the innovation processes by which these results are achieved. Value will be added further by the exploration — in collaboration with Europe's leading business schools — of business scenarios and new value chains, so as to test the commercial potential of new service concepts as they emerge.

The research agenda of the enlarged I³ will constitute a series of thematic domains rather than a list of projects. The identification of research topics and innovative research methodologies are learning processes in themselves.
Different streams of work will be integrated: scanning for new technology; development of blue-sky concepts by designers; explorations of new media by artists; proposals for new services and infrastructures by citizens; development of business scenarios by managers; research observations made by social scientists.

I³ derives tremendous energy from Europe's cultural diversity, with creative individuals, companies, and communities beginning to work together in novel ways. I³ now includes interactive system and technology developers; interaction- and product designers outlining new concepts; interactive media artists developing new media forms; human and social scientists achieving new insight into the relationship between users and technology. An extended research network will be based on a human-oriented vision of the potential of information technology and, if things go well, will foster the emergence of a new innovation culture.

ESCAPE
contact: Tom Rodden
<tom@comp.lancs.ac.uk>
Computing Department
SECAMS Building
Lancaster LA1 4YR, UK
phone: +44 1524 593823
Fax: +44 1524 593608
<tom@comp.lancs.ac.uk>
http://escape.lancs.ac.uk

HIPS
contact: Giuliano Benelli
<benelli@unisi.it>
Dipartimento di Ingegneria dell'Informazione, Via Roma 56
I-53100 Siena, Italy
phone: +39 577 263601
fax: +39 577 263602
http://www.ing.unisi.it/lab_tel/hips/hips.html

LIME
contact: Ingrid van der Zon
<I.vanderzon@design.philips.com>
Philips Design
Building HWD, PO Box 218
5600 MD Eindhoven, The Netherlands
phone: +31 40 2759184
fax: +31 40 2759161
http://www.living-memory.org

MAYPOLE
contact: Kay Hofmeester
<kay@design-inst.nl>
Netherlands Design Institute
Keizersgracht 609
1017 DS Amsterdam, The Netherlands
phone: +31 20 5516500
fax: +31 20 6201031
http://www.maypole.org

MLOUNGE
contact: Thomas Rist
<rist@dfki.uni-sb.de>
Intelligente Benutzerschnittstellen
Stuhlsatzenhausweg 3
D-66123 Saarbrücken, Germany
phone: +49 681 3025266
fax: +49 681 3025341
http://www.dfki.de/imedia/mlounge

PERSONA
contact: Kristina Höök
<kia@sics.se>
Isafjordsgatan 22, Humle,
PO Box 1263,
S-16428 Kista, Sweden
phone: +46 8 7521500
fax: +46 8 7517230
http://www.sics.se/humle/projects/persona/web

POPULATE
contact: Tim Trevan
<tt@3dscanners.com>
London Road 90 London
SE1 6LN, UK
phone: +44 171 9228822
fax: +44 171 9228899
http://www.3dscanners.com/populate/home.htm

PRESENCE
contact: Kay Hofmeester
<kay@design-inst.nl>
Netherlands Design Institute
Keizersgracht 609
1017 DS Amsterdam,
The Netherlands
phone: +31 20 5516500
fax: +31 20 6201031
http://www.presenceweb.org

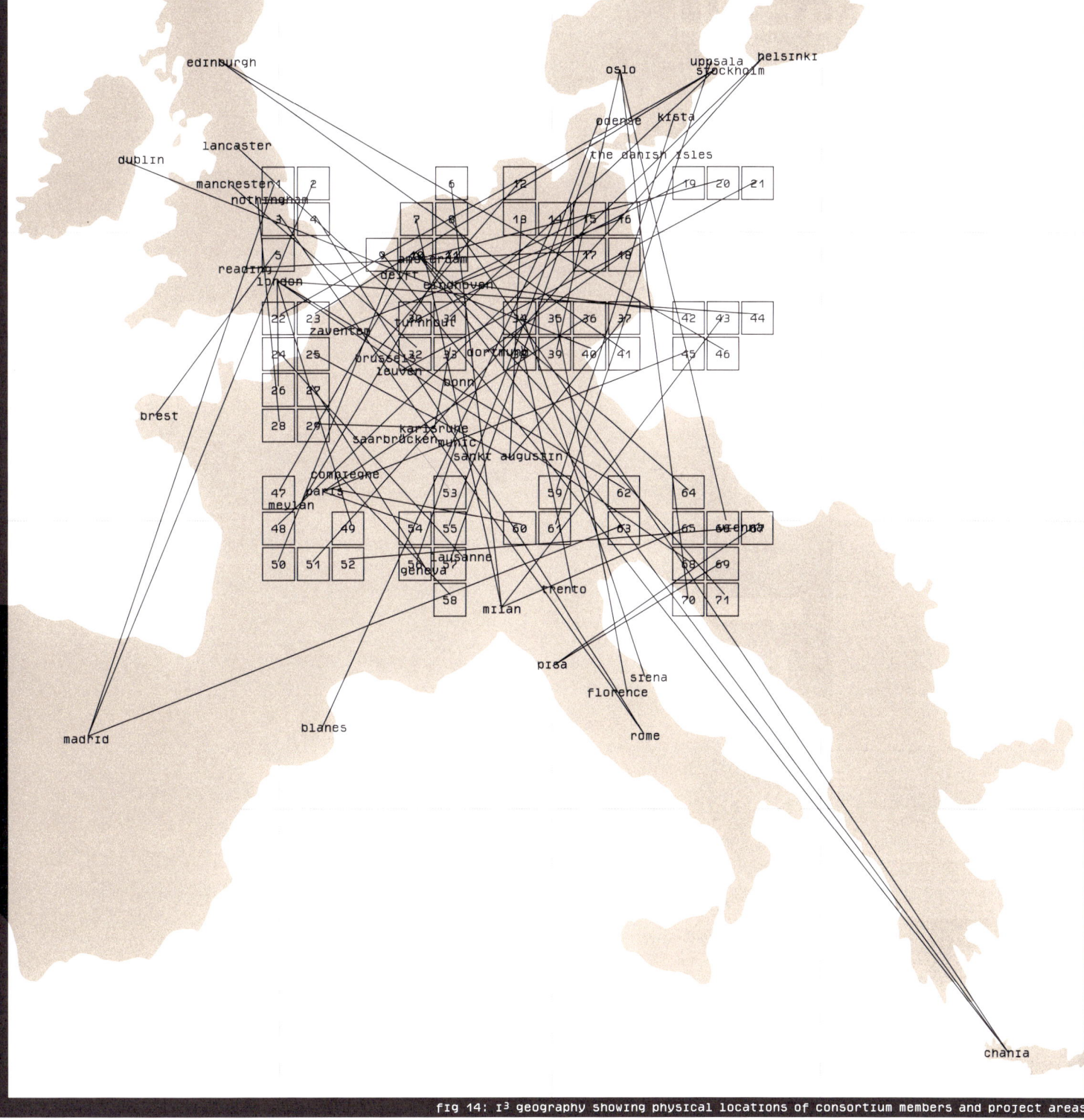

fig 14: I³ geography showing physical locations of consortium members and project areas

(Sankt Augustin)
38. Istituto Trentino di Cultura (ITC) and Istituto per la Ricerca Scientifica e Tecnologica (IRST) (Trento)
39. SINTEF (Oslo)
40. University College Dublin
41. University of Edinburgh

LIME
42. Philips International (Eindhoven, Netherlands)
43. Domus Academy srl (Milan)
44. Imperial College of Science and Technology (London)
45. Université René Descartes (Paris)
46. Queen Margaret College (Edinburgh)

MAYPOLE
47. Netherlands Design Institute (Amsterdam)
48. Helsinki University of Technology (Helsinki)
49. IDEO Product Development (London)
50. Meru Research (Delft)
51. Nokia Research Center (Helsinki)
52. Center for User Rechearch and Engineering (CURE) (Vienna).

MLOUNGE
53. German Research Center for Artificial Intelligence (DFKI) (Saarbrücken)
54. LIMSI-CNRS (Orsay/Paris)
55. The Maersk Mc-Kinney Moller Institute for Production

Technology (MIP) at Odense University
56. SIEMENS AG (Munich)
57. The Danish Isles – User Community
58. UTC Université Technologique de Compiègne.

PERSONA
59. Swedish Institute of Computer Science (SICS) (Kista, Sweden)
60. Napier University (Edinburgh)
61. Pharmasoft AB (Uppsala).

POPULATE
62. 3D Scanners Ltd (London)
63. REM Infographica (Madrid).

PRESENCE
64. Netherlands Design Institute (Amsterdam)
65. Domus Academy (Milan)
66. Human Factors Solutions (HFS) (Oslo)
67. Innovative Devices & Engineering for Automation (IDEA) (Pisa)
68. Royal College of Art (London)
69. Scuola Superiore S Anna (SSSA) (Pisa)
70. Telenor R&D (Oslo)
71. European Design for Ageing Network (DAN) (Amsterdam)

I³: LEGEND

/	physical sites of project case-study
1	member organization
▢	multiple institutes form consortia
●	site in cyberspace
✦	European Union
⊕	north
←	continents beyond the European Union
	xyz-coordinates
	connected community
	inhabited information spaces
	connected community & inhabited information spaces

AMUSEMENT
Virtual amusement space with techniques for collective presence and genetic evolution of virtual representations and behaviours

CAMPIELLO
A range of tools for the dynamic exchange of cultural information and experiences between the local community and visitors

COMRIS
Wearable assistant to enhance participation in large-scale mixed-reality events

CO-NEXUS
Virtual meeting place and new tools for low-literacy adults

ERENA
Electronic interaction spaces support cultural experiences, spanning the arts, performance and entertainment

ESCAPE
Large heterogeneous electronic landscapes in which a diversity of inhabited spaces co-exist

HIPS
A new tool for tourists, for simultaneous navigation of a physical space and a related information space

LIME
New tools for communities to create, share and explore dynamic collective local memories

MAYPOLE
Sharable GSM tools that connect people, objects and places to perform a social activity

MLOUNGE
A virtual meeting place with different levels of interaction for members of a geographically distributed community

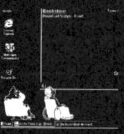
PERSONA
Innovative navigation based on a personalised and social approach

POPULATE
Kiosks for automatic capture of personal avatars, for large numbers of people

PRESENCE
New low-tech and high-tech solutions for integrating the activities of the elderly within their communities

© 1999 / Netherlands Design Institute

no part of this map may be reproduced in any form, by print, photocopy or any other means, without permission from the publisher

designed by LUST, The Hague, for the Werkplaats Typografie, Arnhem

Amusement: emotional responsiveness in interaction

It's only fitting that a project called *Amusement* would look for its proof of concept in a high-tech prank. Hatched by *Amusement* partners at the Universita Politecnica de Madrid, the ploy is called the 'Old Man Experiment'. A video image of an old man on a park bench will be projected at full size on a wall in a public area and, unbeknownst to the public, a hidden camera and microphones will also be placed to detect movements and voices in the vicinity of the projection. When people speak or come near the projection, the man will react in some way — by looking up, hiding behind his paper or walking away. Researchers will observe people's actions around the man, watching whether they continue to badger him or keep a polite distance. The absurdity the *Amusement* team hopes to reveal, of course, is that, simply by programming responsiveness into a video display, its audience can be made to behave as if an electronic creation were alive.

But what does this have to do with the project's primary goal: to develop a virtual amusement centre, in which Net surfers all over Europe can gather to play games? For *Amusement*'s Riccardo Antonini, of Corsorzio Roma Recherche, the experiment yields information on people's need for emotional and instant responsiveness in interaction — a feature all too rare in 3D chat rooms and other virtual spaces existing today. "They look very realistic, but very cold, without expression," says Antonini. Even avatars, the digital figures that are supposed to represent people, seem lifeless compared to *Amusement*'s cagey 'old man'. "We think we have gotten rid of animism, but we haven't," Antonini adds, referring to the atavistic belief that things that move and respond must be living. "Future interfaces have to take this into account."

Amusement's solution is to design an avatar that automatically responds to others — looking up when a new avatar enters the room, for example — without any direction from the person it represents. Instead of responding to its user like a puppet, explains Antonini, this avatar is driven partly by the user's actions, and partly by a set of personality and mood controls that the user sets in the software. By defining both the avatar's basic personality and how it feels that day, the user determines whether he will greet his mates in the Amusement Centre with a smile or a snarl, a big hello or a cold shoulder.

In another feature *Amusement* is working on, avatars are able to 'remember' and imitate the behaviours of other avatars. Based on principles of genetics, avatar actions evolve in reaction to what other avatars do, depending on the rules of the game they are playing. The same design principle allows avatars to become 'fashion victims', automatically adopting the dress styles of others they meet.

According to the *Amusement* partners, once users cede some control to the computer, they can emote through their avatars without thinking about it, making the online world more interesting and unpredictable. "You don't need a puppet," says Antonini of avatars. "You need an intelligent friend."

This is the premise that guides most of the design work on the project. The emotional component of play is of central importance in the Amusement Centre, celebrated in everything from the richly-appointed digital environment to a card game for avatars that can be won by bluffing or by exhibiting one emotion while actually 'feeling' another (the proverbial 'poker face,' for example).

Some i³ participants expressed concern that *Amusement* is a belated attempt to enter an online entertainment market already stuffed with virtual-world production companies and amateur VRML hackers. Defending the project, Antonini calls it "a tool box in which all the tools have been reinvented." Instead of creating variations on the usual online battlezone — "more *Dooms*" — *Amusement* aims for a new mode of experience, one not limited to entertainment. "*Amusement* is just a test bed" for more general applications, he says. Others at i³ voiced a more serious criticism that *Amusement*'s simulation of real-world feelings could be interpreted too literally by users. While a card game at the Amusement Centre may be virtual, the emotions arising from playing it are quite real, and having them generated by a computer could be every bit as disconcerting as it is amusing.

Campiello: inside information on 'cultural cities'

Europe's 'cultural cities' face a double-edged sword as they attract hordes of tourists from all over the world. With the crowds comes social friction, as residents find themselves forced to share their municipal services, public spaces and cultural events with thousands of visitors. In Venice, one of the two *Campiello* sites, the problem is 'extreme', says Domus Academy's Marco Susani: locals see tourists as 'invaders', who in turn see them as evasive and 'mysterious'. Of course, observers of European life have reported this problem for centuries.

Campiello proposes a uniquely contemporary response: change the way tourists get information about a 'cultural city', and you will change the quality of life there. Most tourist information deals with the fixed, long-term features of a place, notes Susani. A visitor standing in the Piazza San Marco with her nose in a guidebook experiences "a kind of Disneyland, a frozen city" as he puts it.

By contrast, Susani's favorite term for *Campiello* is "dynamic." The proposal calls for a constantly changing 'knowledge base' of digital information about the city, which visitors and locals can access from devices located around town — large information screens, printers, even their own portable digital assistants — indoors and out. This database contains official information from cultural institutions, but adds to this the personal views of community members, from restaurant reviews to anecdotes and gossip.

The idea is to "hide warm data behind cool data," says Susani. "You go there to find out where a restaurant is, and then you get involved in an annotation by a person who says, 'Restaurants today in Venice are not exactly the real Venetian cuisine... go to the small trattoria around the corner,' and so on." All users of *Campiello* would be encouraged to contribute as well as receive information — an exchange made practical by the use of paper as an interface. But not just regular paper: using a paper-encoding technology developed by *Campiello* industrial partner Xerox, users can submit information on handwritten forms that incorporate 'data-glyphs,' an experience pleasingly closer to writing a postcard than data-entry.

Paper in *Campiello* is not just a medium, but the metaphor the designers have relied on in envisioning how users, and the market, will regard the system. *Campiello* storyboards created by Domus Academy show interfaces that resemble posters, newspapers and even diaries — traditional means of urban information exchange that have clearly inspired Susani.

"What comes out of *Campiello* is the potential with this technology to create a medium that is like an exciting version of a local paper. The excitement comes from it being more dynamic, and built around the model of exciting gossip about the city." He adds that "within *Campiello*, we often think our real potential client is a publishing company."

Campiello is about publishing — not in the traditional sense, but as reformulated by the Internet. The traditional hierarchy of reliable sources is replaced with an information flow that is instantaneous, collaborative, and ongoing — a city of conversations overlaid on the real one.

Unlike Venice's artwork and monuments, the conversational city is not an easily manageable asset. Its value is unpredictable, rising and falling with the quality of its gossip, and dependent upon its residents' motivation to reach out to their temporary fellow occupants. But *Campiello* could convert these parallel urbanisms into a mutually-rewarding exchange, interweaving the grain of everyday life into the well-trodden circuit of sightseeing destinations.

PORTRAIT COMPOSED USING 'DATAGLYPH' PAPER-ENCODING TECHNOLOGY DEVELOPED BY XEROX, CAMPIELLO'S INDUSTRIAL PARTNER

Comris: your own personal parrot to navigate oceans of data

THE COMRIS DATA 'PARROT' LINKS REAL AND VIRTUAL CONFERENCE CENTRES

"Are you aware of your wearable or is your wearable aware of you?" quips Walter Van de Velde of *Comris*, alluding to the hidden perils of the portable communications devices that have become our constant companions.

The cellular phone, for example, has been so successfully miniaturised that it's quite possible to forget you've got it with you. But by catching their wearer unawares, gadgets like these can turn the wired life into a comedy of errors. "Imagine you did not want to be disturbed and suddenly your phone starts ringing," says Van de Velde. "Even worse: the person calling you is exactly the one you wanted to avoid. But what did your wearable know about that?"

If only it could gauge your current situation, such a device could smooth your way in business encounters instead of tripping you up. At least, that's the premise of the *Comris* project, which is developing a wearable to enhance communication among conference participants.

Dubbed a 'parrot,' it consists of a portable computer with a voice generator that talks to its user through an earpiece — rather like a parrot on the shoulder of a pirate captain (though as yet the prototype is not fleshed out with beak and bright plumage). Instead of the shark-filled high seas, the user navigates conference centre corridors and ballrooms crowded with current and prospective colleagues and competitors. Connected by wireless network to a database, her parrot relays helpful facts about fellow delegates and personalised information based on her priorities and interests, like who she knows or who she might want to meet.

Like Mission Control for an astronaut, the parrot also conveys data on the conference room-plan and schedule, keeps track of the user's movements and interactions, and offers succinct hints on how to proceed. Its computer-generated voice might reveal, say, that a session of interest is about to begin in the room down the hall on the left. The parrot can also sense the proximity of certain other parrots, perhaps alerting its wearer that an old friend or prominent venture capitalist has just walked into the room.

Not just a fount of cues and reminders, the parrot also provides a link to a parallel, virtual world that mirrors the conference — a world inhabited by teams of software agents representing each human participant. By accessing outside networks and interacting with one another, these agents can perform such tasks as calling a taxi for an appointed time, making dinner plans with other delegates, or exchanging electronic documents at the user's direction. The parrot conveys the instructions and reports the results.

This upstairs/downstairs set-up recalls traditional diplomacy, with the high officials in the banquet hall and their minions negotiating on the periphery. It is possible that the real business of such a conference could be accomplished not by those actually attending sessions all day, but by their tireless agents. The more animated those agents get, the more *Comris* users may have to heed their synthetic pets, since only *they* will really know what's going on.

According to Van de Velde, one idea behind *Comris* is that of "trying to avoid navigation" as the means of gathering information. At a conference or "in any complex society," he continues, "information should be automated, supporting you wherever you are." Context-sensitivity is hardly a new idea in the design of wearable electronics, but the parrot's intimate and potentially secret connection to its user could make for interesting social scenarios.

How might the quality of conversation change when everyone has parrots at their ears? Could social instincts be trumped by emergent imperatives from the other, virtual, world where 'interest-based' connections (algorithmically determined) are the guiding principle?

"The parrot's not meant to control you," Van de Velde hastens to assure. "I'm against bio-implants that directly control your behaviour. I want the brain to remain in the loop." Nonetheless, future *Comris* users might be well advised to keep an eye on the electronic creature whispering in their ear.

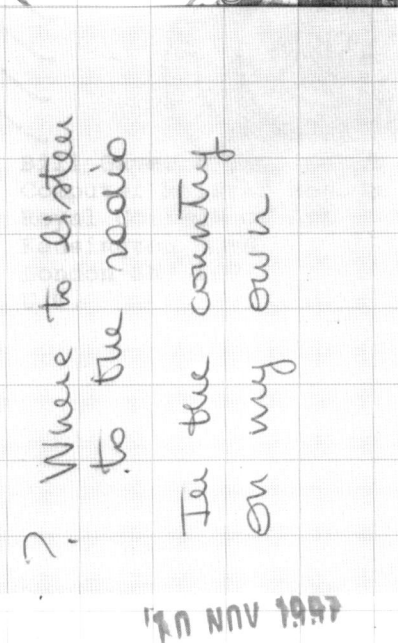

RESPONSES TO THE 'CULTURAL PROBES' SENT OUT BY THE
PRESENCE DESIGN TEAM AT THE ROYAL COLLEGE OF ART,
LONDON

Presence: (inter)active roles for elderly people

In the low-income, multi-ethnic Bijlmer housing project outside Amsterdam, senior residents imagine what it might be like to talk to friends across town through their television sets. In an affluent district of Oslo, another group of elderly people creates an advertisement for a 'Nonnogotchi', an imaginary electronic 'pet' that would allow their grandchildren to remind them to take their medicine. In the small rural town of Peccioli, in the heart of Tuscany, elders hatch a plan to attach radio transmitters to their free-range chickens. Three very different communities, three very different sets of ideas but all part of *Presence*: an i3 project that defies widely-held stereotypes of old people in fear of new technology.

Bringing together designers, psychologists, and technologists, *Presence* envisions various new forms of public and personal media that could help older people remain active in their communities and be 'present' in the daily lives of their neighbours, families and fellow citizens. "Older people aren't interested in technology for its own sake, but as a means to better communication," says Kay Hofmeester, *Presence* project manager at the Netherlands Design Institute. "*Presence* sees older people as a resource to society rather than as disabled people who need taking care of."

The project began with community research conducted in collaboration with groups of representative users: surveys and informal visits that yielded demographic and socio-economic 'portraits' of the three communities. But for the *Presence* design partners — the Domus Academy and the Royal College of Art (RCA) — this aggregated, factual view of the users was insufficiently-rich ground for innovation.

"In traditional user research, you see what people's problems are, and you propose ways of solving them," observes the RCA's Gillian Crampton-Smith. "But that tends to lead to mapping solutions to what exists already. We were trying to look for opportunities, rather than solutions."

The designers needed a way to gather what they called 'inspirational data' — the sorts of qualitative impressions from residents of the three communities that could help them design more imaginatively. To capture this data, they devised and sent out 'cultural probes' to all three sites, to be return-mailed to the design partners. The 'probes' consisted of packets of materials that invited users to portray their lives in assorted media, by taking photos with a disposable camera, annotating maps, writing postcards and keeping media diaries. "It really was touching how much response we got," says Bill Gaver, an RCA designer and former experimental psychologist who helped develop the probes. "People let us see into their lives so much. We asked them to think very hard, and they responded so generously."

This trove inspired a broad range of idiosyncratic and often whimsical design concepts; many of the devices, especially those conceived by the Domus Academy *Presence* partners, respond to or complement people's emotional states.

Bedecked with photo and video clips of elders, an outdoor 'Grandpa Totem' courts public pride and nostalgia; meanwhile, the 'Active Portrait' alleviates loneliness by enabling grandparents to see what their grandchildren are feeling.

As *Presence* documentation records, users' responses to the concepts have been equally emotional — from horror at the possibility of being shown on a public video screen, to delight at the prospect of being contacted via a 'Nonnogotchi'.

Some i3 members at the Denmark first-year summit found the mix of emotions and infrastructure a bit too volatile. One reviewer expressed doubt that most of the concepts could be adequately validated without a thorough-going implementation from the start; others wondered how communities would learn to share the public devices amicably. Acknowledging the real-world perils of *Presence's* lofty thinking, Hofmeester remarked, "We are inventing a new process, and finding the answers as we go. Maybe we'll know next year."

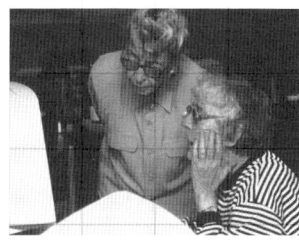

MEMBERS OF THE PRESENCE COMMUNITY IN OSLO

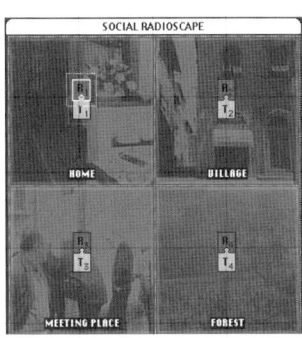

SOCIAL RADIOSCAPE INTERACTIVE SOUND ENVIRONMENT PROPOSED FOR PECCIOLI, ITALY, BY RCA RESENCE TEAM

ABOVE AND RIGHT: INTERACTIVE PUBLIC SIGNAGE, PROPOSED FOR THE BIJLMER HOUSING ESTATE IN AMSTERDAM, BY THE ROYAL COLLEGE OF ART PRESENCE TEAM LED BY TONY DUNNE, BILL GAVER AND GILLIAN CRAMPTON-SMITH.

If:

-Afraid of everything you have forgotten, you randomly decide that page 31 and 32 will be black with at least two things you've done on Sunday November 1,

Then:

Spoke with Jean-Marc about some chairs for his flat.

Had a drink with TANIA

Populate: raising the avatar nation

Virtual space may be the stuff of science fiction novels and high-profile research programmes, but it's a frozen wasteland without you. Or as Tim Trevan, project manager of *Populate*, puts it: "Virtual interactions will not be widely adopted if they are seen as alienating or cold. A key component for creating a warm and human environment will be clearly recognisable and realistic images of individuals." That's why he's betting that avatars — digital representations of people — will eventually colonize the networked world.

That forecast puts him in famous company. Prognosticators from William Gibson to Bill Gates have envisioned a world where people from all walks of life shop, learn, play and relate to one another as avatars. What sets Trevan and *Populate* apart is that they've actually devised a plan — and designed the equipment — for raising the avatar nation. They propose to build and install avatar-creation booths (rather like passport photo booths) in which anyone will be able to follow instructions, pose and assemble an avatar that looks recognizably like themself, from a series of photographic views and body calibrations.

Having birthed your digital twin, you'll be able to take it home in a bundle of software and load it on to your computer where your surrogate self can deliver email messages to friends and colleagues; serve as a size-accurate model to try on virtual fashions; and even stand in for the star of your favorite video game. And things won't stop there: Trevan predicts that commercial software makers will quickly develop new applications to extend the avatar's uses. Because the avatars will conform to the popular VRML standard for 3D computer models, even amateurs can build and enter their own virtual environments.

The measurement of man required to create such avatars is unprecedented for a self-service booth, and the technical challenges are many. Unlike a photo-booth, the avatar booth will require several different steps and poses. "This booth has to be idiot-proof," says Trevan, explaining why the project has been working with an industrial psychologist on the user interface.

There's also the touchy matter of clothing: for the avatar to move realistically, the booth's cameras must be able to record not just bodily dimensions, but also the locations of the major joints: the armpits, crotch and head-position are the strategic coördinates. Ideal subjects, Trevan says, will be wearing a tight fitting outfit so that their silhouettes are "as close to the naked avatar as possible." Unusual body types — amputees, people on crutches or in wheelchairs, or just with 'big hair' — pose their own difficulties.

"The computer needs to capture certain points, and it assumes a clean-shaven individual. If you have a very big beard, it will assume the beard is actually the outline of the jaw — so you'd have an extraordinarily inflated head."

Explaining to passersby why they need an avatar will be just as great a challenge. Trevan plans to wow them with digital footage of avatar 'actors' incorporated, say, into the latest James Bond movie. Beyond such enticements, it's clear that a leap of consumer imagination will be needed if the new avatars are to be understood as well as sold like hot cakes. Most avatars today are fantasy figures used for play by on-line gamers, chat room junkies, and other computer-literate subcultures. *Populate* hopes to encourage a new, practical mainstream of users who would trust their avatars to arrange business meetings as well as flirt in virtual bars. That's where the photographic realism comes in.

The new users are expected to want serious, straightforward avatars — surrogates in inhabited information space. Making one's avatar could perhaps become a rite of passage, like getting a passport or drivers license. One bonus of the i³ summit was Trevian's meeting with Dr Antonio Camurri of the University of Genoa, who is developing an infra-red camera for real-time motion capture — a potential solution to one of *Populate*'s technical problems. "To get a good-quality texture-map to go on the avatar surface, you need even lighting of the whole body," Trevan explains. "If their camera can capture motion, it can certainly capture silhouettes. That could potentially obviate the need for the back-lighting or flash-lighting and make our solution a lot cheaper and easier."

Will broad-based avatar societies really take shape? "We're not trying to second-guess the market. It may be a fad application," admits Trevan, adding, "If you believe in markets, you believe that people will find their own uses." For now, *Populate* is playing it safe. The first sites for avatar booths will be shopping malls, those spawning grounds for trends and novelties.

Persona: couch-potato commentators lead 'social navigation'

Thanks to the *Persona* project, i3 participants got a refreshingly altered view of the Internet. Switch on your browser and your computer desktop is transformed into the living room of *Frieda and Agneta*, two icon-sized cartoons who sit on a couch at the bottom the screen, watching the action on the Web as if it was a home-movie. As the Web pages appear, the characters comment dryly to one another about the site, and jeer at the error messages that come up from time to time. "These Yankees are so self-centered. They talk in a loud voice," says Agneta, commenting on a movie Web site. At one point, Frieda even wanders off-screen for a cup of tea.

This charming application is the most fully realized prototype to emerge from *Persona*, one of the smaller-scale i3 projects. Two institutions, Napier University in Edinburgh and The Swedish Institute of Computer Studies (SICS), are conducting a think-tank-like study of navigation, trying to discover how people find things and orient themselves in digital information space. The characters on the couch are linked to *Persona*'s mission by a question: what makes us feel comfortable in the digital world?

Persona's inquiry has uncovered vast differences in people's ability to find their way in an information space — and not just across cultures and backgrounds, but within fairly homogenous groups. Psychologist Kristina Höök, of SICS, wants attributes like delight, curiosity, irony, and humour to be taken more seriously as criteria for measuring the useability of these realms, rather than the usual quantitative parameters such as 'efficiency of task', time spent, and number of errors made. Höök cites a study measuring the ability of male engineers at one company to find their way through a particular virtual space: their performances ranged from assured to stumbling. There was a 20:1 difference between the fastest and the slowest. When the *Persona* team asks 'why do some people get so lost?' the usual suspects are rounded up: differences connected with age or gender, expectations of the system and of oneself.

Making one of the few critiques of 'information space' voiced at the i3 summit, Höök points out that not everyone is inclined to think of information spatially, and that there are significant limits to the metaphor of information as an undiscovered country that the user wanders through, explores and conquers. As an alternative to this spatial notion, *Persona* proposes narrative-based or 'social navigation', in which orientation is established by observing and interacting with other people or agents.

Some aspects of this argument sound suspiciously like a transplant into the digital world of that old dichotomy between men who travel by blind reckoning and women who ask for directions. Nonetheless, *Persona* makes a valuable distinction between different types of navigation: interaction with others can make an experience more linear, and thus more manageable for some users.

Equally important, the presence of other people navigating the same world creates the opportunity to joke about it, even subvert it a bit. "New media always take themselves very seriously," says Per Persson, creator of *Persona*'s couch-commentators. "You see very little irony and reflexivity on the Web. *Frieda and Agneta* are quite bitchy and reflexive about the medium itself." In the informal and not too overbearing atmosphere of the ladies' living room, new moods and modes are possible.

Persson explains that the characters' gaze-direction is very important in establishing their engagement with the Web pages shown. And nor are they one-trick ponies: additional behaviours and comments are loaded in for repeat visits to a given Web site.

Frieda and Agneta surely represent not just a way to create a comfort zone in cyberspace, but also an entertainment in itself (quite possibly more compelling than the Web-content they're 'viewing') — providing a meta-narrative much like the characters in *Beavis & Butthead* or *Pop-Up TV*, which Persson cites as influences. One unintended consequence may be that products like *Frieda and Agneta* become popular as add-on modules while failing to influence the design of the software they overlay.

FRIEDA AND AGNETA WATCH THE WEB

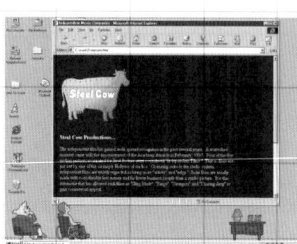
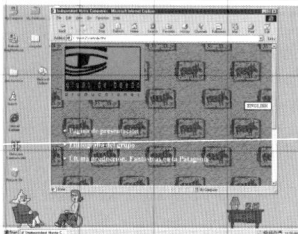

eRena: linking real and virtual performance spaces

A SCENE FROM *MURMURING FIELDS*, ONE OF THE ERENA PROJECTS.

In the i³ vision, the future of the performing arts in the digital age is packed hopefully into something called the 'electronic arena'. *eRenas* are seen as the virtual gathering halls of digital crowds where tomorrow's art and entertainment will play; the vast *eRena* project is charged with developing the first of these spaces and, gradually, inviting artists and audiences in. But what *is* an electronic arena? That depends on which *eRena* participant you ask. The project's broadcast media contingent see it as *Inhabited Television*, in which TV shows are shot in networked virtual worlds and aired in the real world. For project members from the theater and fine arts, the starting point is the auditorium or gallery, where groups physically assemble before making virtual connections. In *eRena*, each of these visions has been allowed to develop independently on paper and in real-world trials.

"For us, a virtual space is like a rehearsal space where we can try things and make 'as if' situations," says Monika Fleischmann of the Media Arts Research Studies (MARS) department at GMD (Germany's huge national computer laboratory), and one of the creators of *Murmuring Fields*. She describes this installation as "a virtual stage, or a framework for extended performance. We work on the theatrical concept of 'mixed reality', which brings together actors on the Internet with actors in real space." In *Murmuring Fields*, as people move through a single gallery, cameras and sensitive flooring track each person's movements and record them as 'trace avatars'. Through their traces, the players both communicate with one another *in*, and construct a virtual space *on* the Internet, allowing connections to others outside the room.

A similar concern with language and improvisation shows up in *World Generator: The Engine of Desire* by American artist Bill Seaman in collaboration with ZKM, the Karlsruhe Media Centre. In this project, groups in different nations were linked both by live video and through a virtual world that they could change by moving a set of digital wheels.

The first *Inhabited Television* venture was a series of virtual worlds on the Internet, collectively known as *The Mirror*, produced by the U.K. production company Illuminations. Online interactions of *Mirror* visitors were recorded and later shown as clips on a Net-themed TV show broadcast on Britain's Channel 4 — a sort of online *Candid Camera*. That experiment laid the groundwork for *Heaven and Hell - Live*, described as 'a TV show staged inside a collaborative virtual environment'. Net surfers logging on to *H&H* were also stepping in front of live TV cameras, as the action in the virtual world was shown in real time on Channel 4.

"We're going a stage further than interactive TV," says *eRena* participant Steve Benford, of the University of Nottingham, referring to the call-in shows and video-on-demand experiments so roundly hyped in the early '90s. "This is a way of engaging socially in TV. It's no longer just about you, your television and your credit card."

But *Inhabited TV* responds also to the formlessness of most social interaction on the Internet, by insisting on the narrative structure of a broadcast TV show.

According to Benford, people want something to do together on the Net. "Do you author or engineer their interactions," he asks rhetorically, "or do they just chat?" To this end, *Inhabited TV* borrows some production roles from broadcast TV, such as digital set designers who build the space, and directors who decide what part of the action the broadcast audience will see. A director can also control the virtual environment, influencing players' actions through the software. As Benford points out, interaction in virtual space depends both on who and what you can see, and on how many others can see *you*. "Using effects like spotlights, directors can potentially shape narrative or create surprise."

From these descriptions, *eRenas* certainly seem capable of challenging expectations and changing the relationship between creator and audience. But, in practice, the lack of preconceptions has been disabling as well as exciting for *eRena* participants. When artists and audiences must find their footing with each new event, disorientation is inevitable, and the performance can seem arbitrary. Steve Benford recalls watching as visitors from the Internet first entered the *Heaven and Hell* virtual space, and quickly e-mailed their first impressions. "I'm in shot," read one user's distress call. "Why can't I see myself?"

Maypole

Informal communication - sharing jokes, teasing each other, asking what kind of day you've had - is an important part of everyday life. Most families also do a lot of comunicating to organise and schedule shared resources: car pools and school runs in the morning; ferrying kids to sporting events after school; getting in touch for help with homework in the evening. A high proportion of the 100 billion minutes of telephone calls made each year are short-distance - so the market for any service that adds value to local, intra-community communications is potentially vast. This is why *Maypole* focuses on new ways to enhance social communications among an extended family in the community.

Early on in this project, two real-world communities were researched by a variety of methods (see picture) at a secondary school in Vienna, Austria, and among a scout troop in Helsinki, Finland.

In looking for communication dysfunctions in this context, the *Maypole* team realised that some logistical tasks, like car sharing, were too complex - and too riddled with security issues - to be tackled in this kind of project. It decided instead to focus on social communication: the constant chatting, verbal 'grooming' and bonding that keep families and communities healthy.

Maypole researchers discovered that communication through pictures fosters unexpected forms of social interaction. Images are already used socially in lots of different ways, and on a vast scale: more than 2,700 photographs per second were taken worldwide in 1997. Designers and community members came up with lots of new ways to use images. Early ideas ranged from pure fun ('This is Daddy with the head of Mr. Bean') to the need for reassurance ('Look, our baby is happy in the daycare centre'). Working with children and parents,

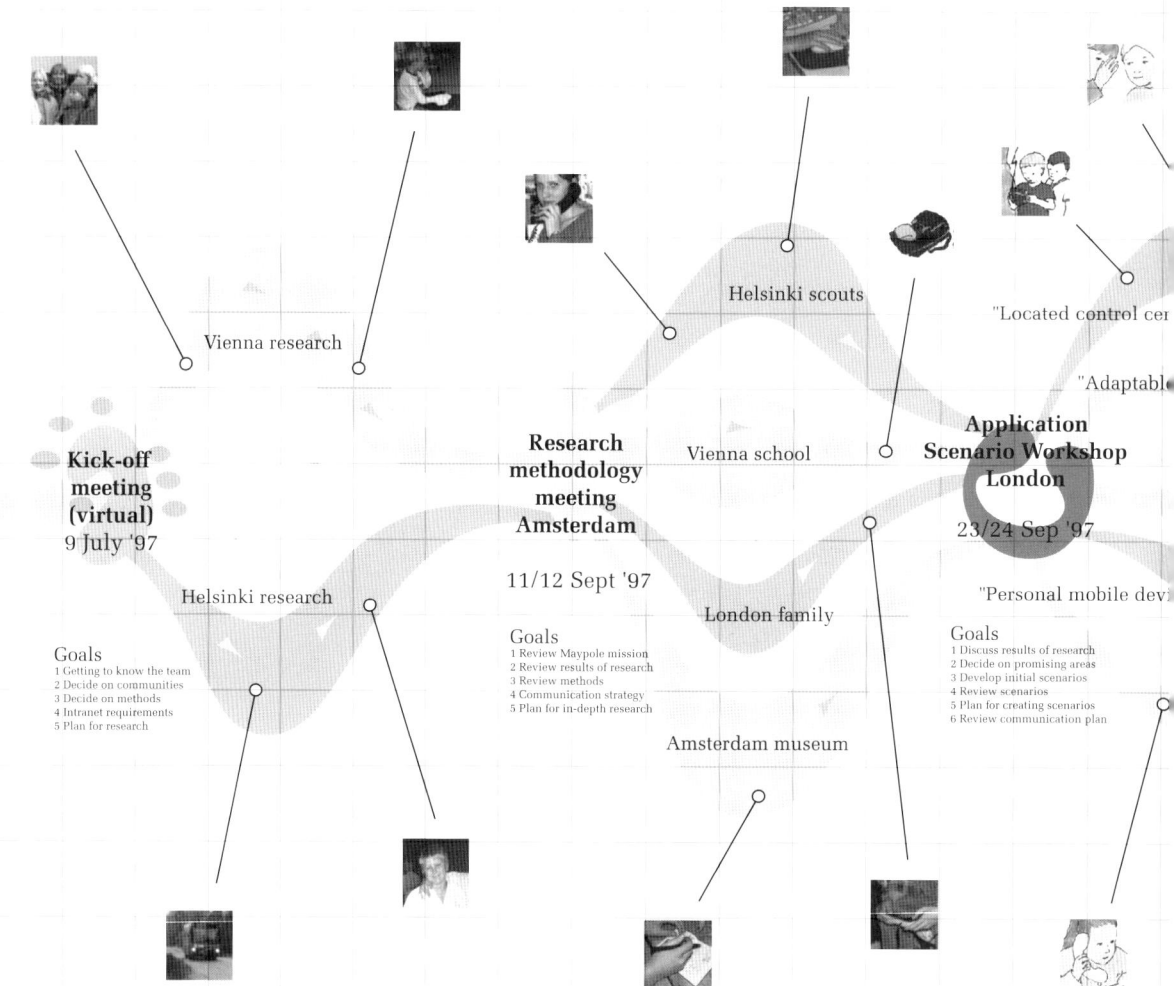

Maypole partners developed dozens of scenarios before selecting the four most promising concepts for pictorial communication devices that talk to each other in a local network. These will now be developed, prototyped and tested in field trials.

The final year of the project (through to late 1999) involves the development of these prototypes. These will be working models, developed by *Maypole's* technology partner, Nokia, the Finland-based consumer electronics company; or interaction designs made by IDEO, a leading interaction design company. The Centre for User Research & Engineering in Vienna, and the Helsinki University of Technology are leading the project's user-research; Meru Research, in the Netherlands, researches process methodology. The project and its results are managed and communicated by the Netherlands Design Institute.

On the *Maypole* project chart - nicknamed 'the courgette plant' by team members - different strands of work progress on their own for weeks at a time, but team members come together and interact with each other at three-monthly project meetings. The collaboration has worked because different disciplines are asked to compromise only at certain intervals. There has of course been tension between single-discipline work and inter-disciplinary synthesis - but so far the tension has produced mainly positive energy, say Maypole team members.

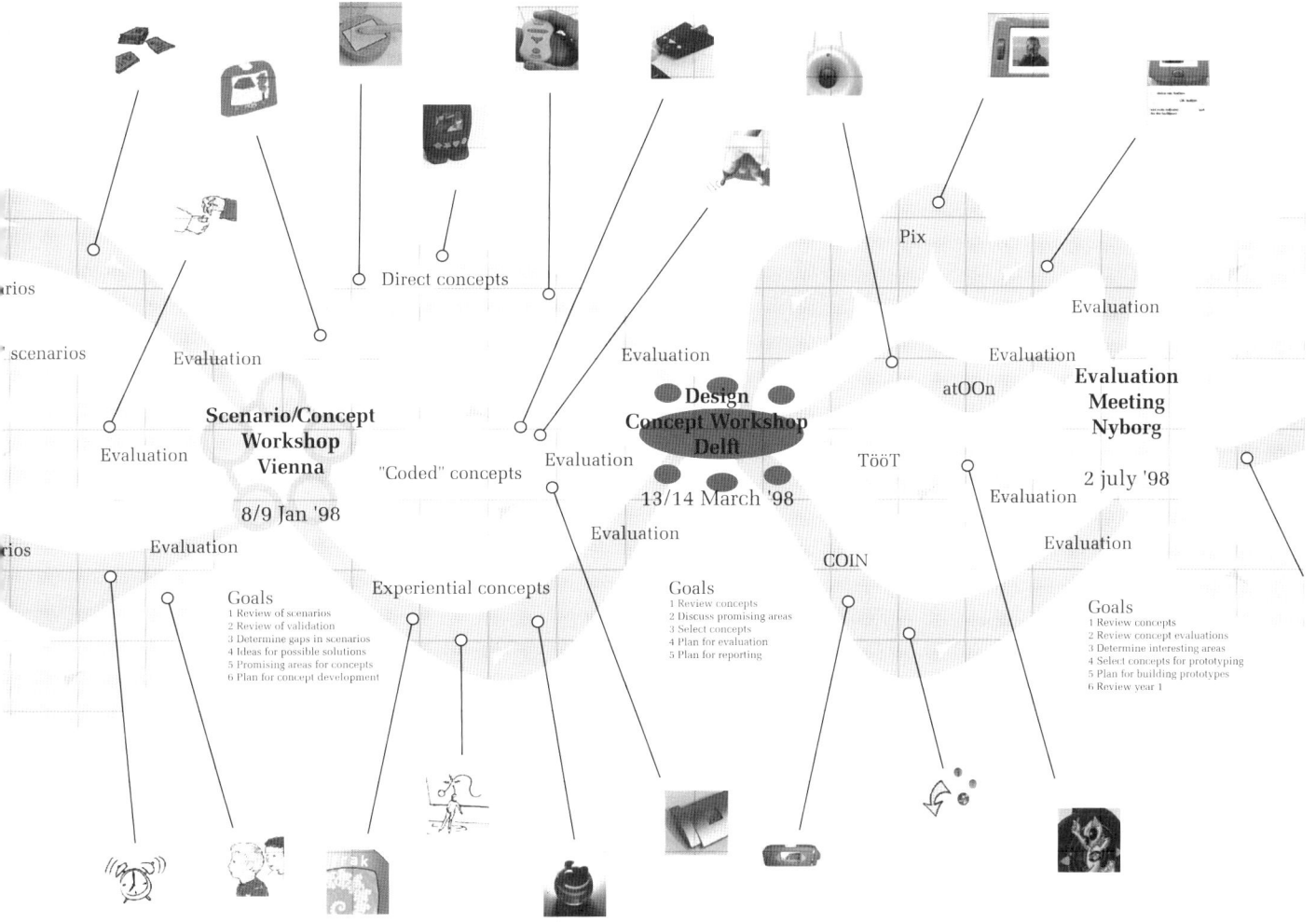

Europe's Virtual Media Lab

Operating as a Europe-wide research and development laboratory, the i³ programme aims to identify new paradigms for interface designs to enhance everday life. In a short time, i³ has established a distinct organisational culture that reflects the plurality of national outlooks among its participants, and contrasts in both its research methods and social goals from the prevailing spirit of most new media ventures in the U.S. **Andrea Moed** reflects on the initial findings of this trans-European consortium.

In Heaven, goes the old joke, the French do the cooking, the British are the police, the Swiss keep the books, and the Italians are the lovers. Switch those roles around, and what you've got is Hell. When it comes to the disciplines of information technology, however, national stereotypes fall auspiciously away. We are left with an open question: How does Europe, in all its diversity and in the midst of economic unification, imagine the digital age? i³ is the European Union's answer to that question.

With participants drawn from academia, industry, design and the fine arts, this two-year-old consortium is working to define the role of emerging information technology in European communities of all kinds. i³ is designed to function like an R&D lab with a Europe-wide campus, producing in-depth studies and reports followed by innovative designs for communications products and infrastructure.

In the best hopes of its founders, i³ will become a magnet for telecommunications industry research funds that currently go overseas to places like the MIT Media Lab; i³-developed products will be taken up by corporate sponsors and give rise to new consumer markets.

Initially, i³ committed resources to thirteen different research projects, each of which involves scientists, artists, designers and business-people at collaborating institutions in several different countries. In June 1998, all the inaugural i³ participants came together for the first time in Nyborg, Denmark, to take stock of each project's progress and of the group as a whole.

"The positive thing about i³ is that all points of view are represented," commented i³ coordinating group member Marco Susani. "At this meeting, we've heard from academics and researchers who say, 'We want to be free, we don't even want to work for companies.' It's an extreme stance, but why not respect it? After all, some nice things come out of isolated, dreamy reserves — even in technology. We've also heard from people from companies with very strategic goals who are here because these i³ projects fit into their planned strategies — so they will aim for something absolutely business-oriented. And then, offering a kind of balance between the two, we have members of the design community — focused on users, and on ideas that come from life. There's no reason to take apart this balance."

To observers at the June 1998 summit, two things were clear from the outset. First, in spite of its short history and widely dispersed membership, i³ already has a distinct organisational culture. Second, that culture bears little resemblance to anything you might find at, say, a new media conference in the United States. Not that the technology outlook was different: i³ project managers employed many of the current buzzwords, including 'virtual environments', 'intelligent agents', 'avatars,' and 'wearable computers'.

But where other media think-tanks talk of business models and target-markets, the i³ speakers envision 'Connected Communities', 'Inhabited Information Spaces', and interfaces to be used by 'ordinary people' in their 'ordinary lives'. Worker productivity and consumer satisfaction, the holy grails of the corporate IT world, were nowhere in evidence among the participants' research goals.

i³ projects address our much neglected higher-order needs: bolstering the informal society that arises in cafés and gaming parlors (*Amusement*), encouraging communication across generations (*Presence*), making cities of antiquity more vital and hospitable from visitors' and residents' points of view (*Campiello*), and promoting widespread literacy in emerging media (*Co-Nexus*, *Populate* and *Persona*). Whatever the technologies they featured, the project presentations had less to do with the possibilities of digital devices than with the principles of traditional humanism.

In keeping with that tradition, almost every i³ project sees itself in terms of public space. Whether it's the physical terrain of ancient cities, the rambling geography of conference centres, or the ethereal construct of a 'magic lounge' in cyberspace, i³ members clearly feel a mission to create digitally-enhanced versions of the great *agoras*, performance centres, pubs, and other time-honoured human gathering places.

The preference for a spatial metaphor to describe human-computer interaction may be the most quintesially European aspect of i³. After all, so much of the continent's cultural capital is fixed in space, from treasured historic cityscapes to café society and village life. But, as the various projects were described in depth, the metaphor simply could not contain all the ideas in play.

For example, *eRena* project representatives defined everything from experiments in 'Inhabited Television' to small-group participatory theatre as an 'electronic arena.' This did not disguise the incredible diversity of digitally-augmented performance paradigms on which *eRrena* members have been working, but neither did it make the project more understandable.

More critically for i³ as a whole, the focus on the specifics of place tended to highlight the lack of cohesiveness of some projects; it also created tension between the concern over recognising cultural differences (among the assorted case-study communities), and the need to be able to draw widely-applicable conclusions from often highly-targeted research. As Kristina Höök of *Persona* wondered at one point, "Do the peculiarities of Danish Isles or Edinburgh pubs help you get to a model of a 'Connected Community'?"

Where geography was less of an issue, different projects that converged around the same themes often had a great deal to say to one another. For example, a technical session on avatars illuminated diverse but complementary approaches among the *Amusement* researchers at Consorzia Roma Ricerche and U. Politecnica de Madrid (designing avatars with personalities and emotions), the *Populate* partners at UK-based 3D Scanners (creating photo-realistic avatars for download in public places), and *eRena*'s University of Nottingham researchers (whose avatars can form crowds), and their partners at IG and EPF Lausanne (making avatars that can dance with one another). In cases like these, even the apparent duplication of work across projects has had a worthwhile outcome.

Unfortunately, not all presentations testified to the benefits of i³'s distributed research model. In some cases, the geographic remoteness of research team members from one another led to projects too wide in scope to have definitive impact, or to research clearly behind the curve of private-sector product development.

As the projects' relative strengths and weaknesses emerged, one couldn't help but begin handicapping their chances of success in the world beyond i³. This was hindered by most presenters' lack of experience in helping an audience to visualise how their projects might look or feel in the real world. Out of line with the demonstration-oriented culture of telecommunications research, the June 1998 i³ presentations mostly offered formal academic papers, supported by visual documentation that varied widely in quality and graphic effectiveness.

Still, the most innovative projects stood out through their power to inspire hard questions and imaginative speculation among the audience. The *Amusement* presentation led one person to ask whether an avatar can ever convey emotions with respectful fidelity to the human heart. Others wondered how communities using the *Presence* or *Lime* systems would learn to present their collective memories democratically. And what it would be like to talk to someone with a *Comris* parrot whispering in her ear.

While these questions revealed just how far most of the projects are from implementation, they also demonstrated how vividly and readily one could imagine oneself into i³'s future scenarios. This very human orientation represents i³'s best chance of bridging its cultural gap with industry and the public. To be successful, the program must further develop its capacity to share its visions with those outside the hot-house.

In summer 1998, the Netherlands Design Institute held three open evening seminars entitled *Getting On!* about the design of devices and interfaces that determine our experience of the 'information revolution' — kiosks and furniture for public access to the Internet, portable digital assistants, and the transaction technologies of the future. Photos: **Bart Hendriks**.

GETTING ON!

1 furNETure

2 DATABUTLERS

3 BREAD/CIRCUITS

Getting On!
1. furNETure

One-part telephone kiosk to two parts cyberspace launch-pad, tomorrow's street furniture aspires to look and act smart. At the first *Getting On!* session in June 1998, **Ineke Schwartz** heard contrasting opinions about design for public access to the Internet.

About two years ago, the first pieces of furNETure started to show up in public spaces: street furniture that provides Internet-access, these specially-designed hybrids sprouted in airports and shopping malls, hotel lobbies, cafés and libraries. FurNETure pioneers were not even sure that people would want to access the Internet in public space. Would seasoned Netizens consult the Internet in stations or on the street? Would non-computer owners bother to go outdoors to send an email or surf the World Wide Web?

The first session of the Netherlands Design Institute's *Getting On!* series looked at three different species of furNETure: the *Leestafel* (Reading Table) designed for the café in De Waag, the Medieval gateway to the heart of Amsterdam; the Internet *zuil* (column) that appeared unexpectedly on streets and squares around Holland over the last two years, courtesy of the Dutch telecom company KPN; and its UK counterpart, designed for indoor use, British Telecom's Touchpoint Kiosk.

All three artefacts offer strikingly different scenarios for social experience of the Internet. The Touchpoint kiosk opens up only a small portion of the World Wide Web, namely those shops and commercial services that pay BT to be included in the interface. At KPN Telecom's internet *zuil*, experienced net-users can surf and send email outdoors. The *Leestafel* at De Waag offers the same possibilities but here, specially-designed software helps the inexperienced user find their way through the morass of the Net. In direct contrast to the KPN *zuil*, the *Leestafel* was developed by a non-profit organisation, the Society for Old and New Media (which is based at De Waag) without reference to target groups or market-research, and on a very limited budget. After two years in use, initial conclusions can be drawn about the first crop of furNETure.

The starting points for the *Getting On!* discussion concerned useability, and the difference between Getting On in a domestic or a street setting. But the real question that quickly emerged was a different one: why is most of the hardware and software for public access to the Internet so ugly and difficult to use? Should furNETure look familiar, as a collage of recognisable parts, or just the opposite? Does it need specially designed, easy-comprehensible new interfaces? Where should those public connections be placed: at the same spots as public phones? The Net poses different demands: people tend to prefer getting personal email or replying to a newsgroup in a quiet, intimate place, whereas looking at a listings agenda or checking a railway timetable can be done anywhere.

As an experiment in providing commercial services through the Net, BT's *Touchpoint* was declared a success although by the end of 1998 BT had withdrawn its test-models, saying it would incorporate lessons from Touchpoint into its next genreation of multimedia payphones. Two hundred kiosks were produced and placed in high-traffic, high-visibility locations, such as shopping malls, airports, universities, hotel lobbies and motorway service centers. Information (about all kinds of goods and services, from opera tickets to lottery numbers and horoscopes) was free, though some services had to be paid for.

With hardware designed by Fitch (the London consultancy), Touchpoint was a hybrid of recognisable parts and looked rather like an open telephone booth with friendly curving walls. Next to the touchscreen a slot for coins; underneath it were a credit-card slot and a laser printer outlet for print-outs of requested information. The handset to the left — intended for access to helpline operators and call centres to purchase goods and services — caused lots of problems because users frequently confused it with a normal phone. Nor was the printer ideal: most people forgot to take the pages they'd printed. The kiosk could have had a more unified look, admitted Gordon Butler, BT's multimedia design manager, but he was concerned it would get too large and wanted to use existing parts to give it a familiar look.

The fact that the Touchpoint interface looked more like a TV channel than like Netscape was one of the project's most successful aspects, according to Butler. Since, as he put it, "technicians aren't able to design user-friendly interfaces," he turned to Brand Union (formerly Tutssels), a London design consultancy with extensive TV design experience, for interface and branding design; the underlying applications were developed jointly by BT Research Labs and ICL, on an ICL platform. "We felt it had a lot more to do with television experience than PCs," Butler explained. Unattended, the screen played eye-catching images; as soon as someone touches the screen, an opening menu appeared. And people managed to

http://www.waag.org/maatschap/projects/readin/presentatie/leestafel.html
http://www.touchpoint.bt.com/home.htm

THE KPN INTERNET ZUIL IN USE
PHOTOGRAPHS JANET ABRAMS

BT TOUCHPOINT KIOSK
SHOWING SCREEN AND
HELPLINE PHONE HANDSET TO
ITS LEFT

THE **LEESTAFEL** AT THE WAAG
PHOTOGRAPH JANINE HUIZENGA

use it, despite the cluttered look of the interface: in addition to the menu with 24 different options, it featured a toolbar, advertising information and a newsfeed.

The KPN-Internet *zuil* is the complete opposite of Touchpoint. A clearly-composed design, slender and high-tech looking, it is in a direct lineage to the series of public telecommunication kiosks that the Dutch consultancy Landmark Design had developed earlier for KPN Telecom, but includes no existing parts. KPN had previously experimented at Schiphol airport with 'Spider,' an integrated communication terminal from which to fax, phone or use the Internet. But this hybrid was not successful at communicating these different services. So the KPN Internet *zuil* was developed as a single-function machine. Ianus Keller (who worked on its design while at Landmark) does not believe in integrated terminals like Touchpoint: "loose parts like handsets and keyboards make a new product like this hard to understand. It must be able to communicate what it can do in a single glance." The interface of the KPN *zuil* got much less attention, however: a somewhat stripped-down version of Netscape, with a clearly marked e-mail option, makes it practical for experienced net-users only; others simply did not understand how to operate the system.

In spite of this and the stiffness of the built-in keyboard (slightly angled and with hard-to-press keys), the KPN *zuil* was initially quite popular. Some people spent up to seven hours on it, showing off their homepages and consulting information services — though one reason for its popularity might be that the payment system (via a phone card) could easily be hacked. After some time, interest dropped. KPN removed the columns and now sells them to municipalities as information kiosks.

Rolf Pixley knows why interest in the KPN Internet *zuil* waned. Who wants to dive into the immeasurable depths of the Net standing up in all weather? So far as he is concerned, the whole idea of an Intenet kiosk is wrong-headed. "We wanted to make reading the Net as easy as reading a book and give the user a homely feeling," said Pixley, referring to the *Leestafel* at De Waag, of which he was one of the principal designers. "As long as kiosks are ugly and cybercafés are a threat to most people, the Net remains restricted to a very small group of people. That should *not* be the case. The Net is more important than computers, we reckoned, so let's skip all the computer stuff we don't need to see or use. Software should be something pleasing, especially when you spend hours a day with it."

Following these principles, Pixley and two other designers (Janine Huizenga and Mieke Gerritzen) developed the *Leestafel* for Old and New Media, which won the Rotterdam Design Prize in 1997. Sale of goods, services or telephone time is not the ambition here. Instead, the goal is to make the Net as easily accessible as the newspapers and magazines on the reading table at De Waag's café — opening it up for everybody, not just the 20 per cent of technophiles who already know how to use it. Even kids are not excluded: under the table is a screen specifically for children, with a big fat trackball and a black and white interface to *Welcome to Wonderland*, by the Japanese interaction designer Thoru Yamamoto.

The long table — meant for old media like newspapers and magazines *and* the Net — is reminiscent of the reading tables traditional to many Dutch cafés. The *Leestafel* is a hybrid, though the different parts are built-in wherever possible. The table's archaic design (wooden surface on a dark steel frame, supporting back-to-back slanting steel planes in which the screens are fitted) is adapted to De Waag's interior. The liquid crystal screens can be tilted, using a bellows-like angle adjustment. Every screen has a touchpad with a click-button built into the table-leaf. The small plastic keyboards are deliberately *not* built-in; in a 'wet' space like a café, they have to be easily replaced — average life-expectancy

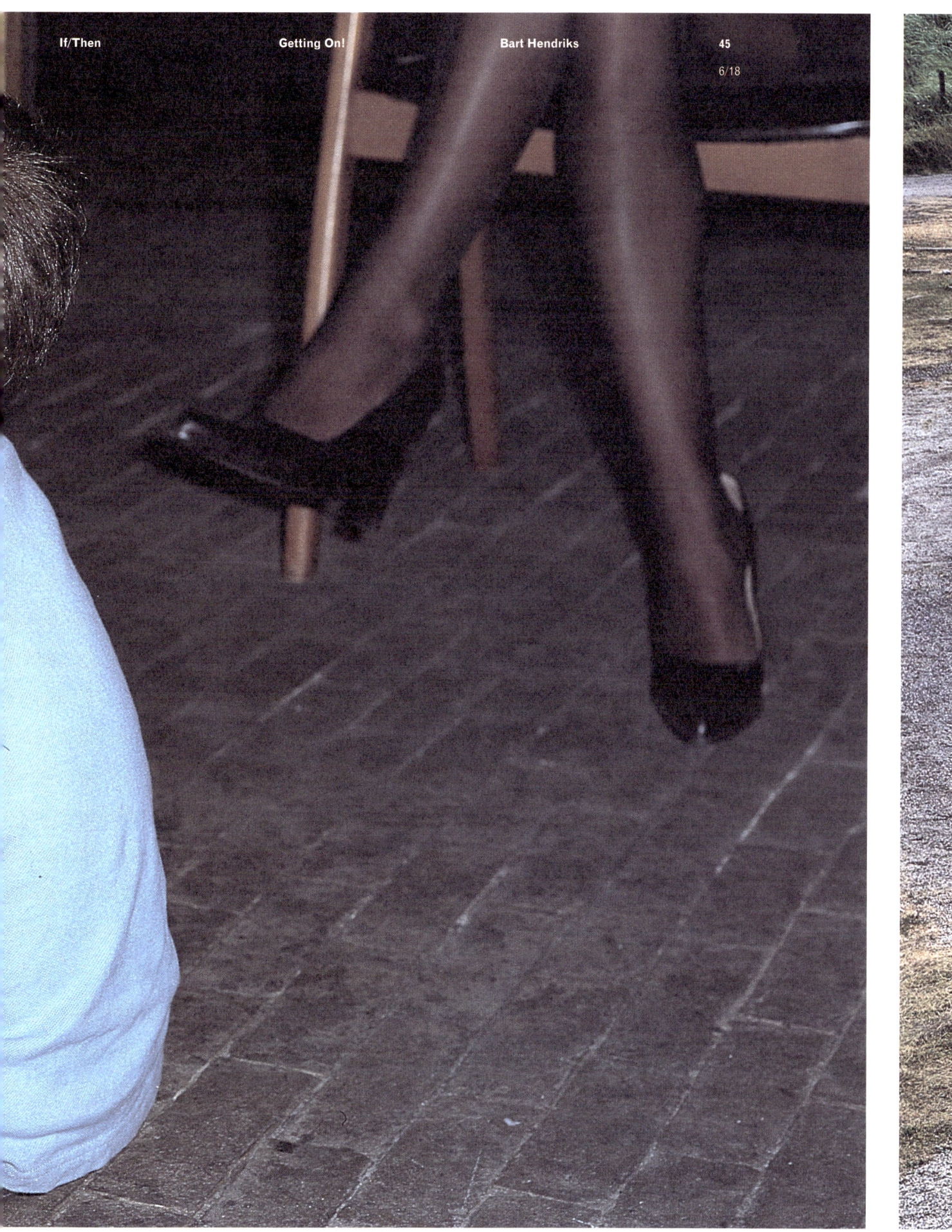

AT DE WAAG, AMSTERDAM, A CHILD PLAYS *WELCOME TO WONDERLAND*, UNDERNEATH THE *LEESTAFEL*

is two months before they give up, having been doused with one-too-many beers.

Touching the keyboard or touchpad, you are confronted not with the jargon of Netscape or Internet Explorer, but with virtual pages that turn themselves. An environment free of scrollbars or menus follows: only fields of bright colour with a limited number of clickable choices, on slowly revolving discs. But the entire Net remains accessible, in addition to free email (via dds.nl) and newsgroups. The cursor follows exactly what your finger does on the touchpad — no double-clicking or dragging. If you go to the bottom of a list, it begins to scroll automatically. Options and buttons are reduced to a minimum. Once you've finished your email, for instance, there are only two possibilities: *send* or *cancel*.

The international jury of the Rotterdam Design Prize was enchanted. "This is not a cyberpunk world," they wrote. "The interface looks friendly, not intimidating; it has nice colors, images and movement. And even more important: it is comprehensible to outsiders in the field of new media, who don't need to feel embarrassed because of their inexperience." In De Waag this concept works perfectly. The table is used by people from the neighborhood of all ages: youths come with their grandma or neighbor to teach them how to use the Net. In the social context of the café, asking for help is easy, even for the highly-educated — who don't usually dare ask questions like 'How do I get on?'

Although the *Leestafel* got plenty of media attention and was highly praised (a mobile version was developed for the Rotterdam Design Prize), it is so far the only one of its kind: the only order that came in was for a more corporate version, from the Dutch bank Rabobank, and the company that was to have mass produced the table went out of business.

Nevertheless, the *Leestafel* — or its type of easy-to-use software — does represent the future for public access to the net, according to KPN Research Manager Jans Aasman, speaking at the same session of *Getting On!* The KPN Internet *zuil* was for technophiles, and KPN is now focusing on the 80 per cent of technophobes, he explained. Two years ago he visited De Waag and was very impressed: "This was the first time I saw someone who had dared to dump the standard user-interface and succeeded in removing a lot of features. We copied most of the elements, although for a very different set of services." KPN is now developing an interface like that of the *Leestafel*, which will work on different devices, including kiosks, Internet-TV and the newest screenphones. The consumer, he believes, will accept and understand a new interface so long as it is simple and has as few options as possible.

Keller and Aasman have different views of the future. The *Leestafel* interface is still pretty abstract. Aasman considers Web TV — which offers web access on TV via the remote control, and which KPN has used in its customer research — a much better interface, being direct, familiar and easy to use, without cursor or scrollbars. "The average person doesn't think about information in the abstract," said Aasman. "Most interfaces are incomprehensible to them. Designers develop new iconography all the time, which means people are continually having to learn completely new alphabets. TV has been doing what it should do for 30 years now, and does it well."

Keller even goes further. "As a designer you have to realise that the user is not interested in interfaces, but in the services that lie behind them." Having designed the hardware for a public network to obtain services via smartcards at bus stops and billboards, he is convinced the user should be able to "just put their card in, push a button and get what they want." The fact that those services are actually carried by the Internet is not significant to them, Keller thinks.

Already, the vision of what can be provided at a public internet access point, and how it should be presented, seems to be quite narrow: TV remains the dominant model. But having only just begun to design hardware and software for the Net, what else is possible? Interfaces do come between the user and what they want, but this could be a plus. Limiting the interactivity of the Net would be a pity for both furNETure-providers and users, since each has information to offer the other. And, to judge by the audience response at the first *Getting On!* session, the latter certainly have ideas, opinions, and feedback that could be invaluable for the next generations of furNETure design.

KIOSKS PRODUCED BY FACTURA, SHOWN BY ROLF PIXLEY IN HIS *GETTING ON!* PRESENTATION

http://www.waag.org/mieg/lezingtafel/36reasons.jpg

Getting On! 2. DataButlers

Like an electronic Jeeves, the DataButler puts information in its owner's hand with unobtrusive diligence, and in places and times the desk-bound PC can't match. **Nico Macdonald** reports back from the second *Getting On!* session which explored the nitty-gritty of portable interactivity — from the minimum size of the QWERTY keyboard to tomorrow's networked wearables.

In his most recent book *The Invisible Computer* technology useability guru Donald Norman claims that the complexity of computers is out of control.[1] What's needed, he says, are information appliances better fitted to people's lives; consumers are ready for products that offer "convenience, ease of use and pleasure." According to Marc Weiser, chief technologist at Xerox PARC, the best technology is technology we don't notice – seamlessly fused with our physical and social worlds, and capable of fostering new models of work and play[2]. Are 'DataButlers' (as the Netherlands Design Institute dubs portable digital assistants) a step towards realizing these visions? What lies behind the recent proliferation of handheld electronic devices? And do they promote a more connected community or a culture of info-nomadism?

The second session of the *Getting On!* series brought together three people to explore these questions: Martin Riddiford, of London-based Therefore Design consultants, designer of the Psion 5 handheld organiser and all its predecessors; Irene McWilliam, head of Design Research at Philips Design, Eindhoven; and this author.

From being tools for creating and processing information, computers have graduated to serve a far wider range of activities – information exchange, delivery of services, two-way communication, collaboration and coordination – all intensified by the growth of the Internet. Desktop personal computers may be fine for the former tasks, but they are completely ill-suited to the latter, time-sensitive functions. The value of information changes over time and many services demand immediate action. While PCs will continue to be the way most people understand computing for some time to come, they won't make much more headway in their current form, since they don't adapt well to most environments, don't have integrated connectivity, and are forever crashing and rebooting.

The concept of the handheld electronic device has been around for many years (see *The DataButler through (PC) History* p 48) but recently, several factors have laid the basis for new kinds of computing. Improved chip design has come from PCs; laptops have pushed the envelope in displays and compact hardware engineering; consumer electronics has brought cheap, high-quality manufacturing; and the Internet has provided a solid, worldwide network has for DataButlers to connect to, and a way for keen shareware developers to distribute their product. The final element was improved software design and engineering.

Today, DataButlers fall broadly into two categories: cut-down PCs and electronic Filofaxes. The Psion – really the pioneer in this class of device – falls into the first, as does the Apple Newton. In the latter category are the 3Com Pilot; devices running Microsoft's Windows CE operating system (though clamshell-style models also are potentially 'cut-down' PCs); the new mobile phones with built-in diaries, address books and email; and Franklin's credit card-sized Rex, which can only be 'read' on the move and updated via PC.[3]

A few myths...
Technologies alone do not create social change, but DataButlers do open up exciting possibilities for new forms of collaboration. Traditional working practices have already been shattered, first by corporate down-sizing, then by the 'flattening' of organisations, and the passing of responsibility to employees, particularly in teams. What was once a job for life today can easily be just collateral damage in a corporate merger. So workers are becoming more pragmatic and self-reliant, finding flexible ways of working — from self-employment to contracting and tele-working. DataButlers fit these scenarios well: contact details are always to hand, whether the next meeting is in the nearest coffee shop or hotel lobby. The transportation crisis — particularly acute in the UK — is also promoting the use of Data-Butlers, since travel-time is increasingly work-time: getting there is now half the job done.

But DataButlers have not yet done away with the office and are unlikely to do so in the future. As Esther Dyson – a clas-

---

1 Donald Norman, *The Invisible Computer*, MIT Press, October 1998.
2 *Red Herring* July 1998, p134; *World Link*, January/February 1998, p 48
3 See Nico Macdonald, 'Palm Reading' *I.D. Magazine*, March/April 1998, p 93
4 Esther Dyson, *Release 2.0*, Broadway Books, 1997, p 74

If/Then Getting On! Bart Hendriks

The Databutler through (PC) history

Alan Kay and the dynabook
Computer as a personal tool environment

SoftBook and NuvoMedia's RocketBook
The arrival of the electronic book

Corel-type agendas
Data should be mobile and easily accessible

Psion series
A pda-computer that wears the mantle — good size, medium price. Windows like but prior to the master.

Microwriter Agenda
Creative attempt to get around the keyboard

Notebook computers
Full computing power on the move

Magic Cap (and March)
The first iteration of the hand-held Butler.

Newton (and Sharp Group)
More than a person al organizer — but mobile computing + handwritten recognition

BellSouth Simon
Users understand phones

Palm Pilot
Smaller than a PDA, and cheaper than the next step

Windows CE
Follow-the-Dad for mobile computing

Franklin Rex
Portable filer with pc connection

Sun-minibook
Just a full-function PC as small as a notebook

Electronic writing pad
Pen-input tablet (see existing use with nomadic sales division of per olam a writing pad that sends sent that happens so that the page can be treated in a PC)

Palm-sized PC
Microsoft's attempt to also extend its control. Perhaps more complex than the Palm, but also more rich. Perhaps too literal

AT&T Internet enabled phones
Email on telephone as standard

Nokia and Siemens phones with computing
Mobile memory needed for contact and other data. Evolution from it and the designers. Getting on!

Alcatel One Touch Com
PDA which mimics filo + medium + phone/email from and browsing

THE PSION ORGANISER 2 (TOP), PSION 3A AND PSION 5 (BOTTOM) WITH ITS QWERTY KEYS SPACED 16 MM APART, DESIGNED BY THEREFORE LTD.

sic info-nomad – points out in *Release 2.0*, information technology simply increases the road warrior's range, rather than freeing them from the office completely.⁴ In fact, the more remote workers there are, the greater the number of organisations will be needed to act as 'Houston Mission Control' to myriad information-age 'Eagles'.

Another criticism of the new portable digital devices is they are not easily personalised in the way a Filofax becomes characterfully scuffed with age. True, DataButlers are not yet capable of revealing their owner's physical imprint, but each person's use is unique: one need only think how laborious it is to use someone else's computer. The related argument, that DataButlers ruin your handwriting, is at least partially proven by the stories of Palm Pilot users who find themselves writing in 'Grafitti' (the glyph-based shorthand used for stylus input) on the rare occasions they put pen to paper.

Technologies rarely succeed at the specific task for which they were intended. Indeed their subversive use is often the most telling, as one *Getting On!* audience member pointed out, citing Japanese schoolgirls who use the infra-red links in their kids' electronic organisers to beam notes to one another when they are supposed to be listening to their teacher.

Where do we need to go (today)?

For DataButlers to succeed, several conditions are essential: network access via fast built-in modems with Internet connectivity; cheap, global mobile telephony (which may be provided by global satellite networks such as Teledesic and Iridium); better communication between devices (PC, DataButler, phone, printer) using infra-red or part of the radio spectrum; Web sites that accommodate their greyscale, letterbox-shaped screens; and software capable of the rich formatting customary in 'office' documents (at present one can start a document on a DataButler but not continue work on an existing one). Rather than simply mimicking PCs, tools and techniques are needed for specific DataButler-oriented activities such as brainstorming, project development and management, and for new ways of sifting and sorting data. Beyond today's 'docking stations', synchronisation probably means better use of wireless messaging and cellular networks. But as DataButlers become more like network computers — capable of loading applications and data off a central server — this may become academic.

For computing to be useful to more people, it will probably take a different form even from successful DataButlers like the Pilot, instead following the models described by Norman and Weiser. 'Wearables' will be an important step towards 'ubiquitous computing', taking advantage of the body as a network.

This was the terrain explored in Irene McWilliam's presentation: as Manager of Design Research at Philips Design, her perspective on DataButlers is informed by broad research into user-behaviour, cultural anthropology, and concerns such as privacy.

McWilliam explained that while the relationship between a user's actions and their outcome was quite self-evident in pre-electronic products, their electronic successors need more conscious interface development. In a striking series of diagrams, McWilliam laid out a 'Powers of Ten' schema explaining the exponential evolution of interface design, beginning with the domain of the expert user and the programmer (the two-dimensional user interface, already established), via agents, multi-media and multi-user environments (the third dimension, rapidly becoming familiar) and virtual reality (the fourth dimension). In the fifth dimension, the separation between the user and the interface (usually the screen) begins to blur, creating a 'crossover zone', so embedded data becomes more available to be designed into objects. In the sixth dimension, networked, mutable objects with behavioural systems begin "doing things for us," as McWilliam puts it. And in the seventh dimension, these devices interact and communicate with one another in a constellation.

Portability and wearability constitute the eighth dimension, with augmented wearables connecting us to other people and or objects. The tenth dimension brings in the time factor, and takes into consideration how we pass through information environments, what people are prepared to carry with them (in terms of weight and size), and cultural specifics — the 'who, what, when and how' of social behaviour — in different countries around the world. Illustrating this last 'dimension' with a diagram of her own journey to work from Utrecht to Eindhoven — which encompasses five modes of transport, four transitory spaces, and a various durations in each — McWilliam pointed out that people traverse multiple environments in their daily itineraries and carry out different activities 'on the move' — presenting complex challenges for designers.

One designer who has definitely risen to this challenge is Martin Riddiford, who has designed each successive edition of the Psion handheld organiser, in a remarkable 15-year association with the company. Psion's CEO, David Potter, encouraged him to set up Therefore Ltd, with Psion as a founding client.

As Riddiford explained in his presentation, Therefore is involved in all aspects of design, including circuit boards, operating systems and keyboards, allowing more effective integration of the various elements of the final product. The first Psion was intended for the non-

QWERTY literate user, and designed to be 'pocketable' to protect the keys. Used in 'field force integration' (data collection and retrieval outside the office, especially by sales staff), with printer and radio connections added on, this model had to be rugged and waterproof. Business consumers soon demanded PC connectivity; thus augmented, the Psion 2 sold 1.5 million units.

The first QWERTY keyboard was added in the Psion 3, along with the now familiar 'clamshell' form factor; the batteries were housed along the unit's hinge to avoid adding depth to the whole profile. For the keyboard to fit the form factor, one column of keys had to be eliminated and cursor keys embedded. The new operating system now enabled switching between running programs (multi-tasking) and 'flash cards' added memory and extra applications. The still-popular Psion 3a had a larger, grayscale screen and sold over a million units.

The most recent Psion, the Series 5, incorporates a pen interface (so as to be competitive with the Newton and the Pilot) although, for licensing reasons, the software had to remain fully functional using only the keyboard. The Psion 5 has an unusually long stylus – its design inspired by a dart – that allows the user to reach over the keyboard to the screen, holding the pen halfway along the shaft.

With keys spaced 16mm apart, the Psion 5's keyboard is the first on a handheld PC to be practicable for touch-typing. Unable to convince any manufacturer to invest in the design process for the requisite new keyboard mechanism, Therefore did the work in-house. Balance was also critical: to prevent the weight of the screen from tipping the unit over, a cantilever mechanism allows the keyboard to shift toward the user as they open it, while the screen pivots around its axis.

The elegance and useability of the Psion products are a testament to a mature relationship between the designers and the client, resulting in sophisticated integration of 'soft' and 'hard' design.

Getting On! 3: BREAD/CIRCUITS

The design of financial services is perhaps the most abstract and multi-disciplinary task in modern design, involving software designers, psychologists and economists, in addition to traditional graphic skills. In a fast-changing networked economy, the stakes are commensurately high. **Jules Marshall** was at the third *Getting On!* session to hear experts on e-commerce and communication researchers forecast the future of banking.

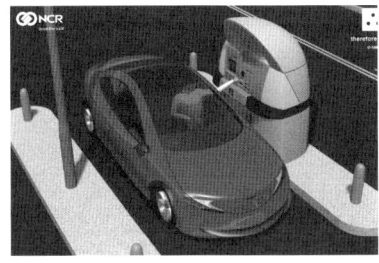

 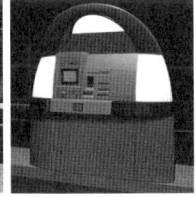

DRIVE-THRU ATM MACHINE, DESIGNED BY THEREFORE LTD FOR NCR CORPORATION

They used to say that knowledge is power. I used to think so, but I now know that they mean money.
　　　　　Lord Byron, 1788-1824.

There's a sense of almost evolutionary inevitability to the way money is shedding its last illusory atoms of tangibility and becoming purely digital. Banks and their large corporate clients initiated the transubstantiation of cash into blips of light some 30 years ago. Through a combination of strategy, fashion, and market pull, new services have been added ever since. The impact of new technology-enabled channels has, to date, been relatively low because much of the technology has been proprietary, that is to say, bank-based (e.g. ATM), and because consumer uptake of new technology has been relatively low. But the explosion of Internet use in the mid-1990s has been harder for banks to cope with, leaving them "playing catch-up," according to Geert Roggen, project manager at the Dutch bank Rabobank, and one of the speakers in the third *Getting On!* session in July 1998.

Stephen Emmott, director of the NCR Financial Services Knowledge Lab, based in London, believes things are going to change even more in the next ten years, because of the accelerating rate of change in the channels through which financial services are provided.

Twenty-five years ago, financial services were delivered primarily via the branch. Ten years ago, the only significant

| If/Then | Getting On! | Bart Hendriks | 52 |

URLS Products
Geofox palmtop http://www.geofox.com
Seiko MessageWatch site http://www.messagewatch.com
NuvoMedia's RocketBook http://www.nuvomedia.com
SoftBook http://www.softbook.com
Motorola Marco
http://cgi.ebay.com/aw-cgi/eBayISAPI.dll?ViewItem&item=70879723

URLS Services
Dutch services for Seiko MessageWatch
http://www.minimail.com
GSM Information Network (Dutch GSM-based services)
http://www.gin.nl/service/index.htm
Advanced Buzzer Services http://www.callmax.com
Unwired Planet http://www.uplanet.com/
UPlanet Cellularphone surfing article
http://www.sjmercury.com/business/top/008040.htm

URLS Browser
Unwired Planet Browser
http://www.uplanet.com/tech/products/upbrowser.html

URLS Reference
'wireless' links http://winwww.rutgers.edu/pub/Links.html
Mobile computing http://www.volksware.com/mobilis/
Wireless Application Forum http://www.wapforum.org

addition was the ATM. Today, thanks to changes in both technology and consumer behaviour, financial services are now delivered via a panoply of channels: branches; fixed and wireless telephones, the Internet, proprietary PC-based services, interactive kiosks, magnetic and 'smart' microprocessor-based cards, and non-branch, non-bank physical locations such as supermarkets.

From the banking perspective, technology cuts costs and makes things easier, and leads to new revenue streams and markets which can be accessed virtually; the synergy will ultimately be enabling, resulting in more efficient markets. As Anton Martens, e-commerce manager at Cap Gemini put it: "The revolution in banking is primarily a channel revolution." Is multiplicity good? The supply-side assumes so, but consumers (at least, to judge by the audience at all three *Getting On!* seminars) frequently say no.

Technological innovation is merely the second most radical change, says Emmott, who argued that "the technology is less important than the relationship." The problem for banks is more psycho-social: how do you engender the same feeling of trust in a customer on the Net, on the phone, or at a home terminal, as you can in a branch? How do you capture and retain their attention?

The problem for designers is no less tricky: how do you capture attention and create trust when the bank's card has become the only link with the customer — when, effectively, its logo *is* the branch and the contact?

Are designers confined to creating the look of the cards, or should they be involved in the whole process? Fred van Haaften, research director of telebanking at Rabobank, characterised design in financial institutions as, traditionally, "a battle between boring bankers and mad designers." One need only look at existing interface design of automated transaction devices, from ATMs to ticket machines, to see who has had the upper hand.

According to Emmott, the task of capturing and retaining consumers through an expanding number of technology channels requires a relationship not dissimilar "to that with a lover." Besides trust, he suggests that communication, affinity, attention and understanding are all "relationship technologies," vital if banks and others are to become 'trusted brokers' in e-commerce. Little money is to be made in simple transactions any more, so it is in relationship technologies that NCR believes the future of banking lies.

Emmott illustrated his points with examples of over-the-horizon products his Knowledge Lab team is working on. The growing ubiquity of computing power will shortly mean all consumer goods may have their own IP address. Since much family business is conducted in the kitchen, NCR is looking at a microwave oven with a flat-screen monitor serving as

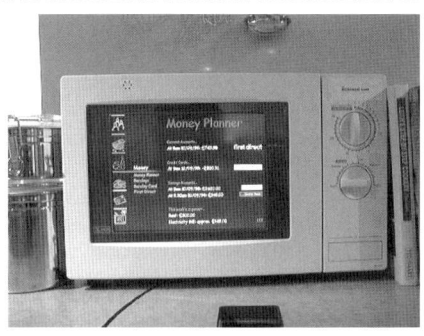

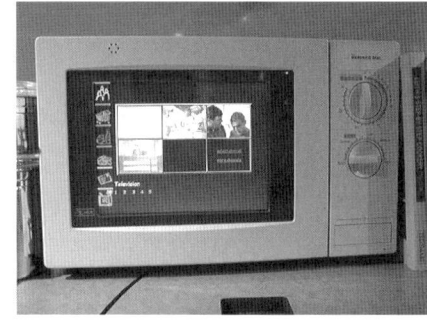

THE MICROWAVE BANK PROTOTYPES © NCR KNOWLEDGE LAB 1998

Ready cooked interfaces: from touch to hold

Sarah Woods is one of the pioneers of 'physical computing'. J.J. King finds out how she is helping the NCR Knowledge Lab think up the banking facilities of the future.

Interface is the next wild frontier of technology. Continuous advances in processor speed have not yet translated into better user-experience, which remains limited by mouse, keyboard, screen and the ubiquitous desktop metaphor. The computer's raw potentiality already outstrips what can actually be done with the commercial applications running on it. Only with more direct and intuitive interfaces can this problem be overcome, and the heavy hitters are already laying their bets on the next generation of interface technology: Microsoft backs speech recognition (for now, at least), while Sun's gurus see the future in gesture-recognition. Whichever approach wins out, the challenge to go 'beyond the screen' will — along with networking and interconnectivity — define thinking about computing in the coming decade.

Sarah Woods is well placed to take up that challenge, having graduated from the Royal College of Art's Computer Related Design (CRD) course in 1995 with *Buggies*, a piece that employs coloured blocks to trigger musical notes produced by a computer. By playing with the blocks, children also play music: rather than the holy trinity of keyboard/mouse/screen, the blocks are their interface with the machine. *Buggies* was borne out of Woods' frustration, while working on a children's CD-ROM, at the limitations of 'interactivity' — still largely confined to clicks and keyboard strokes, despite the rhetoric of multimedia.

Buggies' physical interface, by contrast, allows users to manipulate the sound application in a direct tactile and three dimensional way — a technique that has proved as popular with adults as with children when employed in exhibition design, encouraging exploration and collaborative play. "Several quite creative pieces of music have been generated," says Woods, "and on one occasion I've found children fighting over them. No-one seems to have any problems grasping what to do with *Buggies*." And, as she quickly realised, interfaces that allow users to operate in real space may have distinct advantages over those that rely upon the traditional modality.

After leaving the Royal College of Art, Woods went to work for the Interval Research

a door, allowing Net surfing and financial transactions to be conducted while dinner warms up.

Soap operas grab people's attention, so NCR has created a Net-based soap, the *Virtual Idol Opera*, in which the characters are downloadable intelligent agents who offer financial advice. You can also drag the CD from the V-actor's virtual CD player and order it, or try on her clothes and ask her what she thinks (and then order them).

As computer screens become flatter, lighter and bigger, NCR speculates that financial transactions such as car-buying will be conducted at home via 'video wallpaper' and software agents — perhaps in the guise of celebrities such as model Liz Hurley or England football captain Alan Shearer. "I'd trust Shearer more than an anonymous face from a bank," confessed Emmott, touching on an issue that design alone may be unable solve.

As many members of the *Getting On!* audience confirmed privately afterwards, when the networked economy's smart, all-in-one health record/library ticket/cashcard/credit card comes of age, banks will not be very near the top of the list of trusted parties to be made privy to and responsible for this data.

Trust is a dissipating resource in contemporary society. From church to state, all hallowed institutions are suffering. Banks were once paradigms of virtue and sobriety, but well-publicised scandals (Barings, BCCI, the US Savings and Loans collapse) and the social practices predicated by banks' 'responsibility to shareholders' (including eviction of mortgage-defaulting home owners, and bankruptcy of US farmers) means that trust cannot be simply slapped on a card as a superficial afterthought.

Banks may need relationships with their customers akin to a lover's, but the general impression is that they are actually more like that between acrimonious divorcees: painful, reluctant and mediated by lawyers.

The problem with NCR's vision, and with most other analyses of e-commerce, is that they are linear extrapolations of multi-variable, synergistic, chaotic, exponential change. When national reserve banks became the sole guardians of national currencies, they doled out licenses to creditable institutions that duly built large, solid-looking headquarters and huge networks of branches staffed by sober individuals. That trust-affirming network of bricks, mortar and people is being rapidly being 'disintermediated' — to borrow a current buzzword. All sorts of retail enterprises, from supermarkets to entertainment companies, are offering financial services, while many corporate customers have developed in-house banking capabilities. For example, Ford — ostensibly a car manufacturer — currently makes 80 per cent of its profits from financing deals, as Emmott noted.

Innovations such as micropayments and non-financial exchange of goods and services — from Local Economy Trading Schemes (LETS) to Air Miles to pay-to-view ads — are re-defining the nature of money and value, and their relationship to work. Developments in finance are not evolving in a vacuum, but as part of a far wider ongoing redefinition of the relationship between work/non-work and their relative rewards. Trust is in effect being (re)democratized.

The harder and faster banks struggle towards pervasive e-commerce, the more competition they open up for themselves. It's a Chinese finger puzzle from which they hope design can free them, but it's a task the banks hand over reluctantly.

PERSONALISED ATM, PROTOTYPE
© NCR KNOWLEDGE LAB 1998

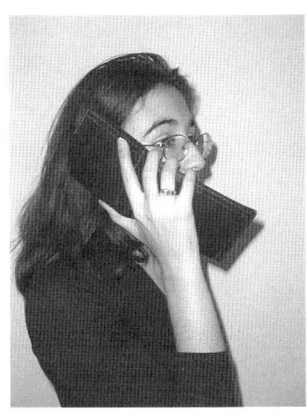

INTERACTIVE WALLET PROTOTYPE
© NCR KNOWLEDGE LAB 1998

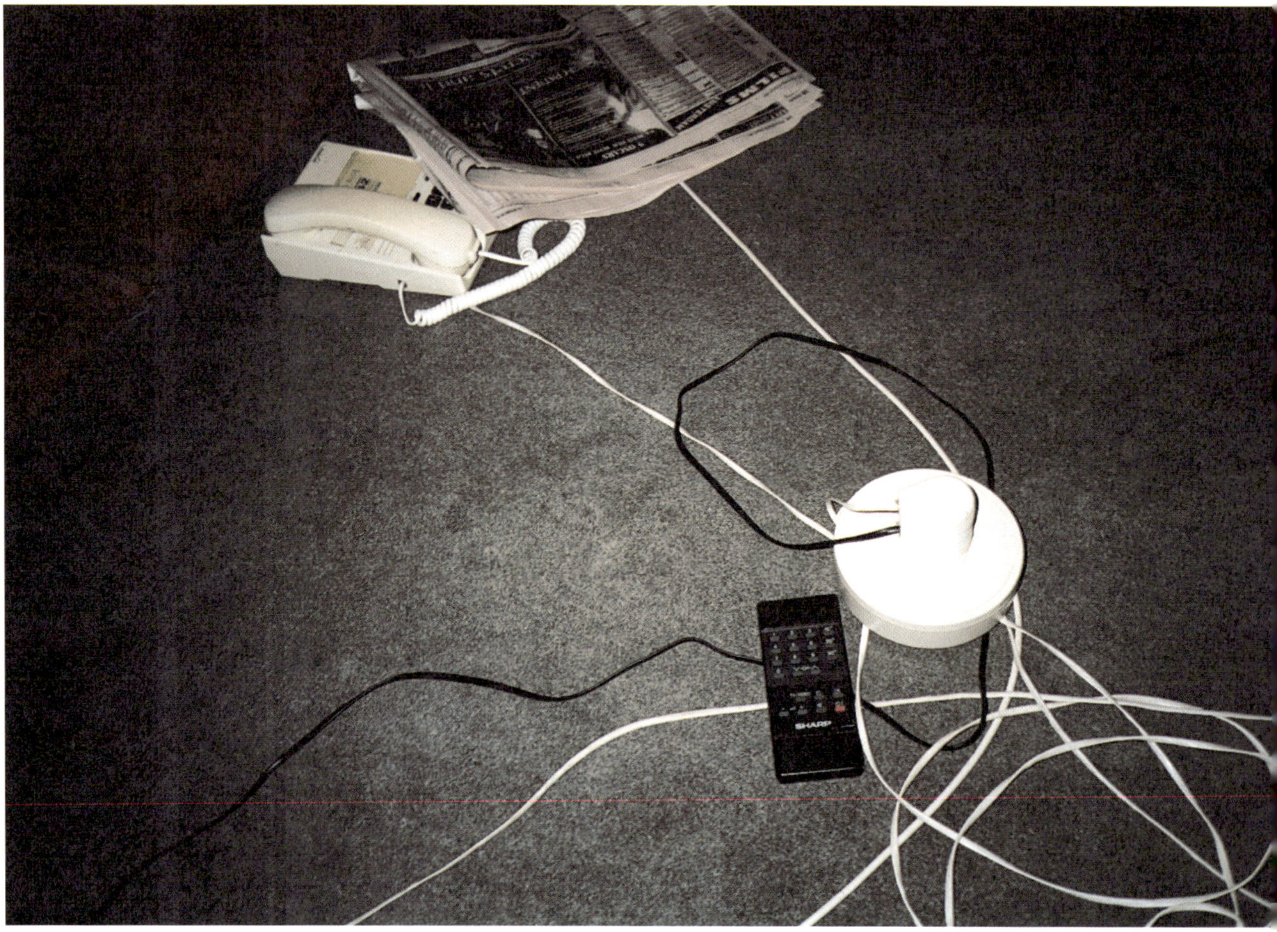

キ
イ
カ
カ
…
三
キ
ラ
三
」

ヌ ハフスミ/ハフスイ

ツ   ヨキカキコクリメスト

フ   コス/キラメ/ニスノフニカト

Knowledge Management is the buzz phrase in business these days, as companies restructure themselves to compete in the global economy. Information, rather than objects, is becoming the primary source of corporate value, so the pressure is on to keep track of it: where it resides, how it flows through an organisation, how it becomes knowledge.

But knowledge is hard to map when corporate personnel are geographically dispersed — and especially when individual employees strategically prefer to keep it to themselves. So companies increasingly need maps capable of representing intangible assets that are in constant flux and connected in complex, dynamic relationships.

When knowledge managers got down to business with interaction designers at a Netherlands Design Institute seminar on Knowledge Maps last April, they found that — despite all the contemporary rhetoric about 'flattened hierarchies' — Darwinist principles are still at work in the workplace.

If conflicts of interest are inherent in any social organisation, will designers inevitably find themselves asked to make knowledge maps that represent companies as more harmonious than they really are? **Marek Kohn** reports.

"You might have heard a lot of businesses talking about simplifying their business. I'm really worried about that," said David Smith, Unilever's Head of Knowledge Management and Development, addressing an invited group of knowledge managers and digital designers at the Netherlands Design Institute's Knowledge Maps seminar in April 1998.

"I think we have the opportunity to make businesses more complex, more knowledge-rich, knowledge-intensive, and to provide more creative products and services," he told his fellow participants. "Anything that produces complexity, that's a good thing. That's how you compete."

Whether you like it or not, he might have added. Smith had pointed to a key truth about profit. For companies in developed economies, value increasingly resides in information rather than in objects. The higher the level of the information, the more valuable it is likely to be. At the highest level is knowledge, according to the practical definition widely used by knowledge managers. In David Smith's phrasing, knowledge is the capacity to transform information and data into value. As well as needing a base of low level information, knowledge requires structures to support it. So even if what a company thinks it needs is simplicity, it's going to have to face up to increasing complexity. And if that's the way a business has to go, it's going to need a map.

The modern company has already become largely unknown territory. A mapmaker assigned to draw a map of it would be forced, like the cartographer of old, to label much of it *terra incognita*. But at least the old cartographers knew where the unknown territory began, if not where it ended. And as far as their masters were concerned, what was not known might well be of no value. Modern managers and executives, by contrast, live in a world where what they value most is hardest to chart.

A century ago, organisations had the tools they needed for assessing themselves and mapping where their assets lay. The techniques of accountancy did a good job of identifying the value of machinery, buildings and labour. Today, such assets may constitute perhaps a fifth of a company's worth. The other four-fifths lie in intangibles. Brands will account for part of the balance; the rest is knowledge. Yet companies still have to rely largely on 19th-century organisational tools designed for a world powered by steam. It is as if the men who charted Britain in the early part of the 19th century had been obliged to conduct their Ordnance Survey at night.

Enter knowledge management. A small proportion of executives, the kind who attract the label 'visionary', has embraced it. Others dismiss it as just the latest fad, albeit one with a more elegant name than 'business process re-engineering.' Between them is a large number of business professionals who can see the point of knowledge management in theory, but have done little about it because they are not aware of practical tools for implementing it. This group, perhaps the silent majority, stands to gain most from the development of knowledge maps.

These elusive charts were the subject of the seminar at which the knowledge managers and the information designers came together, under the auspices of the Netherlands Design Institute and Kenniscentrum CIBIT. At the invitation of John Thackara, the Institute's director, the knowledge managers took turns to introduce themselves over a working supper that opened with the following question: 'Is it possible to design a dynamic and multi-functional map of knowledge resources in an enterprise or network of enterprises?'

It soon became obvious that, however keenly aware they are of the bottom line in business, knowledge managers are free — not to say profligate — with their metaphors. David Smith invoked quantum theory, the science of complexity, and the ratio of an organism's surface area to its volume. Several other managers compared the modern business organisation to a living organism. Remo Pareschi of the recently privatised Telecom Italia remarked that reconstructing staff on modern business lines was like turning squirrels into apes. After a while it began to look as though the managers wanted to meet zoologists, not cartographers.

Nor were they keen to take their models straight off the shelf from an atlas. Esko Kilpi, of the Helsinki management consultancy Sedecon, struck a chord when he said that knowledge workers should not be too concerned with what was available, but should concentrate on what was *not* available. Dick Rijken of TBWA/E-company, a digital communication consultancy in Amsterdam, denied that he even wanted maps of knowledge. Instead, he wanted maps of *people* — which need not even be in graphic form. All that is required, Rijken suggested, is a 'knowledge Yellow Pages', a list of who knows what, and where to find them. Nice resource if you can get it.

What nobody much wanted was a rigorous philosophical definition of knowledge. It became clear that knowledge was a loose concept, something that could mean different things for different organisations, and that this looseness was necessary for knowledge to be of practical use in business. Whatever it constitutes in a particular company, it always signifies the translation of information into action. As the management theorist Peter F. Drucker put it in *The New Realities*, "Knowledge is information that changes something or somebody".[1] Although it can rarely be pinned down, it can be sorted into categories. Rudy Ruggles, knowledge management research director at Ernst & Young's Center for Business Innovation in Boston, would call 'Knowledge Yellow Pages' a form of catalog knowledge. Ruggles also identifies process knowledge, ('recipes for doing things well'), basic factual knowledge (the easiest to deal with, but least valuable), and cultural knowledge ('knowing how things actually get done in an organization'). All these forms come in two flavours, tacit and explicit. Philosophers and knowledge managers recognise that tacit knowledge is fundamental to understanding complex problems, but difficult to represent because we don't know we know it, and so 'we know more than we can tell'.[2]

Victoria Ward, who used to be Chief Knowledge Officer for NatWest Markets and now runs a consultancy called Spark Knowledge in London, related an anecdote about a company which shut down a depot in the course of rationalisation. This left its technicians without a place to meet and swap notes. They began to call at a local café, whose proprietor kindly agreed to keep a book in which they entered useful information, thus alleviating the problems that mobile workers face in getting together at a particular time. Taking the cynical view, it also seemed an ideal solution for the company, since the workers were organising the system and bearing its costs themselves, in conjunction with the café proprietor. Employees may not always be so obliging, though, and other enterprises would perhaps prefer to make sure of a solution by using their own information technology. That way the company would retain ownership of the knowledge, too.

Hans Lipman of KPN Telecom, formerly the publicly owned Dutch PTT Telecom, provided a break from the visionary thing with his refreshingly candid remarks about life in the telecommunications industry. The impact of technological upheaval and the deregulation revolution is particularly intense in telecoms, most of all in those that are being taken from public monopoly into the private sector. Lipman pointed out that constant change means staff are constantly moving, which makes it especially hard to keep track of people with knowledge about particular issues. Lipman also noted that it may be against individuals' interests to share knowledge. If knowledge is becoming the most valuable resource a company can possess, then its value to individual knowledge workers will also increase. Under conditions of permanent revolution, individuals may feel they can rely on their knowledge more than they can on their employers. Maintaining a monopoly over local knowledge may seem like a good way of avoiding an unwelcome redeployment. If individuals are uncertain that they have a future within a company, they may prefer to keep knowledge buried in their portfolios as a nest egg.

At this point, I felt the discussion had really got down to business. One of the attractions of the visionary style in management discourse is that it is idealistic. The contemporary ideology of business invokes a vista of freedom and creativity, in which all hierarchies are flattened and all members of staff are 'empowered'. This is widely seen as an inevitable consequence of modern business structures and the technology that supports them. The telecommunications prophet George Gilder, for example, declared in his 1991 *Harvard Business Review* article "Into the Telecosm" that "new computer systems decentralize control and empower people all along the information chain." He coined the term *heterarchy* to imply that hierarchies are being flattened out of existence altogether. It seems to be a *faux pas* to mention that somebody still owns the company and somebody is in charge. Having won the class struggle, business is unwilling to recognise that conflicts of interest are inherent in any form of social organisation.

In this respect, the metaphors that the managers borrowed from the natural sciences were revealing. If what really matters is the bottom line, it seems almost perverse to appropriate ideas whose major implication is uncertainty. It is not as though complexity or quantum theory are the only games in town. Evolutionary theory is equally dynamic, and it shares a common language with economics, of cost and benefit. Unlike the more esoteric domains of physics and mathematics, however, it offers little to those who wish to see each entity as a harmonious whole. Modern evolutionists do not believe that competition takes place just between individuals. They expect to find conflict within organisms, between the genes contributed by each parent, and between the

---

1 "Knowledge is information that changes something or somebody - either by becoming grounds for actions, or by making an individual (or an institution) capable of different or more effective action." Peter F. Drucker, *The New Realities*, HarperBusiness, 1994.

2 Rudy Ruggles, "Knowledge Tools: Using Technology to Manage Knowledge Better," Working Paper, Ernst & Young Center for Business Innovation, Boston, 1997.

mother and the offspring in the womb. For Darwinists, communication is a matter of the bottom line: a signal will be sent if the benefits to the sender outweigh the costs; if the costs outweigh the benefits, it will not. Similar calculations will determine whether signals are truthful, and whether they are believed. Darwinists are never surprised to encounter deception — especially among humans, the champions of the art.

Many forms of knowledge are not amenable to transfer or concealment. Much knowledge exists only in the context of a specific organisation, and is of no value outside it. But as organisations buy more services from external sources, knowledge will become increasingly detached from specific organisations, and therefore more portable. And while it will generally be impossible to keep large bodies of knowledge private, humans are exceptionally adept at manipulating information in subtle ways. By the astute use of nuance and omission, knowledge workers can maintain a position of advantage for themselves while appearing to be loyal team players.

Responding to Hans Lipman's observation, David Smith gave examples of very different approaches to the problem. One American CEO, of a major manufacturing corporation, had a policy of sacking any employee caught hoarding knowledge. Fujitsu, by contrast, had gone for the carrot rather than the stick. It instituted an internal market in which ideas could be bought and sold. Their cash value was modest; the real incentive was the prestige that came with being seen to offer ideas. Smith commented that each solution was probably specific to each company's culture, and would not necessarily work elsewhere. But the examples illustrated the strength of incentives and the weakness of threats. Incentives encourage disclosure; threats may only encourage concealment. The American CEO's methods were also a clear example of the kind of 'command and control' strategy which David Smith had dismissed as obsolete.

Victoria Ward doubted that people hoard knowledge because it is power. "The reason people won't share their knowledge is because while it's theirs, they are the guardian of its quality," she said. "If they give it to somebody else, they can't control the quality or what is done with it." She also came up with an excellent example of knowledge with a capital K, in the shape of *The Knowledge*, the famous understanding of routes that London taxi drivers have to master. At the lowest level it is data, the names of roads and streets; above that it is information, about the spatial relationships between the streets. Above all it is knowledge about how to actually get from one place to another, incorporating contextual information about matters such as traffic congestion and local bottlenecks, and how to modify the Highway Code to London conditions. And, of course, it is a set of maps.

Unlike London cabbies, knowledge managers live in a world where the watchwords are speed and change. As CIBIT director Rob van der Spek pointed out, mapmakers live in a fixed world. In the old days, objects stayed put long enough to be worth mapping. Nowadays, it is the currents rather than the coastline that matter.

The following morning, it was the turn of the information designers to set out their stalls. Martin Dodge of University College London's Center for Advanced Spatial Analysis showed examples from his *Atlas of Cyberspace*, a collection of maps of the Internet, the World Wide Web and their burgeoning social enclaves. These representations were drawn up by people other than geographers, he noted, and in cyberspace there are no agreed grids or metrics. Among the slides was a 'satellite view' of *AlphaWorld*, a virtual townscape in the ActiveWorlds online environment where subscribers can stake out territory and build upon it. Dodge pointed out the literal-minded way in which virtual homesteaders put roofs on their buildings, thus reducing the information content and the interest of the satellite view.

Yuri Engelhardt, based at the University of Amsterdam, discussed the visual grammar of information graphics. Among Engelhardt's points of reference were the 18th-century Turgot Plan of Paris, and Harry Beck's 1933 map of the London Underground (see pages 72-74). Paul Kahn and David Durand of Dynamic Diagrams (based in Providence, Rhode Island) also drew on these classic designs for their MAPA system, which helps Web users orient themselves by mapping Web sites (see pages 68-69). From the Turgot Plan they took the idea of an orthographic projection, which looks like a perspective drawing but has no vanishing point, minimising visual distortion. The Beck map taught them the value of bold colours, a regular grid and space for labels. Traditional values in a modern setting, to coin a phrase. In contrast, Lisa Strausfeld's San Francisco-based company Perspecta embraces three-dimensional interfaces with 'fly-through' capabilities, in a system — called

http://www.cybergeography.org/atlas/

If:

-All things being equal, you randomly decide that page X will show one photograph of a situation which reminds you of Y, to her Z, and the photograph which evokes nothing in particular.

Then:

Pierre Bismuth, If/Then January 1999. Page 63

Pierre Bismuth. If/Then January 1999. Page 64

SmartContent™ — designed to bring automated expertise to the extraction of information from databases (see pages 66-67). Gong Szeto and Steve Cannon — respectively vice president for design and lead technologist at New York-based i/o 360 Digital Design/Rare Medium — demonstrated their *Parasite* project, an attempt to turn email into a more dynamic and re-usable body of knowledge. Although all the information designers showed maps, Szeto and Cannon were the only ones to present a prototype knowledge map (see pages 70-71).

When the designers' presentations were complete, Rob van der Spek set three questions for the afternoon workshops: What kind of information should be on knowledge maps? What kind of design principles will make them work? And what kind of tools for knowledge can we give to people in organisations? These questions met with a mixed response. One group decided to start from business process models and fell into a discussion of how to devise icons, how to identify communities with shared practices or interests, and how to track flows of activity. A second group emphasised the importance of tacit knowledge and irregular knowledge — such as whom to bribe — that are not written down. The third, uncomfortable with the questions to begin with, highlighted the need to map gaps in knowledge.

In his concluding remarks, John Thackara observed that managers and designers had mutual interests aplenty. But, he wondered, did they have mutual understanding? Lisa Strausfeld admitted she did not feel ready to make a knowledge map, because she had not yet grasped the knowledge managers' needs. She spoke for others who were not quite so candid. It wasn't that the managers appeared not to need the kind of assistance a map can provide, but that they spoke a language in which the designers were not yet fluent.

My own feeling was that the project of knowledge mapping would be hampered by the reluctance of modern business to admit conflicts of interest. The most valuable maps would be those that charted the interests of agents within an organisation, so that mutual interests could be designed in, and conflicts designed out — or at least recognised. But, just as a sensible Renaissance cartographer would give his royal patron a map showing what the ruler wished to see — putting the royal palace at the centre of the world, say — a smart modern design company might be inclined to give its corporate clients maps that depict organisations as more harmonious and less hierarchical than they really are.

An important strategic question for knowledge cartographers is whether they should be trying to sell their products to the princes of industry, for whom an overview of a large organisation could be a powerful asset. In his talk during the opening session, David Smith offered a striking insight about an organisation in a mere couple of sentences. He observed that Shell, the petrochemical company, has two knowledge cores: one is geoscience, which produces knowledge about where to find oil; the other is knowledge about negotiating with governments — the biggest resource of its kind outside governments themselves, he suggested. All of Shell's other knowledge is generic; its competitors know as much as it does about processes such as refining and distributing petrochemical products.

Whether knowledge maps could add value to a brilliant précis like this is an open question. Instead of trying to tackle the big pictures, knowledge mapping projects might do better to concentrate on providing tools with which individual knowledge workers can make their own local maps. That would be in the spirit of empowerment so widely vaunted in contemporary business rhetoric, after all. Once the mapping tools have been honed on small patches of knowledge terrain, it should be that much easier to see how they could be applied to the landscape as a whole.

On the other hand, if the prophets of networks and flattened hierarchies are right, they may already have done the job by then.

PERSPECTA
Discreet 3D

Cutting-edge digital design has often looked to the skies for its metaphors, invoking a vision of graphics not as a surface but as a space through which the viewer flies. But If God had meant us to fly through immersive environments, He would surely have given us wings. Playing three-dimensional computer games is one thing, but designers have had a lot more trouble presenting serious information in three-dimensional formats.

Carrying the spirit of the MIT Media Lab into the world of new media start-ups (two domains in which the familiar laws of gravity do not apply, either to economics or graphics) the San Francisco-based Perspecta team has gone some way toward making 3D information graphics a reality.

With its discreet translucent layers, the company's *PerspectaView* interface delivers the benefits of three dimensions without making a big immersive deal of them. The technology has its roots in more spectacular visualisation efforts, such as the *Financial Viewpoints* project that co-founder Lisa Strausfeld created while studying at the Media Lab's Visible Language Workshop. Designed to provide business professionals multiple perspectives on a large financial database, it yielded an image like an ethereal skyscraper at night. Never before has a mutual fund portfolio looked so beautiful.

A *PerspectaView* front end can also look like a conventional Web table if the designer using Perspecta's *SmartContent* system prefers. What really counts is the connections the System makes behind the scenes in the database. The *SmartContent* system is basically an engine for intensifying metacontent — that is, information about information — which comes from three sources: any meta-information already present in the database to which it is applied; extra meta-information added by its operators; and connections within the database that it makes by itself.

One of the key tools with which the operators can raise the level of the information is the Concept Editor, which is used to create a Concept Database. At the user's end, the *PerspectaView* software (a Java client which can be downloaded from Web sites using the Perspecta system) delivers the graphic representation created by the metacontent machine. The information it supplies is somewhat like a smart version of what conventional Web search engines offer. If you ask a search engine about Mr X, and one of the hits refers to Ms Y, this is often the spurious result of a dumb reading of data. If Perspecta comes up with such a response, it should be because there is a connection between Mr X and Ms Y — for example, they work for the same company — of which you may be not aware. And it should also be able to tell you why you should be interested in Ms Y, instead of leaving you to work it out for yourself.

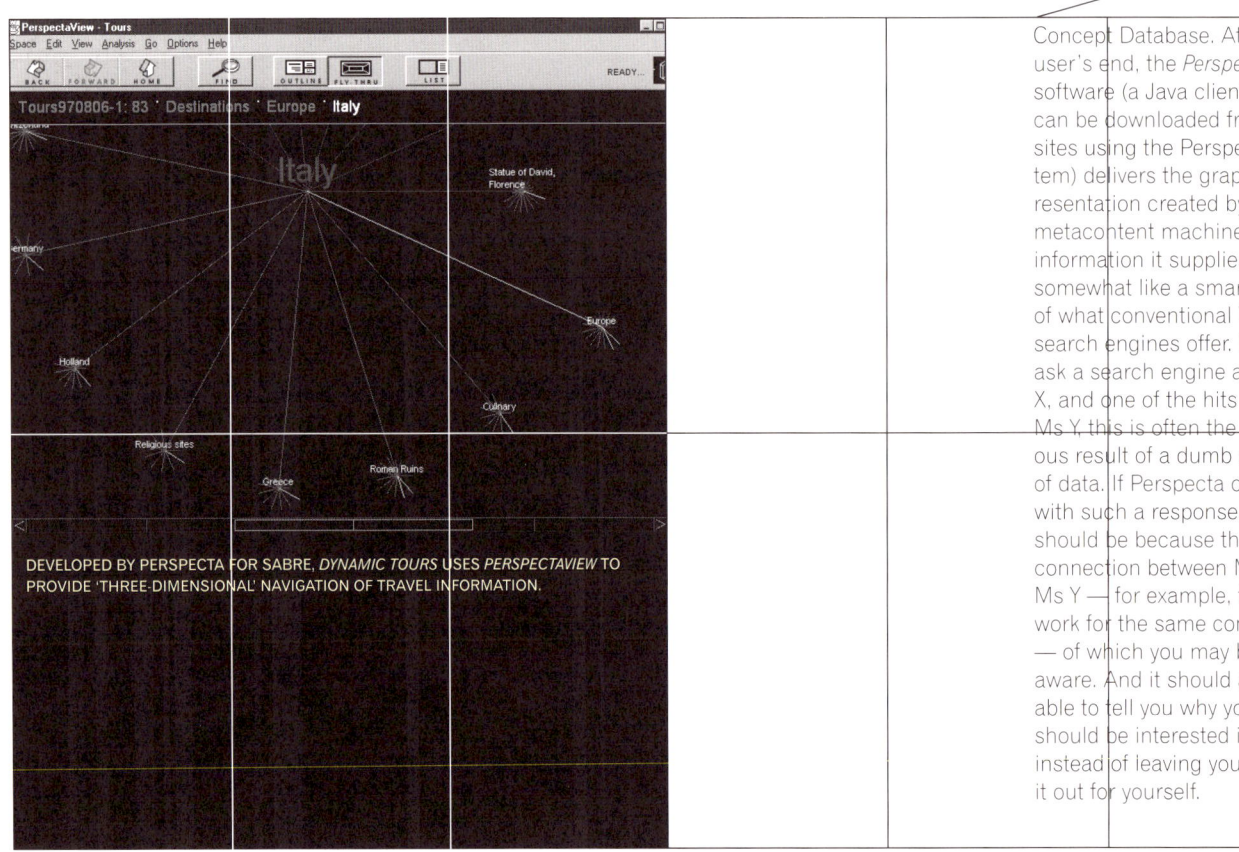

DEVELOPED BY PERSPECTA FOR SABRE, *DYNAMIC TOURS* USES *PERSPECTAVIEW* TO PROVIDE 'THREE-DIMENSIONAL' NAVIGATION OF TRAVEL INFORMATION.

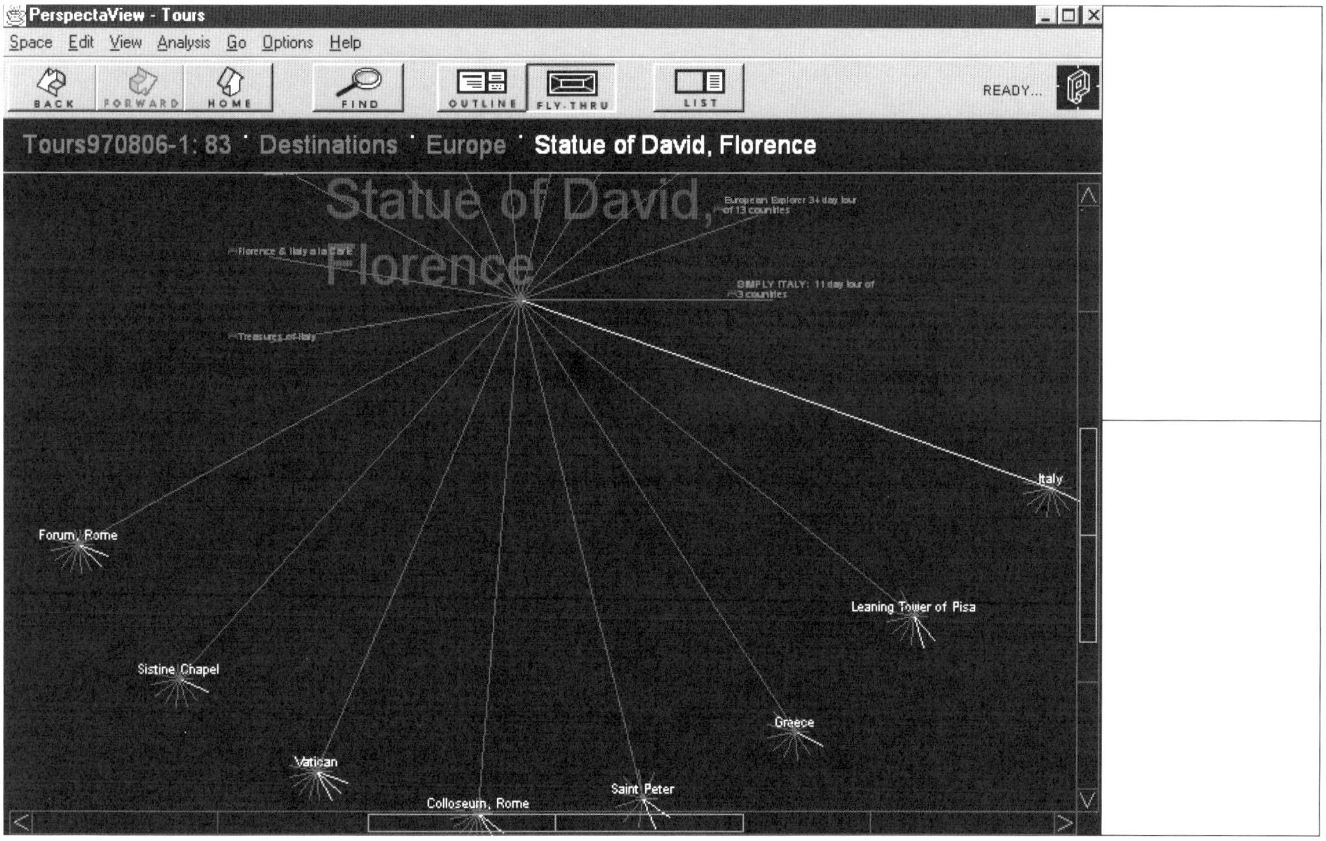

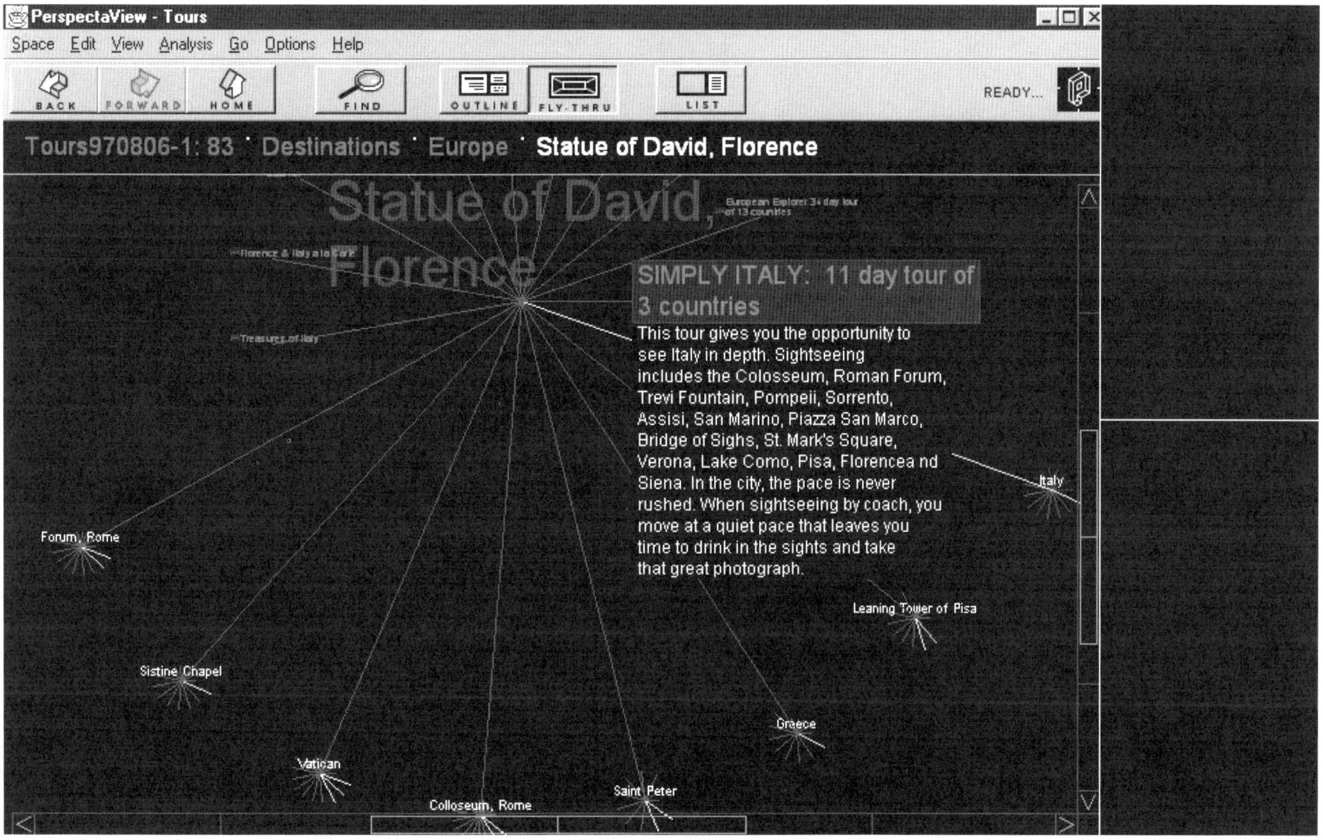

DYNAMIC DIAGRAMS: You Are Here

Internet publicist Douglas Rushkoff thinks today's kids understand the new world of fractals, chaos and infinitely complex webs, which they blithely surf through with skateboards and joysticks. In his book *Children of Chaos*, he advises the rest of us to "take a remedial course in postlinear, visual communication. We should read comics."

For those of us with work to do, however, Dynamic Diagrams have looked at the Web through a classical, linear, hierarchical prism, and come up with a mapping system, MAPA, that imposes a calm order on what can often seem like chaos.

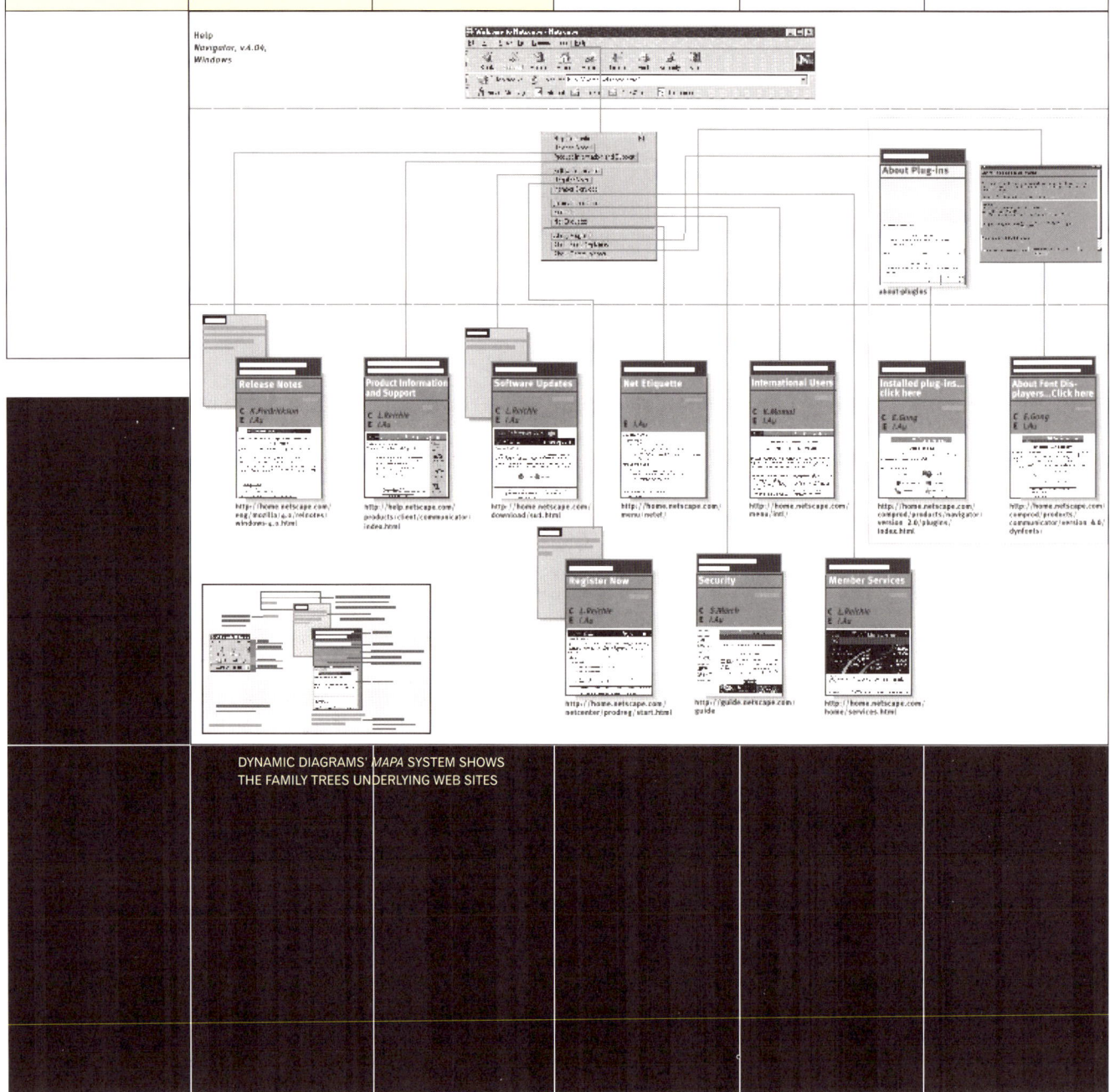

DYNAMIC DIAGRAMS' *MAPA* SYSTEM SHOWS THE FAMILY TREES UNDERLYING WEB SITES

David Durand and Paul Kahn of Dynamic Diagrams aren't against complexity, but they realise that the Web's great attraction can also be its great disadvantage. The difficulties arise, they argue, not because the environment of the Web is too complicated or because it contains too much information, but because there is no physical context, and a lack of clear organisational ground rules. It helps to know where you are, how the page you are looking at relates to others in the site, and how it relates to the site as a whole. MAPA's software traces the boundaries of the site and visualises the links within it, giving the user something like the sense of the parts and the whole that a reader derives from a printed document.

MAPA generates two treatments from its survey: a list of links related to individual documents, and a map. Both are based on hierarchy, which Dynamic Diagrams believe to be the clearest and most comprehensible way of visualising large sites, rather than webs or spatial structures. Hierarchies, they observe, "support a strong notion of place."

MAPA designates relationships between pages in family terms, automatically identifying any pages with outgoing links as 'parents'. Webmasters can mark pages that 'belong to' parents as 'children', and label certain parents as significant. MAPA calculates the 'ancestry' of each page, tracing its lineage back to the site's home page. When a viewer moves to a new Web page, MAPA generates a new display based on that page.

Dynamic Diagrams considered three-dimensional visualisation systems, including those produced by Perspecta, but then turned to an older prototype for a key element of the MAPA display. Freed from the constraint of a vanishing point, the Turgot Plan of Paris (1734-39, see figure 3, p 73) was able to present a large array of elements with a minimum of visual distortion.

MAPA adopts this orthographic projection so its viewers can see an array representing several hundred Web pages in a single 640 x 480 pixel display, without having to scroll or zoom. The program as a whole can cope with sites of more than 50,000 pages. MAPA draws its page-icons up on parade, their relationships indicated by colour (orange for ancestry, green for children, blue for grandchildren) and spatial ordering, in the space freed by the use of orthographic projection. There are no lines joining up icons, making MAPA displays far less cluttered than many Web maps. Orthographic projection also makes the display of text easier, as the designers of the Turgot map appreciated. So does a regular grid, as London Underground map designer Harry Beck realised (see figure 2, p 73).

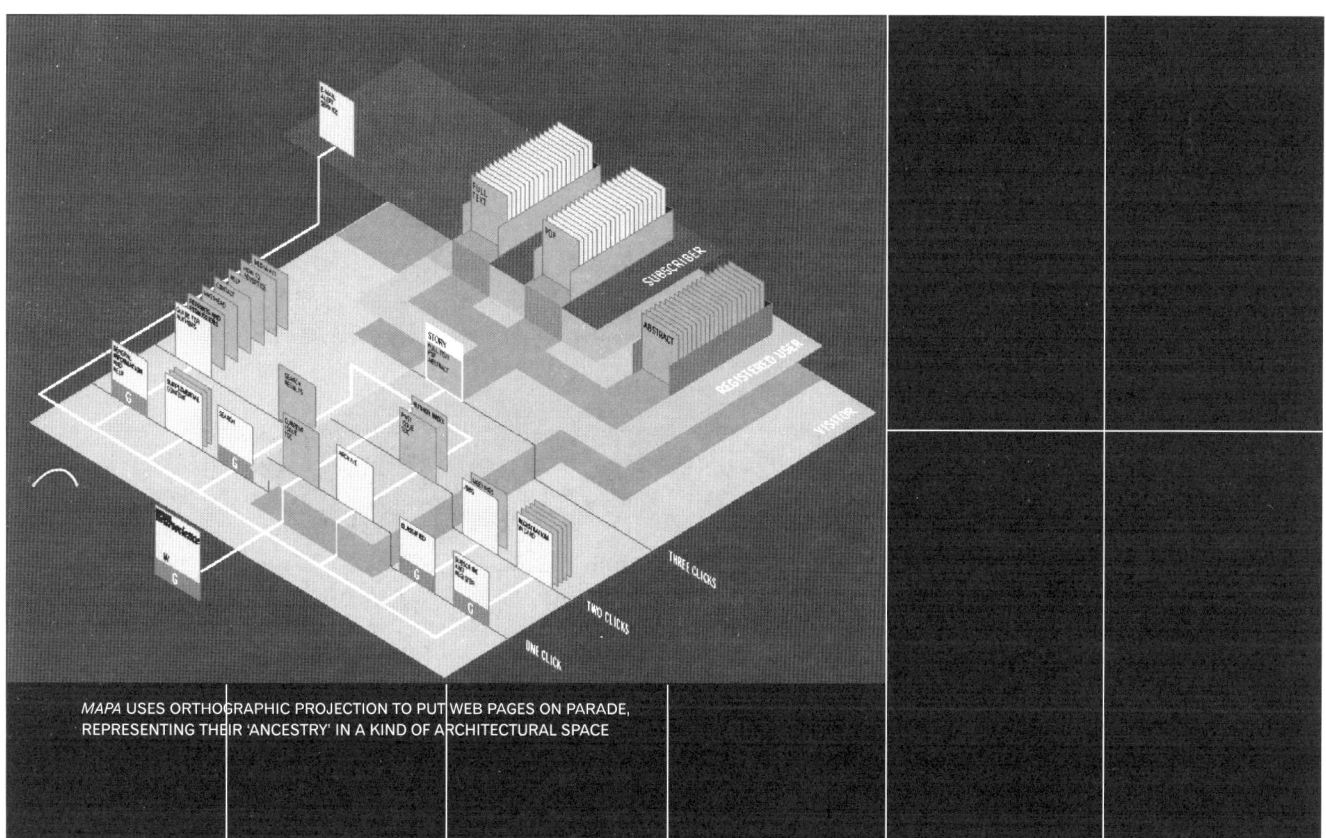

MAPA USES ORTHOGRAPHIC PROJECTION TO PUT WEB PAGES ON PARADE, REPRESENTING THEIR 'ANCESTRY' IN A KIND OF ARCHITECTURAL SPACE

I/O 360/ RARE MEDIUM
Knowledge from your emailbox

WHORLS ON THE RADIALS INDICATE INTENSE BACK-AND-FORTH CORRESPONDENCE BETWEEN TWO PARTIES, IN THE *PARASITE* EMAIL INTERFACE

If there is one thing on the typical knowledge worker's computer desktop that is crying out to be restructured, it is the mailbox, whose principal contents are conversations. In the words of Steve Cannon, lead technologist of i/o 360/Rare Medium, the goal of *Parasite* is to turn these conversations into re-useable resources. In the process, remarks and notes will be transformed into knowledge.

Gong Szeto (i/o 360/Rare Medium's vice president for design) points out that people are very protective of their inboxes. Email is a highly effective way of exchanging concise information. Its tactics include drastic editing, minimal organisation and *ad hoc* decisions. A typical email may include statements without any indication of what questions they answer, statements about unrelated matters, or statements of different qualities, such as technical information and remarks about people. Decisions about what to leave in or out are made by senders on the basis of what they believe their recipients will know about a given situation, rather than following a system of protocols. One message may be important for several different reasons, none of which may be apparent from the subject line.

The result is that inboxes are much easier to fill than to empty. Messages tend to be either deleted immediately, or to hang around indefinitely. They remain in the inbox because they contain information whose potential value is difficult to realise.

Standard email programs allow messages to be sorted by the names of correspondents, by date or by subject line. They can be filed but they cannot be mapped. Steve Cannon observed that no matter emails are presented as lists, tables, or three-dimensional graphics, the context is lost. Methods like these under-appreciate the links or relationships between pieces of data.

Cannon and io/360/Rare Medium's designers do not see a third dimension as an essential element of advanced displays: *Parasite* uses a two-dimensional interface, structured by Feynman diagrams. The Nobel physics laureate Richard Feynman invented these as tools for use in quantum field theory, replacing pages of algebra with a simple graphic. The secret of their success was that they represented interactions graphically, while also giving numerical information.

In his biography of Feynman, *Genius*, James Gleick observes that the Feynman diagram is "an aid to visualization. But it serves physicists mainly as a bookkeeping device." This seems to capture what is required of an email program with aspirations to knowledge-creation: it has to serve as a ledger, while also adding value by analysing its contents at a higher level.

Parasite substitutes emails for fundamental particles; the relationships between them are shown by the lines which Feynman used to represent 'force bosons'. At first glance, it might look as if you would need to be a quantum physicist to make sense of *Parasite* diagrams. But i/o 360/Rare Medium's designers see them as a means of simplifying the user's task, by replacing overlapping windows and menus with an interface sensitive to the context of the user's behaviour. *Parasite* may indeed be a glimpse of a world beyond Windows.

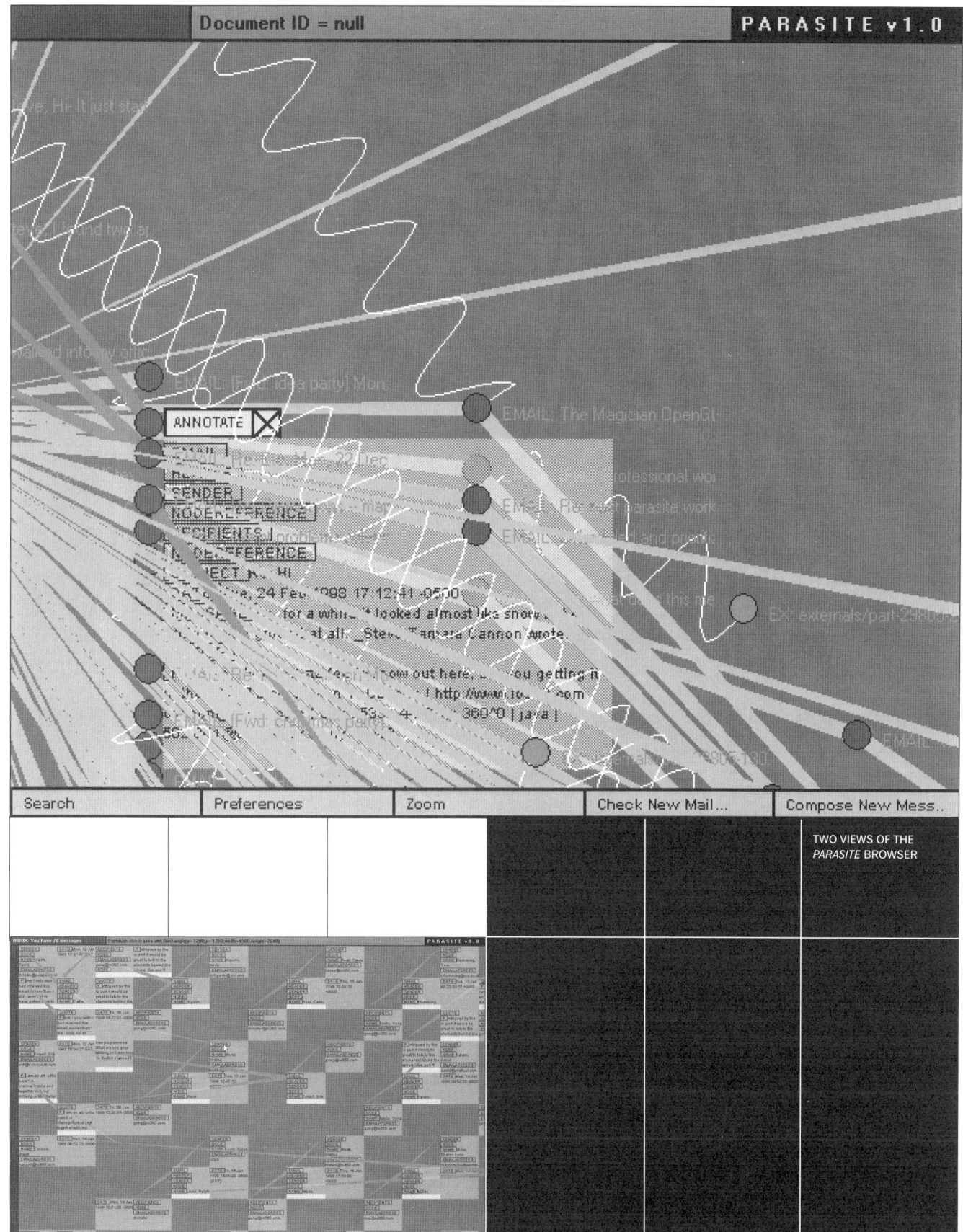

TWO VIEWS OF THE *PARASITE* BROWSER

YURI ENGELHARDT
Meaningful Space

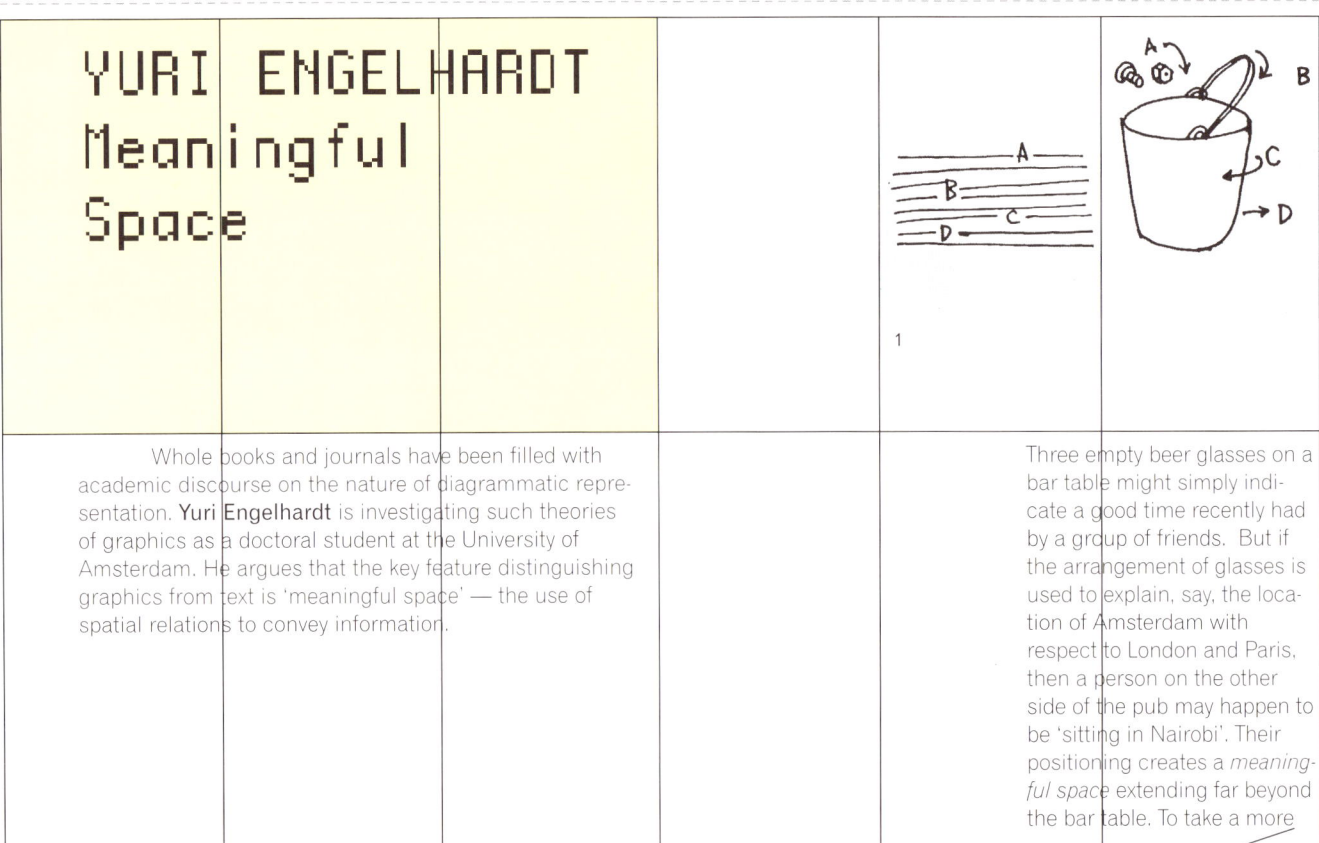

1

Whole books and journals have been filled with academic discourse on the nature of diagrammatic representation. **Yuri Engelhardt** is investigating such theories of graphics as a doctoral student at the University of Amsterdam. He argues that the key feature distinguishing graphics from text is 'meaningful space' — the use of spatial relations to convey information.

Three empty beer glasses on a bar table might simply indicate a good time recently had by a group of friends. But if the arrangement of glasses is used to explain, say, the location of Amsterdam with respect to London and Paris, then a person on the other side of the pub may happen to be 'sitting in Nairobi'. Their positioning creates a *meaningful space* extending far beyond the bar table. To take a more work-related example, a mark drawn at a certain position in the meaningful space of a financial chart might serve to indicate that the company in question earned $500,000 in 1996. A mark drawn higher would imply that the company earned more than that amount.

The use of meaningful space distinguishes diagrammatic representations from text. The spatial positions of words in a text (marked A,B,C,D in left part of 1) are not meaningful in themselves; rather, they are determined by linguistic grammar, and by the particular column width in which the text happens to be set. In contrast, in most diagrammatic representations (right part of 1), the spatial positions of elements *are* meaningful.

Meaningful space comes in two sorts, represent-

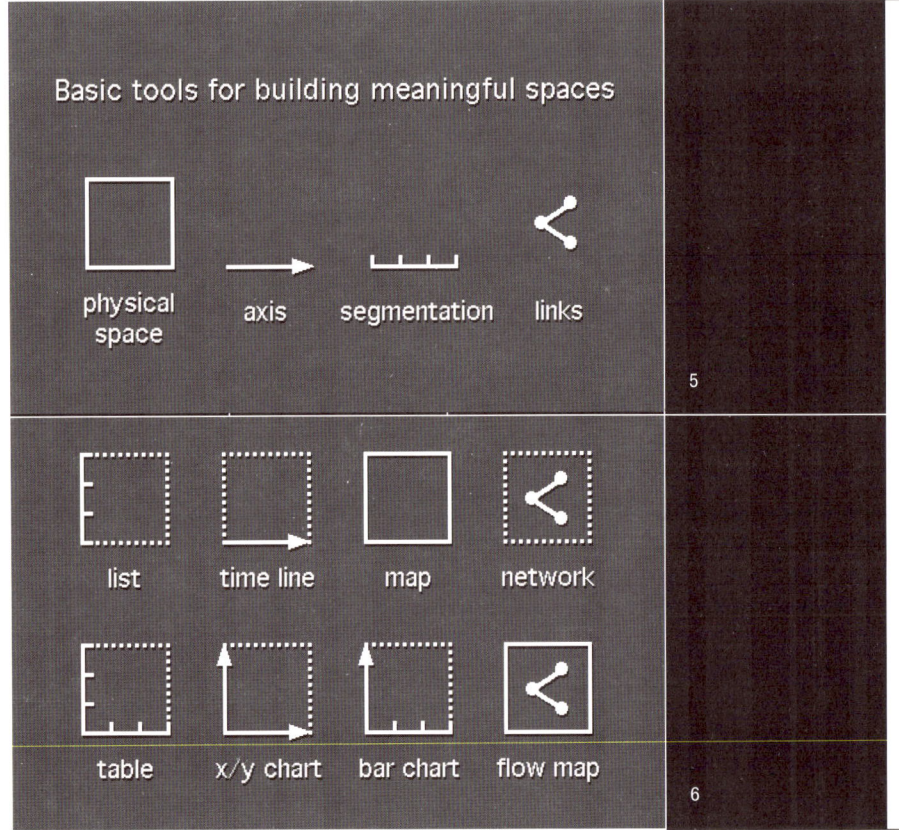

5

6

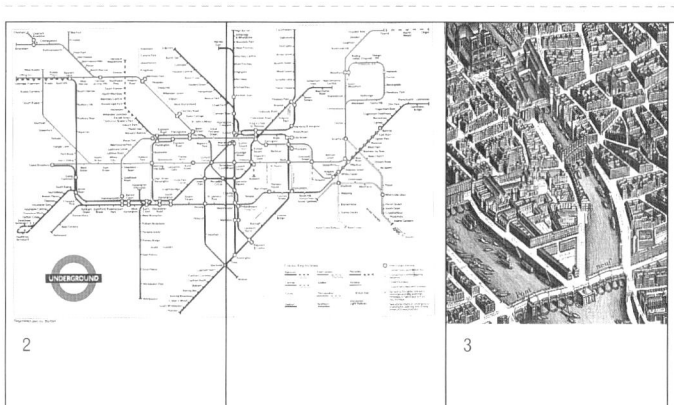

2

3

4

ing either *physical* space or *conceptual* space. The former is represented in maps and drawings of physical objects, while the latter is represented in graphics such as statistical charts, time lines and family trees. When *physical* space is represented, the spatial relationships may be manipulated to various degrees. The London Underground diagram (2) obviously distorts the topographical distances between stations, but even the Turgot drawing of Paris (3) greatly exaggerates the width of many streets, in order to minimize the degree to which buildings visually occlude each other. *Conceptual* spaces are involved when graphical space is used metaphorically in order to create a spatial representation of non-spatial information.

Many graphics use *hybrid* spaces — combinations of physical and conceptual space. For example, in the three-dimensional 'landscape' of population density in the U.S. (4), the two horizontal dimensions represent a physical space (the surface of the U.S.), while the vertical axis represents a conceptual space (population density).

In my research, I have identified a few basic organizational tools for building meaningful spaces (5). Conceptual spaces can be constructed by *segmentation*, by *axes*, and by the use of *links* (e.g. arrows); used in combination, these account for the structure of most graphics (6 and 7). The project planning chart (8) combines segmentation into sub-programmes (vertically) with a time axis (horizontally) with the use of links (arrows). The import/export flow map of the world (9) combines the representation of physical spaces (the continents) with

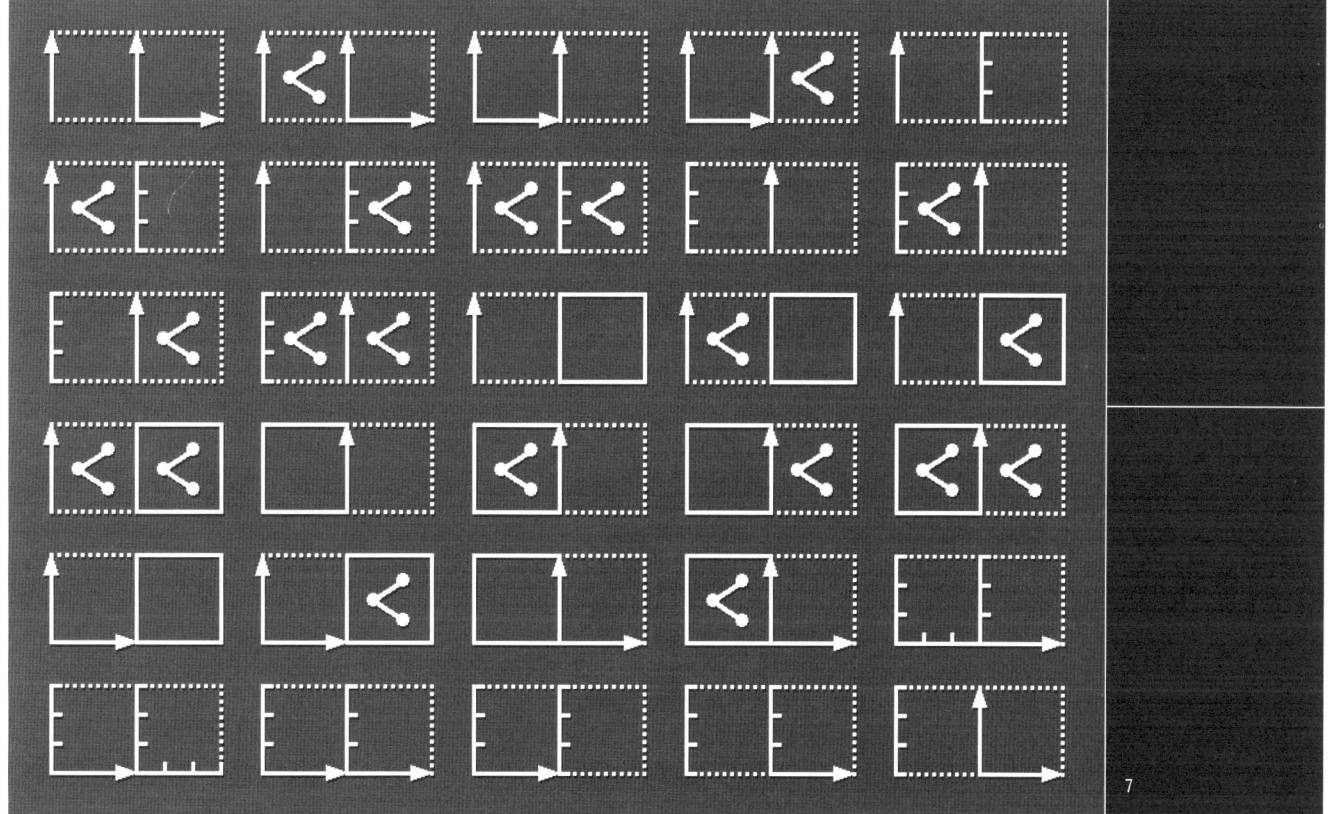

7

the use of links (the coloured 'ribbons' between major ports). The diagram about evolution (10) is constructed along a vertical time axis (running from bottom to top), combining a cross-segmentation (table on left side) with the use of links/arrows (tree of evolution, right side).

Most graphics, however complex, are constructed from these basic tools of meaningful space. An awareness of these tools and their possible combinations can help designers to explore a wide variety of alternatives when designing information graphics.

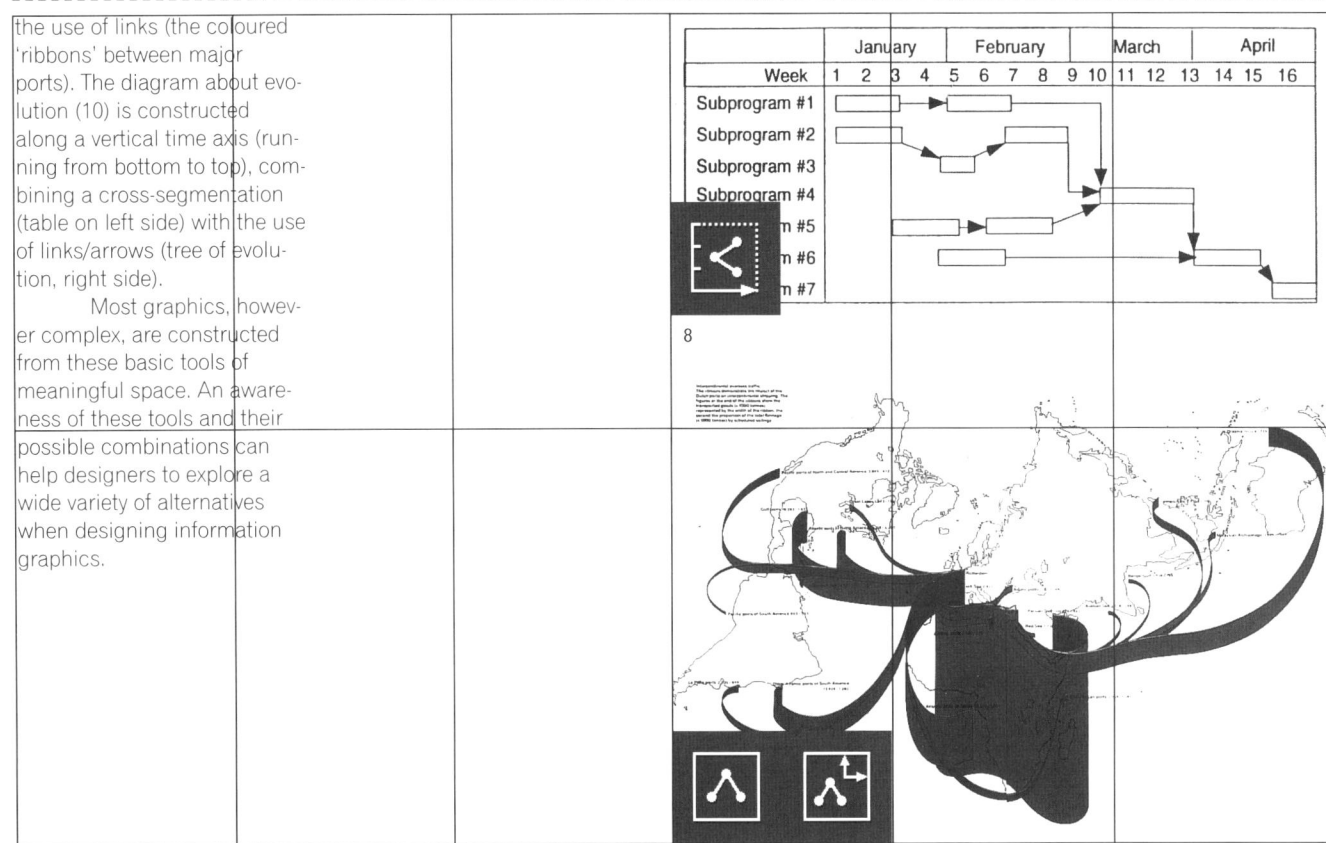

1 Larry Gonick *The Cartoon Guide to (Non) Communication*, HarperCollins, 1993, p 175

2 London Underground diagram, Harry Beck/London Transport 1989

3 Turgot and Bretez (1739), *Plan de Paris* (from Edward Tufte *Envisioning Information*, Graphics Press, 1990, p 36)

4 Harvard Laboratory for Computer Graphics Mapping Service (from Nigel Holmes *Pictorial Maps*, Watson-Guptil, 1991, p 162)

5 The basic tools of meaningful space, Yuri Engelhardt, 1998

6 and 7 Examples of simple graphics, obtained by combinations of the basic tools, Yuri Engelhardt, 1998

8 Robert Harris, project planning chart, *Information Graphics*, Management Graphics, 1996, p 413

9 Benno Wissing, John Stegmeger *Impact of Dutch Ports on Intercontinental Shipping* (from Peter Wildbur *Information Graphics*, Trefoil/Gaade, 1989, p 67)

10 Larry Gonick *The Cartoon History of the Universe* volumes 1-7, Doubleday (with minor adaptation), 1990, p 20

Tracks

Max Bruinsma reads between the lines of 's declarations.

It takes a second look to affirm what you thought you saw in the first place. They're letters, or at least that's what they *have* been, before they became this rhythm of rectangles that is dynamising the pages. And if you're type-smart (or saw the title), you can even read them: No Image No Message. Or the other way around: No message No image. That's a clear and simple double statement. No image without a message; no message that is not an image.

For these pages, Martijn Sandberg has re-arranged the elements of an earlier work, which was silk-screened in silver on reflective film mounted on metal — an artwork like a painting, a canvas. Meticulous, rarefied: only five copies were made. Another version covered an entire wall at an independent art fair. Printed in silver on white paper, the rectangles and their font shimmered like enormously enlarged 'ons' and 'offs' on the surface of a CD. They became a pattern, energetic and decorative, almost to the point of triviality — purely abstract forms repeated to produce an ornamental field. But once you know, or see, that the ornamentation is based on letters, and that the letters form words, then the repetition acquires another quality. The single slogan becomes a chant. Over and over again, a thousand voices shout: No Image! No Message!

This thin line between image and message, between meaningful sign and abstract form, is where Martijn Sandberg produces what he calls his 'image-messages'. The basic question is 'When does an image stop being a text?' For all texts are images, formally and principally, but not all images are texts. When does a text become a pure and abstract image?

Sandberg stops just short of that point. He is not interested in making what semiotics refers to as 'empty signs'. His work researches the balance between the meaning of letters and words, and their image character. When you walk the streets of the city, he says, you see a lot of words on buildings, on billboards, everywhere. What do you see before you read them? Or do you read them, before you see them? It's hard to tell. Sometimes it seems that the image is erasing the text. Sometimes it's the other way around. It's like those drawings used in psychology, in which you can see either a rabbit or a duck, but never both at the same time.

The Song Remains the Same is another typographic work by Sandberg. Its title can be read as a motto for his work in general — what changes are the sequences. In this respect he shows a marked affinity for Techno and House music, and more than just in terms of obvious stylistics. It's not about virtuoso solo performances. What counts is the sound of the entire thing, the complete field of experience, from the nihilistic and punk-like double slogan 'No Message!', 'No Image!', to the more auspicious combination that can be summarised as 'there is no image that is not a message' and vice-versa.

The spreads in this issue can be 'read' as a remix of those sample image-messages: a track with the same structure as an earlier version, but looped in different ways — extended with differently shifting rhythms. In the background, there is still the choir, chanting the recitative, 'No Image No Message'.

Femke Wolting previews *Exploding Cinema*, the showcase for digital media at the upcoming 1999 International Film Festival Rotterdam.

melting media

Ideas about media and content are colliding, causing hybrid forms to emerge at the intersection of traditional media and the digital world. *Exploding Cinema* 1999 will explore this convergence, looking at new life forms that are blurring the edges of old and new media, and at the role of artists working at this intersection. How is the relationship between consumer and producer shifting? In what ways are our interactions with content changing? What will happen to traditional distribution channels for art and culture — whether museums, newspapers, shopping malls or film festivals — once they begin to shed their material bases and become virtual places?

Cultural convergence is more than just the merging of computers with television: chips can be embedded in many objects, and computers share common protocols, so artists and performers (whether in fashion, music, graphic design, architecture or media) can now work together using the same software. And when previously unconnected professions share tools, and different technologies are integrated, the results will surely be more than the sum of the parts.

With the merging of delivery platforms — from museums to government, broadcasters to bookstores — the very notion of 'content' is changing, becoming more fluid. Audience interaction is also: in the *Star Trek* Web sites, for example, fans of the TV series situate themselves as characters in self-written narratives no TV station would dream of broadcasting.

And since animation requires only a limited flow of data, there is exciting potential for making interactive characters available, live, to Internet users.

The audiovisual industry is extremely concerned about ownership of ideas, characters, copyrights and the way content can be reworked — as witness the film studios' legal actions against the producers of fans' Web sites for *StarTrek* and *South Park*. At the same time, the industry is learning to capitalise on this cultural convergence, profiting from the audience's interest in archiving and transforming content. Today, films are primarily trailers for marketing a whole range of products and experiences, from computer games to toys and theme park rides.

"The Web has enormous potential for creating a more diverse and democratic popular culture, one that allows much broader opportunities for grassroots participation. That is what makes the digital revolution a cultural revolution," says Henry Jenkins, professor of Comparative Media Studies at Massachusetts Institute of Technology. A test-bed for new communities of media producers, the Internet is changing the balance between media producers and media consumers. The question arises as to where the content producers' domain ends and where the users' begins. This shift is apparent in all areas of culture, from techno dance parties in which the audience is part of the stage experience, to new artforms in which the art only exists by virtue of users' participation. These are among the issues to be examined in *Exploding Cinema*.

The Digital New Wave
In a special program at IFFR 99, the *Digital New Wave* will focus on how cinema is being transformed by digital production technologies. A filmmaker can now modify individual frames or whole scenes,

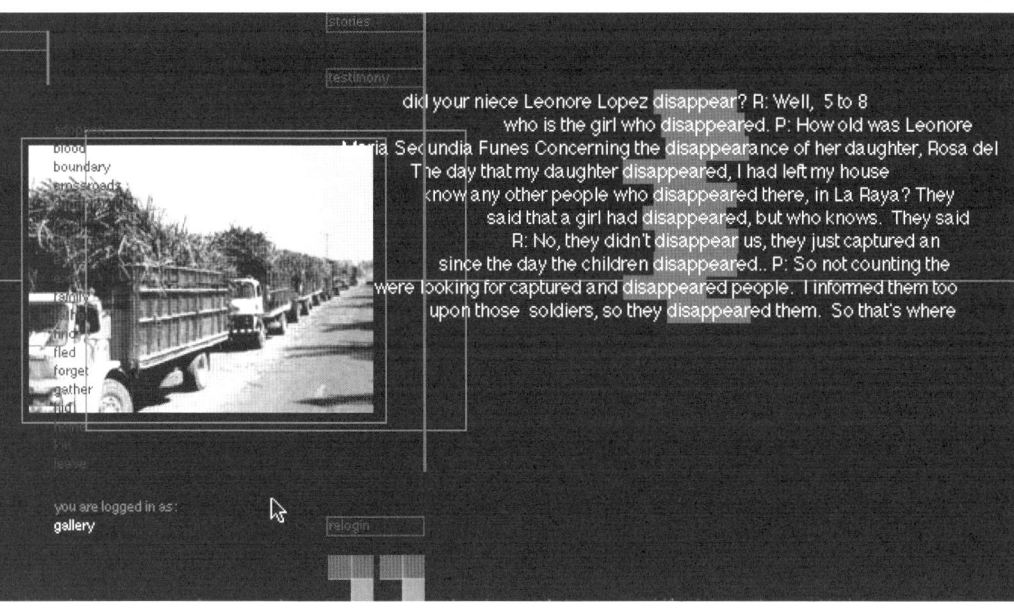

Designed by New York-based web designers Beth Stryker and Sawad Brooks, *DissemiNETion* (first presented in *body mechanique* at the Wexner Center in Columbus Ohio, from September 1998) draws parallels between social diasporas and the dispersal of meaning over the World Wide Web.

Conceived as a repository for personal and social memory, the *DissemiNETion* installation links the *DissemiNET* Web space to local stations for multiple input, allowing people to add their own stories of displacement to the database. Key concepts are automatically indexed throughout the system, so users can pursue themes across the storyspace as it evolves. Video vignettes shuttle horizontally under the surface of the texts, and are reconfigured as themes shift, according to the viewer's movements between stories.

When a keyword is selected, the system searches for and returns fragments of texts containing words that are visually or syntactically similar, and displays them on the Crossroads interface (shown here), creating new crossroads/ connections between stories.

using a digital paint program to cut, bend, stretch and stitch images so they have perfect photographic credibility — the only difference being that these images were never actually filmed. Shot footage is no longer the final point but merely the raw material for computer-manipulation. The main work of filmmaking begins in the editing room where 'real' and modified images are brought together and assembled into the final film. In short, production has become just the first stage of post-production. Cinema can no longer be clearly distinguished from animation or a sub-genre of painting.

In view of the recent adoption of digital video cameras by filmmakers, can digital technology be seen as just a cheap replacement for film, or does it offer new production and aesthetic potential? Is digital editing changing the notion of montage, taking advantage of the image-layering capabilities of non-linear editing systems, or is it simply an economical expedient?

The *Digital New Wave* will investigate the emerging aesthetics of digital film production, with screenings and a lecture by film and television professor Lev Manovich, based on his forthcoming book on digital cinema.

New media masterclass

In collaboration with the Stimuleringsfonds voor Culturele Omroepprodukties, the Netherlands state fund for broadcasting projects, IFFR 1999 will hold a week-long new media masterclass entitled *The Future of the Small Screen*. Teams of professional television and film directors, producers and new media designers (including participants by open submission) will spend the week before the film festival, from January 25 to 31, in Rotterdam, developing innovative concepts for the intersection of the Internet and television. Focusing on narrative as well as non-linear programs, in fiction and documentary genres, the masterclass aims to identify concepts for programs that could not be made in traditional media or on television alone.

How can television and the internet reinforce each other? What kinds of interactivity are relevant, and what kind of interface designs are needed? How can the user become involved as an editor or participant? How can time-based experiences be designed within an on-line environment?

Program concepts and prototypes will be developed during the week under the direction of Dutch and international directors and mentors, including new media designer Sawad Brooks (see caption story, above), film and new media director Douglas Gayeton, and University of Southern California professor Marsha Kinder. The results will be presented the following week during the 1999 International Film Festival.

International Film Festival Rotterdam
Exploding Cinema
http://www.iffrotterdam.nl

http://www.wexarts.org/thefold/disseminet

ANATOMY LESSONS

Shu Lea Cheang's multimedia project *Brandon* slices open the digital body with a year-long series of installations, live debates and online discussions about the nature of gender identity — focusing on the real case of a murdered American transsexual. Two cities, Amsterdam and New York, are joined at the hip for an experiment in new media art — but is *Brandon* more than an Internet-enabled freakshow? Dick van Dijk dissects the project's launch in Amsterdam, at the beating heart of an inter-cardiac link...

...and Peter Hall caught up with the ongoing debate in New York...

AMSTERDAM

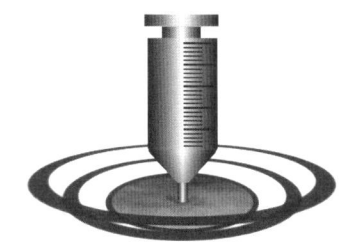

Identity, and sexuality, are hot topics these days, especially in Amsterdam — all the more so in summer 1998 with the buzz surrounding the Gay Games held in early August, and associated events such as the Stedelijk Museum's summer exhibition on 'queer art'.

Kicking off this season of sexual multiplicity, the Taiwanese-American media artist Shu Lea Cheang begat virtual siamese twins on June 30 1998, when her interactive installation project *Brandon* opened simultaneously in the early evening at De Waag in Amsterdam and early afternoon at the Guggenheim Museum SoHo in New York. With the two cities connected in real time through the *Brandon* Web site, a year-long discussion on gender identity and the internet was launched with speeches and Bloody Marys.

Brandon, like the recent *Partywalker* in Brussels, is an example of the proliferating genre of Web/live projects that combine online activities with events in the real world. Exploring boundaries between male and female, virtual personae and transsexuality, it is based on the true story of 21-year old Teena Brandon, an American woman who dressed, lived and loved as a man, and was raped and brutally murdered in 1993 when her/his female anatomy was revealed.

This gruesome tale-for-our-times – which has made Teena Brandon an icon for gender activists — was aptly-sited at the Theatrum Anatomicum at De Waag, a historic building in the Nieuwmarkt district that was the epicentre of Dutch 17th century human dissections. Cheang's temporary installation was mounted in the same attic space in which Rembrandt painted *The Anatomy Lesson* in 1632. Designed by artist Joep van Lieshout's Atelier van Lieshout, the *Brandon* installation was reminiscent of an operating table. A beautiful, horizontal video screen was centred within three large, concentric metal rings at different heights — like a planetary orrery — on one of which a small remote-controlled camera circled to capture glimpses of the live audience. These images were then relayed by the Internet and projected onto an enormous 75-screen video wall in the Guggenheim's SoHo branch, where

NEW YORK

Given the incendiary status of topics like gender politics, hate crimes and cyberbodies, it wasn't surprising that a good 70 actual bodies showed up at last September's *Brandon* forum at New York's SoHo Guggenheim museum. Despite its current puritanical mayor, New York City remains a body politic proud of its liberal organs, with a community defiantly supportive of the right to do as we wish with our flesh, be it dance topless or change sex.

The bait was most probably the *Brandon* Web site, both seductive and confusing, loaded with system-crashing Java applets, an array of alternative navigation interfaces and accompanying cyber cul-de-sacs. The forum promised a 'textual surgical operation on the theory and construction of technosocial bodies'. Elaboration was available in an essay by the forum's moderator, culture critic Lisa Cartwright, whose took as her premise the theory that gender is not a natural property of bodies but, as Teresa de Lauretis puts it, a "product of social technologies, institutional discourses, epistemologies and critical practices." In an age in which surgery and hormone

http://www.guggenheim.org

http://brandon.guggenheim.org
http://www.waag.org

AMSTERDAM

passers-by could also watch the action from the street. Van Lieshout's concept for the installation is recapitulated in part of the *Brandon* website's interface.

During August 1998 a live debate was held in August in Cambridge, Massachusetts, in collaboration with Harvard University's Institute on the Arts & Civic Dialogue. The debate featured a cast of five actors playing the roles of victims, perpetrators and legal personnel, and court proceedings conducted by renowned legal scholars. A second debate took place at the SoHo Guggenheim in September 1998 (see Peter Hall's report, below). Another tribunal will be held in Amsterdam in mid-1999, again staged by Harvard University, focusing on sexual assault cases in real space and cyberspace (not limited to that of Teena Brandon), the meaning of identity within the judicial system, and the extent to which words can really harm people – or constitute 'virtual rape'.

An online discussion forum and virtual court – debating gender as a matter of freedom of choice – feeds the live events. So allowing everyone with an internet connection can enter the debate — offering judgement on Teena Brandon and others like her/him, or coming to their defense. The virtual court and its system for public engagement will be further developed for the Guggenheim's forthcoming Virtual Museum.

Though the exploration of identity in cyberspace is, in itself, nothing new (Sandy Stone, for one, has written extensively about human identity in electronically-mediated spaces) Shu Lea Cheang's *Brandon* offers a simultaneous analysis of physical identity and mental space. By using a true story, she allows the real world to break in on the virtual world, as in her earlier projects that also probed issues of desire and control in collaborative, technologically-hybrid installations.

At the Amsterdam opening in June 1998, however, expectations raised by the project were dampened by low attendance and the banality of the online discussion, which barely went beyond 'you show me yours and I'll show you mine'. As with so many live electronic/IRL ventures, there was a pal-

NEW YORK

therapies enable one to change gender, and in which we can easily change our digital self-representations, is there a case to be made for resisting the various social technologies and taking pleasure in 'incompleteness'?

As one might have predicted from the deft deployment of the word 'technosocial', these relatively interesting ideas were to be revisited during the forum with increasing levels of obtuseness. To add to the performance, a carnival of malfunctioning communications media had been assembled in the Guggenheim foyer to frustrate all sensible attempts at face to face discussion. On the room's central monitor, the chat feed from Amsterdam came in as a scrolling assemblage of half-formed thoughts and mis-spelled words, frequently interrupted with automated entries: 'Shu Lea enters the conversation', and 'Shu Lea leaves the conversation'. For those who couldn't see the screen, the textual operation was read aloud by the indefatigable roving MC, Ms Cartwright, who posed questions to the panelists between pauses for diagnostic updates from the technical troops at the back of the room on the state of the forum's ailing tele-nervous system.

Occasionally, a panelist, someone on screen or a member of the rapidly diminishing live audience raised a half-interesting question. Can we ever really escape ourselves when we reinvent them in an online persona? Is the world of the flesh ultimately incompatible with the cold binary logic of the computer? How can Net communication be both intimate and isolating? Do organs have memory? But to little avail. The promise of discourse was swiftly dashed by the apparition of a new communication: the disembodied laugh of Sandy Stone from the University of Texas via two-way radio, descending upon the room in a sea of static. The technotroops immediately scrambled to better (or worsen — who knows?) the radio connection, while Cartwright attempted to commune with the voice: "Sandy, have you been reading the chat? Sandy, are you there? We've lost Sandy. Maybe we can catch up on the chat. Where did it go?" Suddenly, a phone rang. The audience began secretly to wish for carrier pigeons.

pable gap between the advance hype and the actual event.

The *Brandon* Web site employs a roadtrip metaphor to illustrate Brandon's travels through cyberspace, and provides space for artists to participate in the Web narrative at various points along the route. Though it took me along several surprising detours, I got lost before reaching any interesting discussion.

Revisiting the Web site a few days later, I found a completely new set of interfaces, one of which lead to the virtual court, where people had joined the Cambridge debate on sexual assault, but thus far without any trace of results or proceedings. Once again I signed off, unsatisfied. But Cheang still has the better part of a year to develop the project, so hopefully in the upcoming debates, the dilemmas of gender fusion and techno-identity will be more fully 'fleshed out'.

DIGITAL DISSECTION AT DE WAAG. PHOTO DERK JAN WOOLDRINK

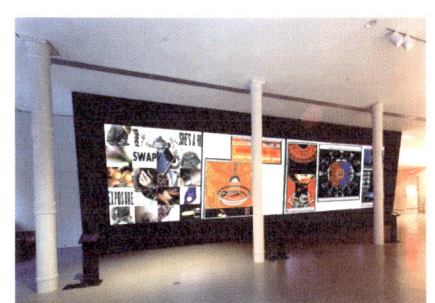

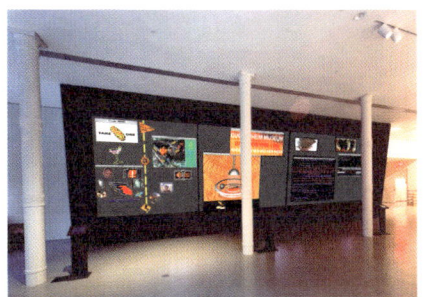

Ultimately, we are left to wonder whether, in this post-McLuhan decade, digi-discussion has become somewhat overly obsessed with the reigning communications medium. Were similar forums held in the 1950s to discuss the relation between people and their telephone personas? Perhaps it is time to let the Internet assume its role as an embedded tool in our society, a channel rather than a place. By now, whenever I hear the words 'forum' and 'technosocial', I reach for the wirecutters.

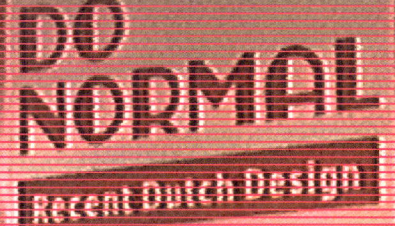

Americans are enraptured by Dutch design, as the recent *Do Normal* exhibition at San Francisco Museum of Modern Art proved. But is the design grass really greener in the Low Countries? **Max Kisman**, transplanted from Amsterdam to San Francisco, appraises this showcase with the clear eye of an expatriate familiar with design practice in both countries.

STRANGE ENOUGH ALREADY

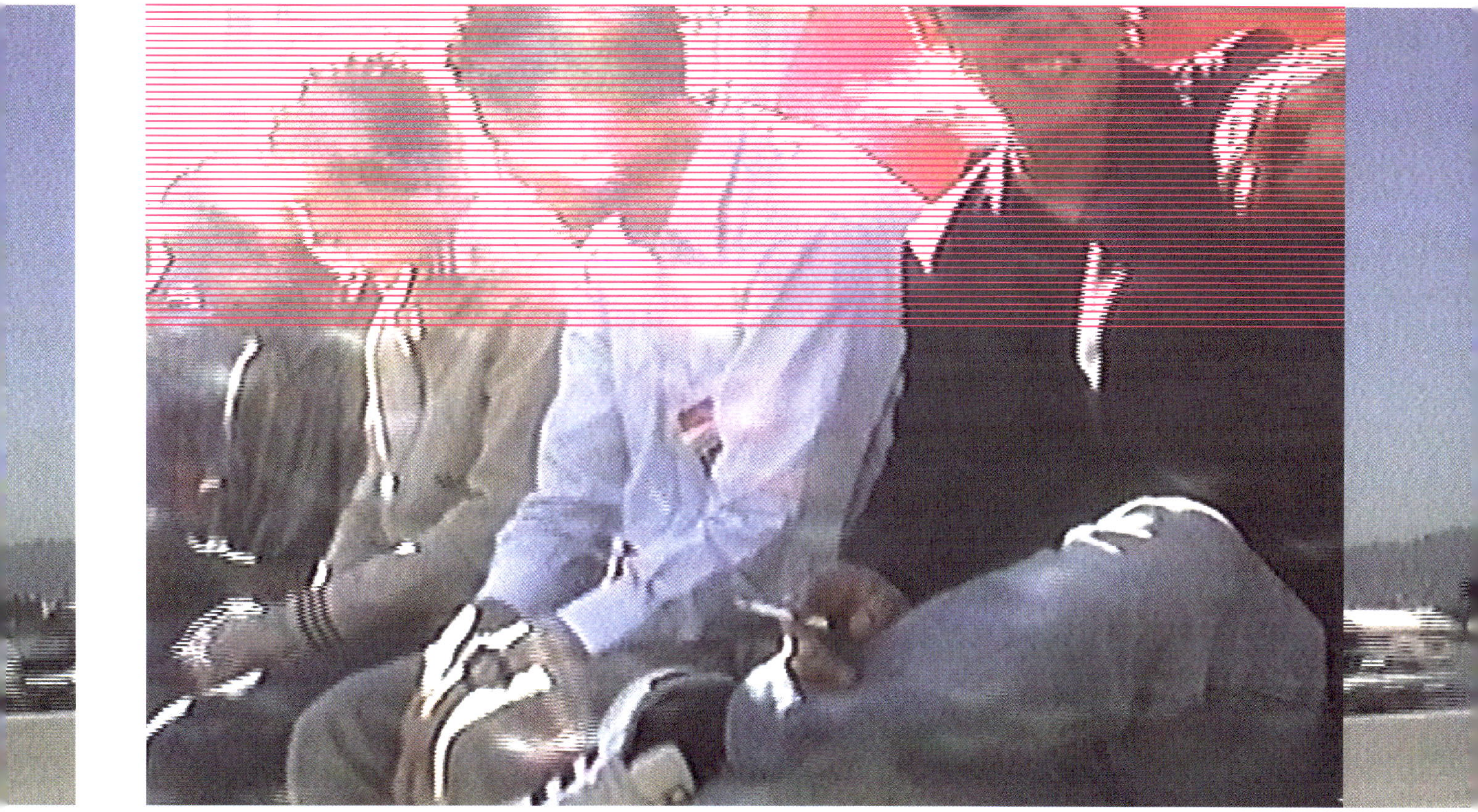

American designers look enviously at Dutch design which, in recent years, has been showcased in several major cultural institutions in the United States. The result is that, ironically, Dutch design has received more critical acclaim outside the Netherlands than in the Netherlands itself.

That good design is an everyday fact of life in the Netherlands comes as quite a pleasant shock to most Americans, who find it fascinating that such a tiny country can offer such broad support to design in all its professional fields. Whether individually or as a whole, Dutch architecture, product and graphic design, fashion and new media catch the eye as being well-considered and well-executed.

As an expatriate Nederlander living in a technologically innovative and 'futuristic' environment like the Bay Area, and San Francisco in particular, it has been amazing to see how much design here is still so very conventional: cars, buses, trains, architecture, publicity are all very much the confirmation of a certain American lifestyle. There seems to be quite a split between the technological identity and the cultural identity of this country. The exhibition *Do Normal: Recent Dutch Design* held at San Francisco Museum of Modern Art [1] attempted to show that a well-balanced approach to design pays off with excellent results on all levels. Without exception.

American designers envy their Dutch counterparts who over the years, seem to have been able to ignore the demands of commerce, thanks to their State-subsidised commissions. Such a comfortable situation is hard to imagine in a country where marketing and advertising are God.

In the U.S., the approach is more market- and technology-driven. Design itself becomes an invention, rather than a tool with which to invent. Artists and designers are often little more than cannon-fodder for marketing, their brains picked by advertising agencies for the sake of a campaign. Sirens whose talents are used to seduce consumers with something new, they willingly sacrifice originality in order to 'sell'.

Artists and designers may know how to speak, but it's the agencies who know when to speak the language and what to say. Examples abound in the campaigns for Nike, Reebok, Coca Cola, Microsoft and Calvin Klein. But money speaks loudest: even successful designers will go for it. The effects are becoming apparent in Europe too, where young design studios now proudly list big corporations and advertising agencies as clients on their CVs.

There is a significant historical difference between the U.S. and the Netherlands. Dutch graphic designers generally get to have more 'editorial' responsibility and are often involved in the entire design process, from account acquisition through conceptualisation, content-development and visualisation, to design and production. They are backed up by confidence in their roots in typography and design — a tradition that has become an organic and natural part of their approach.

The lack of the expressive element is what makes Dutch design so attractive and inspiring to Americans. In recent years it has been imported (via various practitioner-educators) to several major U.S. design institutes, including Cranbrook, Rhode Island Shool of Design, Cal Arts and Cooper Union. Probably the most influential magazine on typography in post-war America, *Emigre*, is edited by an expatriate Dutchman, Rudy Vanderlans. Ironically, Dutch Design has done better outside of the Netherlands (at least in terms of critical or peer-group esteem) than within the Netherlands itself.

Recently, new generations of designers and a general shift away from typography to imagery have given Dutch design a renewed charisma. Aaron Betsky, the curator of architecture and design at the San Francisco Museum of Modern Art, was brought up in the Netherlands. He therefore has a first-hand appreciation of how design is so much a part of daily life there. Together with the Los Angeles-based Dutch journalist Adam Eeuwens, Betsky visited a wide variety

1 *Do Normal* was at San Francisco Museum of Modern Art from July 17 until October 20 1998
http://www.sfmoma.org

of studios to gather material for a show on recent developments in Dutch design. Its title, *Do Normal*, is based on the colloquial phrase *Doe maar gewoon, dan doe je al gek genoeg* ('Just act normal and that will be strange enough').

Betsky's primary goal was to demonstrate that the everyday presence and awareness of design can lead to a more pleasant and efficient society. Supporting evidence for this argument was marshalled from a range of practitioners in several fields: Eek, Hutten and Scholten in furniture; Van der Veer, Engbers, Scheffer, Droog and Van der Meulen in product design; Gerritzen, AAP and Grootens in interactive media; Mijksenaar and Inklaar in public signage; Ninaber van Eyben, Drupsteen, Oosterhof, Martens, Kisman, Joseph Plateau and DEPT in transactional tokens, such as currency, stamps and smart cards; Mevis & Van Deursen, Boom, Gonnissen/Widdershoven in books; and Caulfield & Tensing, Lucas and Experimental Jetset in magazines and flyers.

Few such exhibitions are held in the U.S. and this was an excellent opportunity to show the innovation in various fields of Dutch design. However, the initial proposal for this show promised something more defined than the actual outcome. Despite all good intentions, *Do Normal* missed out on some essential vibrant qualities of Dutch design, especially in omitting work by Wild Plakken and Hard Werken (only mentioned in the catalogue), Marten Jongema, or Just van Rossum and Erik van Blokland of Letterror.

Admittedly it is almost impossible to convey a representative image. But overall the show seemed to have narrowed its focus to the marginal area of club culture and art productions. Even then, the excitement was lost in a static and distant presentation of the material, all framed and displayed behind glass. In a rather sterile installation, the selection showed a strong preference for 'constructed' design in typography, furniture and products, rather than the more lively and diverse imagery typical of contemporary Dutch design.

Speakers at the seminar accompanying the show's opening must have felt that there was more to Dutch design than the show put across. Jelle van der Toorn did a good job in supplementing it with his slide presentation spanning from De Stijl to Total Design, van Toorn and Beeke, Hard Werken and Wild Plakken. Eugene Bay made clear that design studios are becoming more and more involved in product marketing (Holland as a brand: landscape = straight lines, colour = orange, material = water, object = wooden shoe). Marketing is more common in the U.S., where graphic design studios often have links to major advertising agencies, but Bay showed that this relationship can be more equally-balanced between client and studio. An unpretentiously amateur video, hosted by Tirso Francés, introduced start-up studios in Utrecht, like Dietwee, De Designpolitie and AAP.

At first glance, the *Do Normal* catalogue (designed by Rebeca Méndez and edited by Adam Eeuwens) is chaotic, but humorous captions and quotes from individual designers offer insight into the illustrated work. Betsky's short essay on recent Dutch design unfortunately lacks supporting images to create a visual context. From my point of view (and gratified as I am to be included in both the exhibition and publication), *Do Normal* offered an interesting snapshot of contemporary currents in the landscape of Dutch design — albeit taken with a throw-away camera.

All stills taken from *Holland International - The Video*, 1998

Holland as a brand: landscape = straight lines
colour = orange
material = water
object = wooden shoe

Virtual Platform: Real Progress in Dutch New Media Culture
Cathy Brickwood reports

An umbrella group of Dutch non-profit organisations is lobbying to ensure that policy makers recognise the role new media culture plays in shaping the information society.

In 1997, the Dutch Ministry of Education, Culture and Science took two steps towards the support of new media culture in the Netherlands by funding the establishment of a new media laboratory at the V2 Organisation in Rotterdam; and by awarding 300,000 NLG ($150,000) over a three-year period to the Virtual Platform, a group of advanced small organisations active in the field of new media and cultural policy in the Netherlands.

The Platform's nine members are: V2 (interdisciplinary platform for art and new media); The Society for Old and New Media (cultural research and development centre for communications technology); The Netherlands Design Institute; STEIM (developing of new instruments for software and performance of audio and performance art); De Balie (political and cultural centre with a key interest in technological culture); MonteVideo/TBA (laboratory developing, producing and distributing electronic art); Media-GN (interdisciplinary centre specialising in computer graphics, computer animation and interactive multimedia); Paradiso (venue for music and digital technology); and the Interfaculty for Image and Sound, Royal Conservatory, The Hague.

Organisations in the Virtual Platform share a conviction that the cultural and social dimensions of the Information Society should be given as much weight as technological and economic considerations. They argue that the work of artists, performers, media activists, designers, theorists and others involved in new media culture plays a vital role in maintaining a critical approach to these developments.

The Virtual Platform, set up in 1995, provides a focal point for co-operation between these organisations. It sets up regular meetings, produces policy documents, lobbies for funding, establishes joint programmes and shares technical facilities and expertise. The Virtual Platform is based on the notion that a network of centres of expertise with long-standing contacts and reputations can be more

If:

-Wanting to do something you have never done before, you randomly decide that pages 97, 98, 185, 186 will be, respectively, golden yellow, orange, green and light green,

Then:

Pierre Bismuth. If/Then January 1999. Page 98

effective than a monolithic, centralised, national new media centre. Its first policy document, *From Dada to Data*,[1] (1996) argues that "the government's task is principally to support networks and intermediary connections," rather than the creation of any new institution specifically dedicated to new media. *From Dada to Data* sketches the plans of Virtual Platform member organisations and proposes a role for cultural policy in "guaranteeing space for a democratic structure for new media in the public sector" by supporting independent developments.

While this document focuses on the Netherlands, the Virtual Platform also has a European outlook. In November 1997, together with the Council of Europe, it broadened the debate by organising a conference in Amsterdam, *Towards a New Media Culture: From Practice to Policy*.[2] This conference brought together 24 organizations from across Europe, most of them from the non-profit sector and many facing similar experiences with regard to both national and European policy. The findings of these closed discussions were presented to a group of policy makers invited to a supplementary seminar, in a document entitled the *Amsterdam Agenda*.[3]

Stressing the evolutionary potential of new technologies for industry, education and 'social quality', the *Agenda* calls for new media culture to be recognised as a field of cultural activity alongside the more traditional arts. It demands improved access to public media and free bandwidth on the networks. According to the *Agenda*, funding and policy-making structures need to be adapted to the interdisciplinary nature of new media culture and to the research and development being carried out in this field — much of it *ad hoc*, small scale and international in nature.

A key message emerging from the *Practice to Policy* conference was that a great deal is already being achieved, but often remains invisible to the outside world, and that this existing practice need to be nurtured and supported. With new funding from the Dutch government, the Virtual Platform has set up a secretariat based at the Netherlands Design Institute in Amsterdam, to help implement the recommendations in the *Amsterdam Agenda*. Currently, the Virtual Platform is undertaking a survey of new media activities in the Netherlands. This audit will serve as the basis for policy advice on the quadrennial Arts Plan (the government's funding policy for arts organisations) as well as for policy makers in economic, social, education and technology policy, both domestic and international.

The Virtual Platform will also produce a Web site/shared workspace that will provide information about Dutch new media culture. A book based on the *Practice to Policy* conference is due to be published in the spring of 1999 and, in the longer term, the Virtual Platform plans to produce a follow-up to the 1997 conference, to ensure that the debate continues.

1 *From Dada to Data* (English and Dutch versions) http://www.dds.nl/~virtplat
2 P2P conference site http://www.dds.nl/~p2p
P2P journal http://www.dds.nl/p2p/journal
3 *Amsterdam Agenda*
http://www.dds.nl/~p2p/p2p_journal/agenda.html

PLAY

If/Then play 101

Sharon Lockhart
Audition

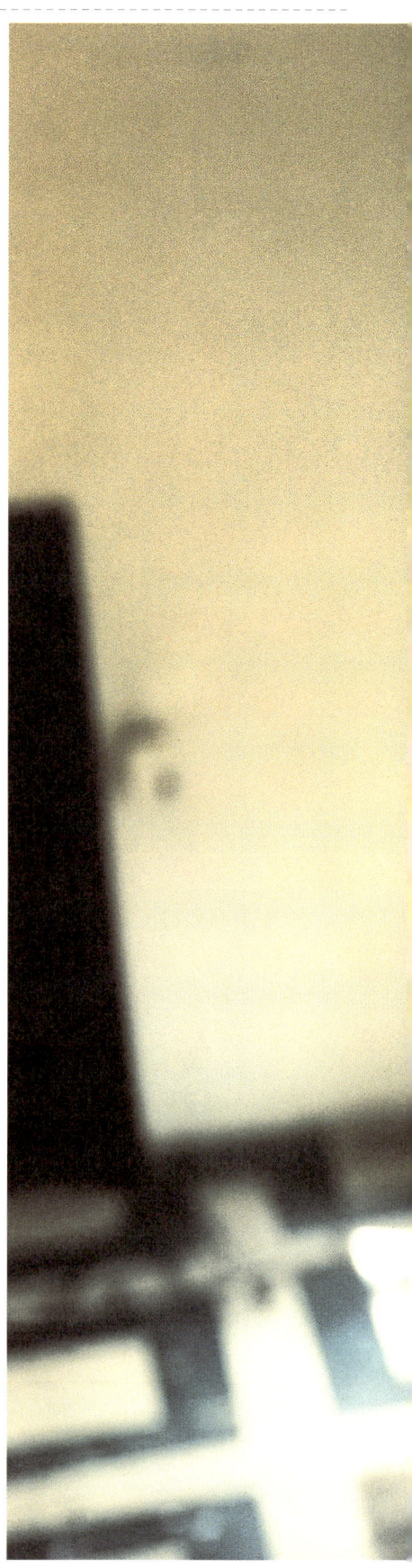

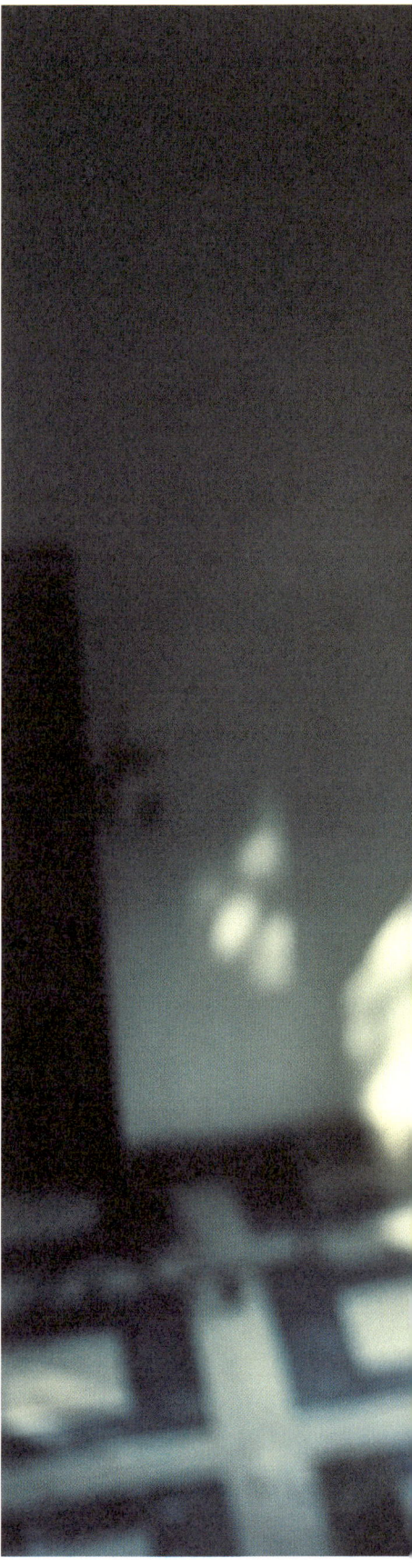

Audition Four
Kathleen and Max
1994

STRATEGO MILTON BRADLEY 1977

Real-time multi-player games existed long before the Internet. **Eric Zimmerman** rummages through his personal archive collection of boardgames — from the morally uplifting to the gratuitously garish — and explains how flat planes of four-colour printed cardboard (plus a few other bits and pieces) can provide engaging 'immersive experiences' that give pleasure to millions — no modem required.

ZAXXON MILTON BRADLEY 1982

SORRY! PARKER BROTHERS 1979

CAREERS PARKER BROTHERS 1971

If/Then   The Rules of the Game   Eric Zimmerman
Boardgames

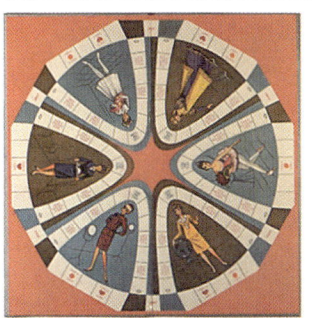
WHAT SHALL I BE? SELCHOW & RIGHTER CO. 1966

OF

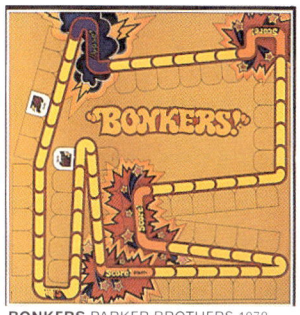
BONKERS PARKER BROTHERS 1978

WWF WRESTLING CHALLENGE GAME MILTON BRADLEY 1989

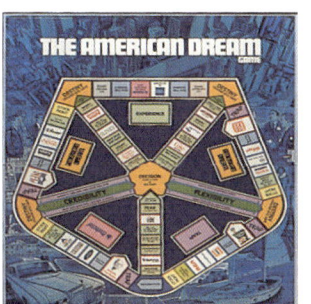
THE AMERICAN DREAM MILTON BRADLEY 1979

Boardgames. You've played them. Those long, flat boxes stuffed full with the accoutrements of childhood play: a pair of dice, a deck of cards, a handful of brightly coloured plastic pieces, maybe even a spinner or two. And don't forget the centrepiece: the board. There is an endearingly klunky, undeniable appeal to boardgames. But from what? Flashy graphics? Addictive gameplay? Sheer nostalgia? It's time to dust off those long, flat boxes, break out the boards, and find out.

Games within games

Every game has two parts: rules and materials. The rules tell you how to play and the materials are the things you play with. Flat and rectangular, the board is the essential component of a boardgame, the physical and metaphorical space in which the game occurs, the foundation and ground for all of the action. Every game is an artificial representation of conflict and the hard edge of the gameboard is the exact delineation of the zone of engagement. When your rook gets captured in chess, what do you do? You take it out of the fray. You take it off the board.

The conflicts modeled in boardgames tend to be economic or military, which is why so many boards take the form of maps — from the global conquests of *Risk* and

BARETTA GAME UNIVERSAL TELEVISION 1976

PAYDAY PARKER BROTHERS 1975

Time and space, work and play, the comic and the pitiful — all are conflated in *Payday*'s ironic homage to the drudgery of a work economy.

CANDYLAND MILTON BRADLEY 1978

Diplomacy to the iconic national economy of *The Game of the States*. The classic, unadorned grid gameboard represents territory in the abstract. Many of the earliest known games (Chess, *Go*, the Norse *Hnefatafl*) are grid-bound military simulations. *Stratego* takes the grid literally: the contested terrain is painted as a backdrop to the squares of the board.

Sure, games are inherently competitive. But they're also inherently cooperative: game conflict is productive conflict. The board is the shared space for the stylized discourse of play, where the participants' experiences overlap and intermingle.

In *Candyland*, the board is literally the world of the game. By placing your piece at the starting position, you enter its surreal, sugar-coated realm. Compelled by the rules, you draw cards and move your pieces forward in a race to the finish line. But why? Who really cares which plastic token reaches the end first? The other players, of course. Like you, they give meaning to the game by talking the talk and walking the walk of *Candyland*. Translation: the first face-stuffing, sugar-hungry kid to the finish line wins big!

Flat systems

Gameboards recline supine on a table — and there is a reason for this. As the common ground for social interaction, the gameboard is a plane of possibility, at right angles to more dominant representational media, such as the perspectival window of renaissance painting, the vertical cinema screen, or the computer monitor.

All these vertically-oriented rectangles traffic in naturalistic visual immersion. What the boardgame offers, by contrast, is immersion into a system — the system of a game. Unlike painting, film, or even a computer game, a boardgame requires constant and dedicated participation from several players to move the experience forward. There is no perceptual illusion, no hidden projector, no computer software operating behind the scenes. At every moment, boardgame denizens inhabit the rules, playing them out, iterating the system to its next step.

At odds with vertical immersion, the flat board plays a strange game with representation. Rather than depictions of pictorial space, game boards are diagrams for interaction — so it's impossible to consider their visual aesthetics apart from the system of rules that they embody. In *Payday*, the board appropriates the graphic system of a calendar month. Players trudge through work-week after work-week, accumulating and spending money as they await the glorious payday at month's end. Time and space, work and play, the comic and the pitiful — all are conflated in this ironic homage to the drudgery of a work economy.

Chutes and Ladders is a contemporary update of the pedagogical Christian boardgame *Snakes and*

In the twisted logic of hip nostalgia, there is an inverse relationship between fun and retro-fascination: the 'good' games are eclipsed by the bad, the awkward, the mercilessly cheesy.

CHUTES AND LADDERS
MILTON BRADLEY 1972

GO TO THE HEAD OF THE CLASS
MILTON BRADLEY 1977

GAMBLER PARKER BROTHERS 1977

EASY MONEY MILTON BRADLEY 1936

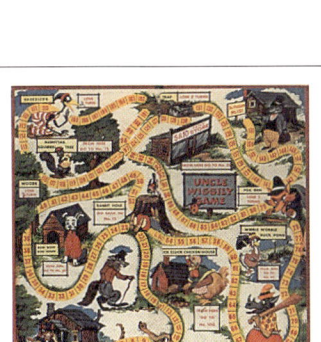
UNCLE WIGGILY GAME
HOWARD R. GARIS 1954

Ladders, published in 1870 and one of the first boardgames produced in the U.S. Your utterly random progress through the game is assisted and hampered by climbing up ladders and sliding down chutes. Ladders are framed by good deeds (such as rescuing a cat from a tree) and Chutes by bad deeds (such as disastrously dangerous bicycle tricks). As you struggle to reach that final square of redemption, the narrative geometry of the board conflates ethics with mathematics. The moral: follow the rules, roll the die, move your piece, and trust in the Higher Order to mete out your rewards and punishments.

Gameboards are a functional part of a larger game system, their structure and layout an effect of the rules. That's why, when they're presented as isolated aesthetic objects (such as in these pages), they seem curiously incomplete. The gameboard is the negative space of play, the artifact that remains when players are taken out of the equation. Only when a gameboard is filled with activity is it truly complete.

The *Go To the Head of The Class* gameboard is a lonely place: empty rows of desks define a space of pedagogical possibility, waiting patiently for the pupils/players to enter. And despite its aggressively wacky graphics, the gameboard for *Bonkers* is also more empty than full — the wide ochre spaces on either side of the path become crowded with cards, but not until the game is actually played.

Pop cult

Even as structural residuals, boardgames possess an undeniable graphic appeal. Because they have to operate as the ground for a system, they have an intrinsically modular and iconic design. *Easy Money*'s alternating tricolor stripes, *Uncle Wiggily*'s brightly numbered squares, and *Gambler*'s self-contained funky illustrations demarcate clean, understandable spaces that belie their underlying complexity.

Far from the simple grids of the classics, today's boardgames are eccentric and colorful spaces, loaded with the transitory signifiers of pop culture. Typically, boardgames are tied to content from other sources. *The Incredible Hulk Game* hails from a comic book. The *G.I. Joe Game* and the *Barbie Queen Of the Prom Game* link up with action figures and dolls. *The Baretta Game*, *The Jetsons Game*, The World Wrestling Federation's *Wrestling Challenge Game* and *The NBC Game* are all television properties. And in a curious case of game-about-game, the *Zaxxon* boardgame is derived from (of all things) the *Zaxxon* arcade videogame.

All these products desperately try to do justice to the visual punch of their parent media, with varying degrees of success. *The Hulk* and *GI Joe* boards translate well: both appropriate the force of comic book cover art with centralized character-based compositions, strong contrasting colors, and prominent skewed type. Others, such as the uncomfortably ornate *Barbie* game and the bleak, ugly disk of *World Wrestling Federation* stars, are less than perfunctory — merely cheap frames for garishly-branded content.

Graphic successes or not, the most striking thing

> From roadside flea markets to specialty pop-culture stores, overpriced boardgames can be found sandwiched between lunch boxes, action figures, and the occasional Colorforms set.

BARBIE QUEEN OF THE PROM GAME MATTEL 1991

G.I. JOE GAME HASBRO 1986

THE INCREDIBLE HULK GAME MILTON BRADLEY 1978

about all of these pop culture boardgames is that, as games, they stink. Nobody plays them anymore. But despite this fact, emotional attachment remains. From roadside flea markets to specialty pop-culture stores, overpriced boardgames can be found sandwiched between lunch boxes, action figures, and the occasional Colorforms set. An overwhelming postmodern nostalgia rejects the games as games. Swept up in the museology of pop culture, they are valued as kitsch icons rather than as designed interactive entertainment.

The most memorable and evergreen boardgames — the ones that are actually fun to play, such as *Mouse Trap*, *Monopoly*, *Trivial Pursuit* — usually define their own content. Others, like *Pictionary* or *Scrabble* let players create their own. In the twisted logic of hip nostalgia, there is an inverse relationship between fun and retro-fascination: the 'good' games are eclipsed by the bad, the awkward, the mercilessly cheesy.

The future of fun

Increasingly, boardgames are dinosaurs from an era in which 'multimedia' meant four-colour printing and cute plastic tokens. Boardgames today support comic books, TV, and film, rather than the other way around. They don't lead pop culture trends; they follow them. In the Information Age, the word 'game' signifies something digital: a computer or video game. And as technology increasingly implicates play as the dominant form of activity for the wired civilization, the future of fun becomes a serious question.

Spacewar! (1971) and *Pong* (1972) were the first two bonafide videogames and, strikingly, both of them require two simultaneous players.[1] But in the decades since these were created, the single-player game has come to dominate digital entertainment design. From the solo-typing of early text-based adventures to the button-thumping of *Mario* to the lonely shores of *Myst*, computer, console, and arcade games have been predominantly single-player experiences. A few game genres, such as multiplayer MUDs and arcade fighting games, encouraged interaction — but they were the exceptions and not the rule.

Why the ubiquity of single-player games? In the days before personal computers, game coders were synonymous with game players: the one-to-one interaction between programmer and terminal was hardcoded into the tropes of computer play. There were technical limitations as well: without net connectivity, multi-player games meant several players had to crowd in front of a single computer monitor.

With the skyrocketing rise of the Internet, all that is changing. Once a special

---

1 see *Remote/Involved*, by Alex Wilkie and Noortje Marres, pp 206-217

THE JETSONS GAME HANNA-BARBERA 1962

treat in a CD-ROM title, a multi-player mode is now a 'must have' feature for computer games. Arcade manufacturers are experimenting with networked play. And all the new game consoles have a modem jack.

The vertical screen of the single-player game is a narcissistic mirror for the solo computer user. But connect that computer to others on a network and what you get is a flat grid: the horizontal connectivity of net play. Sounds a lot like a gameboard, doesn't it? From the ultra-violent battles of *Quake* death matches to the witty contests of *Acrophobia*, games are returning to their multi-player roots as enablers of social interaction. And for designers struggling to invent new ways to play, here's a well-kept secret: interactive culture predates computers — by centuries. It's always amusing to see the digital give a nod to the analogue, whether or not anyone is really paying attention.

Boardgame, anyone?

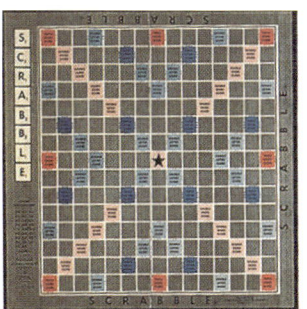
SCRABBLE SELCHOW & RIGHTER 1953

The gameboard is a plane of possibility, at right angles to the perspectival window of renaissance painting, the vertical cinema screen, or the computer monitor.

HALMA PARKERS BROTHERS CIRCA 1940

Soothed by a key in its back rather than a pacifier in its mouth, the latest in life-like dolls is programmed to cry at random intervals, and designed to teach some tough lessons to potential teenage moms. A weapon in the battle against unwanted pregnancy, the Baby Think It Over™ doll is emphatically 'not intended as a toy for children', according to its manufacturers. **Pauline Bax** spent a day in New York taking care of an 'infant simulator' and experienced the glories and despairs of digital parenting. Photos by **David Rinella**.

Pauline thinks it over

The United States has always ranked high on the scale of extremities —

prison population, suicide rates, car ownership per capita, number of professional bounty hunters. So it comes as no surprise that the U.S. also lists the highest number of teenage pregnancies of all industrialised nations. Although the rates have declined over the past five years, the U.S. government still considers teen pregnancy to be a significant problem. One million American girls under the age of twenty will find themselves pregnant this year, and more than half of them — 512,000 — will take their pregnancy to term. The Baby Think It Over doll is an immaculate conception for our times, a response to these statistics that puts the burden of parenting literally into the hands of teenagers, giving them a cautionary (and reversible) electronic trial-run at motherhood.

Coming from the Netherlands, a country with the lowest global percentage of teen pregnancies, and having scarcely given the idea of motherhood the time of day, the Baby Think It Over program struck me as another evangelical idea at best; the hyperbolic strategy of correctional zealots, at worst. A computerised baby, I imagined, would induce in me about the same maternal feelings as a week-old dirty diaper.

But in the U.S., Baby Think It Over has proved to have a profound appeal. An estimated 40,000 'infant simulators', sold to high schools at a pricey $250 apiece, have been shipped all over America since the company's launch in 1993. In a climate of understaffed family planning centers and politically-ambushed abortion clinics, Baby Think It Over is ingenious in its simplicity. Young girls are provided with a realistic baby doll that cries at irregular intervals, demands attention and care, and thus imbues them with the sense of responsibility that comes with actual parenthood. Most of all, they realise that having a baby will change their lifestyle overnight. Baby Think It Over is an alternative to the more common eggs and flour training, in which high school kids have to tend a handful of raw eggs for a week. The love-child of technological progressivism and political correctness, Baby Think It Over is not only digitally-programmed, but also comes in different versions, modeled after newborns of five different ethnicities.

While babies are generally understood to arrive via storks, and most American babies come from hospitals, this Baby is delivered by Federal Express. Anxious to get my parenting experience going, I set aside the instruction manual and immediately insert the batteries in the electronics box. A small computer that can be set on three different modes — *cranky*, *easy* and *normal* — this device is Baby Think It Over's lifeblood, registering both the quality and quantity of care given. Dr. Spock defined the newborn as a "reasonable, friendly being," and one with a normal temperament to boot, but I have yet to find out how much a *normal* baby tends to cry, so I set the box in this mode. Held in place by strips of Velcro in Baby's back, the electronics box can be pulled out by a pink satin ribbon —

pink corresponding with this Baby's modestly sculpted genitals.

In contrast to the rectangular box, Baby looks surprisingly cuddly. Little creases curl around its neck, limbs and vaguely distinguishable nipples, while the monochromatic vinyl skin feels soft to the touch. I have opted for a milk-chocolate brown model, or rather, I picked a light-skinned African-American female, to deviate slightly from the norm. (American Indian, Asian, and Hispanic infant simulators are also available in both genders, and, for teenagers in particularly underprivileged neighborhoods, a drug-affected premature baby has also been designed, albeit only offered in Caucasian editions.)

When I insert the electronics box in its back, nothing happens. I wait in silence. I decide to shake Baby, just a little. Still nothing happens. Did I do something wrong? I quickly scan the operating instructions as if they were Dr. Spock's maternity bible. *Baby Think It Over begins its cycle by simulating sleep.* Phew.

At 10.30 a.m, right when I'm standing in line to buy a subway token, Baby wakes up and comes to life. It breaks out in a winding, repetitive wail only slightly muffled by the towel in which I keep her wrapped. Everyone looks up. The lady in the token booth hurriedly gives me my change, as if I'm some mentally deranged person who could just as easily be carrying a machine gun as a baby doll. My embarrassment shifts into panic. I grab my tokens and hide in a corner, fumbling for the care key — a small plastic stick that should stop the crying as soon as it is inserted in the electronics box. I may have to hold it in place for up to thirty minutes, never certain how long it will take for Baby to shut up: it is programmed to cry for randomly-varying durations.

There! Peace regained. I'd like to wipe the sweat off of my forehead, but I can't, since I'm using one arm to steady Baby and the other to keep the key turned. A black woman comes up to me and whispers: "You need to breastfeed your baby?" I say I don't, really. She shoots me a puzzled glance and walks away. I feel bad. I sit there, hunkered down in the subway, ministering to my charge.

Twenty minutes later, Baby starts crying again. This is the signal to take the care key out. I have loosened my grip on it several times, hoping that my 'care time' might be over. But being a mom apparently requires patience and obedience. I adjust the doll's T-shirt, emblazoned with the same symbol (a cartoon cry-baby, all mouth and no face) that appears on all the other accessories — or in company parlance, 'product extensions' — sold by Baby Think It Over, Inc.

A woman and her daughter enter the train and sit down in front of me. The girl, about four years old and with pigtails adorning her curious little face, points at my bundle of vinyl. "Baby," she says, "Baby." The mother smiles at me. "If that was a real baby," she replies, "do you think she would hold it like that?" Obviously, I have forgotten to support baby's head. "Baby doll," the girl continues. "Baby doll."

I get off somewhere downtown to walk ten blocks to a bookstore. If a

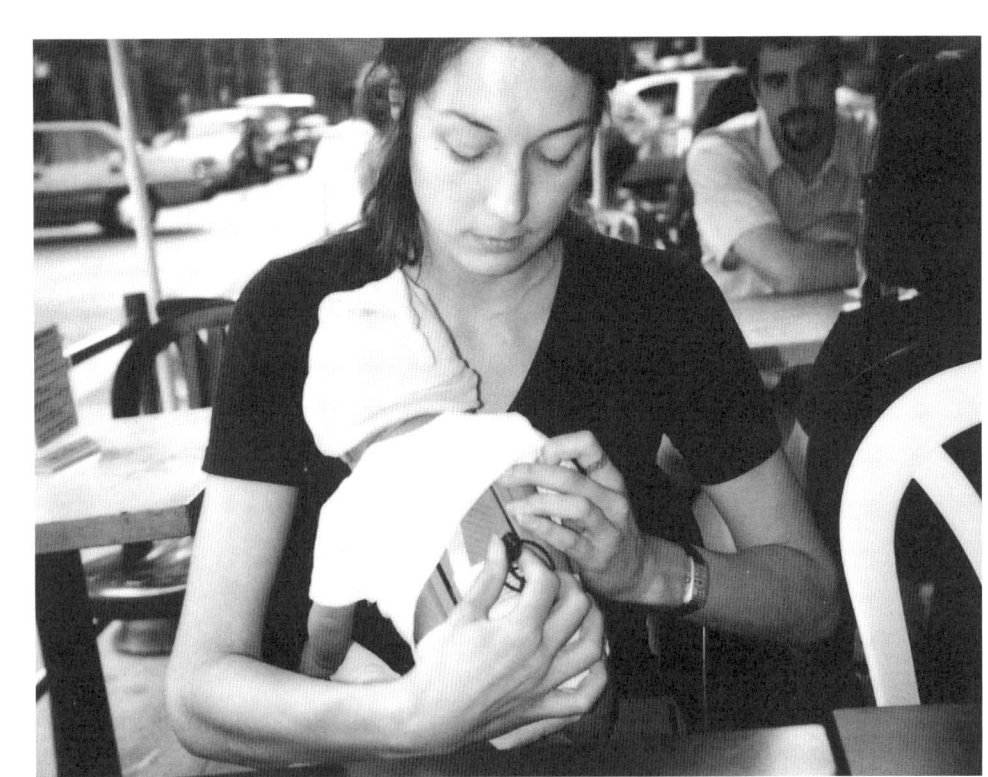

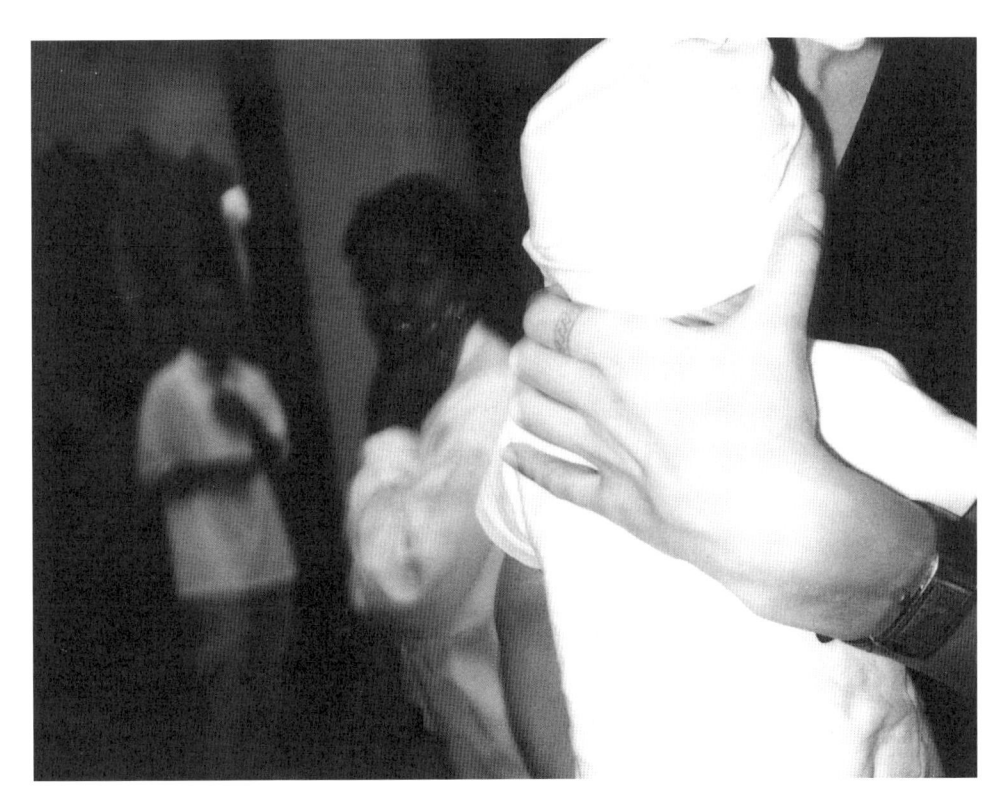

real newborn baby is a weighty seven-pound burden, this one is a very close approximation. I cradle its 21 inches in the curve of my left arm, my right hand holding its skull. Head support is crucial for handling Baby Think It Over. The neck can fall back suddenly: it is designed to do so. This and Baby's subsequent crying are the features of which the manufacturer is most proud. Unfortunately, the horizontal gap between the neck and the back scores low on realism, so I decide to buy a hat in a cheap clothing store. Baby's skull needs covering, too: the plastic swirls that are meant to signify hair don't do a very good job. Baby Think It Over, Inc. concedes that hair would make baby more human, but having had 'cleanliness issues' with earlier models that did sport hair, the company decided instead to go for a smooth skull.

I spot a hat for my synthetic baby, displayed (appropriately) amid assorted knock-offs of designer brands. Jordansport backpacks hang from the ceiling; DSNY (sic) jeans are shelved next to a glass showcase for COBY walkmans. "Is that a real baby?" the security guard marvels. "Get outta here!" The checkout clerk, a young woman, shrieks "O my God! For a split second I thought it was real." With all but its face covered, Baby can virtually pass for a living, breathing infant.

In company literature and on its web site, Baby Think It Over, Inc. strenuously insists that this product is a serious educational program, and "NOT intended to promote abortion or to pressure pregnant teens into adoption instead of self-parenting."

But the disclaimer cannot compete with the love some students bestow on this most realistic of all baby dolls. Some teenage girls have apparently tried their hairdressing skills on Baby; others, worse still, have returned Baby, defunct, after being given a bath. "It's incredible," Carol Lambert, Baby Think It Over's head of marketing and PR tells me by phone from the company's Eau Claire, Wisconsin, headquarters. "Sometimes they almost mistake them for real babies." I realise that it has become less important how real Baby seems to me than how realistic it appears to others.

"That is the littlest baby!" a woman comments from across the street. Many women, I notice, are now paying me attention. I have never received so many friendly, encouraging smiles – not even from men. Curiously enough, whenever a baby in a stroller or carrier passes by, I intuitively glance over and compare. I have somehow begun to feel protective of my computerised offspring.

In the bookstore, almost as a matter of course, it starts to cry again. The quiet hum of the air-conditioning fades to the background and here I am, embarrassed all over again. Caring for Baby takes fifteen minutes this time. If it doesn't prepare me for motherhood,

tending Baby might at least condition me for owning a mobile phone which, similarly, can go off anywhere, anytime.

Having a child must be a nerve-wracking business. It dawns on me that I haven't been rewarded with a coo yet — the only positive response Baby can give, and only if it has been properly cared for.

But Baby just keeps on drawing attention for the rest of the afternoon, no matter how stiff its limbs or how dispassionate the stare from its narcissistic, sunken brown eyes. Two ladies on a cigarette break laugh in a mixture of disbelief and endearment when I approach. "You scared the heck outta me," says one of them, "I though it was real." Her friend bends forward and pokes her finger at Baby's cheek. "O how cute," she gushes. "What a cute boogie-boogie! Aren't you the cutest boogie-boogie! Oooo...Where did you find this darling?" At last someone is cooing. "Thank you, miss. My ovaries are cringing now!" she calls after me.

Back in the subway during rush hour, another woman stands up, gesturing to me to take her seat. I feel like a con artist and show her what's underneath the hat. "Ah, you want to be a mama soon," says a young Korean man, assuming I am practising with Baby. He asks if he can hold it. Relieved to be able to stretch for a moment, I hand it to him. He holds Baby at arm's length, grins, and, to my surprise, starts shaking it. Once again I have overlooked an important instruction. *Don't let other people hold Baby unless you would trust them with your own child. Some people think it's funny to abuse Baby*, the manual reads.

My favorite comment of the day is that of an elderly man, who wishes me luck with "frozen baby." At home, Baby continues to cry at irregular and inconvenient intervals. I manage to extract a coo after another fifteen minutes of care time. The coo, which resembles a happy, drawn-out hiccup, was recently added at a customer's request. The company assures me that the sound is deliberately not encouraging enough to make girls want a real baby, and it probably isn't. So much for positive reinforcement.

What settles the matter is the interruption of my dreams. At 6 am the next morning, having been woken three times by Baby's relentless wail, I decide to terminate my rehearsal of motherhood. After reading my score (ten 'failures to support the head', one 'rough handling event', four minutes of 'neglect' and 21 minutes of 'crying due to any of the above mistakes') I remove the batteries from the electronics box. Baby is put to sleep: not the simulated sleep of a digital infant, but

the eternal sleep of an incapacitated doll.

High school students don't have it so easy: they can be stuck with Baby for more than a week. I still don't know how to raise a child, but at least I'm left with the temporary illusion that parenting is a clear-cut task at which one can improve, a reassuring-enough promise. If anything, Baby Think It Over is an excellent example of applied science in our competitive age of silicon chips. Stroking Baby's head one last time, I enjoy the irony of returning this 52-centimeter crying machine to the same plastic bag in which it arrived. *Danger,* warns the red lettering. *To avoid suffocation please keep this bag away from infants and children.*

With her late husband Peter, **Iona Opie** compiled the most comprehensive record of children's playground behaviour ever attempted: sixteen books spanning from 1951 to 1997, including *The Lore and Language of School Children*, their legendary 1959 trove of games, rhymes, jokes and taunts.

Matilda Blyth tracked down Iona Opie in Liss, Hampshire, and found out why the Opies' historical studies still have a great deal to tell us about contemporary play. And why playground fads, from computer games to Tamagotchis, still spread like wildfire.

Games Children Play

IONA AND PETER OPIE AT WORK, LISS JUNIOR SCHOOL PLAYGROUND, 1962

> Children have their own set of norms through which they rehearse adult life. Using complex oral codes, they swear the truth, formally declare themselves sincere friends, tease others or subject new friends to vicious initiation rights.

"Child's play is human nature, but today's children are overprotected — fact!" declares Iona Opie, with unexpected vehemence for a woman in her mid-seventies. She has reason to be resolute. After a lifetime of research with her late husband Peter, Mrs Opie is the leading expert in Britain on children's play. She has collected every rhyme, chant, jeer and custom that children use while they play, and has documented the history of popular childrens' games. Yet she still thinks most adults just don't understand it.

Born in 1923 in Colchester, Essex, she was raised mainly by her mother, since her father, a pathologist and director of the Wellcome Research Laboratory in Sudan, only made occasional visits home. She met her husband, the young writer Peter Opie, while serving in the Women's Auxiliary Air Force (WAAF) during the Second World War. "I read his autobiography, *I Want to Be a Success*, and was so impressed that I immediately struck up correspondence with him." Peter proposed marriage to her twice, but she stubbornly turned him down, claiming there were "so many other things I wanted to do." Eventually she gave in to his "conventional caveman tactics," and married him in a state of resignation, anxious about losing her independence. When she became pregnant she left the WAAF and looked for a new way to occupy her time.

The Opies' lifelong obsession with the history of nursery rhymes began with a small epiphany. A ladybird landed on Peter's finger during a walk, and he instantly recited a familiar ditty:

Ladybird, ladybird, fly away home
Your house is on fire and your children all gone.

As always, the ladybird dutifully flew away. The couple found themselves wondering how they had known the rhyme since childhood, yet had never questioned what it meant, where it came from or who had written it. From that moment, they set about recording the folklore of children's play.

The Opies' work is best understood in the context of three traditions. One was the study of Folklore, which had been revived by leading British theorists — such as Sir Laurence and Lady Alice Gomme, Charlotte Burne and Cecil Sharp — at the end of the 19th century. Fearing that the arrival of a mass culture would mean the irretrievable

Nicknames and Epithets

What's your name?
Mary Jane.
Where do you live?
Down the lane.
What do you keep?
A little shop.
What do you sell?
Ginger pop.
How many bottles do you sell
    in a day?
Twenty-four, now go away.
    Swansea, skippingsong

Skinny-malinky long legs
    Big banana feet,
Went to the pictures
    And fell through the seat.
    Boy, 12, Helensburgh

Red hair, carrot nose,
Pull the string and up he goes.
    Versions throughout Scotland

> The Opies brought to light the clandestine world of schoolchildren's lore, making it accessible to adults who had forgotten what it meant to be a child.

loss of entirely oral traditions, they sought to record and preserve these historic cultural products. The Folklorists' interests focused primarily on the culture of English folk songs and dances, but some work — such as Lady Alice Bertha Gomme's two volumes of her seminal study *The Traditional Games of England, Scotland and Ireland* (1894, 1898) — concentrated specifically on children's games.

The Opies' research also has an affinity with the 1920s British documentary movement and the Mass Observation project founded in 1937. The documentary movement thrived on a belief that the truth could be found by capturing the ephemeral world, and sought to collect transient information from ordinary people. Similarly, the Mass Observation project, led by Tom Harrison, Charles Madge and Humphrey Jennings, cajoled volunteers to write down detailed diaries of their thoughts, as they experienced them. In this way researchers believed they could collect evidence of everyday practices and attitudes. The Opies applied all these methods to their study of children's play, amplifying their first-hand observations with traditional library research. They examined and recorded playground behaviour, bringing to light the clandestine world of schoolchildren's lore, and making it accessible to adults who had forgotten what it meant to be a child.

After spending long hours scouring historical records, the Opies compiled the first extensive record of nursery rhymes, *The Oxford Dictionary of Nursery Rhymes* (1951). In the course of researching this work, they realised that many rhymes were passed on not from adult to child, but *between children*. "The school rhyme circulates simply from child to child, usually outside the home, and beyond the influence of the family circle… a rhyme may be excitedly passed on within the very hour it is learnt; and, in general it passes between children who are the same age, or nearly so".[1] To study this secret lore that was hidden from adults, the Opies changed their methods of data collection. They began to travel around, frequenting local school playgrounds in Hampshire where they recorded songs and games. They 'hung out' with children playing on street corners and conducted longitudinal surveys into play behaviour with over 70 schools in England, Scotland, Wales and one in Dublin. Representing a cross-section of the schools in Britain, their sample included "small village schools in remote village districts…and grim barrack-like buildings to be seen in nearly every city."[2]

Bargain Making

Ring a ring a pinkie,
Ring a ring a bell,
If ye brake the bargain
Ye'll go to hell.
    Forfar

Secret Keeping

Can you keep a secret?
I don't suppose you can
If you mustn't laugh or giggle
While I tickle your hand.
    Girl, 11, Market Rasen

---

1 *The Lore and Language of School Children*, Oxford: Clarendon Press, 1959, p 8
2 *ibid*. vii

In *The Lore and Language of Schoolchildren* (1959), a unique compendium and perhaps their most celebrated work, the Opies suggest that "Like the savage, [children] are respecters, even venerators, of custom."[3] By gathering together the rhymes, riddles, nicknames, chants and pranks of schoolchildren, they show that children have their own set of norms through which they rehearse adult life. Using complex oral codes, children swear the truth, formally declare themselves sincere friends, tease others or subject new friends to vicious initiation rights. No one had previously collected juvenile lore and language through oral tradition, and for the first time a large number of Britain's schoolchildren were being listened to.

Iona also suggests that "playground rhymes and chants can behave like Chinese whispers, starting in one small community but quickly sweeping the nation." Rhymes and jokes from a school playground mutate as they spread, often picking up speed across the country. One example they give is the speed of transmission of 'scurrilous verses' in 1936. At this time rumours of abdication were endemic in Britain, and gossip about King Edward and Mrs. Simpson was rife. The rhyme,

Hark the Herald Angels sing,
Mrs. Simpson's pinched our king,

was so scandalous that it could never have been printed or broadcast. Yet youths in London, Chichester, Liverpool, Oldham and Swansea were singing the verse well before the end of the Christmas term that year. New fads are spread through intimate playground networks, and the arrival of a new pupil at a school can bring fresh rhymes, jokes or toys which are adopted and adapted by their schoolmates at a rate faster than any marketer's dream. Perhaps this is why more recent crazes, such as the Tamagotchi and its more aggressive counterpart, the Digimon, have become such successful marketing phenomena despite small advertising budgets.

Throughout the Opies' joint endeavors, Iona's input was vital. She obtained access to young children that Peter would never have gained as a man, and regularly worked till ten at night, having also completed the housework. Although research became the epicentre of their life, Iona doesn't romanticise the incessant labor. "Writing down the fifty-seven

> New fads are spread through intimate playground networks: fresh rhymes, jokes or toys are adopted and adapted by schoolmates at a rate faster than any marketer's dream.

Making Friends

Make friends, make friends,
Never, never break friends.

Make up, make up, never row again,
If we do we'll get the cane
    South Molton and Cleethorpes

---

3 *ibid*. p 2

IONA OPIE PHOTOGRAPH NORMAN MCBEATH

minor variations of 'I'm a Little Girl Guide dressed in blue' was tedious beyond words," she recalls unsentimentally. But her depth of her involvement and commitment meant she was continually drawn back to "loving the lifelong monster" of her work.

Iona believes Peter married her as a "willing slave," and assumed he would work with his wife throughout his life. "If I had not loved him, in the idiosyncratic way I did, I could of course have escaped, and would never have become entangled in the first place," she reflects of her marriage. In return, Peter gave her status. He suggested that she was the author of *The Oxford Dictionary of Nursery Rhymes*, and he made Iona, rather than himself, a member of the Folklore Society. This meant she gained the prestige of membership, and Peter could only visit it as her guest. She believes this was his way of "making amends for having submerged me in motherhood."

The couple mainly worked in their house in Liss, Hampshire, in adjoining studies, popping in and out to consult each other as the day went by. Iona would sift and analyse the material that came in, often writing a summary of a particular game, while Peter wrote a section and gave it back for comments. At times this close working relationship in companionable solitude became a bit too intense. Peter's dictatorial behaviour once caused Iona to seek refuge for a night in the local pub, where she contemplated a new career as a school teacher. But she bumped into her bank manager who made her realise that she enjoyed her work, even if she and her husband only earned as much as a police constable.

After Peter's death in 1982, Iona published *Children's Games with Things* (1997), completing a trilogy (including *Children's Games in the Street and Playground*, 1969, and *The Singing Game*, 1985) that brings together their lifetime's study of the games children play. This last book shows how children's games are subject to 'seasons' determined not by

Jeers

I know a little girl sly and deceitful,
Every little tittle-tat she goes and tells the people.
Long nose, ugly face, she ought to be put in a glass case,
If you want to know her name her name is Heather Lee.
Please Heather Lee, keep away from me;
I don't want to speak to you, nor you speak to me.
Once we were friends, now we disagree,
Oh Heather Lee, keep away from me.
It's not because you're dirty,
It's not because you're clean,
It's because you've got the whooping-cough,
Pooh! You awful thing!
    Versions from 15 schools
    throughout Britain

Telling a Lie

Criss cross the Holy Bible,
never tell a lie.
If I do I'll cut my throat, and then I'm sure to die.
    Aberystwyth

Clasp my hands,
Look at the sky,
Cross my heart
and hope to die.
    Penrith

> Children's games are subject to 'seasons' determined not by the weather, but by waves of enthusiasm or the whims of fashion. Some games die out, while others return into playground culture with cyclical reliability.

the weather, but by waves of enthusiasm or the whims of fashion. Some games do die out, while others return into playground culture with cyclical reliability. An unparalleled overview of the nature and history of games, *Children's Games with Things* places current children's games in a wide social context and gives the lie to widely-expressed concerns that today's children have lost the ability to play.

Today, media pundits constantly complain that television, the cinema, and computer games have blunted children's imaginations, leaving them unable to entertain themselves. But Iona Opie will have none of it. "The truth is that, unless they are seriously undernourished or in a state of fear, children will always play when they are on their own, unsupervised, in the freedom of an open space." In *Children's Games with Things*, she attacks the negative rhetoric surrounding new forms of play. Iona thinks that "Children are as creative as they ever were. Child's play is instinctual. Whatever toys they have, children will continue to play."

    Dismissing the notion that children have become passive, she criticises adults' response to new game technology and the ever-present cry that children don't play like they used to. "The much-reiterated phrase is, 'We used to make our own amusements.' At the same time [adults] all but prevent their children from making their own amusements by supplying them with generous pocket-money, and giving them expensive toys... Human nature being what it is, a child would rather play with glamorous glass marbles than with cherry-stones picked up from the gutter."[4] Or more likely today, with an alluring Nintendo Gameboy.

    The Opies demonstrate that indignation over new childrens' games stems purely from ignorance, since adults are often unable to recognise emerging forms of children's games. "Teachers on playground duty have their minds on things other than identifying games, and in any event cannot always recognise which game is which, amid the criss-crossing melée of the playground. A chasing game superimposed on a game of *May I?*, and both games intersected by a diffuse game of *War*, can look like 'children running about aimlessly'."[5] This is a common accusation levelled today at computer games. To an adult, a group of children gathered around a Sony PlayStation may appear to be wasting time developing rapid finger movements, rather than playing a game with clear rules or team skills. Adults' fear of the unknown can blind them to the range of

4 *Children's Games with Things*, Oxford and New York: Oxford University Press, 1997, p 13
5 *ibid*. p 9

social and imaginative skills which are involved, such as turn-taking or creative fantasy, which children can develop as they play in electronic worlds.

Peter and Iona's obsession with children in general did not prevent them being reticent about raising their own. The three Opie offspring were all sent to boarding school throughout their childhood, but seem nevertheless to have thrived on the family belief in the sanctity of child's play. Having grown up amid heaps of books, toys and recordings, their subsequent careers reflect a familiarity with the notion of maintaining a collection: James is a leading toy soldier expert at the auctioneer Phillips, Robert runs the Museum of Advertising and Packaging at Gloucester Docks, and Letitia is a finance manager of a Further Education college in Cranbourne. Adamant that she has given her last lecture and written her last book, Iona herself now revels in the "wonderful sense of freedom" afforded by retirement: still living in Liss, she has recently taken up kite-flying, maintains an acre of garden, and cares for her bantams, ducks and geese.

Some of the Opies' studies now date back nearly fifty years. And yet, throughout the sixteen books they published, they rarely theorise their work or speculate on how it might inform a modern understanding of child's play. They always assumed that the facts — children's own statements — would speak for themselves. The neutrality with which they laid out over 20,000 written accounts from children gives the Opies' work a timelessness, and makes it a fundamental source of primary data about play behaviour — frequently cited and still relevant to those who are interested in understanding child's play today. No one else has ever attempted such extensive research into the way children conduct themselves in the playground. Their collection of rhymes, games and songs are vital for providing a historical context to contemporary thinking about how children interact with each other, and how they make sense of the worlds in which they play and live.

But what does Iona think? Her voice softens. "Many of the things we wrote about are just as applicable to now. But, however hard we try to understand, adults will never quite remember what it was like to be a child."

Books by Iona and Peter Opie

Christmas Party Games. New York: Oxford University Press, 1957.

The Lore and Language of School Children. Oxford: Clarendon Press, 1959.

Children's Games. New York: Oxford University Press, 1969.

Children's Games in the Street and Playground. Oxford: Clarendon Press, 1969.

Three Centuries of Poetry and Nursery Rhymes for Children. London: Oxford University Press, 1973.

A Nursery Companion. Oxford: Oxford University Press, 1980.

The Singing Game. Oxford and New York: Oxford University Press, 1985.

Children's Games With Things. New York: Oxford University Press, 1997.

As compilers

I Saw Esau. London: Williams and Norgate, 1947.

The Oxford Nursery Rhyme Book. Oxford: Clarendon Press, 1955.

The Puffin Book of Nursery Rhymes. London: Penguin, 1963.

The Oxford Book of Children's Verse. Oxford: Clarendon Press, 1973.

The Classic Fairy Tales. Oxford: Oxford University Press, 1974.

The Oxford Book of Narrative Verse. Oxford and New York: Oxford University Press, 1983.

As editors

The Oxford Dictionary of Nursery Rhymes. Oxford: Clarendon Press, 1951.

Ditties for the Nursery. London: Oxford University Press, 1954.

"Writing down the fifty-seven minor variations of 'I'm a Little Girl Guide dressed in blue' was tedious beyond words," Iona Opie recalls unsentimentally.

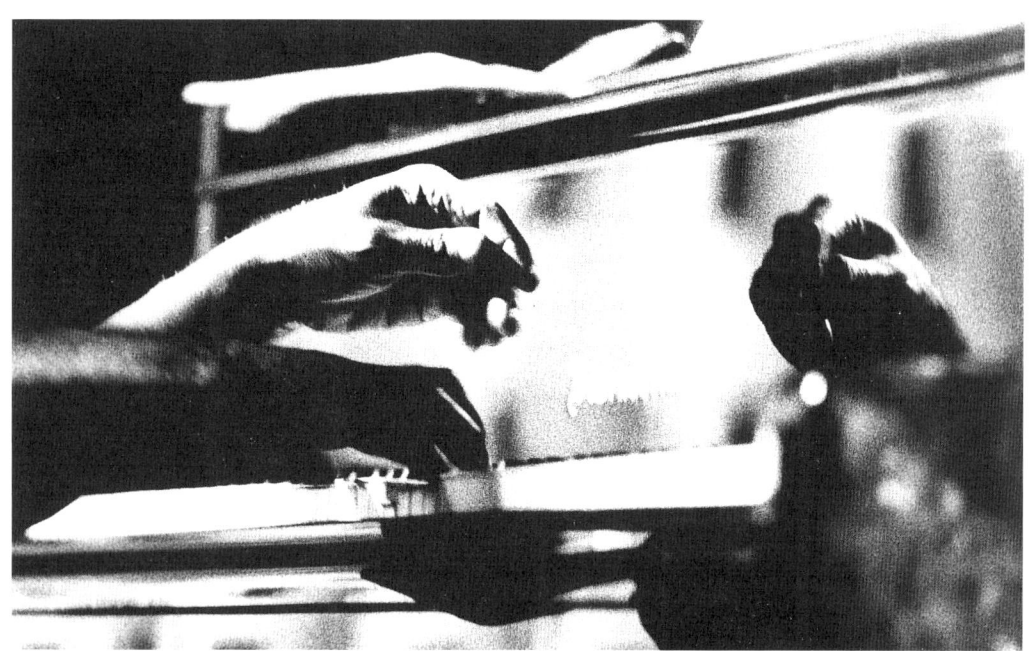

MUHAL RICHARD ABRAHAMS PHOTOGRAPH KARL HEINZ BECHHOLZ

discovery in digital craft

In what ways can we play in the digital realm, a medium of non-physical manipulation and limitless 'original copies'? Malcolm McCullough, author of *Abstracting Craft: The Practiced Digital Hand*, argues that working with pixels offers opportunities for skills and dexterities that are familiar from traditional craft practices — whether throwing clay pots or playing jazz piano. Outlining the various kinds of play to which we are already accustomed in the 'real world', he shows that principles of structure and improvisation, and hand-eye coordination, still matter in the developing sphere of digital design.

In almost anything you might do today, you have got to improvise. There is simply too much change for tradition to handle; there are too many possibilities for any methodology to anticipate in advance. So improvisation plays a major role in serious matters with real stakes, from business plans to scientific research. In all kinds of work, people take pride in thinking on their feet, inventing solutions when under pressure, and practicing originality in the face of risk. They just don't call it play.

But it is a distinct advantage of computation to introduce play: this is a natural consequence of working in bits. The irreversibility of so many traditional processes is rooted in the physical laws of material— in the atoms. You can only move atoms around so much before material starts to break down. Testing, in particular, is often destructive. Thus you cannot play around indefinitely with a physical medium: you have to get to work. But when rearranging bits, processes may be reversed completely without any loss of quality or affordance. Furthermore, true copies are possible, and these are just as good as the original— indeed every copy is an original. This is important, for it means that tentative processes may be applied without risk to extra, throwaway copies. Finally, the very structure of the medium contains variables that invite modification along established parameters. You might recall that when spreadsheets popularized personal computing, very much on the basis of these advantages, the exploratory process was simply referred to as 'What if?'

Play and Learning
Play is for learning: that is why children do it most. Yet adults play too, for simple relaxation, for learning about one another, and for continued skill development. Play lets us search for some lost sense of wonder. A philosopher might argue that in some higher sense, all is play. The cycle of becoming, replete with Sisyphean setbacks, is like a game of fetching the ball. "Some Hilarious God in charge of us," wrote the beat poet Ferlinghetti after a day of whitewater rafting on the Rogue.

Adult play we call recreation. So much work involves so little play that after we work hard, we must also play hard. Although it is more usually physical sport, sometimes recreation still involves making things, and this is the one surviving form of traditional craft. To the artisan, this same process was work. But in comparison to the chaotic work of today, and relieved of the tedium of repetition for earning a livelihood, craft becomes recreation. Yet to its proponents, it is no mere frivolity. Recreational craft is more satisfying than mere amusement, precisely because it is merged with work.

If productive play or serendipitous work fill an inner need, then perhaps there is some truth to the axiom that the basic material every craftsman works with is himself. Popular literature is full of books on getting in touch with a medium as an allegory for finding oneself: "what is the craft of being human?" [1] Given that people are becoming involved with creative computing for recreation, it is probably only a matter of time before we see books on *The Tao of Photoshop* or *Zen and the Art of AutoCAD*. Yet the inner component of work is more than indulgence: it is, as much as any engagement of the senses, exactly what sterile computer usage lacks. If we are to conduct some sort of personal work amid the one-time

---

1 Carla Needleman, *The Work of Craft*. New York: Knopf, 1979.

> Play serves learning though experimentation without risk. Learning occurs through quick, imprecise actions, conducted within understood rules of a game, and free from threat or consummation. Play does not use up so much as build.

military-industrial world of computing, one important way to do so is to play.

Play takes many forms. For example, it can be individual or social. According to one classic taxonomy, individual play includes pursuit of sensations, exercise of motor apparatus and experimentation with higher mental powers. This mental play includes exercise of attention, emotion and will. Attention play includes tests of memory, imagination, focus and reason. On the other hand, social play includes fighting and rivalry, loving and courtship, imitation and status seeking. Imitative play includes movements, drama, behavioural constructions and emulation of inner states. [2]

Crafts and craft learning embrace quite a range of these playful forms. Arguably, no productive process combines so many so well. Sensation, skilled motion, attention, involvement, will — all must be balanced, and this is the basis for craft as recreation. Craft learning is a form of imitative social learning. Movements are physical skills taught directly, whether by demonstration or coaching. Drama is a lesser component here, although it may be understood in the willful suspension of disbelief that allows participation in an abstract medium. Constructions are the artifacts. They are the plastic play, the visual examples, the operational learning. Finally the inner state is the patience, reflectivity and intent that distinguish the master.

Play serves learning though experimentation without risk. Play often lacks any immediately obvious aim other than the pursuit of stimulation, but functions almost instinctively to serve the process of development. Learning occurs through quick, imprecise actions, conducted within understood rules of a game, and free from threat or consummation. Play does not use up so much as build. One thing it builds is common sense. Play's endlessly variable series of awkward, exaggerated motions seeks out the approximate arena for later development of true competence.

There is much to be said for play in a medium. If a medium is defined by its affordances and constraints, then learning consists of exploring these properties. Experimentation is especially useful for becoming familiar with constraints: we learn from our mistakes. We must accept that beginning work in a new medium will be full of setbacks. There will also be fortuitous discoveries, however particularly of affordances. Design is not only invention, but also sensitivity to a medium. Craft cannot be merely in service of technique, or of inappropriately conceived ends. The craftsman must begin to feel something about the artifacts, and only certain moves will feel right.

Of course when it comes to computation, we all must learn. In a sense, we're all children— the medium is *that* new. And of course, the most fluent experts here are often quite young. As all of us learn about this promising new domain, a chain of developments should be clear: play shapes learning; learning shapes the mind; mental structures shape software; and software data structures afford work and play.

Structure and Improvisation

The master at play improvises. Consider the jazz pianist. In *Ways of the Hand — The Organization of Improvised Conduct* (1978), the musician David Sudnow gives us a rare description of otherwise tacit knowledge in action. Improvising on a piece takes much more talent than simply playing from a notation or learning by rote, Sudnow explains. Moreover, improvising begins with a sense of structure, from which it builds a cognitive map. For example, the 'way in' to an arpeggio is mentally mapped. The structure of the keyboard presents a physical map of a chord, which may be modified in countless ways by physical moves. One could play the adjacent keys, for example, or one could translate by any arbitrary interval. One could transpose or invert. One could change the order in which the notes were played, or the

---

[2] Karl Groos, *The Play of Man*. New York: Appleton and Co., 1901

the same pitches as the first, the doubled back and went fast again, but over different pitches... There were innumerable variations possible; looking at 'structure' in this way and corresponding to various continuity practices, ways of the hand were cultivated that were suited to the performance of such manoeuvres... Transposition of such a figure to a new segment and correct repetition with respect to pitch, without slowing it down or slowing down parts of it, involved coping with the topography of the terrain by the hand as a negotiative organ with various potentials and limitations. [3]

tempo, or the attack and decay. Of course one could substitute dominant, major and minor chords.

Sudnow argues that because these variations are sequences of physical positions, they are learned as active skills no longer necessary to be understood at a mental level. Each becomes a handful. That the hand gets a hold of a variation on a chord is indicated by observed tendencies to start into particular sequences with certain fingers on certain keys. The manoeuvre is known by the hand, and the mind only maps the way in. The ability to modify the run note by note — which would require conscious attention — only comes later. Even without attentive intellectual guidance, however, the natural tendency of the hand is not to repeat itself, even in a series of figural repetitions. Thus once a sufficient repertoire of runs is learned, this tendency inherently ensures a richness to the sound. The hand searches its territory for sequences, which process replaces a faithfulness to the score, and that makes jazz. For example:

The new run could be in various other ways only 'essentially related' to the preceding run. Say the first started slow and went up fast, then doubled back and went fast again, while the second started slowly and came back down through

Although jazz is the obvious case, it is hardly alone. Improvisation plays a role in many contemporary practices, and in many traditional crafts. Few of these worlds employ such a singular instrument as the piano; few are able to turn so much over to the hands, but all involve playful response to a structure. For example, of industrial design, Herbert Read insisted that "Art implies values more various than those determined by practical necessity." [4] As a modernist and industrialist, he felt admiration for fundamental structural laws, such as the golden section also admired by his contemporary Le Corbusier. He was convinced, however, that metrical irregularities based on a governing structure, rather than slavish adherence to the laws in their precision, was the basis for pleasurable expression. He cited Ruskin's line that "All beautiful lines are drawn under mathematical laws organically transgressed." [5] He held that this was the case even in the useful (industrial) arts.

Consider the case of processing a digital photograph. The makeup of the raster image file, the various tone scale and filtration operators, provides a very clear structure in which to work but demands no particular order of operation. The complex microstructure of the sampled pixels provides a sub-

> The natural tendency of the hand is not to repeat itself, even in a series of figural repetitions. Thus once a sufficient repertoire of runs is learned, this tendency inherently ensures a richness to the sound. The hand searches its territory for sequences, which process replaces a faithfulness to the score, and that makes jazz.

---

[3] David Sudnow, *Ways of the Hand—The Organization of Improvised Conduct*, Cambridge, MA: Harvard University Press, 1978, p 7
[4] Herbert Read, *Art and Industry—The Principles of Industrial Design* New York: Horizon Press, 1954 [1934]
[5] *Ibid*.

stance upon which to act. (Compare the more difficult situation of sitting down to a blank screen with a paint system.) Patterns of these pixels may be modified and replicated within the image in all variety of ways. Moreover, the ability to copy and paste particular groups of pixels (which you might understand as figural objects, but to the software are just pixels) between multiple files provides excellent capacity to play with compositions. You might process several different images separately, for example, to bring them into the same level of contrast and similar color balances, then extract and compose elements from them into one new image or on top of one existing image chosen as a background. The overlay process can be used to experiment not only with the relative scale and position of several elements, but also with masking and degrees of transparency. You might cross-fade between two backgrounds. You might paste a figure into a limited area of a background, with the effect of it appearing behind the background. You might drag several elements around on different layers and experiment with the order in which they are overlaid. You might flip or stretch some elements to get their foreshortening right or to have the shadows falling in the appropriate direction. Tone scale adjustments alone provide enough means with which to improvise variations in an image for hours. Components of red, green and blue can be controlled separately, as can relatively lighter or darker areas. Intensity distribution graphs can be manipulated to control particular thresholds and ranges. Adjustments can be applied to selections of pixels.

Potential results of each individual step can be previewed, often quickly enough for the work to feel continuous.

Filters themselves are improvisations by programmers. Aside from a few obvious ones such as sharpening and despeckling, there is no clear repertoire. Rather, they are possibilities: pure affordance. More become available all the time, and from these you might establish and explore your own particular collection.

All of this is to say nothing of the improvisatory nature of finding one's raw material for image processing. Sources abound: direct shots from digital cameras, scanned pieces of traditional prints, 35mm slides, video stills, scanned objects, found images on the Internet, commercial clip art. The emphasis is on sampling, but many sources may be the result of pure synthesis: raytraced renderings, charts and graphs, polygonal maps, views of geometric models — indeed anything that appears on your screen.

At the level of devices, skilled people improvise with astonishingly crude instruments. For example, these many image operations are controllable through quick keyboard combinations. All else being equal, one's sensory-motor knowledge of these key combinations can affect one's choice of moves: we tend to do what we know. But what some people get out of a simple keyboard is quite remarkable, and the same is true for an ordinary mouse. For the future, better devices will assure richer improvisation.

Of course the impetus to improvise is deeper than the availability of moves by reflex or the assurance that one can undo any given step. The artifacts themselves invite speculation in the form of moves. Even — perhaps especially — when the goal is a single, studied composition, improvisation plays a role in study. Finished artifacts may go through inchoate stages, and separate study artifacts may be prepared. By nature, study artifacts are always incomplete and contingent. As is commonly understood among designers, the particularities, eccentricities, and implications of intermediate objects influence the outcome of the creative process.

Thus if we could say that improvisation is a manner of inhabiting design worlds, we must note that those worlds are populated by evolving objects. You try things using these elements and operators, and if you like them, you keep the results, and the object of your work evolves. You develop a style based on emphasising particular processes, but you also try processes in response to the state of the artifact.

The ability to navigate a continuum of possibilities is a fundamental advance over the slower iterations of traditional design. We have seen one example in the excursions through a continuum of parametric variations. In this case the mental model of the design world builds a corresponding space of solutions (not necessarily limited to three dimensions), and the physical action consists of moving along design vectors through that space. The eye is engaged in appraising the changing condition of the artifact as the hand modifies one of its design variables in real time. Note that despite its tremendous fluidity, this method is quite structured. The individual parameters shape the kinds of variational excursions that may be made. Moreover, the initial establishment of all parameters frames exactly one design world, and nothing the variational process can do will change that. Thus the design process really occurs in two stages: composing a structure, and then exploring the consequences of that structure.

One could conceivably improvise at a higher level, however, by swapping structures. To continue the case of theme and variations, this means looking for the right theme. When describing an artifact, it means parsing the artifact, or more accurately the formulation of the artifact, in different ways. That is, the same artifact could have many different potential parameterizations. This in turn means understanding the design problem in different ways. Substitution is a normal element of play, and so this fundamental challenge of seeing as, so basic to creativity, involves improvisation in its own right.

Converse to swapping structures of the same artifact, we can swap different artifacts having the same structure. This is essentially a matter of syntax. The usual context is the ordering and relation of discrete elements, for example, windows in a facade. Consider that animation software takes the metaphor of actors on a stage: elements with individual character are subject to a structure of moves, blocking relationships, and scene transitions, and this overriding structure, which is represented in a score, can be enacted with different cast members. This same idea applies in many media: instead of modifying individual dimensions or positional relationships, one can quickly substitute elements in a given armature. To do so involves a playful grasp of structural equivalence that is essential to human outlook.

Finally, just as there is play in applying the software tools within a particular medium, there can be play in choosing the medium in which to work. This is different for digital media, which as we have seen share many more concepts and techniques. We have

> If improvisation is a manner of inhabiting design worlds, we must note that those worlds are populated by evolving objects. You try things using these elements and operators and, if you like them, you keep the results. You develop a style based on emphasizing particular processes, but you also try processes in response to the state of the artifact.

seen how the capacity to realise the affordances presented by a given structure was presented as a means of guiding explorations, or workmanship.
Furthermore, each medium is distinguished by particular vocabulary, constructions, and modifiers, and these together establish within it a limited but rich set of possibilities. This has been referred to as a design world. Working in a digital medium consists of experimenting in a design world, and as we have also seen, doing so involves certain suspensions or assumptions that allow one to enter the representation.

Generative Systems
Syntactic structure can serve as a recipe for growing entire formal systems. As is an increasingly common image thanks to contemporary discussions of genetics, the identity and integrity of the system are encoded in the structure. It becomes an interesting proposition, then, to invent generative structures, albeit less marvelous than those found in nature, which incorporate patterns of growth as in the dynamics of natural systems. We see this in the growing interest in fractals and biomorphic form. Growth algorithms, of which fractals are just one example, seem to offer an interesting future for design.

Time factors add a rich source of algorithmic beauty. Form may evolve in uninterrupted time, or in artificial intervals (as in game cycles), or as a frame of the design process (for example version history). Note that although craft depends on the impetus of the craftsman, elements of the work may have dynamism of their own, like material spinning on a lathe. Although the choice of what to do when belongs to the craftsman, the rate at which the work occurs has a timeframe of its own, based on the meeting of the craftsman's skill with the workability of the material. Nevertheless, there are dynamic representations where not having to exert control over lower-level operations yields a higher sense of control over a complete process. One can work at the level of derivatives, for example, controlling velocity rather than position. By altering the settings of a dynamic system (for example the coefficients of a system of differential equations), one can improvise within the context of a simulation. Probably the most prevalent example of playing style in simulations is the 'builder' games such as *SimCity* or *Civilization*.

The popularity of simulations without explicit winning conditions may reflect a constituency that also keeps a playful attitude in productive computing. As a measure of this, consider the proliferation of multimedia animations in applications ranging from product design to education to crime reconstructions. In this world, generative systems sometimes replace finished artifacts as the tokens of creative arts and entertainment. These configurable worlds of generative action need not exactly mimic corresponding physical worlds. In particular, they may allow better crossovers between different media and representations and therefore allow for the practice of higher-level meta-techniques. Alan Kay:

> The protean nature of the computer is such that it can act like a machine or like a language to be shaped and exploited. It is a medium that can dynamically simulate the details of any other medium, including media that cannot exist physically. It is not a tool, although it can act like many tools. It is the first metamedium, and as such it has degrees of freedom for representation and expression never before encountered and as yet barely investigated. [6]

This may mean that one can simultaneously inhabit and redesign a design world, an idea that is especially interesting with regard to generative structures. One can tweak the algorithms as they run.

> Working in a digital medium consists of experimenting in a design world, and as we have also seen, doing so involves certain suspensions or assumptions that allow one to enter the representation.

[6] Alan Kay, "Computer software," in *Scientific American*, 251: (3),1984, in Brenda Laurel, *Computers as Theater*. Reading. MA: Addison-Wesley, 1991 p 32. See Alan Kay's 'Why The Computer Revolution Hasn't Happened Yet', pages 198-205.

> Like the hand, the eye is playful. It loves computing, where it comes up with such improbabilities as flying toasters. How else but with the eyes can you tell when you have found something?

Structure is revealed in transformation. Notational structure suggests transformations, independent of content. Interface structure invites the application of specifically focused software tools to abstract digital media. Design worlds are structured by distinct repertoires of operations on particular vocabularies. Pushing the stuff of medium, be it bits or atoms, reveals affordances and constraints, and invites workmanship. All of these are forms of exploration, improvisation, and, to use the simplest word, play.

Recognition and Discovery
Both vision and computation are quite prone to abstraction, and the point is to get them to coincide. Here is where this can happen: the eye, more than the hand, can sense algorithmic beauty, see evolution in action, and recognise desirable states in the dynamic flux of forms.

Computation and vision combine playfully for invention and discovery. Like the hand, the eye is playful. It loves computing, where it comes up with such improbabilities as flying toasters. How else but with the eyes can you tell when you have found something?

In traditional craft, the eye constantly monitors the effect of the hands to guide the work toward some abstract vision. One might argue that the ability to recognise correctly emerging results was intrinsic to traditional crafts. If you had seen enough similar artifacts before and lived with them all your life, it was fairly easy to make another one. Because each piece was slightly different, there was always room for a bit of experimentation. Because the conduct of the work was less mediated, there was a shifting back and forth between work and play.

Now the same may begin to occur in computing, but under slightly different the conditions. First, as noted much earlier, the eye is elsewhere than upon the hand itself: hand-eye coordination changes. Second, the effect of the hand is given leverage by generative structures. One might say that the hand need only steer. This acceleration, amplification, or transformation makes the role of the eye all the more important. The hand even if fully, sensuously engaged cannot feel its way. The eye is the monitor of abstraction.

What the eye does best, especially in comparison to computers, is to recognise. We come upon configurations. We see more than we can think of. We appraise. We come upon structural equivalencies - through 'seeing as'. We discover. Here again, craft is more sensitivity than invention.

Hand-eye coördination has its particular ways of learning, play and discovery. The reversible and proliferating nature of operations on structures of bits enables this coordination to develop. The algorithmic beauty of generative structures gives new meaning to the truism that vision is the innate sense of order.

Playful coördination produces the best single record of craft. The beauty of the object derives from the quality of the work: not only workmanship but also playful vision. Outer beauty reflects inner beauty, and rediscovering aesthetic and intellectual pleasure is part of the design and craft process.[7] The relation of work and play is the source of style and beauty.

Excerpted from Malcolm McCullough, *Abstracting Craft: The Practiced Digital Hand*, © 1996 MIT Press, by permission.

[7] Needleman, *The Work of Craft*.

Helen Levitt captured the vibrant emotions and vicious battles of childhood in her classic photographs of 1940s New York streetlife. **Susan Delson** traces the influence of Surrealist cinema on Levitt's eye, and explains how her images summon a lost era of unselfconscious play in the public domain.

PHOTO PLAY

HELEN LEVITT

> Her streets are as intimate as a kitchen table, as elegant in their design as any stage set. And on that stage, children are transformed into an ancient and enduring tribe.

As Helen Levitt is quick to point out, she didn't only photograph children — but children are perhaps the defining element of her work. Her unobtrusive and discerning lens captures the utterly absorbing, day-to-day work of childhood, and the artless grace of those who perform it. No one has portrayed children in quite the same way, before or since.

Levitt began photographing in the mid-1930s, a shy, unassuming young woman in her early twenties. Almost from the beginning, she staked out New York City's streets as her photographic turf. Inspired by friends and colleagues — Henri Cartier-Bresson, Walker Evans, and James Agee, among others — she photographed the people and neighbourhoods of upper Manhattan well into the 1940s. She then moved on to filmmaking for more than a decade, returning to photography in 1959.

What kind of world does Levitt's eye conjure up for us? A not-quite-Arcadian vision, where life is lived publicly, communally, and — to a greater extent than is even conceivable in today's media-saturated culture — unselfconsciously. Her streets are as intimate as a kitchen table, as elegant in their design as any stage set. And on that stage, children are transformed into an ancient and enduring tribe. In his essay for Levitt's book, *A Way of Seeing*, James Agee notes that "The cardinal occupations of the members of this culture are few, primordial, and royal, being those of hunting, war, art, theater and dancing. Dancing, indeed, is implicit in nearly all they do."

And Levitt dances alongside them, in graceful, split-second timing. For her early street work, she always used a Leica — a small, lightweight camera that required an almost athletic precision. To it she added a right-angle viewfinder, enabling her to aim the camera unobtrusively while she herself faced a quarter-turn away from her subject. At times, she would cradle the camera in her arms so that people remained unaware of her shooting — a manoeuvre she has regretfully acknowledged as utterly useless these days.

Occasionally, Levitt's camera finds its subjects looking directly into the lens, as with the four boys, legionnaires in some imaginary army, who fill the frame with their mugging. But in most cases, the children in her photographs remain intent on their own business — the serious business of play.

The play that Levitt chooses to depict is not of the bat-and-ball variety, but the free range of the imagination. For her, the street is nothing so much as theatre, and a surrealist one at that. In 1935, she became acquainted with the photographer Henri Cartier-Bresson, who was then spending several months in New York. From him, Levitt absorbed a keen eye for surrealist juxtapositions, and for the 'Decisive Moment', that fraction of an instant when the picture comes together before the camera with heightened intensity.

As an avid movie-goer — especially to foreign films — Levitt found another surrealist influence in *Le Sang d'un Poete (Blood of a Poet)*, the 1930 film by Jean Cocteau. A series of loosely related vignettes based on the inner life of a poet, the film is filled with haunting, deliberately disorienting images. Among the many sequences that affected Levitt deeply was a scene that takes place in a courtyard-like street. A deadly snowball fight among schoolboys is followed by a dreamlike, life-and-death card game, in which the street literally turns into a theatre. The facade of the building across the plaza fills with crowds of elegant, blasé theatregoers; they occupy the bal-

conies as if they were loges, looking on through opera glasses, and sweeping the snow from the ledges with their fans.

Levitt saw *Blood of a Poet* some time after she had begun photographing in the street. As she remembers it, the film utterly changed the way she saw her own streets, casting a surrealist aura over the slightest encounter. Other films influenced her as well, including Soviet filmmaker Dziga Vertov's classic 'city symphony' film, *The Man with a Movie Camera* (1929). While most admire the film for its innovative cinematic techniques and complex formal structure, for Levitt it simply reaffirmed the desire to shoot in the streets, at as close a range as she could manage.

A surreal theatricality touches Levitt's shot of children soberly ranged around a broken mirror frame — street-level Cocteau at its most delicate. On a more slapstick note (Chaplin was another of her favourites) is the image of an enormous box, a scrum of boyish legs emerging below.

But while Levitt's view of children may be fond, it's unflinching. The glorious animal energy, unexpected tenderness, and great, swooping glee are tempered with a darker streak. Every so often, her photographs catch children lost in ineffable sadness, or recoiling in pain from each other's blows.

Nothing reveals this dark side so much as an episode from *In the Street*, the short film Levitt made with Janice Loeb and James Agee. Shot in East Harlem in the mid-1940s, the film is a jazz-like arrangement of fleeting moments: Levitt's photographs sprung into syncopated motion. In one of the longer sequences, a group of boys celebrates Halloween by pelting each other with cloth bags filled with flour. But the good-natured fighting turns vicious; the film shows not only the wounded warriors choking back tears, but the indignant, apron-clad matriarch who breaks up the melée.

Still, not every pain goes unconsoled. Elsewhere in the film, an unprovoked punch in the eye — from the youngest in a family of gypsy children — elicits the comforting attentions of two older sisters. Later, the miscreant redeems himself with a beguiling, energetic dance. To Levitt's great satisfaction, when James Agee showed *In the Street* to Charlie Chaplin in 1949, not only did he appreciate the film, he imitated the little gypsy's frenetic dance to perfection.

Now in her mid-eighties, Levitt continues to photograph as the vicissitudes of age permit. Last year, New York's International Center of Photography bestowed on her the Infinity Award for Master of Photography, and presented a retrospective of her work. This year, an exhibition of her Mexican photographs — taken during a 1941 trip — has been touring American museums, and a book of these works, *Helen Levitt — Mexico City* was recently published by Doubletake/W.W. Norton. And the ICP exhibition has been touring several museums in Germany.

Rarely one to comment on her own work, Levitt is reluctant to say much about the photographs that made her reputation. "When those early photographs were made," she says, "the streets were like playgrounds. And that explains why those pictures were taken." Her voice trails off, implying the rest: things ain't what they used to be, and those streets aren't playgrounds anymore.

In the end, though, any discussion of 'play' in Levitt's work must come to rest with Levitt herself. For her, always, photography is play: something to be pursued for personal satisfaction, for the fulfillment of her creative vision, and for the sheer pleasure of it. Public recognition is merely a by-product of her fun. But if there's anything that her photographs tell us, it's that playing together beats playing alone. And, like the savvy, street-smart kid that she is, Levitt knows how to share.

> While Levitt's view of children may be fond, it's unflinching. The glorious animal energy, unexpected tenderness, and great, swooping glee are tempered with a darker streak.

photographs © Helen Levitt
courtesy Laurence Miller Gallery, New York

LET'S PLAY HOUSE

Strangely desolate, but with a strict inventory of interior props, these are Ideal Homes as children make them. At youth playgrounds on the eastern and western outskirts of Amsterdam, photographer Johannes Schwartz came across two groups of huts and got to know some of their 'owners' well enough (despite the padlocked doors and voices from within, warning him to 'fuck off') to obtain admission and document the interiors. These photographs record how children — as young as six, up to mid-teens — elect to decorate spaces they can consider their own for a year, for a small membership fee in the grounds, and the cost of electricity.

The structures themselves are permanent (and, from without, painfully similar to the makeshift shacks constructed by the homeless, as recorded by the American photographer Margaret Morton); the interiors are what change. And yet, they reveal a striking conformity about what constitutes the perfect home.

"I was fascinated by the ideas children have about interiors," says Schwartz of the project, which he undertook as his 1998 graduation thesis in photography at the Rietveld Academie in Amsterdam. "There's a certain kind of cosiness, properness they're looking for. It's important that there's no rubbish, no dirt: the rooms are always ready for a visitor." The key furnishings are a sofa, stereo, speakers and artificial lighting, but nothing with which to cook: "No pots and pans, no posters, no mess."

And, in these domiciles, black plastic has unaccustomed caché as a surfacing material. Schwartz recalls visiting one hut that had red walls and reproductions of Dutch Masters on the walls; the following week when he returned, it had been swathed in black plastic. Rather than signifying 'garbage', here its connotations are apparently, more glamorously, to disco.

The slightly eery, deserted look captured by Schwartz betrays distinct ambivalence about what it means to be house-proud. Having lavished considerable care and effort on assembling the decorating materials and furniture, the children don't actually occupy the spaces: "The fun is just to decorate it, getting all the things, making it perfect, and then as soon as it is perfect, changing it."

The absence of people in these images certainly adds to their brooding quality. "I'm not taking portraits," he says adamantly, then admits that taking interior shots "comes quite close." Born in Munich in 1970, and a photographer since he was 17, Schwartz declares himself not interested in typology — that photographic preoccupation of fellow-countrymen such as Bernd and Hilla Becher. But his photographs nevertheless reveal a lingering interest in theme and variation. "The children follow severe rules in building these spaces, about what is good, tasteful, stylish. But in a way, stylish means nothing — because they don't spend a minute in them."

Web Word War

An ungodly alliance of literary theory and arcade game firepower, Alison Craighead and Jon Thomson's *Trigger Happy* offers a cyberspace send-up of Foucault. J.J. King takes a panoptic view.

The 1978 arcade sensation *Space Invaders* is a distillation of America's mid Cold-War psyche: Us vs Them, home team vs bug-eyed alien, in a conflict that demands total vigilance, infinite aggression in the face of eternal attack. *Trigger Happy*, a Shockwave piece by Alison Craighead and Jon Thomson, substitutes paragraphs from Foucault's *What is the Author?* for the invaders, exploiting the game's familiar ideological structure to cast the Foucauldian text as Other: words edge down the screen spitting laser fire, the player's oppositional role parodies the dialectical critical response, and the agonistics of language take form as a brute struggle for survival. A good gag, nicely underscored by the insistently banal ice-cream van jingles accompanying the action.

This critique of the critic, central to the installation version of *Trigger Happy*, also extends into an observation about reader behaviour in a hyperlinked (clickable) environment. The process of the game reduces the player's focus on the text to an abortive, belligerent gaze on individual words: hitting one, you target the next, and so on —until the sentences become punctuated beyond intelligibility. The sense of a whole is elided, detonated by the irresistible urge to click.

The online version of the piece (without soundtrack) takes this critique further, resurrecting keywords from the text as hyperlinks that beckon the user away from the *Invaders* environment, and out onto the web. Craighead and Thomson's crosshair thus targets a central problematic of the network: the Attention Deficit Disorder (as psychologists are now calling it) endemic to a radically interconnected environment.

An overabundance of hyperlinks, the artists seem to say, encourages the substitution of click-through for thorough reading, reducing the critical attitude to a binary: accept/reject, take on/cast off, get bored/click here. In the web environment, as in *Trigger Happy*, the reader's focus on text is constantly and thoroughly aborted, perpetually distracted by the prospect of more specialised, more scintillating, more apropos information.

Thus, in the midst of this play on hits and clicks, *Trigger Happy* gestures towards the basis of a future information economy, in which attention itself — precisely because of its scarcity — may become a central commodity. The most successful constructions, we're left thinking, will be those which, in generating attention and catching the gaze, can take the reader's finger *off* the trigger.

The installation version of *Trigger Happy* was first shown in the *Eyes of March* exhibition at the LEA Gallery in London, curated by Gregor Muir. Thomson and Craighead (respectively, lecturer in Electronic Media and Sound at the Slade School of Fine Art and researcher in Web Specific Art at the University of Westminster) are currently nominees for a Paul Hamlyn Award from the Paul Hamlyn Foundation, which since 1993 has provided five annual grants to artists of £30,000 each. Their newest work, *Speaking in Tongues*, an electro-acoustic piece incorporating radio scanned sounds and a stethoscope interface, was commissioned by London Electronic Arts for the second *Pandaemonium Festival of Moving Images*, held in October 1998 at the LEA Gallery.

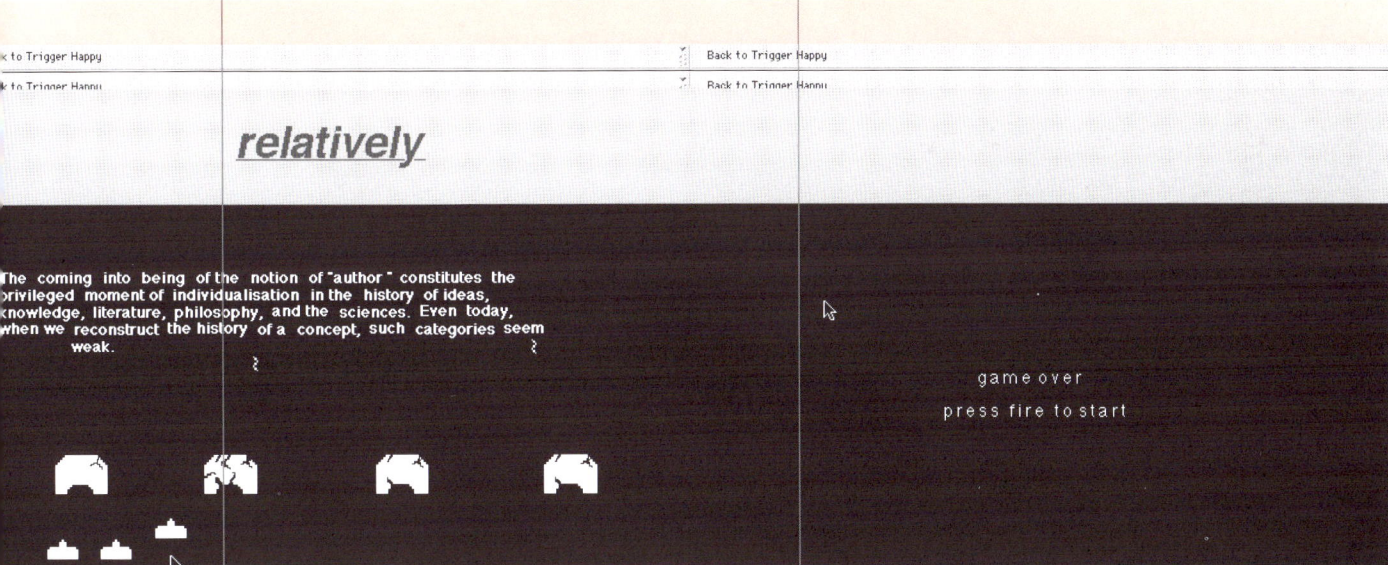

http://www.triggerhappy.org

http://www.lea.org.uk

Toy Storeys

When the going gets tough, the tough go shopping, so **J.C. Herz** made field trips to two Manhattan toy stores — Toys'R'Us and the Store of Knowledge — to find out what their interior design and retailing techniques reveal about children's leisure time, learning and mass entertainment. Photographs by **Kristian Waagner**.

Among educational toy companies, Lego and Galt Toys are household names. Of equal significance and charm, but yet to be recognised among the pioneers of the modernist toy movement, are Abbatt Toys, founded by Paul and Marjorie Abbatt in 1932.

Galt has become syn-

CRAFT TOYS MADE BY FREDA SKINNER FOR ABBATT TOYS, 1932

onymous with well-designed wooden educational toys but when it was launched in 1961, Galt's designer and shop manager had both been poached directly from Abbatt Toys, which had set the standards in this field some thirty years previously.

Today, Abbatt Toys are hard to find. The only examples on general display can be seen at the former home of the late architect Ernö Goldfinger at 2 Willow Road, Hampstead, London (a National Trust property since 1996). The Abbatts commissioned these toys from Goldfinger in 1932 and, in 1936, he designed their shop in Wimpole Street, London.

Fortunately, archive material relating to these formative years has been gathered by Halina Pasierbska, curator at the Bethnal Green Museum of Childhood in London.

Paul and Marjorie Abbatt aimed, by means of innovatively-designed toys, to improve and enlighten the lives of children. Their missionary zeal was shaped by the prevailing utopian-socialist strand of European Modernism, and strengthened through their membership of both The Order of Woodcraft Chivalry and, later, Britain's Communist Party.

Developed in 1917 by Aubrey T. Westlake, The Order offered a new 'social religion' closely aligned with Quaker beliefs, and modelled on Baden-Powell's camp schools. But, unlike the Boy Scouts, this early experiment in 'hippy' communal living invited men, women and children to co-exist freely in defiance of war and technology.

At camp in Sidcot, Westlake promoted the 'lore of the woodman', and here the Abbatts learned the virtues of wood, a 'natural' material that could be used to create 'honest, well-made, crafted objects'. Inspired by The Order, they decided to produce and sell wooden toys as an alternative to mass-produced toys which they deemed poorly-made and representative of the threat of urban modernisation.

The toys they created were not without precedent: the Abbatts borrowed formal elements from those developed by European educational reformers, including the geometric shapes of Friedrich Froebel (Germany, 1782-1852), and the didactic materials of Dr Maria Montessori (Italy, 1870-1852) and Margaret McMillan (Britain, 1860-1931). The latter promoted 'open-air' nurseries with free-arm drawing and sand trays as new methods of learning.

Following their marriage in 1930, Paul and Marjorie embarked on a year-long honeymoon tour of Europe to study progressive educational methods, with an eye to establishing a nursery school on their return. As Paul later recalled, they "taught English in Vienna, wandered through Yugoslavia with a tent and unofficially entered Russia via the Black Sea." Collecting exemplary " wooden objects en route,

THE RIGHT TOY FOR THE RIGHT AGE, INTERIOR DISPLAY AT TAVISTOCK SQUARE, 1932
© BETHNAL GREEN MUSEUM OF CHILDHOOD, LONDON

Child psychologist Dr Charlotte Bühler's dictum, "the right toy for the right age," became the Abbatts' maxim, inscribed on their catalogues for forty years.

Hannah Ford rediscovers Abbatt Toys, whose founders pioneered high quality wooden educational toys in Britain in the 1930s.

"The peasant toy reflects — in a carved block of wood — the weight, the simplicity, the defencelessness of the peasant class.

The peasant has long dark evenings without books to read and turns to toy-making as a hobby."

Paul Abbatt, 1934

IDEOLOGISTS AT PLAY

ABBATT TOYS HAMMER AND PEG SET CIRCA 1971
© BETHNAL GREEN MUSEUM OF CHILDHOOD, LONDON

THE LEGO MINDSTORMS RCX BLOCK IS PROGRAMMED USING RCX CODE, DOWNLOADED VIA THE BLOCK'S INFRA-RED COMMUNICATION PORT. COLOURED PANELS, REPRESENTING COMMANDS, ARE ADDED TOGETHER ON THE INTERFACE LIKE PIECES OF A JIGSAW-PUZZLE.

he uses it in a way that is distinctly different way from what most designers mean. "You're right: it's not so much the look of the finished artefact that I'm referring to, but the process of playing around with the materials. Of course I care somewhat about the look."

Asked what he thinks of the much ballyhooed efforts to put computers into schools, Resnick ripostes, "When I'm asked 'is it good to wire the classroom?' I say, 'Is it good to put *books* in classrooms?' At the conferences I go to on computers and education, there are basically two positions on 'the wired classroom'. The first is, 'hey, this is great because we can find the *best* physics teacher in the country' — basically, a TV broadcast model, centralized and about delivery of information. The second is a database model, which sees the Internet as 'the great library', putting children in control of their learning." Neither of these approaches, in his view, necessarily leads to a vibrant, useful education. "If kids come out of elementary school with a passion for learning, that's more important than any facts or concepts they can learn."

So what defines 'play,' in his view? "I see play as working around at the edges of possibility, a stance towards doing things." One of his criteria for developing LEGO's new construction kit was that it should have a very low threshold of accessibility, "which makes me feel comfortable, emotionally and psychologically, so that as soon as I see the bricks I should be able to start doing things, and have a spurt of new ideas." On the other hand, the system needed to have a "high ceiling of potential development," so as to be capable of growing complexity over time.

He offers a metaphor. "If you had kids, would you rather they learned to play the piano or the stereo? The latter is much easier: in 10 seconds as soon as I learn it, I can play any music I like." Having grown up playing the cello, he learned "what it meant to play with sound: being able to try things out. Music wasn't just something I listened to on the radio."

Likewise, his programmable blocks are aimed at giving kids (his favoured appellation — specifying neither age nor gender) the opportunity to 'doodle' with software, "going back and forth between exploration and focusing."

The turning point in Resnick's own intellectual itinerary came when visiting Xerox PARC as a correspondent for *Bussiness Week*. He realised that he wanted to become more directly involved in creating new technologies, rather than just reporting on them. The transition took him several soul-searching years, but he has obviously found his niche. Of the switch from being a journalist to being a teacher, he says contentedly, "I have a drive to help other people understand things. As it turns out I'm happier making toys and tools to help kids understand the world better, than writing articles to help businessmen understand the world better." His next book may benefit both: a collection of essays based on his Media Lab research, its working title is *Lifelong Kindergarten*.

touch something. Seeing a little robot drive to the edge of the computer screen is far less spectacular than seeing it drive off the edge of the table and falling apart."

In *Turtles, Termites and Traffic Jams*, a slim volume based on his Ph.D., Mitchel Resnick argues repeatedly for the educational benefits of making things. "Many of our richest learning experiences grow out of situations in which we are engaged in designing and constructing personally meaningful things."[3] Why is construction so important? "When you're designing things in the physical world there's a back-and-forth," Resnick replies. "It changes what's in your head so you revise what you make in the world. The type of construction or creativity kit you give to kids makes a lot of difference, but they also need structure to release their imagination. The constraints in the blocks give them greater capability."

Turtles, Termites and Traffic Jams investigates the patterns of behaviour that emerge in large complex systems. (Subtitled *Explorations in Massively Parallel Microworlds*, it appeared in 1994, the same year as Kevin Kelly's *Out of Control: The New Biology of Machines*, which explores not dissimilar territory at compendious length.) The research was primarily conducted via case-study projects undertaken by teenagers using the Star Logo computer program which Resnick developed specifically for this work. Various species of living creatures and apparently chaotic phenomena — such as ant colonies, the spread of forest fires or the motion of cars in traffic jams — are held up as examples of self-organising systems. Disappointingly, whatever the specific character of the subjects, they are uniformly represented in Star Logo's interface by identical coloured specks on the computer screen.

Still, aesthetics are merely incidental: the book is really a polemic in favor of decentralised systems, which Resnick argues are now showing up in various walks of life — from politics to technology to theories of knowledge. In the closing section, he reprises this argument, by way of ratifying his opening statement. Overall, the book is a bit less than thoroughly convincing, but one comes away from reading it with an appreciation of his zeal for decentralisation — a crusade, of sorts. What underlies this motivation?

"I'm interested in moving away from hierarchical power structures," he says. "There's a political sense to this that comes partly from growing up in the 1960s, and a natural reaction against centralised power in the way society is organised, and in the institutions and personal relationships I'm part of. But", he concedes, "just because this framework is applicable in ant colonies, or in the biological world generally, doesn't mean it's necessarily the way we should organise our families or government."

Pressed to say what might have influenced this outlook, Resnick pauses, then recalls a social institution that shaped his adolescence: the Yiddish summer camp that he attended aged 13 and 14, then worked at for three more years as a camp counsellor. Named after a mythical town in a story by Sholem Aleichem , and located near Poughkeepsie, New York, Camp Boiberik was finally closed down in 1979. Resnick recalls that the end of each summer was marked with a *Velker Yom Tov* ('People of the World Holiday') which honoured global culture, rather than any specific ethnic group. Four hundred people, of all ages, showed up at the Camp's reunion in 1998. Now its web-master, Resnick boasts that he's in charge of "the best website for a defunct socialist Yiddish Summer Camp," but more seriously, wonders, "how do we keep Camp Boiberik alive, online? And what is it that remains in our lives?"

One senses that the spirit of Camp Boiberik continues, in modified form, in the Computer Clubhouse that Resnick helped start in downtown Boston: an after-school centre where underprivileged children aged 10 to 13 can try out new technologies as an expressive medium. "There's a lot of talk these days about lifelong learning, but we'd better have lifelong *playing* as well," he says. "Too often when we think about kids learning, it's only concerned with the period from 9am-2pm. We need *daylong* learning as well as lifelong, and a wide range of rich play."

As part of the *Toys of Tomorrow* project at MIT, Resnick and his team have been working on adding computational ability to several other kinds of traditional toys, including beads, balls and badges. "Kids are passionate about beads, so we've extended them to give new capabilities." He shows me a prototype — which still looks like something that's come out of an engineering lab rather than a potential impulse purchase at Bloomingdales' accessories counter. With a built-in microprocessor and light-emitting diode (LED), each bead can communicate with its neighbours by inductive coupling. Depending on how they are strung together, various patterns of flashing lights can be achieved: some beads pass the light along; others bounce it back in the direction it came; still others 'extinguish' it. Resnick argues that this electronically-enhanced jewellery is particularly attractive to young girls, and encourages children to engage in 'probabilistic reasoning' as they work out the likelihood of producing various dynamic patterns from these physical examples of 'cellular automata' (cells that change their state depending on those of neighbouring cells).

In a new project, children develop their own scientific instruments around the MIT programmable brick that is the prototype for MINDSTORMS' RCX block, gaining awareness of the significance of scientific devices and confronting scientific principles hands-on, rather than simply following predetermined classroom experiments. Resnick co-teaches a course with MIT colleague Sherry Turkle entitled *Beyond Black Boxes*, which opens up the field of instrument design and the implications for scientific exploration when much of the functionality is buried in electronics.

"A hundred years ago, scientists built their own equipment," he says. "Today, you order an electronics box, put in some data and retrieve some data. Take a look at current scientific equipment compared to the finely-crafted machines of 200 years ago, and you'll see a distinct lack of aesthetics." Given the long-standing discussion in the product design community about the 'black box aesthetic', it is interesting to hear that technologists are now taking a stand on this topic, albeit from a different perspective.

Resnick uses the word 'design' frequently in describing his work, but

---

3 Mitchel Resnick, *Turtles, Termites and Traffic Jams: Explorations in Massively Parallel Microworlds*, MIT Press 1994, p 47.

ROBOTS BUILT WITH LEGO MINDSTORMS

STORMS RCX block — to which commands could be sent autonomously, using infra-red signals from the computer. So children could now build free-standing (and mobile) 'robots'.

"Being able to 'cut the wires' was a major step forward," says Torben Sørensen, senior vice president for LEGO DACTA, speaking at LEGO'S world headquarters in Billund, Denmark. "Children could now more easily identify these autonomous 'turtles' with a pet, like a cat or dog. Once the creature becomes autonomous — something children can 'give life to' — it activates their fantasies much more."

Indeed, as Sherry Turkle notes in her *Life on the Screen*, children ascribe 'life' to virtual creatures in computer games and robots according to diverse criteria, freely shifting their views as to whether a robotic creature has volition, or whether *they* are making it perform the tasks they have programmed it to do.[2]

"MINDSTORMS is not about technology," insists Sørensen. "It's about a belief that children can develop their cognitive skills, problem-solving ability, and creativity, by constructing with LEGO bricks that have behaviour, using a more visual, less syntax-oriented programming language than Logo. Today with multimedia comput-

ers, we can make them much more child-friendly."

With the rapid penetration of PC's into U.S. and Western European homes, LEGO saw that a market was emerging for a home version of the classroom learning tools developed by LEGO DACTA. But turning the MIT 'Red Brick' into a consumer product posed considerable challenges. "Taking a concept into a prototype as Mitch did, is a major achievement," says Sørensen, "because people in business suits take notice when they can see something physical — more than just an abstract idea. But taking the prototype into the marketplace is also fairly heavy task, because of the cost implications, and quality issues." While LEGO is accustomed to calculating in the world of plastics, for efficient and competitive production of 'conventional' bricks, "when you get into integrated circuits, you need to think in a different way, and to expect a certain learning curve in driving down costs."

Until now, Sørensen says, no company has succeeded in making a product that enables children to use the computer for expressive purposes, as opposed to playing a computer game that takes them through a prescribed path of activities. "To construct on and with the computer: that's the big challenge."

In its graphics, packaging, and the range of creatures to be made with the inaugural extension kits, MINDSTORMS has a definite skew towards boys. While arguing that the system also appeals to girls, Sørensen agrees that this first range is somewhat male-oriented; a new range, specifically aimed at girls, will be launched in 1999. From pre-launch product trials, it seems that girls are inclined to use the programmable brick to make more 'useful' things — from a device to photograph birds that land on a bird-feeder, to weather detection, to feeding a cat when it crosses a certain line, to touch sensors that enable a violin to make a certain sound. If given the chance, boys make "action-oriented things that can shoot or crash into something", whereas girls are more interested in expression of color and sound, not just with motor action," says Sørensen.

MINDSTORMS is not exactly cheap but, he maintains, "LEGO has

long durability and play-value: the cost per play-hour over generations is extremely cheap." From extensive demographic research conducted in 1995-1996 among some 2,000 US and European families, LEGO identified what it calls 'Caring, Conscious and Capable' or 'CCC' homes (roughly 20 percent of U.S. homes) in which parents are very concerned about developing their children's intelligence and spending 'quality time' with them. While there was an obvious correlation between 'CCC' homes and parents with a college degree, education and income were not necessarily the deciding factors: even middle-income and low-income families could afford a cello or a violin if they felt it important for their children's development. It is to these homes that MINDSTORMS is particularly targeted. "In coming years," Sørensen predicts, "children will be surrounded by so much that is only virtual, that there will be an inner need to

THE MIT 'RED BRICK' — PRECURSOR TO THE RCX

THE RCX PROGRAMMABLE BRICK AT THE CORE OF LEGO MINDSTORMS

2 Sherry Turkle, *Life on the Screen*, Simon and Schuster, 1995, p 172

approaches. What we really need is lifelong kindergarten."

So what is it that happens to restrict play after the kindergarten years? "There's a long history of running schools according to an industrial model," he says, "training kids to work, sit in their seats and look straight ahead. It's part of a discipline. In my mind, it's a wrongheaded approach." But while the objects encountered in kindergarten are essential for grasping material fundamentals, they aren't very good at helping kids understand dynamic processes in the world.

This is where the latest LEGO comes in: a new generation of toys with computational abilities which, as Resnick puts it, "extends the range of ideas children can think about while playing, allows them to control things in the world, and get things from it." Aimed at children aged 11 and up, the LEGO MINDSTORMS 'Robotics Invention System' went on sale in autumn 1998, in a kit costing around $200 — approximately two-thirds the price of a Sony PlayStation — which includes the yellow studded RCX programmable brick, plus various peripherals that attach to it (motors, touch- and light-sensor) and the software for downloading behavioural commands from a Windows-based computer. For an additional $50 or so each, the accompanying 'Expansion Sets' ('Extreme Creatures', 'RoboSports' or 'Exploration Mars') allow children to build various robotic creatures, by adding various components to the RCX brick; the latter is the commercial realisation of a prototype developed at the Media Lab.

Behind MINDSTORMS lies a long history of research by LEGO's educational division, LEGO DACTA, and its Boston-based 'radar' on new technology, LEGO FUTURA, in association with various North American institutions, including MIT, Stanford Research Institute and Tufts University. This latest consumer product range — launched in the US and UK in 1998, and due to be launched in selected European and English-speaking Asian countries in 1999 — is essentially a modified home-version of a system that has been available in some 20,000 U.S. schools for several years.

The first computer-controlled LEGO products were developed in 1986. The 'LEGO TC' interface, of 1989, became the basis of the 'Control Lab' system, marketed to schools in the early 1990s at $500 for a complete set. Using 'Control Lab', schoolchildren could build creatures and issue commands to them using the Logo programming language developed by Seymour Papert and others at the Media Lab, in a relationship with LEGO dating back to 1984. Then in 1993-1994, Fred Martin and others at the Media Lab came up with the 'Red Brick' — direct precursor to the MIND-

WITH BRAINS

Fully living up to the proverbial boffin's untidy office, Mitchel Resnick's cubicle at the MIT Media Lab is so cluttered with cardboard boxes and prototype *Toys of Tomorrow* that the visitor must step gingerly between them to reach the only spare chair. The boxes contain computers and bits of computers which, at the time of our meeting, are ready to be shipped to the Boston Computer Museum, where an exhibit is about to open based on his 1994 book *Turtles, Termites and Massively Parallel Processing Systems*. Always with a smile on his face, Resnick explains enthusiastically — often in uninterruptable torrents — why behaviourally-enhanced toys are the coming attraction, and why kids learn more by making things than by having facts rammed into their heads. "I'm interested in helping children engage in new play and learning experiences," he begins. "These two things are closely intertwined. Kids pick up languages very quickly, and they also spend a lot of time playing. That's no coincidence: it's one of the reasons why they are such good learners."

A tall, bushy-bearded man in his early forties, Resnick is associate professor of Research in Education, working within the Lab's Learning and Common Sense Section, headed by Seymour Papert (who, since 1989, has been LEGO professor in Learning Research). Resnick came late to the academy after a long period as a journalist, covering the Silicon Valley beat for *Business Week* in the early goldrush era of new media. Lately, he has found himself more frequently on the receiving end of journalistic enquiries, as one of the leading minds behind MINDSTORMS, the new LEGO system that incorporates computer chips to enable children to build their own programmable devices.

Lying on Resnick's desk, under shelves loaded with books on learning and human evolution, is a copy of *Inventing Kindergarten*, Norman Brosterman's 1997 study of the influential German educational theorist Friedrich Froebel, whose 19th-century innovations Resnick acknowledges in his recent co-authored paper, 'Digital Manipulatives: New Toys To Think With'.[1] LEGO MINDSTORMS bricks-with-brains can be understood as the late 20th-century equivalent of the unadorned wooden blocks and other 'gifts' (a planned sequence of educational playthings for kindergarten children) that were central to Froebel's pedagogical method: they represent the material embodiment of current theories of child development in an age of computer games, 'wired classrooms' and other techno-fetishes.

Likening the Media Lab itself to a kindergarten, Resnick points out that this earliest phase stage of formal schooling is widely regarded as the one part of the educational system that works well, while what comes later is generally seen as problematic. He believes this has to do with its emphasis on construction and direct handling. "Kindergarten is full of physical objects," he explains. "Kids are always making things with pattern blocks, towers of bricks, manipulative materials such as modelling clay. By handling physical objects, they learn about shape, size, scale and color. A few years later, we strip away all those

---

1 Mitchel Resnick, Fred Martin, Robert Berg, Rick Borovoy, Vanessa Colella, Kwin Kramer, Brian Silverman, 'Digital Manipulatives: New Toys to Think With,' presented at CHI '98, the 1998 conference on Computer Human Interaction.

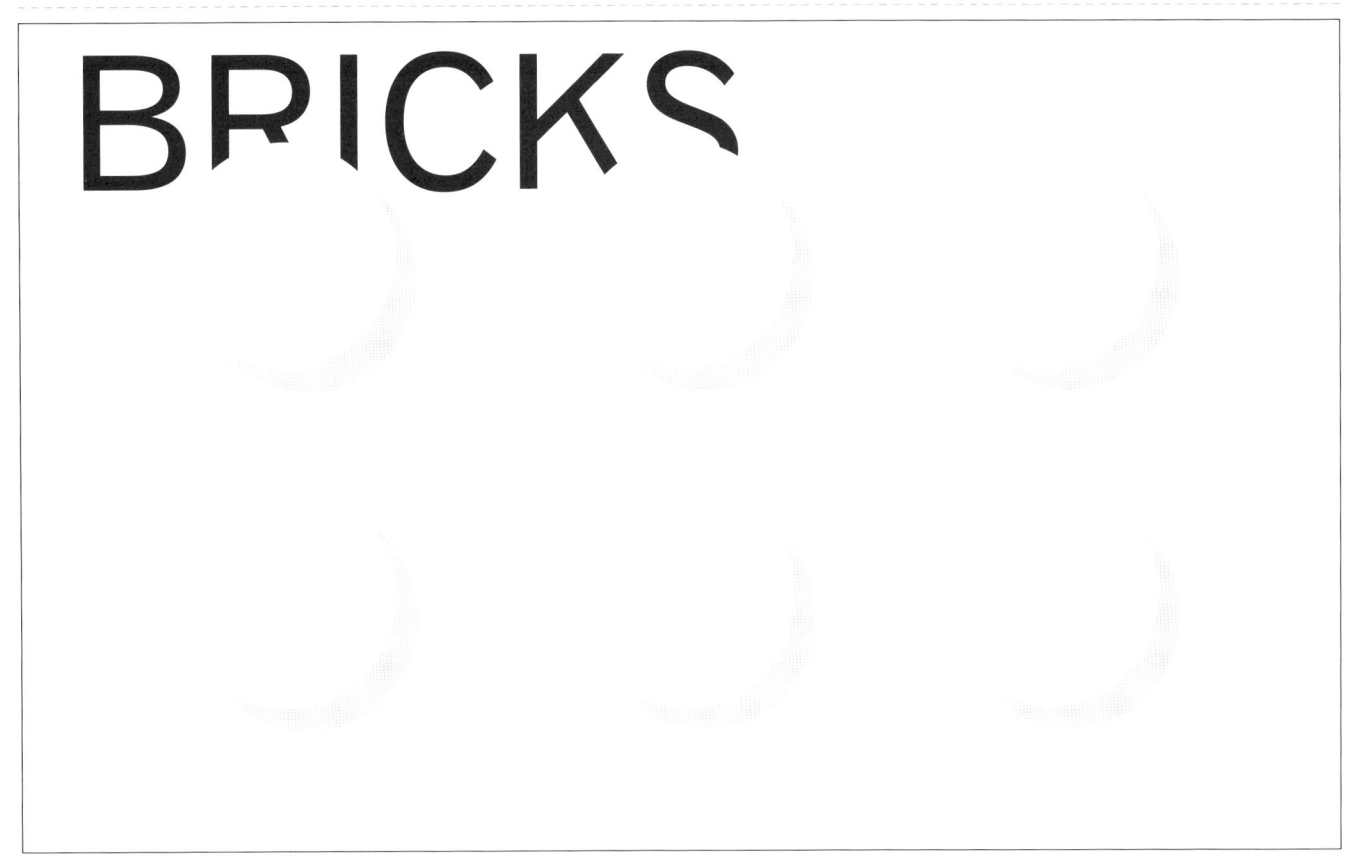

Since its founding by carpenter Ole Kirk Christiansen, LEGO (leg godt = 'play well' in Danish) has evolved from making wooden toys and bricks in the 1930s, to plastic bricks in the 1940s, via mechanically-enhanced brick assemblies in the 1970s, to its most recent product, LEGO® MINDSTORMS™. The result of a long collaboration between the Danish multinational and the MIT Media Lab, the 'electronic' brick at the heart of this system is able to perform various robotic activities. **Janet Abrams** talked to **Mitchel Resnick** and **Torben Sørensen**, two of the brains behind LEGO's bricks with brains, and found some interesting links between European child-development theories, leading-edge U.S. technology and the politics of the 'wired classroom'.

conspicuous lack of frills gives middle-class consumers the impression they're getting a good deal.

In marked contrast is the Store of Knowledge, a 'learning and creativity' boutique toy store on the Upper East Side of Manhattan, a neighbourhood known for pricey real estate, plastic surgeons, and Ladies Who Lunch. Owned by WNET, New York's public television station, the Store of Knowledge presents itself as an alternative to the crass commercial circus of Toys'R'Us. The lighting is subtle. The ceilings are 25 feet high. Instead of escalators and warehouse racks, the store is arranged in an open plan, the upper level elevated by a few steps. The wooden fixtures suggest an upscale bookshop.

There are no aisles, but rather islands of products designed to make children smarter and more knowledgeable. Terraced tables of carefully-selected goods stand as shrines to Howard Gardner's Theory of Multiple Intelligences: a Left Brain island with toys for the budding quantum physicist; a music island for incipient Cecelia Bartolis and Yo-Yo Ma's; a Charismatic Megavertebrate oasis for prospective Steven Jay Goulds and Diane Fosseys. Categorisation is not by gender but rather: *what sort of genius is your little darling?*

And next to each cluster of fun and education, there is a monitor. Because, whatever you're interested in — dinosaurs, space, history, literature, science — PBS has at some point produced a documentary or miniseries about it. The assumption here is that — unlike the plebeian tots frequenting Toys'R'Us downtown — the sons and daughters of Upper East Siders are naturally inquisitive over-achievers, begging to be tutored by National Geographic.

It's very tastefully presented. Instead of the Spice Girls video, on sale for $14.99 at Toys'R'Us, the Store of Knowledge has BBC productions of Jane Austen novels in boxed sets of six for $99.95. Store of Knowledge nudges its customers gently but firmly in the direction of television: you can't throw a koosh ball without hitting a video screen. A toy store run by a TV station (albeit a highbrow public one), it's about learning and knowledge — or more specifically, the kind of things you can learn and know by watching television.

The implicit message is that the merchandise in this store will develop your child's mind so that he or she can get into the right private primary school, the right prep school, and onwards to the Ivy League. Store of Knowledge promises its hard-charging, dual-career knowledge-worker clientele that it will give their offspring some kind of competitive advantage. It speaks to yuppie insecurities about parenting: don't worry if you're too busy climbing the corporate ladder to concentrate on your children. They're not missing out — they have all these great toys to nurture and enrich them. No need to worry that your kids spend all their time watching television, so long as it's the right 'kind' of television. Because, you see, parenting is all about choosing the best products.

But really, this place is just a sophisticated way of flogging videocassettes. Which is ironic, because there's less to be learned from a lavishly produced documentary than from a jar of Play-Doh or a pack of Crayola crayons.

Or, for that matter, from a Super Soaker.*

*The only point of overlap between Toys'R'Us and the Store of Knowledge is, alas, the *Teletubbies*. The Information Economy has its drawbacks.

I am standing in the candy aisle at the Union Square, Manhattan branch of Toys'R'Us — the United States' most venerable chain of megastores. And it occurs to me that this is the most American spot on earth — a place where you can literally consume licensed merchandise. Here, giant mythic creatures are shrunk to miniature edible form, the end of a food chain that begins with special effects movies and ends in hyperactive grade-schoolers' bellies. A dozen varieties of lizard-shaped candy are arrayed on the shelves, with a sign that alerts: YOU MUST EAT GODZILLA CANDY OR...GODZILLA MIGHT EAT YOU!!!!!!!

Meanwhile, a Little Mermaid Spin Pop showcases the latest trend in mass-produced edible toys: motorisation. Press a button and the lollipop actually spins, while Ariel's plastic tail undulates suggestively. Motorised Skittle holders flaunt gears and ejection slots, while the Power Pez rotary dispensing disc looks and functions like a contraceptive pill dispenser. Then there's the usual assortment of Raisinettes and York Peppermint Patties — pacifiers for baby boomers, no batteries required.

Adjacent to the candy aisle, a sign dissects the store's floor plan into the poetry of juvenile mass merchandising:

A diagonal ride up the consumer conveyor belt takes casual shoppers, Chutes & Ladders-style, from the Crayola Sector and the Barbie Zone to a second-floor confrontation with America's most popular water gun: the Super Soaker. From the 70ml Super Soaker XP to the metre-long CPS 2500 ('The Newest Wave in Super Soaker Technology. Adjustable Nozzle for 3 Stream Widths - Up to 20 x More Water Power Than a Super Soaker XP!'), this arsenal represents a kind of aqueous arms race, just in time for summer vacation.

The gender divide is clear here on the second floor, with its separate aisles for action figures, trucks, plastic commando kits, and Michael Jordan basketballs. This is the place for sticks and snails and puppydog tails.

Across from the Godzilla mini-store (non-edible merchandise), board games are neatly stacked — Little Mermaid, Mulan, Cat in the Hat, Elmo, and, yet again, Godzilla. It's not just Monopoly anymore. Every blockbuster entertainment property has been converted into a board game. It doesn't even matter if they don't sell — the margins on boxed cardboard are too high to keep these McGames off the shelves.

Overhead, unshaded light bores down from fluorescent tubes onto putty-colored tiles 15 feet below. Aisle after aisle of metal warehouse racks are stacked up to the ceiling. Toys'R'Us makes no excuses. It doesn't pretend to be anything other than a distribution point for brand-name bits of plastic, manufactured a million pieces at a time in China.

Buying things in warehouses is also very American. Any store stacked with big boxes, and lots of them, filled with anything — office supplies, bath products, groceries, books, athletic equipment or pack-down furniture — is perceived as a temple of bounty and thrift. The idea is that no-one has been hired to set up fancy displays, and the money saved by not hiring effete window dressers is passed onto the consumer. The merchandise is still horrendously over-priced. But the

The Abbatts' missionary zeal was strengthened by their membership in The Order of Woodcraft Chivalry.

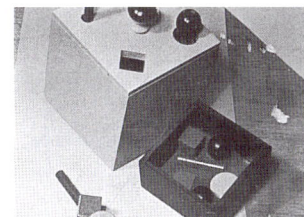

ABBATT TOYS OF THE 1930S SHOWING FORMAL ELEMENTS ('DESIGN TODAY', 1933)

they visited the Pestalozzi-Froebel Kindergarten Centre in Berlin, where they saw Froebel's principles in action. Here, children acquired manual dexterity with the aid of unadorned platonic shapes: painted doors or windows were thought by Froebel to stunt a healthy imagination, and the only decoration allowed was a single primary colour.

In Vienna, the Abbatts encountered the work of Dr Charlotte Bühler, the pioneering psychologist of child's play who had recently claimed in *The First Year of Life* (1930) that "children should be given the right toy at the right age to avoid mental harm in later life." Bühler divided toys into three groups: those for motor activity to stimulate muscular development, such as toys that can be squeezed or grasped; those for constructive and creative play, which mark a connection with the child's material surroundings, such as the posting box and fitting toys; and toys that inspire fantasy and imitative play, to develop the concept of self. Bühler had observed that children under age six generally used household objects and utensils in their play; the Abbatts accordingly bought toy wooden housekeeping tools and construction sets that would help children become useful (by learning to clean) and creative (by making things). Bühler's dictum, "the right toy for the right age," became the Abbatts' maxim, printed on their catalogues throughout the forty-year span of their commercial venture.[1]

In Prague, they were introduced to modernist toy design at Cooperative Work, a small collaborative enterprise producing books and magazines on modernist design, whose art director, Ladislav Sutnar, was also a leading industrial designer. Sutnar had previously exhibited his own wooden toys at international toy exhibitions in Munich and Paris: his first efforts, a series of wooden blocks called 'Factory Town' and 'Grocery Store' (both 1926), displayed a simple design aesthetic in line with contemporary modernism. A year later, in 1927, Sutnar designed a wooden train which he sold along with the blocks at Cooperative Work, and when the Abbatts visited, the shop was also selling products licensed from the Bauhaus.[2]

Touring Eastern European countries, the Abbatts collected peasant toys including wooden farm animals and figures. As a Communist and member of The Order, Paul Abbatt took a decidedly romantic view of the impetus for their creation: "The peasant toy reflects — in a carved block of wood — the weight, the simplicity, the defencelessness of the peasant class," he reflected in 1934. "The shepherd has his knife and dry wood handy on the hillside, his sheep and dog as models, and finds a grateful relief in turning from the spreading contryside to the small particular object in his hands... The peasant has long dark evenings without books to read and turns to toy-making as a hobby."[3] The Abbatts considered this process of toy-making preferable to the industrial model which capitalised on childhood through the mass-production of shoddy toys.

But the Abbatts' ideological stance soon came up against commercial imperatives: keen to attract nurseries and schools as well as local clients, they set up a workshop on the outskirts of London to cope with increased orders, and although the objects were hand-finished, some mechanical production was necessary. The resulting artefacts proved expensive to manufacture, and were sold almost exclusively to wealthy individuals, somewhat defeating their social goals.

Towards the last decade of their business career, the Abbatts began buying in toys wholesale from other companies to meet the increased demand for diversity in product range and competition from the neighbouring company, Galt — leading Paul Abbatt to exclaim, "Blast the educational toy!" The company's demise came shortly after his death in 1973, whereupon their products were relinquished to a large educational toy company, Educational Suppliers Association.

Struggling to reconcile their political beliefs with the demands of entrepreneurial capitalism, the Abbatts never became a true market force, and their name is largely unknown today. Abbatt Toys have yet to enter the auction house, but their sheer durability means that many are probably still in use, having been passed down to younger generations, rather than enbalmed within the museum vitrine.

This article is based on Hannah Ford's 1998 Master's thesis for the V&A/RCA History of Design program, *Modernism in Toy Design: the Story of Abbatt Toys, 1932-1960.*

---

1 Hilary Page, *Playtime in the First Five Years*, George Allen & Unwin, 1939, pp 6-7.

2 Thanks to Paul Makovsky, 1997-98 Peter Krueger/Christie's Fellow, Cooper Hewitt National Design Museum, NY for providing information on Sutnar.

3 Paul Abbatt, "The Evolution of Toys," *Design for Today*, Design and Industries Association, London, 1934, pp 442-444.

Lara j

LARA PHOTOGRAPH SANNE PEPER

Pierre Bismuth. If/Then January 1999. Page 181

Pierre Bismuth. If/Then January 1999. Page 182

corps

Could *Tomb Raider*'s heroine Lara Croft come to the rescue of contemporary dance? Choreographer Krisztina de Châtel is betting on it with her new work, *Lara* — based on the computer game pin-up's primitive gestures and specially presented at *Doors of Perception 5: Play*. **Paul Groot**, who conceived the ballet with De Châtel, takes us beyond the first level.

FROM THE INTERACTIVE INSTALLATION *IMPROVISATION TECHNOLOGIES* BY WILLIAM FORSYTHE/FRANKFURT BALLET WITH ZKM KARLSRUHE © ZKM KARLSRUHE

Lara Croft symbolises the definitive breakthrough of women into the comparatively closed male bastion of the computer world. She is also living proof of another breakthrough: *Tomb Raider*, Core Design's computer game in which she is leading lady, attempts almost consciously to establish a link between computer games and the conventional art world.

As soon as she made her debut, some two years ago, the public immediately fell for Lara Croft: her remarkable presence apparently touched a subconscious nerve. *Tomb Raider*'s initial success was, naturally, accountable to its female heroine, a woman like none other in literature (though Miss Marple is a possible precursor), computer games (invariably peopled by rugged machos and wimpish taxi drivers) or commercial films (though Lara seems partly based on Indiana Jones).

If the love-'em-or-hate-'em Spice Girls arouse the child in us, then Lara Croft awakens the adolescent — thanks in no small part to *Tomb Raider*'s remarkable interface. It may be just a computer game, but because Lara Croft has been designed as a celluloid heroine, she allows you to become both film director and cameraman. You follow her from various angles while she performs her assignments, finding the right perspective and vantage point — responsible not only for her safety but also for establishing the best camera positions.

But Lara offers more. While the first edition broke new ground in game technology, *Tomb Raider II* has definite artistic ambitions. In Part II Lara has real class: she knows what's what and reveals a remarkable familiarity with the habitats of the rich and famous, right from the first level. She negotiates the Great Wall of China and manoeuvres like a virtual Marco Polo through the classical architecture of the Far East and the Baroque ambience of Venice. We see her jump, fight, clamber, swim, dance and shoot her way around the centuries-old city. She climbs the bookcases in the splendid Bartoli palace library, and makes her way via the chandeliers. After a short appearance on stage at the Venetian Opera — not being much of a diva — she vanishes through a gap in the wall!

In some ways Lara is the pivotal figure in today's art scene. Not because of her extraordinary qualities. On the contrary, it is Lara's manifest weaknesses, along with her forceful personality, that make her so fascinating. She is the common factor uniting two different cultures: classical analogue and burgeoning digital, brought together not through tired tradition, but with tongue in cheek. Embryonic elements of continually developing technology are integrated naturally into the established values. So often, technology implies a pristine world to be realised in a vacuum; here, instead, it is built into the remains of the old world.

In her primitive but highly effective way of moving, jumping, running, hitting, fighting and shooting, Lara represents an entirely new art form linked, to some extent, to the unique aesthetic of the nerds and the *otaku* in Japanese culture. While the traditions of Western painting were never likely to inspire the Japanese, Lara provides a dependable element for those who — confused by post-modernist ideas about the durability of modernist dogma — still consider those traditions the standard by which to judge. Because the question Lara poses is the extent to which developments in a whole range of disciplines — including painting, archi-

THE DANCERS ARE SPLIT INTO SIX LARA CROFTS, A SUPERBODY FANNING OUT ACROSS THE STAGE. PHOTOGRAPH SANNE PEPER

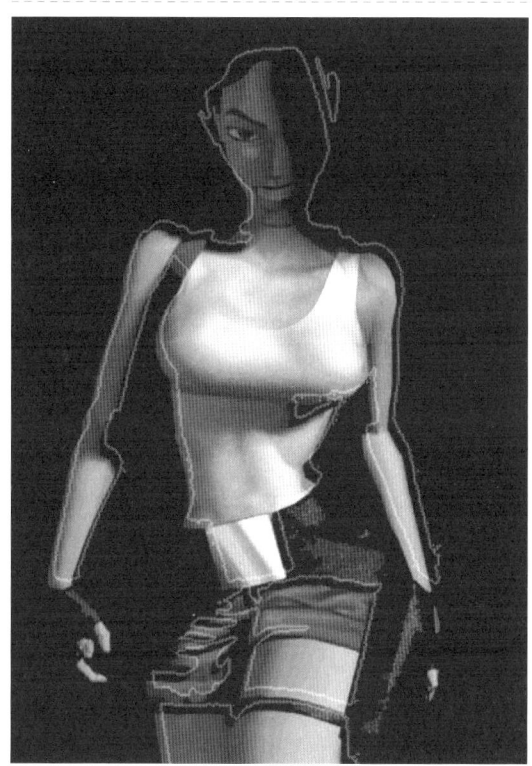

LARA CROFT ILLUSTRATION SANNE SCHUIJREN, PRESENT ARTS

If the love-'em-or-hate-'em Spice Girls arouse the child in us, then Lara Croft awakens the adolescent.

tecture and even dance — can be manipulated. Disciplines which, in this digital age, have had the rug pulled from under them.

Might some underlying logic emerge if you could get people to perform Lara's primitive, yet highly effective movements — as part of a dance presentation, for example? Would it lead to a school of movement that, in the finest tradition of the avant garde, might set new standards in contemporary dance? Given recent developments in the medium, these are no idle questions. Lara's body is a choreographer's dream: in theory, she is capable of performing any movement.

In fact, the ideal companion to *Tomb Raider* is William Forsythe's *Improvisation Technologies*, an interactive installation, soon to be released on CD-ROM. Here, in a series of brief performances, the choreographer of the Frankfurt Ballet sets out his basic principles, offering a masterclass for dancers while, at the same time — through anatomical exercises, reorganisation of space and time, as well as isometrics — laying out guidelines for the design of a ballet for a digital dance group.

Is it possible to get back to degree zero in modern dance? Can you start from scratch, building from an unexpected perspective? With these questions in mind, Krizstina De Châtel and I set out to design a ballet based on the sign language of Lara Croft. An enthusiastic, emotional choreographer with roots in the minimalist tradition, De Châtel has based *Lara* on the computer heroine's gestures. Of course, Lara is no match for her, yet De Châtel's open attitude has ensured at least some mutual exchange.

The dancers start by mirroring Lara's movements and positions, and proceed on the basis of their own physical effort, improvising and attempting to free themselves. Then De Châtel's masterful hand sculpts the dancers' bodies into six split Lara Crofts, to produce a super-body fanning out in all directions. Set against a gigantic video projection of *Tomb Raider* images, an interplay of gestures, movements and choreographed ambiences takes place between the 'real' Lara and her various partners, filled with references to earlier ballets, short dramatic movements, and fantasies of future developments that Lara's virtual body seems to herald. If the dancers (Janine Dijkmeyer, Heike Langsdorf, Massimo Molinari, Tim Present and Peter Kádár) are the representatives of classical dance history, then Lara introduces them to the technological *Umwelt*.

In their dialogue with Lara, the dancers are guided by young Jimmy Petri, a 15 year-old computer-game adept who plays *Tomb Raider* during the ballet, manipulating Lara in real-time on the giant video screen, lending rhythm and structure. Like Lewis Carroll's Alice from *Alice in Wonderland* or Erik from *Erik of het klein insektenboek,* Jimmy enters a wonderland which, until now, he knew only from the outside. His moods colour the show, his insight into the game regulates the ballet, his choices for a given level of the game determine the atmosphere of each performance. The dancers, doubting even their own existence, live in a precarious balance between the digital and the analogue — and indeed they represent a single body, Lara Croft's. Stagnant and wooden, yet simultaneously elegant, their bodies are no longer personal but the expressions of a unique idiom of movement: the limbs of one are the limbs of every other. They move with each other's bodies, feel each other's pain, before returning to their own bodies.

Lara can only function by doing that which justifies her existence: shooting. So De Châtel constantly repeats the one movement that constitutes more than just Lara's existential ambience. The countless variants of the firing position — ubiquitous cliché of film and television — are among the most identifiable images in our subconscious. Everyone recognises them, knows how to interpret and respond to them. Yet the syntax has never been examined. In *Lara* they are a basic ingredient. But with just one missing element: there is no actual gun. Underscoring the absent weapon, this is a ballet based on an empty gesture, its movements focused on the unarmed hand.

Early in his writing career, **Paul Auster** came up with an idea he hoped would catapult him out of literary penury: a deck of cards with which to play a realistic game of baseball. But he hit no home-run. Here, in this extract from his memoir *Hand To Mouth*, Auster recalls his brief flirtation with the U.S. toy industry.

ACTION BASE BALL

In early December, a friend came up from the city to visit for a few days. We had known each other since college, and he, too, had turned into a struggling writer—yet one more Columbia graduate without a pot to piss in. If anything, he was having an even rougher time of it than I was. Most of his work was unpublished, and he supported himself by bouncing from one pathetic temporary job to another, aimlessly traveling around the country in search of strange, down-and-out adventures. He had recently landed in New York again and was working in a toy store somewhere in Manhattan, part of the brigade of surplus help who stand behind the counters during the Christmas shopping season. I picked him up at the train station, and during the half-hour ride back to the house, we talked mostly about toys and games, the things he sold in the store. For reasons that still mystify me, this conversation dislodged a small pebble that had been stuck somewhere in my unconscious, an obstruction that had been sitting over a tiny pinprick hole of memory, and now that I was able to look down that hole again, I found something that had been lost for nearly twenty years. Back when I was ten or twelve, I had invented a game. Using an ordinary deck of fifty-two playing cards, I had sat down on my bed one afternoon and figured out a way to play baseball with them. Now, as I went on talking to my friend in the car, the game came rushing back to me. I remembered everything about it: the basic principles, the rules, the whole setup down to the last detail.

Under normal circumstances, I probably would have forgotten all about it again. But I was a desperate man, a man with my back against the wall, and I knew that if I didn't think of something fast, the firing squad was about to fill my body with bullets. A windfall was the only way out of my predicament. If I could rustle up a nice large chunk of cash, the nightmare would suddenly stop. I could bribe off the soldiers, walk out of the prison yard, and go home to become a writer again. If translating books and writing magazine articles could no longer do the job, then I owed it to myself and my family to try something else. Well, people bought games, didn't they? What if I worked up my old baseball game into something good, something really good, and managed to sell it? Maybe I'd get lucky and find my bag of gold, after all.

It almost sounds like a joke now, but I was in dead earnest. I knew that my chances were next to nil, but once the idea grabbed hold of me, I couldn't shake free of it. Nuttier things had happened, I told myself, and if I wasn't willing to put a little time and effort into having a go at it, then what kind of spineless shit was I?

The game from my childhood had been organized around a few simple operations. The pitcher turned over cards: each red card from ace to 10 was a strike; each black card from ace to 10 was a ball. If a face card was turned over, that meant the batter swung. The batter then turned over a card. Anything from ace to 9 was an out, with each out corresponding to the position numbers of the defensive players: Pitcher=ace (1); Catcher=2; First Baseman=3; Second Baseman=4; Third Baseman=5; Shortstop=6; Left Fielder=7; Center Fielder=8; Right Fielder=9. If the batter turned over a 5, for example, that meant the out was made by the Third Baseman. A black 5 indicated a ground ball; a red 5 indicated a ball hit in the air (diamond=pop-up; heart=line drive). On balls hit to the outfield (7, 8, 9), black indicated a shallow fly ball, red a deep fly ball. Turn over a 10, and you had yourself a single. A jack was a double, a queen was a triple, and a king was a home run.

It was crude but reasonably effective, and while the distribution of hits was mathematically off (there should have been more singles than doubles, more doubles than home runs, and more home runs than triples), the games were often close and exciting. More important, the final scores looked like the scores of real baseball games — 3 to 2, 7 to 4, 8 to 0 — and not football or basketball games. The fundamental principles were sound. All I had to do was get rid of the standard deck and design a new set of cards. That would allow me to make the game statistically accurate, add new elements of strategy and decision making (bunts, stolen bases, sacrifice flies), and lift the whole thing to a higher level of subtlety and sophistication. The work was largely a matter of getting the numbers right and fiddling with the math, but I was well versed in the intricacies of baseball, and it didn't take me long to arrive at the correct formulas. I played out game after game after game, and at the end of a couple of weeks there were no more adjustments to be made. Then came the tedious part. Once I had designed the cards (two decks of ninety-six cards each), I had to sit down with four fine-tipped pens (one red, one green, one black, one blue) and draw the cards by hand. I can't remember how many days it took me to complete this task, but by the time I came to the end, I felt as if I had never done anything else. The design was nothing to brag about, but since I had no experience or talent as a designer, that was to be expected. I was striving for a clear, serviceable presentation, something that could be read at a glance and not confuse anyone, and given that so much information had to be crammed onto every card, I think I accomplished at least that. Beauty and elegance could come later. If anyone showed enough interest to want to manufacture the game, the problem could be turned over to a professional designer. For the time being, after much dithering back and forth, I dubbed my little brainchild Action Baseball.

Once again, my stepfather came to the rescue. He happened to have a friend who worked for one of the largest, most successful American toy companies, and when I showed the game to this man, he was impressed by it, thought it had a real chance of appealing to someone. I was still working on the cards at that point, but he encouraged me to get the game in order as quickly as I could and take it to the New York Toy Fair, which was just five or six weeks down the road. I had never heard of it, but by all accounts it was the most important annual event in the business. Every February, companies from around the world gathered at the Toy Center at Twenty-third Street and Fifth Avenue to display their products for the upcoming season, take note of what the competition was up to, and make plans for the future. What the Frankfurt Book Fair is for books and the Cannes Film Festival is for films, the New York Toy Fair is for toys. My stepfather's friend took charge of everything for me. He arranged to have my name put on the list of "inventors," which qualified me for a badge and an open pass to the fair, and then, as if that weren't enough, set up an appointment for me to meet with the president of his company—at nine o'clock in the morning on the first day of the fair.

I was grateful for the help, but at the same time I felt like someone who had just been booked on a flight to an unknown planet. I had no idea what to expect, no map of the terrain, no guidebook to help me understand the habits and customs of the creatures I would be talking to. The only solution I could think of was to wear a jacket and tie. The tie was the only one I owned, and it hung in my closet for emergency use at weddings and funerals. Now business meetings could be added to the list. I must have cut a ridiculous figure as I strode into the Toy Center that morning to collect my badge. I was carrying a briefcase, but the only thing inside it was the game, which was stowed inside a cigar box. That was all I had: the game itself, along with several Xeroxed copies of the rules. I was about to go in and talk to the president of a multimillion-dollar business, and I didn't even have a business card.

Even at that early hour, the place was swarming with people. Everywhere you turned, there were endless rows of corporate stands, display booths decked out with dolls and puppets and fire engines and dinosaurs and extraterrestrials. Every kiddie amusement and gadget ever dreamed of was packed into that hall, and there wasn't one of them that didn't whistle or clang or toot or beep or roar. As I made my way through the din, it occurred to me that the briefcase under my arm was the only silent object in the building. Computer games were all the rage that year, the biggest thing to hit the toy world since the invention of the wind-up jack-in-the-box, and I was hoping to strike it rich with an old-fashioned deck of cards. Maybe I would, but until I walked into that noisy fun house, I hadn't realized how likely it was that I wouldn't.

My talk with the company president turned out to be one of the shortest meetings in the annals of American business. It didn't bother me that the man rejected my game (I was prepared for that, was fully expecting bad news), but he did it in such a chilling way, with so little regard for human decency, that it still causes me pain to think about it. He wasn't much older than I was, this corporate executive, and with his sleek, superbly tailored suit, his blue eyes and blond hair and hard, expressionless face, he looked and acted like the leader of a Nazi spy ring. He barely shook my hand, barely said hello, barely acknowledged that I was in the room. No small talk, no pleasantries, no questions. "Let's see what you have," he said curtly, and so I reached into my briefcase and pulled out the cigar box. Contempt flickered in his eyes. It was as if I had just handed him a dog turd and asked him to smell it. I opened the box and took out the cards. By then, I could see that all hope was gone, that he had already lost interest, but there was nothing to do but forge ahead and start playing the game. I shuffled the decks, said something about how to read the three levels of information on the cards, and then got down to it. One or two batters into the top half of the first inning, he stood up from his chair and extended his hand to me. Since he hadn't spoken a word, I had no idea why he wanted to shake my hand. I continued to turn over cards, describing the action as it unfolded: ball, strike, swing. "Thank you," the Nazi said, finally taking hold of my hand. I still couldn't figure out what was going on. "Are you saying you don't want to see any more?" I said. "I haven't even had a chance to show you how it works." "Thank you," he said again. "You can leave now." Without another word, he turned and left me with my cards, which were still spread out on the table. It took me a minute or two to put everything back in the cigar box, and it was precisely then, during those sixty or ninety seconds, that I hit bottom, that I reached what I still consider to be the low point of my life.

Somehow or other, I managed to regroup. I went out for breakfast, pulled myself together, and returned to the fair for the rest of the day. One by one, I visited every game company I could find, shook hands, smiled, knocked on doors, demonstrated the wonders of Action Baseball to anyone willing to spare me ten or fifteen minutes. The results were uniformly discouraging. Most of the big companies had stopped working with independent inventors (too many lawsuits), and the small ones either wanted pocket-sized computer games (beep-beep) or else refused to look at anything connected with sports (low sales). At least these people were polite. After the sadistic treatment I'd been given that morning, I found some consolation in that.

Some time in the late afternoon, exhausted from hours of fruitless effort, I stumbled onto a company that specialized in card games. They had produced only one game so far, but that one had been wildly successful, and now they were in the market for a second. It was a small, low-budget operation run by two guys from Joliet, Illinois, a back-porch business with none of the corporate trappings and slick promotional methods of the other companies at the fair. That was a promising sign, but best of all, both partners admitted to being avid baseball fans. They weren't doing much at that hour, just sitting around their little booth and chewing the fat, and when I told them about my game, they seemed more than happy to have a look at it. Not just a peek, but a thorough viewing—to sit down and play a full nine-inning contest to the end.

If I had rigged the cards, the results of the game I played with them could not have been more exciting, more true to life. It was nip and tuck the whole way, tension riding on every pitch, and after eight and a half innings of threats, rallies, and two-out strikeouts with the bases loaded, the score stood at two to one. The Joliet boys were the home team, and when they came up for their last turn at bat, they needed a run to tie and two to win. The first two batters did nothing, and quickly they were down to their last out, with no runners on base. The following batter singled, however, to keep them alive. Then, to everyone's astonishment, with the count at two balls and two strikes, the next batter hit a home run to win the game. I couldn't have asked for more than that. A two-out, two-run homer in the bottom of the ninth inning to steal a victory on the last pitch. It was a classic baseball thriller, and when the man from Joliet turned over that final card, his face lit up with an expression of pure, undisguisable joy.

They wanted to think about it, they said, to mull it over for a while before giving me an answer. They would need a deck to study on their own, of course, and I told them I would send a color Xerox copy to Joliet as soon as possible. That was how we left it: shaking hands and exchanging addresses, promising each other to be in touch. After all the dismal, demoralizing events of that day, there was suddenly cause for hope, and I walked out of the Toy Fair thinking that I might actually get somewhere with my crazy scheme.

Color Xeroxing was a new process then, and it cost me a small fortune to have the copies made. I can't remember the exact amount, but it was more than a hundred dollars, I think, perhaps even two hundred. I shipped the package off to them and prayed they would write back soon. Weeks passed, and as I struggled to concentrate on the other work I had to do, it gradually dawned on me that I was in for a disappointment. Enthusiasm meant speed, indecision meant delay, and the longer they delayed, the worse the odds would be. It took almost two months for them to answer, and by then I didn't even have to read the letter to know what was in it. What surprised me was its brevity, its utter lack of personal warmth. I had spent close to an hour with them, had felt I'd entertained them and aroused their interest, but their rejection consisted of just one dry, clumsily written paragraph. Half the words were misspelled, and nearly every sentence had a grammatical error in it. It was an embarrassing document, a letter written by dunces, and once my hurt began to wear off a little, I felt ashamed of myself for having misjudged them so thoroughly. Put your faith in fools, and you end up fooling only yourself.

Still, I wasn't quite ready to give up. I had gone too far to allow one setback to throw me off course, and so I put my head down and plunged ahead. Until I had exhausted all the possibilities, I felt duty bound to continue, to see the whole misbegotten business through to the end. My in-laws put me in touch with a man who worked for Ruder and Finn, a prominent New York public relations firm. He loved the game, seemed genuinely enthused when I showed it to him, and made an all-out effort to help. That was part of the problem. Everyone liked Action Baseball, enough people at any rate to keep me from abandoning it, and with a kind, friendly, well-connected man like this one pushing on my behalf, it wouldn't have made sense to give up. My new ally's name was George, and he happened to be in charge of the General Foods account, one of Ruder and Finn's most important clients. His plan, which struck me as ingenious, was to get General Foods to put Action Baseball on the Wheaties box as a special coupon offer. ("Hey, kids! Just mail in two Wheaties box tops and a check or money order for $3.98, and this incredible game can be yours!") George proposed it to them, and for a time it looked as if it might happen. Wheaties was considering ideas for a new promotional campaign, and he thought this one might just do the trick. It didn't. They went with the Olympic decathlon champion instead, and for the next umpteen years, every box of Wheaties was adorned with a picture of Bruce Jenner's smiling face. You can't really fault them. It was the Breakfast of Champions, after all, and they had a certain tradition to uphold. I never found out how close George came to getting his idea through, but I must confess (somewhat reluctantly) that I still find it hard to look at a box of Wheaties without feeling a little twinge.

George was almost as disappointed as I was, but now that he'd caught the bug, he wasn't about to quit trying. He knew someone in Indianapolis who was involved with the Babe Ruth League (in what capacity I forget) and thought something good might happen if he put me in contact with this man. The game was duly shipped to the Midwest again, and then followed another inordinately long silence. As the man hastened to explain to me when he finally wrote, he wasn't entirely responsible for the delay: "I am sorry to be so late in acknowledging receipt of your June 22 letter and your game, Action Baseball. They were late reaching me because of a tornado that wiped out our offices. I've been working at home since and did not get my mail until ten days or so ago." My bad luck was taking on an almost biblical dimension, and when the man wrote again several weeks later to tell me that he was passing on my game (sadly, with much regret, in the most courtly terms possible), I barely even flinched. "There is no question that your game is unique, innovative and interesting. There may well be a market for it since it is the only table-top baseball game without a lot of trappings, which makes it faster-moving, but the consensus here is that without big league players and their statistics, the established competition is insurmountable." I called George to give him the news and thank him for his help, but enough was enough, I said, and he shouldn't waste any more time on me.

Things stalled for a couple of months after that, but then another lead materialized, and I picked up my lance and sallied forth again. As long as there was a windmill somewhere in sight, I was prepared to do battle with it. I had not the least shred of hope anymore, but I couldn't quite let go of the stupid thing I had started. My stepfather's younger brother knew a man who had invented a game, and since that game had earned him a pile of money, it seemed reasonable for me to contact him and ask for advice. We met in the lobby of the Roosevelt Hotel, not far from Grand Central Station. He was a fast-talking wheeler-dealer of around forty, a wholly antipathetical man with every kind of bluff and angle up his sleeve, but I must admit that his patter had some verve to it.

"Mail order," he said, "that's the ticket. Approach a major-league star, get him to endorse the game for a share of the profits, and then take out ads in all the baseball magazines. If enough orders come in, use the money to produce the game. If not, send the money back and call it quits."

"How much would a thing like that cost?" I asked.

"Twenty, twenty-five thousand dollars. Minimum."

"I couldn't come up with that much," I said. "Not even if my life depended on it."

"Then you can't do it, can you?"

"No, I can't do it. I just want to sell the game to a company. That's all I've ever had in mind—to make some royalties from the copies they sold. I wouldn't be capable of going into business for myself."

"In other words," the man said, finally realizing what a numskull he was talking to, "you've taken a shit, and now you want someone to flush the toilet for you."

That wasn't quite how I would have expressed it myself, but I didn't argue with him. He clearly knew more than I did, and when he went on to recommend that I find a "game broker" to talk to the companies for me, I didn't doubt that he was pointing me in the right direction. Until then, I hadn't even known of the existence of such people. He gave me the name of someone who was supposed to be particularly good, and I called her the next day. That turned out to be my last move, the final chapter of the whole muddled saga. She talked a mile a minute to me, outlining terms, conditions, and percentages, what to do and what not to do, what to expect and what to avoid. It sounded like her standard spiel, a furious condensation of years of hard knocks and cutthroat manoeuvers, and for the first several minutes I couldn't get a word in edgewise. Then, finally, she paused to catch her breath, and that was when she asked me about my game.

"It's called Action Baseball," I said.

"Did you say baseball?" she said.

"Yes, baseball. You turn over cards. It's very realistic, and you can get through a full nine-inning game in about fifteen minutes."

"Sorry," she said. "No sports games."

"What do you mean?"

"They're losers. They don't sell, and nobody wants them. I wouldn't touch your game with a ten-foot pole."

That did it for me. With the woman's blunt pronouncement still ringing in my ears, I hung up the phone, put the cards away, and stopped thinking about them forever.

From the book *Hand to Mouth: A Chronicle of Early Failure*. Copyright © 1997 by Paul Auster.
Used by arrangement with Henry Holt and Company, Inc., and with Faber & Faber, UK.

Description

Action Baseball is a card game for 1 or 2 players, consisting of two decks of 96 cards, a playing field with pegs, and a scoreboard. It is suitable for both children and adults, and one game can be played in approximately twenty minutes.

Without elaborate charts or complicated rules, Action Baseball simulates baseball as it is played on the field and allows players to make all the important strategy decisions of a big-league manager. Pitch by pitch, the results are uncannily true to life, and every outcome reflects the statistical possibilities of real baseball. From the final score to the ratio between balls and strikes, from the number of hits and errors amassed by each team to the number of successful and unsuccessful stolen bases, sacrifice bunts, and double plays, Action Baseball unfolds with all the excitement of a flesh-and-blood game.

How to Play

The traditional rules of baseball are followed at all times. There are nine innings in each game, three outs in an inning, three strikes for a strikeout, four balls for a walk.

Each card has a triple function: for the pitcher, for the batter, and for strategy situations. The diamond in the center of the card indicates "ball" (green), "strike" (red), or "swing" (black). The second area of information on the card gives the result of a batted ball: groundout to the shortstop, single, fly out to deep left field, error, double, etc. The third area of information deals with strategic manoeuvers.

The players decide who will represent the home team and who will represent the visiting team. Home team takes the red deck; visiting team takes the green deck. The home team pitches first; the visiting team bats first.

The pitcher turns over his cards one by one, calling out balls and strikes as they appear. When a "swing" card turns up, the player at bat turns over his top card and reads off the result. The player at bat keeps track of balls, strikes, and outs on the scoreboard and puts his pegs in the appropriate bases as batters reach base. After three outs have been made, the pitcher becomes the batter and the batter becomes the pitcher.

The cards are shuffled at the beginning of each game and at the end of the fifth inning. If a player comes to the end of his deck before the fifth inning is over, both players reshuffle at that point and the action resumes without interruption. If the game goes into extra innings, the cards are shuffled again after the ninth inning.

Reading the Cards

The red and green diamond cards ("strikes" and "balls") are numbered 1 through 9. Each number represents a different player position: 1 = Pitcher; 2 = Catcher; 3 = First Base; 4 = Second Base; 5 = Third Base; 6 = Shortstop; 7 = Left Field; 8 = Center Field; 9 = Right Field. Green 1, 2, 3, 4, 5, 6 indicate ground balls. Red 1, 2, 3, 4, 5, 6 indicate either pop-ups or line drives. Green 7, 8, 9 indicate shallow fly balls. Red 7, 8, 9 indicate deep fly balls.

The black diamond cards ("swing") include singles, doubles, triples, home runs, and foul balls. Red singles advance runners two bases; green singles advance runners one base. Red doubles advance runners three bases; green doubles advance runners two bases. When the player at bat turns over a "foul ball" card, it is counted as a strike, except when there are two strikes, in which case the count remains the same—as in real baseball.

TAKING A PITCH: The player at bat can declare that he wants to take a pitch (not swing), in which case a "swing" card counts as a strike.

HIT AND RUN: With a runner on first base, the player at bat can declare "Hit and Run." If a "swing" card is turned over, a force out is avoided on a ground ball. The runner advances to second base, and the play is to first. On a single or double, the runner advances one more base than indicated on the card. If a "ball" or "strike" card is turned over by the pitcher, the player at bat must then turn over a card and consult the Stolen Base section at the bottom—SB (2)—to see if the runner is out or safe at second. A green dot indicates safe; a red dot indicates out.

WILD PITCH: With no runners on base, the Wild Pitch is counted as a ball. When it turns up with runners on base, they advance one base. There is no extra advance for runners if it turns up as the fourth ball.

THREE-AND-TWO PITCH WITH TWO OUTS AND RUNNER ON FIRST, RUNNERS ON FIRST AND SECOND, OR BASES LOADED: If a "single" or "double" card is turned over by the player at bat, the runner or runners advance one more base than is indicated on the card.

Reading the Strategy Symbols

E (ERROR): If the player at bat turns over an "Error" card, the pitcher then turns over a card and refers to the E section at the bottom. Green indicates a one-base error, red a two-base error. The number refers to the position of the player responsible for the error.

DP (DOUBLE PLAY): With no outs or one out and a runner on first base. If the player at bat turns over a ground ball card (green 1, 2, 3, 4, 5, 6), the pitcher then turns over a card and refers to the DP section at the bottom. A green dot indicates that the runner is forced out at second base and the batter is safe at first (no double play). A red dot indicates a successful double play: both the runner and the batter are out. Runners on second and/or third base advance one base on a double play attempt.

With runners on first and second, the pitcher can go for an automatic force out at third or declare "Double Play," in which case the runner on second advances to third.

LDDP (LINE DRIVE DOUBLE PLAY): With no outs or one out and one or more runners on base. If the batter turns over a "line drive" card (red 1, 2, 3, 4, 5, 6), the pitcher then turns over a card and refers to the LDDP section at the bottom. A green dot indicates that all runners are safe, and only one out is recorded on the play. A red dot indicates a double play. With more than one runner on base, it is always the least advanced runner who is out.

SacB (SACRIFICE BUNT): With no outs or one out and a runner on first base. Before the pitcher turns over any cards, the batter declares that he wishes to attempt a sacrifice bunt. He then turns over a card and refers to the SacB section at the bottom. A green dot indicates a successful sacrifice: the runner advances from first to second, and the batter is out at first. A red dot indicates an unsuccessful sacrifice: the runner is forced out at second, and the batter is safe at first. A red dot followed by "(DP)" indicates a force out at second and a possible double play: the pitcher then turns over a card and refers to the DP section for the result.

SB (STOLEN BASE): With runner on first base or second base. The batter declares that he wishes to attempt a steal, turns over a card, and refers to the SB section at the bottom. A green dot indicates that the runner is safe; a red dot indicates that the runner is out. The chances of stealing second base—"SB (2)"—are better than those of stealing third—"SB (3)." There are no double steals or steals of home.

SacF (SACRIFICE FLY): With no outs or one out and a runner on third base. If the batter turns over a fly ball card (7, 8, 9), he can attempt to score the runner. He declares "Sacrifice Fly," turns over a card, and refers to the green or red SacF section, depending on whether the fly ball is deep (red) or shallow (green). On a deep fly, the chances of scoring the runner are good; on a shallow fly, the chances are poor. A green dot indicates a successful sacrifice: the runner scores, and one out is recorded on the play. A red dot indicates an unsuccessful sacrifice: the runner is thrown out at home, and two outs are recorded on the play.

EB (TAKING EXTRA BASE ON HIT): After a "single," "double," or "triple," the batter declares that he wants to try to stretch the hit by an extra base. He turns over a card and consults the EB section at the bottom. A red dot indicates that the runner is out; a green dot indicates that the runner is safe. If there is a runner on base at the time of the hit, the red or green dot refers to that runner. The batter takes an extra base automatically, whether the runner is safe or out.

Inf In (3) (INFIELD IN WITH RUNNER ON THIRD BASE): With no outs or one out and a runner on third base. The pitcher can choose to play his infield in to prevent the runner on third from scoring on a ground ball. If the batter turns over a "ground ball" card (green 1, 2, 3, 4, 5, 6), he can declare that he wants to send the runner home—in which case the pitcher turns over a card and refers to the "Inf In (3)" section at the bottom. A red dot indicates that the runner is out at home; a green dot indicates that the runner is safe at home. On a play at home, whether out or safe, the batter is always safe at first. note: With the infield in, certain ground ball outs become singles—which are indicated at the edges of the central area of the card.

With no outs or one out and runners on first and third. If the batter chooses not to attempt to score the runner from third, the pitcher cannot attempt a double play. The batter is out at first base.

With no outs or one out and bases loaded. On a ground ball, the force out at home is automatic. The pitcher need not consult the "Inf In (3)" section.

2 to 3 (ADVANCING RUNNER FROM SECOND BASE TO THIRD BASE ON GROUND BALL): With no outs or one out and a runner on second. On a ground ball to the infield (green 1, 2, 3, 4, 5, 6), the player at bat can declare that he wants to try to advance the runner from second to third. The pitcher then turns over a card and refers to the "2 to 3" section at the bottom. A red dot indicates that the runner is out; a green dot indicates that the runner is safe. If safe, the batter is out at first. If out, the batter is safe at first.

Ground Balls with Runner on Third Base and Infield Back with No Outs or One Out

Runner on third: Runner scores; batter out at first.

Runners on second and third: Runner on third scores; runner on second advances to third; batter out at first.

Runners on first and third: Runner on third scores; normal double play attempt.

Bases loaded: Runner on third scores; runner on second advances to third; normal double play attempt.

(1978)

Demi Dubbel Goes to School

In some Dutch 'wired classrooms', schoolchildren are taking a trip in a time machine, courtesy of a new educational Internet quest. **Pauline Bax** catches up with their adventures.

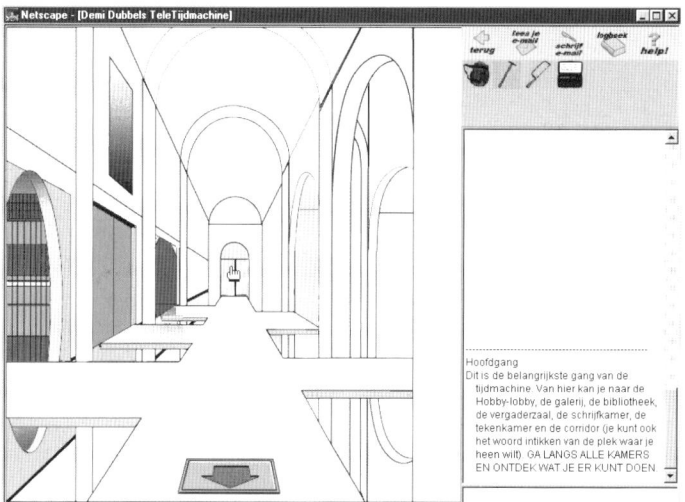

Demi Dubbel Goes to School

Pauline Bax

Art history classes aren't usually taught in Leonardo da Vinci's studio or at the Tower of Babel, but thanks to the Amsterdam-based Society for Old and New Media, at least some schoolchildren will spend a week exploring these antediluvian sites. They might even get to meet the Italian master painter himself, when the *Demi Dubbel* project gets going in early 1999 in eighty Dutch primary schools, with the support of Amsterdam's KunstWeb foundation.

Two separate school classes, ages ten and eleven, will be digitally connected for five strictly-choreographed days, communicating with each other in real time while searching for the elusive character Demi Dubbel. As they are about to embark on their digital quest, the kids will be told by live, in-class actors that the eponymous heroine has traveled to the Middle Ages in a time machine. It is up to them to track her down on their computers as she leaves hints and messages on the Society's secured Internet-pages. During several daily 45-minute shifts, the children have to complete missions, solve puzzles and trace the history of art via assorted hyperlinks, all the while communicating back and forth between schools.

Demi Dubbel is an adventure both for the participating schools — which get to experiment with a hands-on digital educational tool — and for the Society for Old and New Media. Rather than creating a CD-ROM, which would have been a much easier (and cheaper) feat to accomplish, the Society has come up with a friendly-looking, text-based children's MOO (Multi-user domain, Object Oriented) in an unusually elaborate game-like environment, with the aim of reaching a larger audience than just those children who already have access to a computer at home. "We wanted to emphasize the fun aspects of the Internet," says project manager Lara Ankersmit. With *Demi Dubbel*, children learn how to use a computer to find the information they need. For example, they have to complete a mission by making a collage of Bruegel's paintings, which they can find on the home pages of four different Dutch museums.

While art lends itself well to online research, the project could just as easily have taken other subject matter for its theme and storyline, Ankersmit concedes. Geography would have worked just as well. But it so happened that the Dutch Ministry of Education and Science and three different foundations were prepared to provide funding for an art project. Hopefully, the total investment of half a million Dutch guilders ($250.000) will pay off. The first pilot study, using just two Amsterdam schools, proved a success; a second was also held in 1998. "*Demi Dubbel* really came alive for the children," says Ankersmit. "They couldn't wait to get behind the computer and get on with their search." At the end of the week, both schools go off-line, finish their assignments and meet in person. And they might be surprised to find out that, yes, Demi Dubbel really does exist.

DUTCH SCHOOLCHILDREN AT WORK HUNTING FOR *DEMI DUBBEL* DURING THE PROJECT'S PILOT PHASE. PHOTOGRAPHS MELVIN WITTEVEEN

http://www.waag.org/demidubbel
<demidubbel@waag.org>

NEW MEDIA

WHY THE COMPUTER REVOLUTION

FROM

Is the computer more like a musical instrument or the printing press? Computer pioneer, Disney Fellow and amateur pipe-organist, **Alan Kay** compares these three technologies. He argues for a more serious understanding of the computer's capacity to change the way we think and act. Otherwise, he warns, a *Chopsticks* culture will develop — not a more literate society.

CLAVICHORD TO COMPUTER KEYBOARD.

HASN'T HAPPENED YET.

I once had a heckler in a talk about technology, who was an anti-technology-person. I invited him to come up and talk about it. So he came on stage and I said: "Let me relieve you of all the technology that's encumbering you right now." He nodded pretty reasonably when I took his watch from him. But when I started removing his clothes he started protesting. I said "Quiet: language is a technology, it's also one of the things that we make." He didn't have much to do from then on. For people like this, technology is all the stuff that wasn't around when they were born.

There is really nothing you can consider human that isn't based in our formulation of ourselves through constructs like language and culture. Much of what we are comes from fashioning ourselves through our various symbol and representation systems. So technology is just *us*. That doesn't mean it's not dangerous, because we're dangerous. And when you take something dangerous and amplify it, you can get something *really* dangerous. I'm going to take three technologies, one of which — for most people in this room — was just getting started when they were born, or didn't exist.

THE FIRST TECHNOLOGY IS A NEUTRAL ONE: MUSICAL INSTRUMENTS.

1

Being a guitar player, I can tell you: doing simple accompaniments on a guitar in the style of the 17th century really is no mean trick. But to render those same accompaniments on a keyboard is almost trivial. The keyboard was an attempt to automate something tough and expensive. Eventually it paid its way by giving us a new way of thinking about music.

I used to be a professional musician, playing the jazz-guitar for 10 years — stage bands and other kinds of things. I am also an amateur pipe-organist. I have a big, baroque pipe organ at home that we built over six years. It's a big thing, has 1450 pipes, more than 40,000 parts. Building one of these things makes you very aware that it is a machine. Once you get it done, the touch on it is about half the touch on a typical piano — featherlight — even though there are all of these trackers going all over the place. It's the most complicated mechanical thing that people made 250, 300 years ago.

The piano is a more mundane representative of this kind of instrument. A concert-pianist friend of mine was an anti-technologist until I pointed out that his piano was a piece of technology. He had been playing since he was six, gave his debut at twelve with the Philadelphia Orchestra, and his piano was so much a part of him he had not thought of it as a machine. To him it was just an extension. That's what technology is when it's working: an extension of the best we can do. When a musical instrument is working well, it takes the best we have and allows us to do special things with it. There's no music in the piano; the music comes out of *us*. You don't get music just by putting a piano in a home or a classroom.

A clavichord is the most expressive keyboard instrument invented, but so much less expressive than any other instrument. You just can't do that much with the tone. You can play a piano with a rake, because the key is detached from the hammer once it goes down. You can influence the hammer's velocity when it starts off and have the dampers a certain way, but that's it. But if you've ever heard two different pianists play the same piano one right after the other, it often sounds as if they're playing two completely different pianos.

The piano also absolves the player from having to pay much attention to pitch, which makes it not a terribly good first instrument for kids. Drop a rock on a key and it will play that pitch. It's not going to play it sharp or flat; you can't nuance the pitch. This can lead to a mechanical approach, where you don't even have to listen to yourself to play. We've all heard stories about people who practice for hours while reading a book, playing scales up and down.

Why pay any attention to keyboard instruments? The answer is: a human being alone can't do polyphony — only one voice at a time, unless they're a Tibetan monk. Basically we're single-voice instruments. The piano keyboard allows us polyphony and — even more important for western music— harmony, which existed before keyboard instruments, but really came to the fore in the 17th century.

Anyone who has learned the theory of harmony and taken some mathematics will have noticed similarities. Much of elementary geometry is recognizing 'if this thing is this over here, then it has to be the same thing over there.' There are hardly any musical instruments in which the pitches are laid out such that you can see the visual geometry of how sounds relate to each other. When keyboard instruments were invented around the year 1600, they made people really start noticing these patterns: 'This works here and then it works here. This has this interval relationship and this interval relationship…'

Baroque music came about because of the invention of the opera, which required something like a chordal accompaniment, which was done with a lute because it couldn't be done in the church modes that were current back then. Being a guitar player, I can tell you: doing simple accompaniments on a guitar in the style of the 17th century really is no mean trick. You have to be an excellent player. But to render those same accompaniments on a keyboard is almost trivial. So the keyboard became very, very popular. Harpsichords were even built with gutstrings — hard to keep in tune — to imitate the lute. Some of the most gorgeous music ever written for the harpsichord, in 17th century France, was an imitation of the lute style, using the same kinds of ballads. So the keyboard was partly an attempt to automate something tough and expensive. But eventually it paid its way by giving us a new way of thinking about music.

That's why the keyboard is a very important pivotal technology.

> When somebody asks me: "What is the best book to read about computer systems design?" I say: "Read the U.S. Constitution, because you'll see the size of an invention that affects people for hundreds and hundreds of years."

THE SECOND TECHNOLOGY IS PRINTING.

2

Socrates said that writing forces you to follow an argument rather than participate in it. He hated the idea that somebody could write something down, and then go off and die, and you would never be able to argue them back out of it. What we think is so important about writing, he thought was horrible.

The spread of knowledge for which people now look to the Internet was brought about by the printing press. If you are trying to write an argument that will be copied by scribes, you had better couch it in a form that will survive the retelling, like various kinds of allegory and metric schemes. You try to capture the essence of the story. It can't be much of an argument, because the points might get lost, but needs to be capable of constantly repairing itself so as to retain the original. Only long after the invention of the printing press did people realise it meant something very different from manuscript writing and copying. Because the author had corrected the galley proofs, the press could kick out 2,000 copies absolutely in accord with those galleys. This allowed much more complicated arguments to be transmitted accurately.

Page numbers first started appearing in books in western culture in 1516, about 65 years after the invention of the printing press. They had appeared centuries

> Go into a classroom and you discover kids happily doing things on a computer. The teacher is happy, the parents are happy, the principal is happy — everybody is happy. But if you look more closely at what the kids are doing, they are doing nothing of any consequence whatsoever.

before in Jewish writings, because Jews — a marginalised society outside the intellectual world of western culture — were already trying to argue and annotate and cross-reference. When you are building a tightly-reasoned argument, you need something like the press to transmit its nuances exactly as you intended. That was a huge change. And it took hundreds of years.

It took the Catholic Church 100 years to figure out that books might be dangerous. The first on its index of banned books was Copernicus' book about the heliocentric system, about a 100 years after the printing press; 150 years after its invention, the second best-selling book in England was still an astrology book. (Some things don't change!) The best-selling book was of course the Bible. In 1600 science had not yet been invented, but was starting to creak into existence. Then all of a sudden, in the 17th century, this new rhetoric of close argument — and trying to imitate reasoned arguments — started to become very important.

The United States is based entirely on those arguments. I brought one of them along. Tom Paine's *Common Sense* was written in about five or six weeks, and published, anonymously and at his own expense, in January 1776 when we were already at war with the British. A stitched pamphlet without a cover, it's about why monarchies might not be the best way of doing things. It's an attempt to argue not from polemic or rhetoric, but from first causes whenever possible. One of his famous lines was: "A thing long done, becomes so habitual that it seems natural." In the six months after publication, between 500,000 and 600,000 were printed for a grand total of 1.5 million colonists.

A careful study, undertaken about six years ago by a Philadelphia foundation, to estimate the real level of literacy in America, said: 'if you take literacy as the ability to deal with the most important discourse of your civilisation, then no more than 20 percent of Americans can really read and understand and comment on this text.' So we're perhaps less literate now, than we were back then. We really don't know how literate they were.

Then there was something even smaller and tidier: the Constitution of the United States. It's a tiny little book, if you make it into a book, and very interesting to computer scientists because it has admirable parsimony. This is the prescription for a kind of social machine: a machine full of millions of non-cooperative parts, namely us, that has run for hundreds of years without breaking. One of the seven modern wonders of the world, it was prompted by realising: 'We can design a better system than humans do by common sense. Let's try to design the way we live!'

What was in here and what isn't in here? There is a joke that says: 'In America everything that is not against the law is permitted. In Germany everything that is not in the law is forbidden. In Italy everything that is in the law is permitted. And in Russia everything that is okay to do, is forbidden'. Four different ways of looking at the world.

So the guys who framed the U.S. Constitution realized: 'We can't write down how people live, not even today and we can't write it down fifty years from now.' They debated doing one of these every generation, but decided not to — thank goodness, because I think they were better than most of their successors. They decided just to let everything happen as it does and write down how to resolve the conflicts. 'We'll have a wide open system here and we will try and keep it from going out of control, but we won't specify how to control it.' Incredibly wise.

When somebody asks me: 'What is the best book to read about computer systems design?' I say: "Well read *The Federalist Papers*, then read the U.S. Constitution, because you'll see the size of an invention that can organise a complex system of people for hundreds and hundreds of years."

Everybody is comfortable with the idea that music is an elective, though we would hate to force every child in America to learn to play the piano. There was a period when that was almost the case. It would be great if music was pervasive in the culture, but making every child fluent in music seems like going too far. But most European cultures *did* decide that it is absolutely, vitally important for every child in the culture to be fluent with the music of the printing press. That's a big difference, and it brought about state-mandated schooling.

THE THIRD TECHNOLOGY IS THE COMPUTER.

3

The most important thing to understand about the computer is that if it were a book, then it is a book that can dynamically read and write itself.

The hardest thing talking about computers is that things aren't always what they seem. You can do things with a computer for a long time without actually touching their essence, because they are such chameleons: they spend most of their time imitating other media, like paper, television, cartoons, movies. Most people who have used the computer have never touched what it is actually about. What's inside it is not esoteric in the way quantum mechanics is esoteric. Almost everyone can learn to drive a car, to some extent, in about half an hour. But I have never found a way of explaining in a satisfactory manner what the music of a computer is in about half an hour. So I have to make an analogy.

The most important thing to understand about the computer is that if it were a book, then it is a book that can dynamically read and write itself. Its static content is the same as paper. The computer contains just abstract markings, from which you can fashion anything — the symbols for any language, any mathematics, any pictures. But that's too atomic a way of looking at it. Another way of looking at it is that much of its dynamic content is descriptions of media. It is a language machine that deals with things that are like sentences, and can not only move those sentences around and hold those sentences and send them, but also read and write them. In a fairly open-ended way.

It's a whole new way to deal with relationships between ideas. For which the short word is: 'mathematics'. Math is one of those terms to which we've been sensitised. And, unfortunately, because of our school system, most children and now most adults have never had any contact with math whatsoever. Math is actually the science of studying patterns of things: organisations and disorganisations and correlations and relationships between any number of things. Math is a subset of language and we know from the way we use language and the way stories are told that stories don't have to be consistent. We give the special name 'math' to consistent *use* of language.

Math is a larger scheme of trying to deal with relationships or ideas, just like in ordinary language. You don't require algebra examples to do math; you just require an interest in consistency. Of course math is desperately, desperately dangerous. Because it's not about anything more than language is. Language is only about itself. There is nothing about language that forces anybody to tell the truth. You can make up anything you want and put it in there, you can draw any map you want and put it in there. From any English sentence, you can make another sentence with the word 'not'.

The problem with math, in the larger world, is that there is a lure in the consistency of an argument. It still may be complete bullshit, or even worse than bullshit: it may be terribly dangerous to a civilisation. Nothing was more rationalised than Germany's Final Solution in World War Two. They liked the logic of it. Math is context free. On the other hand, science is all about trying to figure out in which context we can use what languages. This is why science is incredibly more important than mathematics.

Another problem with the computer is that it tends to automate too much if we let it. Like a car. Or like a player piano, which you can use instead of learning how to play. Use it to replace playing, and you're subtracting yourself out of the musical process. One of the ethics of the computer community, and for technology in general, is: don't automate the center of your interest, automate the fringes. Then you can usually get the best of both worlds.

LET ME TAKE THESE THREE TECHNOLOGIES AND TRY AND LUMP THEM TOGETHER.

1 + 2 + 3

Let me take these three technologies and try and lump them together.

I've had the following experience all too often over the last number of years. Go into a classroom and you discover kids happily doing things on a computer. The teacher is happy, the parents are happy, the principal is happy — everybody is happy. But if you look more closely at what the kids are doing, they are doing nothing of any consequence whatsoever. It's like putting a piano in a classroom, but not putting any musicians in there. What grows up is a kind of *Chopsticks* culture. The kids are unafraid of these pieces of technology, but the fact that they are happy and doing things is almost always meaningless. Because it actually takes centuries of work to develop the larger ideas about these forms, until it gets to be more than just playing around.

I've been in classrooms where the same thing happens with books, because elementary school teachers are often much less literate than we think. Teachers are for the most part totally illiterate in math and science, I mean *totally*. The fact that they know how to add two numbers together is meaningless — not even math unless you think about it in a particular way. And most Americans don't care. I have a degree in mathematics and what pains me the most going into classrooms is the mathematics textbooks — designed to be bought by totally unsophisticated people, with riots of colours and stuff. Math is cool, not hot. They emphasise coverage and zillions of things, when what you really want is to take one or two things over the year and get to the bottom of them.

One of today's fondly held myths is that 'kids will show us the way'. Adults respond to kids' fearlessness. Kids are able to plunge in and, in a rich enough environment, actually get fluent at some level. But if adults had any sophistication, they would realise that no kid ever invented calculus, or a C-7th chord, or how to really finger a keyboard to get the maximum out of it.

When I was working on personal computers 30 years ago, the one I did looked kind of like an Apple II to come: it had a box set on a desk, a display screen, and a tablet for pointing. When I looked at it, I thought: "Gee, this thing looks just like a time-sharing display terminal, except the time-sharing computer isn't there."

I immediately thought of the Gutenberg Bible, which is made to look as much like a manuscript book as possible. Two hundred and fifty-three different characters in the font to imitate every ligature and abbreviation done by the Medieval scribes. Rubricators were

> When I was working on personal computers thirty years ago, I realised that as long as a computer sat on a desk and looked like a time-sharing terminal, it wasn't participating in the actual revolution. It was participating in the automation of the old. That's exactly where we are right now.

brought in to illuminate Gutenberg Bibles, which at the equivalent of $60,000 today — three years of a clerk's wages — were a lot less expensive than manuscript ones (a couple of million dollars by today's standards). Gutenberg Bibles are big because that was the size of manuscript books. It wasn't until 50 years later, around 1495, that Aldus Manutius in Venice made books the size they are today. Why? Because he measured the saddlebags! The first set of books from Aldus's press was called 'The Portable Library'. Books had now come down to a few hundred dollars by today's standards, which meant they could be lost without it being a disaster. If they could be lost, then they could be moved without peril.

Back in 1968, I realised that as long as a computer sat on a desk and looked like a time-sharing terminal, it wasn't participating in the actual revolution. It was participating in the automation of the old. That's exactly where we are right now. Only when the computer becomes something like an article of clothing, or a pocketbook, will things have developed sufficiently to become a way of life. And that can only happen when there is enough actual content.

We got content in printing by being able to print unbelievably large amounts of bad stuff. The 19th Century is called 'The Age Of Invention' because the total number patents went up by a factor of 80 to 100. Most were absolute crap. Crackpot inventions. But the important thing was that everybody was trying to invent. It was in the air. Some inventions turned out to be very important. The total number of good inventors went up. That's what happens if you go from being a scribe society to a larger society: make the society literate and the quality of writing will go up, even though the total number of good writers still remains rather small.

This is one of the reasons for saying: 'No, The Computer Revolution Hasn't Happened Yet'. It's not going to happen until the kids start learning its music, and particularly the reading and writing of its music, the stuff which is most important to deal with. And that is not going to happen until the technology becomes available in almost throwaway form. So when you're lying on your back in a pool and a 10-year-old comes and overturns you and the computer sinks to the bottom, it's not a tragedy. You just go out and get another one for $19.95. If that happened to your laptop today, you would not appreciate it. It's still a special thing used for special purposes, rather than something you grow up with.

The most important thing to think about the computer revolution is whether it's more like a musical instrument or more like the printing press. If it's like a musical instrument, then we don't have to worry about it too much, because people who are tuned to the music will find it and good things will happen as a result. If it's more like the printing press, then we absolutely have to understand what it is about the music and what it takes to learn that music. Because the continuation of our civilisation could be vitally involved with this new thing.

I think the computer is much more like the printing press than like a musical instrument, and should be taken much more seriously.

From Alan Kay's lecture "The Computer Revolution Hasn't Happened Yet," in the Fall 1997 Franz Rosenzweig Lehrhaus series *Technology: Blessing or Curse?* at the Jewish Theological Seminary, New York.

lift-off!
MIR ASTRONAUT.TIF

te/e/ ved

highlights from outer space

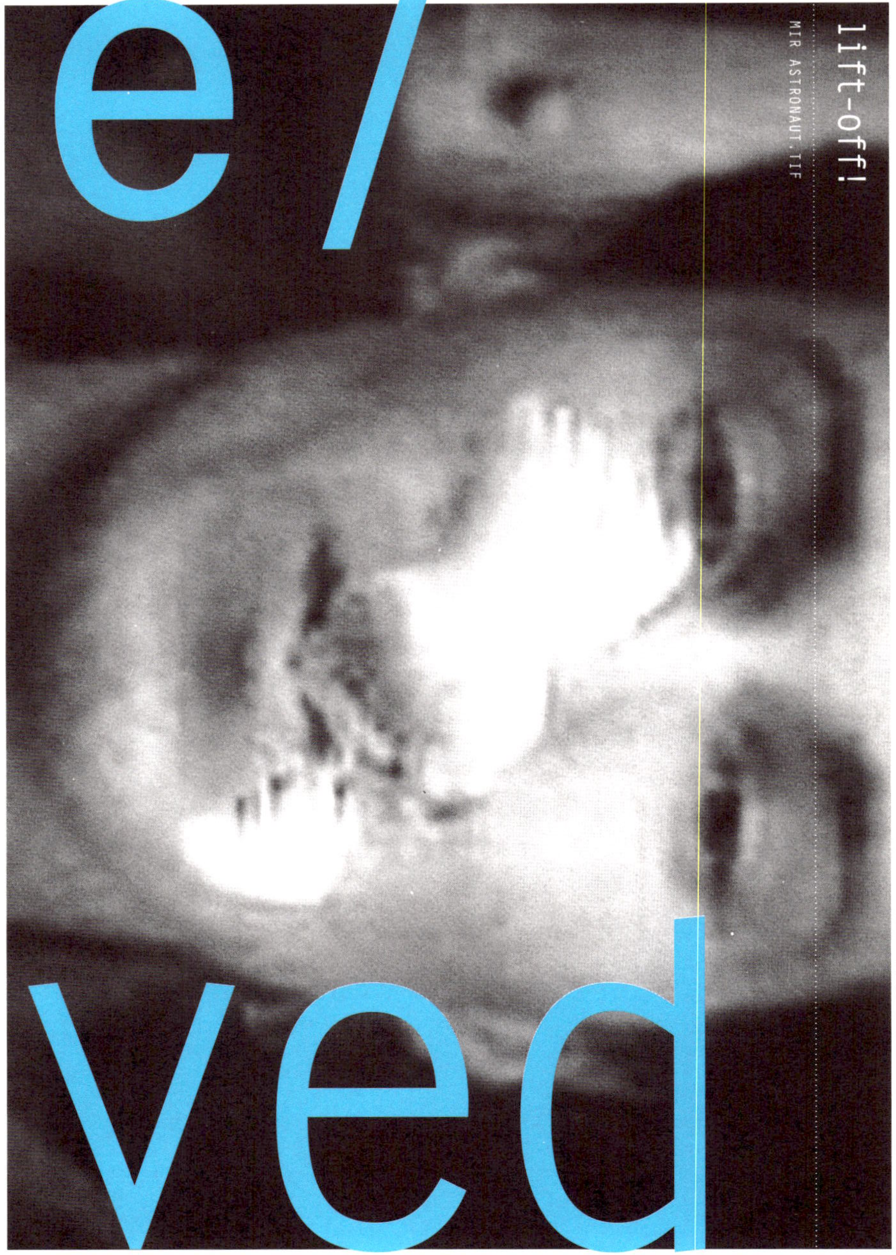

re/mo/ invol

lift-off!
DOOM PLAYER.TIF
fire!

In a joint voyage to the outer limits of the entertainment universe, Alex Wilkie and Noortje Marres present the parallel orbits of the space race and the computer games industry – in a gravity-free countdown of coin-ops and blast-offs, joysticks and jet propulsion, 3D graphics and sky-rocketing sales. At mission control, Maureen Mooren and Daniël van der Velden steer the craft of timeline design.

fly-over

ROCKET.TIF

//downloading images... //waiting for text...

Allow yet another factoid to fly by: later this year, the Japanese Space Agency, NASDA, will launch **Lunar-A**, a lunar orbiter that will shoot three penetrators three metres deep into the moon. Back on Earth, the collected seismographic and thermo-dynamic data will be analysed with an eye to possible future mining on the moon.

Now, computer gamers might think: "Sounds just like **Battlezone 1998**. Space vehicles searching for valuable material? Been there already!"

Such associations seem strangely appropriate, but also somewhat unjustified. **Battlezone** (Activision, US, 1998) is a first-person game in which the player fights and hunts for alien biometals. It features highly detailed and amazingly realistic 3D worlds. A screenshot from **Battlezone** looks uncannily like a photograph of **Lunar-A** – the computer game and the scientific operation display a similar hi-tech aesthetic. But so what? It is unclear what is to be made of these overlaps. How come both game and mission evoke military action, but neither serves military ends? With no Cold War to fall back on, contexts of interpretation are fading.

Or so it seems. The huge stock of space-narratives from the past can still be of use, even now that the performance of high technology in itself appears to be the principal public event in outer space. These narratives simply have to be applied in a different way. For example, the recent history of outer space can be considered as events in which space served as the ideal setting for presenting radical technologies to the public, a setting in which the Cold War was just decorum. Computer space-games and hyped instances of space exploration then served to introduce the advances of technology into people's living-rooms via the television/computer screen. The following time-line proposes such a version of space history.

Sewn together out of images and text-samples taken from the World Wide Web (sites of space-agencies, game companies and interested individuals), this timeline provides an incomplete chronology of the highlights of space-technology available in the mainstream, and a record of the patina they have left in the public realm (the media/the market). History is organised along two planes: portholes display the space-games and space-projects that have been presented to the public, tracing the evolution of imaging techniques and the mutations of space-narratives; enginerooms provide a record of the creative, economic and political shifts that support the portholes.

To a certain extent, the assembled information leaves interpretation open. But by its selection, it forces an attitude on the reader, advancing the proposition that – from a European point of view – both computer-games and space exploration largely come from the outside. And that, in the United States, the mix of narratives and technologies of space agencies and entertainment industries is homemade. In the words of author and scholar Constance Penley, the U.S. takes for granted that "NASA supplies the practice and Star Trek the theory" (NASA/TREK, POPULAR SCIENCE AND SEX IN AMERICA, Verso, 1997). The user-oriented realm of computer games and the politics-driven development of expert-systems have been providing each other with a context from the start, in the first computer game, **Spacewar!** (MIT, 1962), two spacecrafts fire torpedoes at each other while avoiding the gravitational pull of the sun. The Space Race was at its peak around the time of its creation. But no imaging techniques were yet available to capture realistically the presence of man-made objects in outer space.

The timeline also hints at the practical motivations behind so many games' setting in outer space. How to turn a flat black screen into an evocative landscape? A couple of white pixels would do the

job. The 2D black-and-white interface of **Lunar Lander** (Atari, 1979) is about the most famous example from the history of spaceflight, and also a perfect example of basic machine-control. The same pragmatics can be seen in the way space exploration is flavoured with play. How to attract public attention when you land on the moon for the third time? Answer: by having the astronauts of **Apollo 14** play micro-gravity golf on national TV. With recent advances in computer graphics, the exchange of stories, and also of software, has become more direct. Now, the family ties between games and space-exploration can be seen at the level of the interface itself (for example, the internet-presence of NASA's **Mars Pathfinder** and its passenger **Sojourner**, 1997).

The games-market has always been global and, over the last few years, space agencies have also been moving towards international integration. The timeline suggests that Europe has become increasingly involved in both these areas. The **International Space Station** (2004) – whose first components were scheduled to be launched in November 1998 – is the product of a collaboration between the space agencies NASA, RKA (Russia), ESA (Europe) and NASDA (Japan). ESA has generally avoided big media campaigns, but signs are that this policy is changing: in October 1998, the space agency hired advertising agency Saatchi & Saatchi to boost its public profile.

A thousand toy-theories like the above-mentioned can find support in the highlights: stories about the kind of space-realism increasingly displayed in the interfaces of games and projects; about their move from protected institutions out into the market; about the different ways in which they familiarized the public with high speeds and long distances, machine-control and navigation. Get ready for blast off!

Ten, nine, eight...

//start here: portholes

1957 1958 1959

//1957 — SPUTNIK 1, RKA, Earth orbiter
ON OCTOBER 4, IT IS ANNOUNCED THAT THE RUSSIAN SPACE AGENCY RKA HAS SUCCESSFULLY PUT AN ARTIFICAL MOON IN EARTH ORBIT. SPUTNIK 1 IS THE FIRST INFORMATION-TRANSMITTING DEVICE IN OUTER SPACE. ITS RADIO-TRANSMITTERS OPERATE FOR THREE WEEKS, UNTIL THE ON-BOARD CHEMICAL BATTERIES FAIL. THEY ARE MONITORED WITH INTENSE INTEREST AROUND THE WORLD. THE RUSSIAN WORD 'SPUTNIK' MEANS 'COMPANION' ('SATELLITE' IN THE ASTRONOMICAL SENSE).

//1958 — EXPLORER 1, NASA, Earth orbiter
ON JANUARY 31 THE UNITED STATES STRIKES BACK WITH THE FIRST DEVICE IN OUTER SPACE TO MAKE A SCIENTIFIC DISCOVERY. THE 14 KILO EXPLORER I SPACECRAFT CARRIES AN ONBOARD GEIGER-COUNTER TO MEASURE WHAT WILL LATER BECOME KNOWN AS THE VAN ALLEN BELTS.

//1959 — LUNA 1, RKA, Lunar flyby
ON JANUARY 2, RUSSIA LAUNCHES THE FIRST SPACE VEHICLE TO REACH ESCAPE VELOCITY. ON JANUARY 4TH, LUNA 1 PASSES BY THE MOON AT ABOUT 6000 KM/H AND BECOMES THE FIRST ARTIFICIAL PLANET OF THE SUN.

//1959 — LUNA 2, RKA, Lunar Impact
ON SEPTEMBER 14, THE RUSSIAN LUNA 2 BECOMES THE FIRST MAN-MADE OBJECT TO REACH A CELESTIAL BODY. IT HITS THE MOON NEAR THE CRATER ARCHIMEDES.

1960 1961 1962

//1961 — VOSTOK 1, RKA, manned Earth orbiter
ON APRIL 12, THE RUSSIAN SPACE AGENCY, RKA, LAUNCHES THE FIRST MANNED SPACECRAFT. WHEN IT IS OBVIOUS THAT YURI GAGARIN HAS MADE IT INTO LOWER EARTH ORBIT, THE KREMLIN ORDERS THE RUSSIAN NEWS AGENCY TO BROADCAST A PREPARED MESSAGE. THE OFFICIAL ANNOUNCEMENT READS: "THE FIRST COSMONAUT IN THE WORLD IS IN SPACE." GAGARIN SPENDS 108 MINUTES IN EARTH ORBIT.

//1962 — TELSTAR 1, NASA/AT&T, Earth orbiter
ON JULY 10, NASA LAUNCHES THE FIRST COMMERCIAL COMMUNICATIONS SATELLITE. TELSTAR 1 TRANSMITS TWO-WAY FACSIMILE-, VOICE- AND TV-SIGNALS BETWEEN THE U.S., BRITAIN AND FRANCE. AFTER FOUR MONTHS OF SUCCESSFUL OPERATION, SOME TRANSISTORS IN THE COMMAND SYSTEM FAIL. THIS IS DUE TO RADIATION FROM A U.S. HIGH-ALTITUDE NUCLEAR TEST (STARFISH) AND THE EARTH'S INNER AND OUTER RADIATION BELTS. THE SPACECRAFT IS REVIVED FOR A FURTHER TWO MONTHS. TELSTAR 1 IS BUILT BY BELL TELEPHONE LABORATORIES AND ENTIRELY FUNDED BY AT&T.

//1962 — SPACEWAR!, MIT, computer game
After an estimated total of 200 man-hours, Steve Russell, a student at the Massachusetts Institute of Technology, completes SPACEWAR!

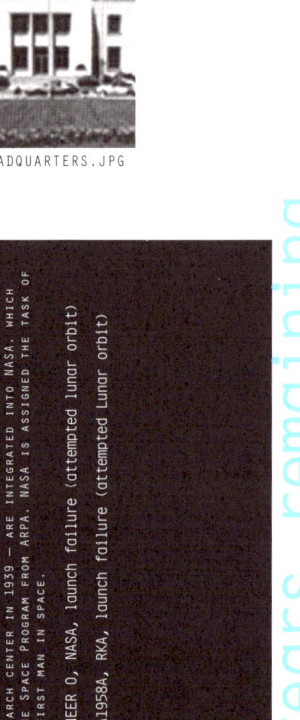
SPUTNIK.GIF

GAGARIN.GIF

TELSTAR.GIF

SPAC

//start here: enginerooms

PDP-1.JPG

KENNEDY.1.MOVIE
KENNEDY.2.MOVIE

NACA_HEADQUARTERS.JPG

//2 years remaining...

//1958 — Foundation of ARPA
SOON AFTER THE LAUNCH OF SPUTNIK 1, PRESIDENT DWIGHT D. EISENHOWER AUTHORIZES THE FORMATION OF THE ADVANCED RESEARCH PROJECTS AGENCY (ARPA). ITS ROLE: TO COORDINATE U.S. MISSILE AND SPACE PROJECTS.

//1958 — NACA becomes NASA
THE NATIONAL ADVISORY COMMITTEE FOR AERONAUTICS (NACA) BECOMES THE NATIONAL AERONAUTICS AND SPACE ADMINISTRATION (NASA). ALL NACA RESEARCH CENTRES — AMONG THEM AMES RESEARCH CENTER, FOUNDED AS AN AIRCRAFT RESEARCH CENTER IN 1939 — ARE INTEGRATED INTO NASA, WHICH TAKES OVER THE SPACE PROGRAM FROM ARPA. NASA IS ASSIGNED THE TASK OF PUTTING THE FIRST MAN IN SPACE.

//1958 — PIONEER 0, NASA, launch failure (attempted lunar orbit)

//1958 — LUNA1958A, RKA, launch failure (attempted lunar orbit)

//1960 — MARSNIK 1, RKA, launch failure (attempted Mars flyby)

//1960 — PDP-1 computer marketed by DIGITAL EQUIPMENT
DIGITAL EQUIPMENT markets the PDP-1, a high speed solid-state digital computer designed to operate with many types of input/output devices, with a computation rate of 100,000 additions per second. The computer occupies 17 sq ft of floor space and consists of four equipment frames, one of which is used as the operating station. Neither airconditioning nor floor reinforcement is necessary.

//1961 — PRESIDENT JOHN F. KENNEDY promises a man on the moon within a decade
On May 25, PRESIDENT JOHN F. KENNEDY, IN A SPEECH TO CONGRESS, DECLARES, "WHILE WE CANNOT GUARANTEE THAT WE SHALL ONE DAY BE FIRST, WE CAN GUARANTEE THAT ANY FAILURE TO MAKE THIS EFFORT WILL MAKE US LAST. I THEREFORE ASK CONGRESS TO PROVIDE THE FUNDS TO MEET THE FOLLOWING NATIONAL GOALS. FIRST, I BELIEVE THAT THIS NATION SHOULD COMMIT ITSELF TO ACHIEVING THE GOAL, BEFORE THIS DECADE IS OUT, OF LANDING A MAN ON THE MOON AND RETURNING HIM SAFELY TO THE EARTH. NO SPACE PROJECT WILL BE MORE IMPRESSIVE TO MANKIND, AND NONE WILL BE SO DIFFICULT AND EXPENSIVE." PRESIDENT KENNEDY MAKES THE STATEMENT UNSUPPORTED BY EXPERT ASSESSMENT OF THE FEASABILITY OF THE OBJECTIVE. THE APOLLO PROGRAM WILL COST THE UNITED STATES $12 BILLION.

//1962 — MARS 1, NASA, Mars flyby (contact lost)

1957 1958 1959   1960 1961 1962

1963 1964 1965 1966 1967 1968 1969 1970

Written and played on a Digital Equipment PDP-1 computer, it is reputedly the first computer game. Two players fire missiles at each other, while piloting the ship to avoid the pull of the Sun's gravitational force. Nolan Bushnell and Bill Pitts, also studying at MIT, spend many hours playing SPACEWAR!, convinced of the great potential in computer-based games.

//1968 – APOLLO 8, NASA, TV-transmission of Planet Earth
ON DECEMBER 23, A BLACK-AND-WHITE VIEW OF THE EARTH IS TRANSMITTED BACK FROM SPACE DURING A LIVE TV TRANSMISSION FROM APOLLO 8. IT IS THE FIRST IMAGE OF THE ENTIRE PLANET, RECORDED FROM THE FIRST LUNAR ORBITS COMPLETED BY A MANNED SPACECRAFT. AT THE TIME OF THE TV TRANSMISSION, APOLLO 8 IS TRAVELLING ON ITS TRANSLUNAR COURSE AT ABOUT 3,254 FEET PER SECOND. THE IMAGE IS INTRODUCED ON TV BY A CITATION FROM GENESIS: "ALL WAS DARKNESS. GOD SAID: LET THERE BE LIGHT. AND THERE WAS LIGHT. THUS GOD CREATED THE HEAVENS AND THE EARTH."

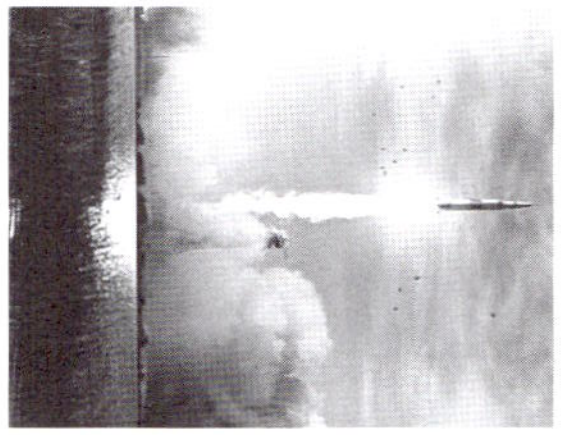

//1969 – APOLLO 11, NASA, manned lunar landing
ON JULY 20, THE EAGLE TOUCHES DOWN ON THE LUNAR SURFACE, MARE TRANQUILITATIS. PLACING HIS FIRST FOOT ON THE MOON, NEIL ARMSTRONG MAKES A STATEMENT BEFORE A TV AUDIENCE OF 500 MILLION PEOPLE: "THAT'S ONE SMALL STEP FOR MAN; ONE GIANT LEAP FOR MANKIND." AT EVA (EXTRA VEHICULAR ACTIVITY) 2 HOURS AND 31 MINUTES, NEIL ARMSTRONG DEPLOYS THE FLAG OF THE UNITED STATES. AFTER THE MISSION, ASTRONAUT EDWIN ALDRIN REPORTS THAT ON LEAVING THE MOON: "NEIL WAS STUDYING THE ALTITUDE INDICATOR, BUT I LOOKED UP LONG ENOUGH TO SEE THE FLAG FALL OVER."

//1970 – VENERA 7, RKA, unmanned landing on Venus
AFTER SEVERAL FAILED ATTEMPTS BY THE RKA AND NASA, VENERA 7 ACHIEVES THE FIRST SOFT LANDING ON ANOTHER PLANET. THE SPACECRAFT SENDS PHOTOGRAPHS AND DATA BACK TO EARTH, INCLUDING A READING OF 470 DEGREES CELSIUS ON THE SURFACE OF VENUS.

//1970 – APOLLO 13, NASA, manned lunar mission (landing aborted)
ON APRIL 13, APOLLO 13 HAS TO ABORT ITS MISSION TO THE SURFACE OF THE MOON DUE TO AN EXPLOSION IN OXYGEN TANK NUMBER TWO. 55 HOURS AND A 55 MINUTES AFTER LIFT-OFF, OXYGEN AND POWER SHORTAGE COMPELS THE CREW TO LEAVE THE COMMAND MODULE (CM) AND TO CONTINUE THEIR FLIGHT IN THE LUNAR MODULE (LM). SINCE THE LANDER IS DESIGNED FOR ONLY TWO PEOPLE, ITS ENVIRONMENTAL SYSTEM CANNOT REMOVE ENOUGH CARBON DIOXIDE

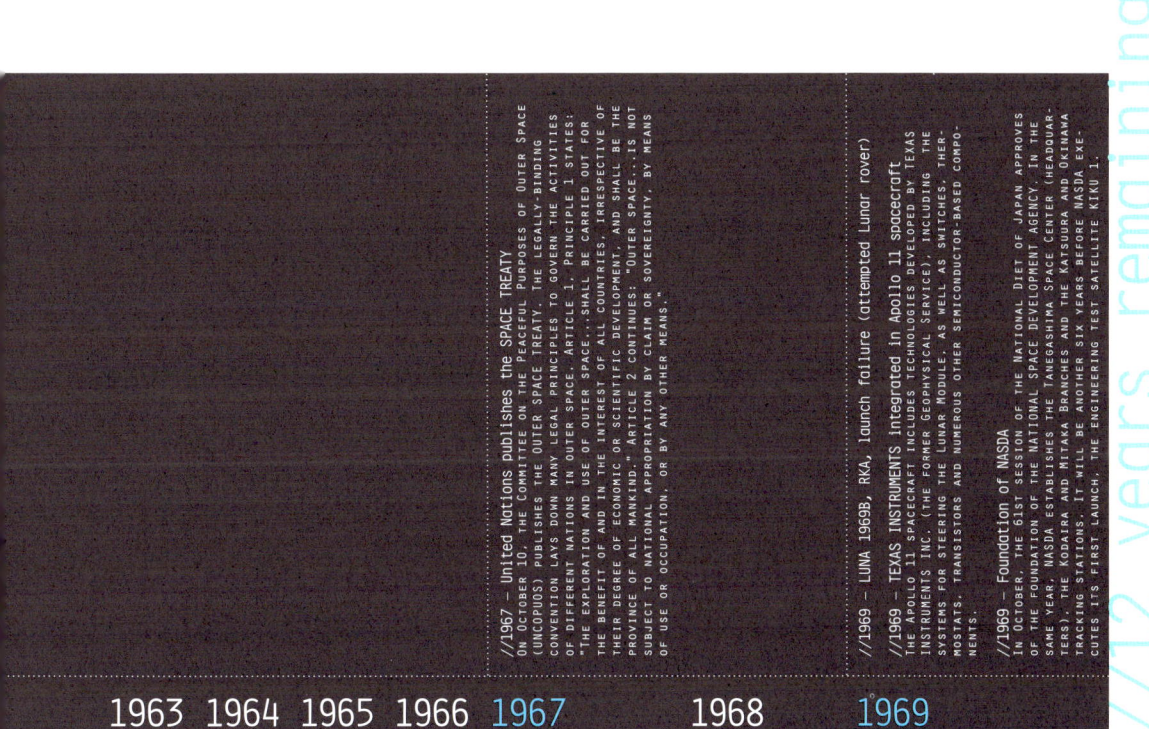

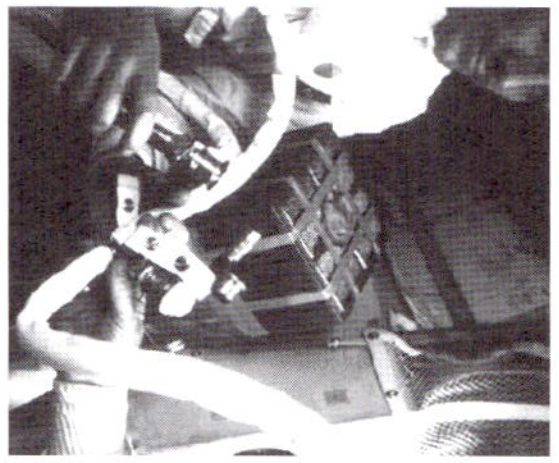

APOLLO 8 LAUNCH.JPG

MOONWALK.JPG

APOLLO_13.GIF

//1967 – United Nations publishes the SPACE TREATY
ON OCTOBER 10, THE COMMITTEE ON THE PEACEFUL PURPOSES OF OUTER SPACE (UNCOPUOS) PUBLISHES THE OUTER SPACE TREATY. THE LEGALLY-BINDING CONVENTION LAYS DOWN MANY LEGAL PRINCIPLES TO GOVERN THE ACTIVITIES OF DIFFERENT NATIONS IN OUTER SPACE. ARTICLE 1 PRINCIPLE 1 STATES: "THE EXPLORATION AND USE OF OUTER SPACE... SHALL BE CARRIED OUT FOR THE BENEFIT OF AND IN THE INTEREST OF ALL COUNTRIES, IRRESPECTIVE OF THEIR DEGREE OF ECONOMIC OR SCIENTIFIC DEVELOPMENT AND SHALL BE THE PROVINCE OF ALL MANKIND." ARTICLE 2 CONTINUES: "OUTER SPACE... IS NOT SUBJECT TO NATIONAL APPROPRIATION BY CLAIM OR SOVEREIGNTY, BY MEANS OF USE OR OCCUPATION, OR BY ANY OTHER MEANS."

//1969 – LUNA 1969B, RKA, launch failure (attempted lunar rover)

//1969 – TEXAS INSTRUMENTS integrated in Apollo 11 spacecraft
THE APOLLO 11 SPACECRAFT INCLUDES TECHNOLOGIES DEVELOPED BY TEXAS INSTRUMENTS INC. (THE FORMER GEOPHYSICAL SERVICE), INCLUDING THE SYSTEMS FOR STEERING THE LUNAR MODULE, AS WELL AS SWITCHES, THERMOSTATS, TRANSISTORS AND NUMEROUS OTHER SEMICONDUCTOR-BASED COMPONENTS.

//1969 – Foundation of NASDA
IN OCTOBER, THE 61ST SESSION OF THE NATIONAL DIET OF JAPAN APPROVES OF THE FOUNDATION OF THE NATIONAL SPACE DEVELOPMENT AGENCY. IN THE SAME YEAR, NASDA ESTABLISHES THE TANEGASHIMA SPACE CENTER (HEADQUARTERS), THE KODAIRA AND MITAKA BRANCHES AND THE KATSUURA AND OKINAWA TRACKING STATIONS. IT WILL BE ANOTHER SIX YEARS BEFORE NASDA EXECUTES ITS FIRST LAUNCH, THE ENGINEERING TEST SATELLITE KIKU 1.

//12 years remaining...

1963 1964 1965 1966 1967 1968 1969 1970

1971

(CO_2). To solve this problem, the astronauts have to succeed in plugging the round opening of the LM's environmental system with a square canister from the CM. The solution is provided by mission control, which puts four engineers in a room with all objects available in Apollo 13. Within 20 minutes, they managed to turn the square filter into a round one. Using only material present in the spacecraft: plastic bags, cardboard, socks and tape.

//1971 – APOLLO 14, NASA, playing golf on the moon. His performance takes place just before lift-off and is broadcast on TV. Apollo 14 is the third manned spacecraft to land on the moon and the first to use a mandcar to collect lunar soil samples. After the mission, Shepard – who became the first American in outer space on May 5, 1961 – reports: "I was intrigued that a ball hit with the same club-head as on Earth, would go six times as far on the moon. And I thought: what a neat place to whack a golf ball!"

//1971 – COMPUTER SPACE, NUTTING ASSOCIATES coin-operated game
Nutting Associates, specialists in coin-operated general knowledge games, purchases SPACEWAR! from Nolan Bushnell. The MIT graduate is hired to realise the game as a commercial product. The game now stages a hostile encounter between a human opponent and a flying saucer. Manufacture of COMPUTER SPACE reaches 1500 units.

1972

//1972 – PIONEER 10, NASA, planetary probe
On March 2, NASA launches PIONEER 10. The probe, developed at AMES Research Center, will be the first to reach an outer planet. Its first to use the gravitational field of a planet to increase its velocity, and the first to leave the solar system. PIONEER's biggest challenges will be navigation of the asteroid belt between Mars and Jupiter, and overcoming Jupiter's radiation environment. The spacecraft has a gold-anodized aluminium plaque bolted on its back. Designed by Carl Sagan, the plaque depicts a man waving, a woman standing by his side smiling faintly, a map pinpointing our solar system amid pulsars, and a 'hyperfine transition of neutral hydrogen' – the most common element in the universe.

1973

//1973 – PIONEER 11, NASA, planetary probe
On April 5, PIONEER 11 is launched to follow its sister towards Jupiter. It will be the first spacecraft to return images of Saturn.

//1973 – PIONEER 10, NASA, Jupiter flyby

1976

//1976 – VIKING 1 and 2, NASA, unmanned landing on Mars
On July 20, the lander of VIKING 1 (launched on August 20, 1975) makes a soft landing at Chryse Planitia. The VIKING 2 lander touches down on September 3. Both landers relay hundreds of images. Their orbiters photograph the entire surface of Mars at a resolution of 150m to 300m, and selected areas at 8m (they are powered down at 1400 and 706 orbits respectively). Among the mission objectives is the search for evidence of life. Experiments testing the presence of carbon monoxide and hydrogen fail, and images show no direct sign of biological activity.

COMPUTER_SPACE.JPG

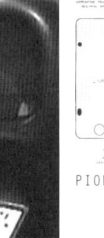
PIONEER_10.GIF

PIONEERCRAFT.JPG

PIONEER_11.JPG

VIKING_1.JPG

4004PROCESSOR.GIF

MAGNAVOX.JPG

FAIRCHILD.GIF

2600ATARI.JPG

//1971 – INTEL INC. introduces the first computer on a chip
In March, the INTEL CORPORATION introduces the Model 4004 microprocessor, the first computer on a chip. Originally designed to drive a desktop calculator, the processor finds its first application supplying on-board computing power to the PIONEER 10 spacecraft.

//1972 – Ralph Baer designs the MAGNAVOX ODYSSEY computer
On January 27 the MAGNAVOX ODYSSEY is introduced, retailing at $100. Designed by Ralph Baer in 1966, assisted by Bill Harrison and Bill Rusch of Sanders Associates (a military electronics firm), the ODYSSEY is manufactured with 40 transistors and 40 diodes – and is consequently capable only of very simple on-screen effects. To simulate sophisticated graphics, the ODYSSEY package includes screen overlays; players are obliged to record scores. The ODYSSEY sells complete with the screen overlays, two controllers, a pair of dice, poker chips, a fold-out scoreboard, a roulette and football play area, six playing cards and toy money.

//1972 – ATARI INC founded
With the profits from COMPUTER SPACE, Nolan Bushnell founds ATARI in the bedroom of his two-year-old daughter. ATARI is incorporated on Tuesday June 27. The name 'ATARI', is selected after first choice 'Syzygy' (the term for a total eclipse of the sun, moon and earth) turns out to be taken by a roofing company. Bushnell's fourth choice, ATARI refers to a position in the Japanese game 'GO' that resembles 'check' in chess.

//1973 – ATARI and LOCKHEED compete over employee.
In June, STEVE BRISTOL is hired straight from school by ATARI INC., accepting their offer over one from LOCKHEED, a company specializing in aeronautics and astronautics technology and one of NASA's principal commercial contractors.

//1973 – ELDO and ESRO become the EUROPEAN SPACE AGENCY (ESA)
In July, the EUROPEAN LAUNCHER DEVELOPMENT AGENCY (Belgium, France, the Netherlands, Germany, Italy, the United Kingdom, Austria) and the EUROPEAN SPACE RESEARCH ORGANISATION (same countries plus Denmark, Spain, Sweden, Switzerland) merge as the EUROPEAN SPACE AGENCY. Laid down in principle by an interministerial conference in Brussels, it takes until October 30, 1980, before a final signature ratifies the convention and gives ESA legal existence. Subsequently, ESA is joined by Norway, Finland and Ireland. Canada is allowed to participate in certain programmes and sit on the ESA Council.

//1976 – FAIRCHILD CHANNEL F introduces cartridge-based games consoles
FAIRCHILD CAMERA AND INSTRUMENTS introduces the console and cartridge ('videocart') formula in August. Additional games can be bought and played on the FAIRCHILD CHANNEL F.

//1977 – ATARI releases VIDEO COMPUTER SYSTEM (2600 VCS)
ATARI launches the VIDEO COMPUTER SYSTEM known as the 2600 VCS, for $199.95. Designed by Joe Decure, Harold Lee, and Steve Meyer, with a 1.19 MHz 8-bit Motorola 6507 microprocessor and 256 bytes of RAM, the VCS remains in production until 1990 – longer than any other digital game console.

1978

//1978 - SPACE INVADERS, TAITO, coin-operated game
On Friday, June 16, the Tokyo-based Taito Corporation publicly debuts SPACE INVADERS. The coin-operated machine breaks video gaming out from the arcade-hall into mainstream environments such as restaurants, ice cream parlours and swimming pools. The player faces a regimented block of advancing alien primitives, spitting laser fire. Within a horizontally scrolling environment, the columns of aliens must be eliminated.

1979

//1979 - PIONEER 11, NASA, Saturn flyby

//1979 - ADVENTURE, ATARI INC, coin-operated game
ATARI INC. releases ADVENTURE for the ATARI 2600 Video Computer System (VCS). Written by Warren Robinett, it is the first graphical adventure game and the first to incorporate an Easter Egg - an unofficial, undocumented function by which the player can discover the name of the game's author. This is in retaliation for Atari's policy of not crediting individuals.

//1979 - LUNAR LANDER, ATARI INC, coin-operated game
In August, ATARI INC. releases LUNAR LANDER, written by Howie Delman. The first arcade game to use vector display technology, LUNAR LANDER challenges the player repeatedly to land a spaceship on the surface of the moon, skilfully exploiting gravity via orientation thrusts. Greater scores are achieved by successfully attempting hazardous vistas and dramatic surface profile close-ups. Due to poor demand, the LUNAR LANDER assembly line is soon devoted to the production of ASTEROIDS. The first 200 cabinets of ASTEROIDS still display the LUNAR LANDER design and artwork. ATARI builds 5,000 LUNAR LANDER games.

//1979 - ASTEROIDS, ATARI INC, coin-operated game
In November, ASTEROIDS (concept: Lyle Rains; programming: Edward Logg) is launched, soon to become ATARI's best-selling coin operated video game. 70,000 cabinets are shipped over at $2,700 each. ASTEROIDS introduces a new level of craft control and freedom; allowing acceleration and 360o of rotational manoeuvring, the spacecraft is charged with destroying waves of randomly-moving planetoid debris. Once hit, the asteroids fragment into smaller and smaller units until they disintegrate. Progression through the game is measured by an increase in the number of asteroids the player encounters. At 100,000 points the score resets to zero. Since the 6502 processor can only render a limited amount of vectors per second, success is rewarded with a noticeable decrease in refresh rates, as valuable processor time is spent displaying bonus ships and debris. As there are no sound-chips available, bespoke circuits are developed to incorporate sound. An Audio/Reg 1 board handles amplification and power regulation.

INVADER_ARCADE.JPG

SPACE_INVADERS.GIF

PIONEER11.JPG

SPEAK.SPELL.JPG

MICROVISION.JPG

//1978 - TEXAS INSTRUMENTS INTRODUCES SPEAK & SPELL
THE FIRST PRODUCT TO IMPLEMENT A SINGLE-CHIP SPEECH SYNTHESIZER IS INTRODUCED BY TEXAS INSTRUMENTS. AT A RETAIL PRICE OF $50. SPEAK & SPELL LEARNING TOYS REPRODUCE HUMAN VOICE WITH INFLECTION AND FIDELITY. USING THE TMS 1000 MICROCHIP AND TWO 128K DRAM, EACH OF WHICH CAN STORE OVER 100 SECONDS OF DIGITIZED SPEECH. WHEN A CHILD TYPES IN A WORD, SPEAK & SPELL PRONOUNCES IT IN STANDARD AMERICAN ENGLISH. CORRECT ANSWERS EARN VERBAL AND VISUAL PRAISE, INCORRECT ANSWERS RECEIVE PATIENT ENCOURAGEMENT TO RETRY. THE SPEAK & SPELL IS USED IN STEVEN SPIELBERG'S FILM E.T.

//1979 - MILTON BRADLEY releases MICROVISION, first portable games console
Designed by Jay Smith, the MICROVISION is the first portable, programmable video games unit. Each cartridge contains the 4-bit microprocessor while the base unit hosts a 2 inch square LCD and a dial switch.

1980

//1980 - ASTEROIDS DELUXE, ATARI INC, coin-operated game
The sequel to ASTEROIDS features minor tweaks: the random hyperjump is replaced by a collision shield; the rocket ship design is updated to a winged shuttle; and motion is faster and smoother.

//1980 - MISSILE COMMAND, ATARI INC, coin-operated game
ATARI INC releases MISSILE COMMAND as a public coin-operated game. Inspired by an article about satellite development, it is programmed by Dave Theurer, and one of the first games to use a trackball; Rob Fulop writes the port to the Atari 2600 VCS. Fulop originally thought of calling it ARMAGEDDON, and planned to include submarines, trains and various other signs of a technologically-advanced state. The final release, though far less encompassing, requires the player to protect an urban landscape from waves of incoming nuclear projectiles. In game 13, when all cities have been condemned to destruction, the city furthest to the far right changes to 'RF' (for Rob Fulop).

//1980 - DEFENDER, WILLIAMS ELECTRONICS, coin-operated game
The ROMs for WILLIAMS ELECTRONICS' DEFENDER are finally burned at dawn on the first day of the Amusement Machine Operators of America (AMOA) trade show. The game is the first 'side-scroller': the playfield extends horizontally beyond the frame of the video-screen. The combat astronaut lurks close to inhospitable terrain with the remit of destroying alien intruders. Alien intelligence has evolved considerably since SPACE INVADERS.DEFENDER will mature as one of the most popular games of the year; WILLIAMS ELECTRONICS goes on to sell 60,000 units.

1981

DEFENDER.GIF

DEFENDER_ARCADE.JPG

BBC_MICRO_ACORN.JPG

ZX_SPECTRUM.JPG

//1980 - MATTEL ELECTRONICS releases INTELLIVISION games console
Introducing downloadable games via a 24-hour home TV cable service, Mattel's INTELLIVISION also delivers a display resolution superior to that of its competitors.

//1980 - SINCLAIR RESEARCH Ltd develops ZX80 computer
Clive Sinclair establishes SINCLAIR RESEARCH Ltd. in Cambridge, UK, and begins developing a small home computer: the ZX80 has 1K of RAM, 4K of ROM and sells for under £100.

//1981 - ACORN releases the BBC MICRO computer.
Designed and manufactured in 1981, the BBC MICRO is the first successful design by ACORN, based in Cambridge, UK. With multiple processors (6502), with an optional Z80) it is capable of (rudimenta-

//22 years remaining...

1982

//1982 — STEVE JURASZEK becomes world DEFENDER champion
On January 18, STEVE JURASZEK, an Illinois high school student, is profiled in Time magazine as the world DEFENDER champion. On the investment of a single quarter, he scores 16,000,000 points during a 16 hour marathon. Adroit players can take advantage of a bug activated by a score of 990,000, yielding extra ships in such quantities that players can take a respite. Play has been known to continue for days. By 1982, 60,000 copies of SPACE INVADERS and 70,000 units of ASTEROIDS have been sold.

//1982 — ROBOTRON:2084, WILLIAMS ELECTRONICS, coin-operated game
Originally dubbed ROBOT WAR:1984, ROBOTRON:2084 is designed by the same team responsible for DEFENDER: Eugene Jarvis and Larry DeMar. Early incarnations involve multiple scrolling screens and a joystick/trackball control configuration. ROBOTRON:2084 ships as a single-screen cabinet with dual joystick control.

//1982 — E.T., ATARI INC, coin-operated game
ATARI begins shipping E.T. in November — a follow-up to the eponymous Steven Spielberg film.

//1982 — ZAXXON, SEGA, coin-operated game
Initially released for a coin-operated machine, ZAXXON is the first fully-rastered diagonal-scrolling game, using isometric bit-mapped graphics to give the illusion of 3D perspective. The player ventures through a luscious hostile conduit, avoiding defensive structures and destroying anti-spaceship installations. The game is later marketed as software for home computers, such as the ZX Spectrum, Commodore 64 and Amstrad CPC.

1983

//1983 — PIONEER 10, NASA, beyond the solar system
PIONEER 10 IS NOW 3.8 BILLION MILES FROM EARTH. AT THAT DISTANCE, PIONEER 10'S 8-WATT RADIO SIGNAL, EQUIVALENT TO THE POWER OF A NIGHTLAMP, TAKE ABOUT 6 HOURS TO REACH EARTH.

//1983 — I, ROBOT, ATARI INC, coin-operated game
Atari Inc. releases I, ROBOT, the first genuine 3D coin-operated game, using 3D polygon graphics (complete with shading), and incorporating an innovative yet unpopular 3D-paint program, DOODLE CITY. A thousand I, ROBOT machines are manufactured, 500 of which allegedly ship to Japan.

//1983 — STAR WARS, ATARI INC, coin-operated game
STAR WARS is programmed and designed by Eric Durfey, Greg Rivera, Earl Vickers, Mike Haily, Jed Margolin and Norm Aveilar. The pilot engages the X-Wing fighter in an insertion operation to remove the Death Star. A first-person, 3-D vector space facilitates free spatial movement. The game's input devices are modified from the controllers on the US military's adaptation of the original (1980) BATTLEZONE.

1984

//1984 — October: SPACE ACE, MAGICOM, coin-operated game
Following Dragon's Lair, SPACE ACE is the second laser disc-based game from MAGICOM, a joint venture between Don Bluth Studios, RDI Video Systems (formally AMS) and Cinematronics; it is created by Rick Dyer and animated by Don Bluth. Assuming the role of Dexter (Ace), the player's aim is to rescue his romantic interest, Kimmie, from the clutches of Borf. SPACE ACE displays sumptuous graphics. For the animation, models are made of Ace's Starship and his motorcycle, which are then filmed traced over and painted. A large-scale tunnel is also built to provide movement for the dogfight sequence. To keep costs down, the creators narrate the characters themselves. Narrator, Michael Rye; Ace, Jeff Etter (animator); Dexter, Will Finn (animator/storyman); Kimberely, Lorna Pomeroy (animator).

//1984 — November: ELITE, ACORNSOFT, computer game
ACORNSOFT publishes ELITE, an interplanetary trading and combat game, for the BBC Micro, in tape and disk format. Written by David Braben and Ian Holmes while they are students at Cambridge University, ELITE demonstrates an 'open' game concept where the player, trades and fights his way through a galaxy, in order to attain Elite combat accreditation. Initially trading with a light spacecraft, the player embellishes the craft with the profits of interplanetary economic exploits; more sophisticated ships increase the player's destructive potential, and thus his status. Using wireframe vector graphics, ELITE offers freedom of movement in a 3D environment, variability of speed, including jumpdrive and hyperdrive, and 3D environment maps. Game states are saved onto tape or disk as rank is slowly gained; failed docking attempts with terminal consequences are common at the early stages of the game.

ROBOTRON.GIF

STARWARS_ARCADE.JPG

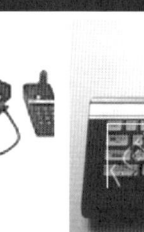
ZAXXON.GIF

LOGO.GIF

ELITE.ADVERT.GIF

COMMODORE64.JPG

COLECOVISION.JPG

VECTREX.JPG

ATARI5200.JPG

7800_ATARI.JPG

NINTENDO.JPG

ry) network support. Its major claim to fame: structured BASIC as its default programming language.

//1982 — COMMODORE releases C64, low-cost home computer
The C64 debuts at the U.S. Consumer Electronics Show (CES) and hits the market in August. It includes a keyboard, 64K of RAM, CPU, graphics and sound chips. The C64 enters 1,000,000 homes in its first year.

//1982 — COLECOVISION joins console market
Released for $199.95, the COLECOVISION consists of 48K of RAM, a 3.58 MHz and an 8-bit Z-80A microprocessor — the first of many announced expansion modules that, together, will form the ADAM computer.

//1982 — ATARI releases 5200 SUPERSYSTEM
The Atari 5200 is the offspring of the 400 and 800 computers, both of which sport cartridge, and built-in joystick ports. Omitting a keyboard, the 5200 is the first machine to accommodate four players via four controller ports.

//1982 — MILTON BRADLEY releases GCE VECTREX games console
Inspired by Jay Smith, the VECTREX is designed by John Ross, Gerry Karr, Mark Indictor and Paul Newell. Priced at $199, the machine incorporates a 9-inch Vector graphic monitor and a Motorola 68A09 8-bit microprocessor.

//1982 — EUGENE JARVIS appears in *Playboy*
Entitled 'What Sort of Man Invents DEFENDER?', Eugene Jarvis, head of the DEFENDER design team, is featured in the July edition of *Playboy*. Later this year, Eugene Jarvis and Larry DeMar form their own company, VIDKIDZ. Their first project: to develop a sequel to DEFENDER, released in 1981 as STARGATE.

//1983 — Mattel releases the INTELLIVISION II games console
The INTELLIVISION II is the successor to the INTELLIVISION.

//1983 — COMMODORE VIC 20 computers sales reach 1 million
COMMODORE also announces a price of $200 for the C64.

//1983 — The 1,000,000th COLECOVISION console is manufactured

//1984 — 4,000,000 COMMODORE computers sold worldwide

//1984 — NINTENDO announces US release of FAMICON with light-gun and keyboard

//1984 — ATARI announces 7800 VCS in January

1985

//1985 — VIRTUAL MARS WALK at NASA Ames Research Center
Mike McGreevy, Lew Hitcher and Warren Robinett develop THE VIRTUAL INTERFACE ENVIRONMENT WORKSTATION (VIEW), WHICH COMBINES A DISPLAY SYSTEM AND INSTRUMENTED GLOVES FOR TACTILE INPUT AND FEEDBACK. ROBINETT IS KNOWN AS THE DESIGNER OF ATARI'S FIRST ADVENTURE GAME, ADVENTURE. VIEW CAN POTENTIALLY BE USED FOR TELE-ROBOTIC TASKS IN OUTER SPACE AND IS PRESENTED AS AN APPLICATION FOR REMOTE ACTION ON MARS. THE DESIGNERS FURTHER PROPOSE SPIN-OFFS FOR ARCHITECTURAL ENGINEERING DESIGN SIMULATIONS, MICROSURGICAL PROCEDURES, ENTERTAINMENT AND EDUCATION.

1986　　　　　　　　　　　　1987　　　1988　　　1989

//1986 – SPACE SHUTTLE DISCOVERY STS-51L, NASA, launch failure (attempted manned Earth orbiter).
ON JANUARY 28, THE STS-51L — BETTER KNOWN AS THE CHALLENGER SPACE SHUTTLE — BLOWS UP 73 SECONDS AFTER LIFT-OFF. ALL SEVEN CREW MEMBERS ARE KILLED, INCLUDING SCHOOLTEACHER SHARON CHRISTA MCAULIFFE. MCAULIFFE HAD PARTICIPATED IN THE MISSION AS PART OF NASA'S 'TEACHER IN SPACE' PROGRAM, WHOSE OBJECTIVE WAS THE ACTIVE INVOLVEMENT OF ORDINARY MEN, WOMEN AND CHILDREN IN THE EXPLORATION OF OUTER SPACE.

//1986 – MIR, RKA, launch of Manned Space Station.
ON FEBRUARY 20, THE LAST MODULE OF THE RUSSIAN MANNED SPACE STATION MIR IS LAUNCHED. AS THE FOLLOW-UP TO RUSSIA'S SALUTE-SERIES OF MANNED EARTH ORBITING STATIONS — SALUTE 1 HAVING BEEN THE FIRST MANNED STATION IN OUTER SPACE (LAUNCH: 1971). THE MIR WILL BE PERMANENTLY MANNED BY THREE COSMONAUTS. REPLACED OCCASIONALLY BY WESTERN ASTRONAUTS. THE ORBITING STATION CONSISTS OF THREE MODULES: A CENTRAL MODULE (HABITATION) SPEKTR (DOCKING) AND KRISTALL (STORAGE). MIR'S PREDICTED LIFE-SPAN IS SEVEN YEARS. DURING THOSE YEARS, HUNDREDS OF HOURS OF HOME-VIDEO FOOTAGE WILL BE BROADCAST ON NATIONAL AND INTERNATIONAL TV, SHOWING THE COSMONAUTS AT WORK AND PLAY IN THE STATION. MIR IS THE RUSSIAN WORD FOR BOTH 'WORLD' AND 'PEACE'.

//1986 – SPACE HARRIER, SEGA, coin-operated game
Re-defining the coin-operated landscape, SEGA releases SPACE HARRIER. Situating the player in a motion cockpit (on the most luxurious cabinets), SPACE HARRIER renders fast, smooth 32,000 colour polygon sprites. Moving continuously forward, the character blasts a corridor through an alien landscape, avoiding projectiles and collisions with the aid of a jet-pack.

//1987 – R-TYPE, IREM, coin-operated game
R-TYPE is the sophisticated and addictive culmination of horizontal scrolling shoot-em-ups. With the open brief: 'BLAST OFF AND ATTACK THE EVIL BYDO EMPIRE!' the player pilots an R-9 Nectarine Battle Cruiser one way through an incessant alien arcade. Graduation to higher levels requires the destruction of an alien 'boss' (the most difficult opponent of the level). Advanced armaments modules include the 'FORCE UNIT', a detachable roving canon, spherical satellite shields, and the infamous main cannon whose force is proportional to the length of time the fire button is depressed. Geiger-esque aesthetics and integral animations are detailed and rich.

MIR.JPG

CHALLENGER CREW.JPG

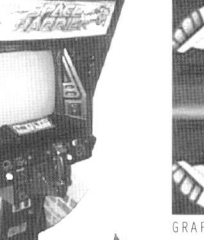
SPACE HARRIER.JPG

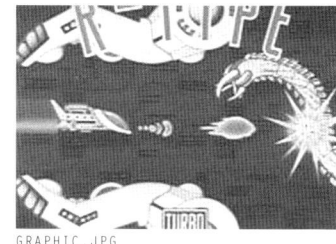
GRAPHIC.JPG

NINTENDO_HARDWARE.JPG

SUPER_NINTENDO.JPG

LYNX.JPG

//1985 – 25,000,000 ATARI 2600 VCS's sold worldwide
Just under half the total (12,000,000) have been sold in the U.S.

//1985 – NINTENDO releases the NINTENDO ENTERTAINMENT SYSTEM (NES)
NINTENDO releases the FAMICOM (Family Computer) in New York City prior to Christmas. It sells with game controllers, R.O.B. (Robotic Operating Buddy) and a light gun. The machine itself is based on an 8-bit 6502 microprocessor with a graphics chip supporting 52 colours; previous consoles could only handle 16.

//1986 – November 10: ATARI introduces the 520ST and 1040ST computers

//1986 – January: NINTENDO begins shipping NES + 15 games to Southern Californian retailers

//1986 – February: Nolan Bushnell unveils TECH FORCES — an assortment of radio-controlled dolls that play video games.

//1987 – September 14: DATA TRAVELLERS OF GERMANY hack into NASA
DATA TRAVELLERS OF GERMANY hack into NASA and publish a political manifesto. Half an hour later, the manifesto is discovered; the site is repaired within an hour.

//1988 – Agreement on INTERNATIONAL SPACE STATION signed by NASA, ESA and NASDA
IN SEPTEMBER, THE UNITED STATES, THE EUROPEAN COUNTRIES, CANADA AND JAPAN SIGN THE INTERGOVERNMENTAL AGREEMENT. A FRAMEWORK FOR THE DESIGN, DEVELOPMENT, OPERATION AND UTILIZATION OF THE INTERNATIONAL SPACE STATION. THEY AGREE THAT THE UNITED STATES SHALL CONTRIBUTE $16 BILLION, ESA $4.2 BILLION, NASA $2 BILLION AND CANADA $1 BILLION. EACH PARTY WILL COVER 25% OF THE OPERATION-COSTS FOR THE COMING 20-30 YEARS.

//1988 – NINTENDO and SONY join forces to create SNES
NINTENDO signs an agreement with SONY for a SUPER NINTENDO ENTERTAINMENT SYSTEM (SNES) CD-ROM Drive combo.

//1989 – WARREN ROBINETT directs VR research
Designer of the first graphical adventure game (ADVENTURE) for the ATARI 2600 Video Computer System (VCS) and co-founder of THE LEARNING COMPANY, WARREN ROBINETT takes up direction of the Head-Mounted Display and Nanomanipulator projects at the University of North Carolina.

//1989 – NINTENDO conducts market research via user groups
NINTENDO puts a video game system in 21% of American homes, the primary users being boys between the ages of 8 to 18.

//1989 – NINTENDO releases the GAME BOY
Designed by Gumpei Yokoi and NINTENDO R&D Team #1, this portable console is released for $100. The cartridge port can now host accessories, such as a digital camera, as well as games. The games run on a 1.1 MHz 8-bit CPU

//1989 – NINTENDO video game sales reach $2.3 billion
According to figures provided by NINTENDO OF AMERICA, video game sales this year are $2.3 billion. NINTENDO Entertainment Systems (NES) sales reach 9.1 million units, and compatible software, 50 million units.

//1989 – ATARI releases the LYNX portable games console
At the summer Consumer Electronics Show (CES) ATARI CORPORATION

1990 1991 1992 1993

//1990 – PIONEER 11, NASA, now beyond the Solar System.

//1990 – HUBBLE SPACE TELESCOPE, NASA/ESA, permanent space-based observatory
On May 20, the first image of a star cluster (in Carina) is received from the Hubble Space Telescope. The 2.4-meter reflecting telescope, deployed in lower earth orbit (600 kilometer) a month previously, includes a wide field/planetary camera (NASA), a faint object camera (ESA), a faint object spectrograph (NASA) and a high-resolution spectrograph (NASA). Hubble's observation time is distributed throughout the international astronomical community by the Space Telescope Scientific Institute at Johns Hopkins University. Images from the 'Window on the Universe' are publicly available world-wide. According to Zolt Levay of NASA's office of public outreach, "Her dramatic pictures provide us with a new sense of awe and wonder about the infinite richness of our universe." In the absence of atmospheric distortion, images at unprecedented high resolution are attainable in outer space.

//1990 – WING COMMANDER, ORIGIN, computer game
In WING COMMANDER, first of a popular series, the narrative interaction is developed with an explicit Hollywood-style plot, and the player is involved in the action (in glorious 3D) at key tactical moments.

//1993 – DOOM, ID, computer game
On December 10, ID releases DOOM (level designers: Sandy Petersen and John Romero). Though not the first first-person 3D shoot-em-up, it nonetheless initiates a new genre: close-combat simulation. Thrown into an inter-dimensional war, the player must disinfect a scientific research facility. Featuring texture-mapping and an advanced real-time interactive multi-user environment, DOOM puts arcade quality resolution and action into the home and office, and is later released in ATARI Jaguar, SEGA 32X, SUPER NINTENDO and SONY PLAYSTATION formats. An estimated 15 million copies are downloaded or exchanged worldwide. More than 250,000 people are registered for the full

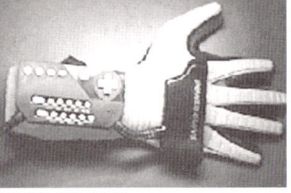

HUBBLE IMAGE.JPG

WING COMMANDER_STATUS BAR.GIF

GAMEBOY.GIF

POWERGLOVE.PICT

3DO.GIF

//32 years remaining...

reveals the new LYNX colour handheld video game. Designed by R. J. Mical and Dave Needle (creators of the advanced COMMODORE AMIGA Home Computer), the device hosts an 8-bit microprocessor and a colour-capable screen.

//1989 – NEC releases first 16-bit games console in the U.S.
One year after its release as the PC ENGINE in Japan, NEC's TURBO-GRAFX-16 is marketed as the first 16-bit games system. In fact, the console houses an 8-bit primary microprocessor with an additional 16-bit graphics chip. The CD-player attachment is a first for dedicated video game systems.

//1989 – SEGA enters 16-bit market
Reconstructing an arcade machine for home play, SEGA releases the 16-bit GENESIS. Known as the MEGA-DRIVE in Japan and Europe, the machine retails for $100 and is driven by a derivative of the Motorola 68000 16-bit microprocessor. 15,000 GENESIS video game systems sell during the year.

//1989 – NINTENDO sales figures sky-rocket
NINTENDO Co., Ltd., Kyoto, Japan generates fiscal revenue of $477 million. NINTENDO sells 7.5 million Nintendo Entertainment Systems (NES), and 70 million compatible software titles. 3.2 million GAME BOYS are sold. 400,000 TURBOGRAFX game consoles are sold in the US and 2.1 million in Japan. 600,000 SEGA GENESIS systems are sold this year in the U.S., and 1,000,000 units in Japan. 9,000,000 video game consoles are sold this year totalling $833 million in sales. Video game sales including computer games reach $2.2 billion. According to figures provided by NINTENDO OF AMERICA, video game sales this year are $3.4 billion.

//1989 – Mattel introduces POWERGLOVE for NES
Originally designed by VPL Labs for NASA for remote repair of satellites (via a robotic armature that moves in tandem with the astronaut's hand), the POWER GLOVE controls on-screen movement by responding to the player's arm and (right) hand movements. Licensed by VPL Labs to Abrams/Gentile Entertainment and in turn to MATTEL, the POWER GLOVE incorporates a keypad and microprocessor that translates information from its sensors and controls on-screen characters' movements.

//1990 – GLOBAL POSITION SYSTEM (GPS) becomes available for civilian users
In July, GPS-receivers go on the market. Civilians can now rely on the Standard Positioning Service (SPS) signals of the 24 satellites comprising the GPS, to determine their space/time coordinates. Owned by the U.S. Department of Defense, GPS served as a navigation and coordination system during the Vietnam and Gulf Wars. Using Selective Availability, the Department of Defense intentionally degrades the SPS-signals transmitted to private receivers. The accuracy of the C/A (Coarse Acquisition) Code is reduced to 100M from its potential radius of around 30M.

//1993 – 3DO releases INTERACTIVE MULTIPLAYER technology
Designed by R. J. Mical and Dave Needle, the 3DO INTERACTIVE MULTI-PLAYER is the first game console based solely on CD technology. Rather than manufacturing the machine, 3DO licenses the technology. One licensee, the PANASONIC REAL FZ-1 3DO, releases for $699.95, featuring a 12.5 MHz 32-bit microprocessor capable of replaying VHS-quality video and CD quality sound.

1990 1991 1992 1993

1995

//1995 — PIONEER 11, NASA, mission ended.
ON SEPTEMBER 30, NASA CEASES DAILY COMMUNICATIONS WITH PIONEER 11. ITS POWER NOW TOO LOW TO OPERATE ITS INSTRUMENTS OR POINT ITS ANTENNAE TOWARD EARTH. THE SPACECRAFT, NOW 4 BILLION MILES FROM EARTH, WILL CONTINUE SPEEDING OUT INTO INTERSTELLAR SPACE TOWARD THE CENTER OF THE MILKY WAY, PASSING NEAR THE STAR LAMBDA (IN THE CONSTELLATION OF AQUILA) IN ALMOST FOUR MILLION YEARS. NASA CHIEF ADMINISTRATOR DAN GOLDIN ENDS THE MISSION BY STATING: "THIS VENERABLE EXPLORER HAS TAUGHT US A GREAT DEAL ABOUT THE SOLAR SYSTEM AND, IN THE END, ABOUT OUR OWN INNATE DRIVE TO LEARN."

//1995 — WIPEOUT, PSYGNOSIS, console game
ON NOVEMBER 21, WIPEOUT is released for the Sony PLAYSTATION format by PSYGNOSIS of Liverpool. WIPEOUT is an instant hit. Set in 2052 AD, the player races round one of eight celestial tracks in an anti-gravity vehicle accompanied by a techno soundtrack, including *Chemical Beats* by The Chemical Brothers, *Afro Ride* by Leftfield and *Wipeout* by Orbital. Displaying a heightened experience of speed and craft control, WIPEOUT features in-race combat with competing opponents. Weaponry — accumulated through the courses — includes missiles, rockets, shields, shockwave and mines.

1997

//1997 — PIONEER 10, NASA, mission ended.
ON MARCH 31, PIONEER 10'S MISSION IS ENDED. AT 6.5 BILLION MILES FROM EARTH (MORE THAN TWICE THE DISTANCE FROM THE SUN TO PLUTO), THE SPACECRAFT IS THE MOST REMOTE OBJECT EVER MADE BY MAN. NOW HEADING TOWARDS THE CONSTELLATION OF TAURUS (THE BULL), IT WILL TAKE PIONEER 10 OVER TWO MILLION YEARS TO PASS BY ONE OF THE STARS IN THAT CONSTELLATION. SINCE THE EMPTINESS OF INTERSTELLAR SPACE OFFERS A NON-DESTRUCTIVE ENVIRONMENT, IT IS PREDICTED THAT PIONEER 10 WILL STILL BE TRAVELLING AMONG THE STARS WHEN THE SUN — BECOMES A RED GIANT AND DESTROYS THE EARTH IN FIVE BILLION YEARS.

//1997 — MARS PATHFINDER, NASA, unmanned Mars landing
ON JULY 4, AFTER A SEVEN-MONTH JOURNEY, PATHFINDER TOUCHES DOWN ON MARS. SIX HOURS LATER, THE LANDER TRANSMITS THE FIRST BLACK AND WHITE IMAGES; ANOTHER 10 HOURS LATER THEY ARRIVE IN COLOR. SOON AFTER, THE IMAGES ARE PUBLISHED ON THE INTERNET AND THE CNN BROADCASTING NETWORK. THE 22-POUND SIX-WHEEL ROVER 'SOJOURNER' IS DEPLOYED THE NEXT DAY: THE FIRST MAN-MADE DEVICE TO MOVE AROUND ON ANOTHER PLANET AND CARRIES OUT GEOLOGICAL MEASUREMENTS. THESE SUGGEST THE PRESENCE OF WATER ON MARS SOME BILLION YEARS AGO. BUT, AS MISSION DIRECTOR RICHARD COOK POINTS OUT DURING A LECTURE AT THE ANNUAL CONFERENCE OF THE INTERNATIONAL ASTRONAUTICAL FOUNDATION IN TURIN (1997), "SCIENTIFIC EXPERIMENT ISN'T MARS PATHFINDER'S FIRST PRIORITY. PATHFINDER HAS AS ITS PRIMARY OBJECTIVE THAT EVERYBODY ON EARTH CAN GET IN TOUCH WITH THE MARTIAN ENVIRONMENT." NASA PUBLISHES A PATHFINDER SOJOURNER ROVER SIMULATION, A WEB INTERFACE FOR TELESCIENCE (WITS) AND HUNDREDS OF PHOTOS ON ITS WEBSITE, ALLOWING WEB-USERS TO "INTERACT WITH THE ROVER JUST AS A SCIENTIST OR MISSION PLANNER WOULD." THE LATTER TWO APPLICATIONS WERE DEVELOPED BY THE JET PROPULSION LABORATORY IN COOPERATION WITH THE INTELLIGENT MECHANISMS GROUP AT THE AMES RESEARCH CENTER, FOURTH PLANET INC. AND SILICON GRAPHICS INC.

//1997 — QUAKE II, ID, computer game
Refining the formal structure of DOOM, QUAKE II enhances play with AI (artificial intelligence) as well as speed and detail. Stroggs (virtual opponents) are programmed with unsophisticated dynamic combat adaptability: even if an enemy is armed, it will try to attack you through a wall as you pick it off. After testing QUAKE II, the German Independent Self-Rating Organisation (USK) decides the game is too violent for even the highest age rating (18 and over), and further deems it "harmful to young people." AI is now used in the majority of computer games.

1998

//1998 — March: STARCRAFT, BLIZZARD ENTERTAINMENT, computer game
On March 31, STARCRAFT, the real-time strategy game from Irvine, California-based BLIZZARD ENTERTAINMENT, hits stores in the United States and Canada. Set at the edge of the Galaxy, the player assumes military command of Terrans, Protoss or Zerg species. Resources are managed from a 3D isometric perspective, with engagements on planetary surfaces and within installations. Thirty single-player missions unfold a space narrative, and networked play is supported via the Internet.

//1998 — BATTLEZONE 1998, ACTIVISION, computer game
BATTLEZONE 1998 commissions the player as Supreme Commander, responsible for either Soviet or US military space operations. Commanding

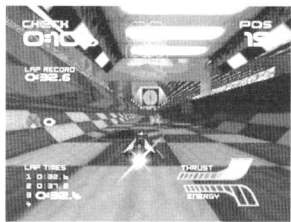

OM STATUS BAR.GIF

WIPEOUT.PICT

PATHFINDER.JPG

BATTLE ZONE.JPG

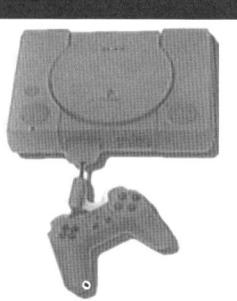

PLAYSTATION.JPG

VIRTUAL BOY.JPG

EUROMOON LOGO.JPG

//1995 — SEGA enters 32-bit arena
The SEGA SATURN deploys twin 28.8 MHz 32-bit microprocessors and parallel processing, feeding on CD-based software. The SATURN is earmarked for many in-house arcade conversions.

//1995 — Launch of SONY PLAYSTATION
The world's most popular 32-bit games console — originally designed as a CD attachment for the NINTENDO Super NES — runs at 33 MHz and is specifically created for polygon graphics. Additional attachments include memory cards, a mouse and a network cable.

//1995 — NINTENDO releases VIRTUAL BOY
Priced at $179.99 on release, the VIRTUAL BOY displays 3D images through a head-mounted display, in red and black, with tiny mirrored screens for each eye. Designed by Gumpei Yokoi and developed in Massachusetts by Reflection Technologies, the machine uses a 10 MHz 32-bit microprocessor to create the illusion of objects in three dimensions.

//1996 — NINTENDO releases N64
Working with Silicon Graphics to produce the 93.75 MHz 64-bit microprocessor, NINTENDO introduces the N64 — the first 64-bit dedicated games console, capable of rendering leading-edge interactive virtual worlds. The machine retails for under $150, including hand-controller.

//1997 — PATHFINDER is effectively cheaper than a movie
MARS PATHFINDER, ONE OF THE FIRST PUBLIC EXAMPLES OF NASA'S NEW POLICY, IS LAUNCHED BY CHIEF ADMINISTRATOR DAN GOLDIN AS "FASTER, CHEAPER, BETTER." PLANNED, DESIGNED AND EXECUTED WITHIN THREE YEARS, PATHFINDER COSTS $250 MILLION — JUST LESS THAN THE PRODUCTION COSTS OF STEVEN SPIELBERG'S *JURASSIC PARK*.

//1998 — ESA's EUROMOON 2000 project is canceled
IN MARCH, THE ESA COUNCIL CANCELS THE UNMANNED LUNAR SOUTH POLE EXPEDITION UNDER DEVELOPMENT AT ESTEC (ESA'S RESEARCH CENTER IN NOORDWIJK, THE NETHERLANDS), WHICH WAS TO HAVE MARKED THE PROGRESS OF EUROPE'S SPACE ACTIVITIES INTO THE NEW MILLENNIUM. EUROMOON 2000 WOULD HAVE PUT A LANDER AT THE CONTINUOUSLY SUNLIT SOUTH POLE OF THE MOON, THE 'PEAK OF ETERNAL LIGHT,' CONSIDERED BY ESTEC THE MOST PROMISING SITE FOR AN INTERNATIONAL MANNED OUTPOST. THE LANDER WOULD HAVE PLACED AN 'ESA PAYLOAD' AND A 'MILLENNIUM CHALLENGE PAYLOAD' ON THE SURFACE, BOTH CONTAINING ROBOTIC DEVICES. THE FORMER FOR THE PURPOSES OF SCIENTIFIC EXPLORATION, I.E. TO SEARCH FOR FROZEN WATER. THE LATTER HAS TO HAVE CONTAINED THREE ROVERS IN WHICH WINNERS OF A MILLENNIUM CHALLENGE CONTEST WOULD RACE TO THE SOUTH POLE. THE PRIZE: TO NAME THE AS-YET UNEXPLORED AND UNMANNED LUNAR SOUTH POLE AND ITS FUTURE HUMAN OUTPOST.

1999

over 30 unique units, the player engages in combat and strategic operations to exploit an alien material. Set on seven distinct moons and planets, BATTLEZONE 1998 presents the "real" space race, featuring highly detailed 3-dimensional worlds and actual imges from NASA space expeditions. (The original coin-op BATTLEZONE [ATARI INC. 1980] was the first game to present an interactive first-person 3D environment; modifications of the coin-operated machine were ordered by Major Dave Robinson of the U.S. Army, to train gunners for the Infantry Fighting Vehicle.)

//1998 – PROJECT VON NEUMANN, Caltech, computer game
Under development at California Institute of Technology, PROJECT VON NEUMANN seeks to create a game, set in the 21st century, with advanced AI enemies: the opponents are endowed with life courtesy of Genetic Algorithms and other Artificial Life techniques. These virtual creatures have their own agendas, motives, weaknesses and needs, which evolve during the course of the game. The interface is standard: in a 2D universe, the player controls a ship that can move forward and backward, turn and fire, and has other capabilities.

//1999 – MIR, RKA, lost mission
IN FEBRUARY 1999, THE LAST MISSION TO SPACE STATION MIR IS LAUNCHED. THE ONLY MANNED SPACE STATION FOR THE PAST 20 YEARS, MIR IS REPLACED BY THE INTERNATIONAL SPACE STATION. FOR WHICH IT SERVED AS A TEST FACILITY. THE RUSSIAN SPACE AGENCY HAD PLANNED TO KEEP THE MIR OPERATIONAL FOR TWO MORE YEARS, BUT GIVES IN TO NASA'S DEMANDS TO DISASSEMBLE THE STATION. SINCE NASA WILL CEASE FUNDING MIR AFTER 1999, THE STATION WILL THEN HAVE SPENT 13 YEARS IN SPACE. ALMOST TWICE ITS PREDICTED LIFE-SPAN, HAVING COMPLETED APPROXIMATELY 72,000 EARTHS ORBITS.

2000 2001 2002 2003 2004 200

//2004 – INTERNATIONAL SPACE STATION, NASA/RKA/ESA/NASDA, assembly complete
AT THE END OF THE YEAR 2004, THE IN-ORBIT ASSEMBLY OF THE COMPONENTS OF INTERNATIONAL SPACE STATION ALPHA, BEGUN IN NOVEMBER 1998, IS COMPLETE. THE STATION COSTS MORE THAN $50 BILLION, WEIGHS 500,000 KILOGRAMS AND EXCEEDS THE SIZE OF A FOOTBALL FIELD (108M BY 78 MM) UP TO SEVEN PEOPLE WILL LIVE IN THE SPACE STATION. EACH SPACE AGENCY HAS ITS OWN RESEARCH MODULE DEDICATED TO CHEMICAL, BIOLOGICAL AND MEDICAL RESEARCH. SEVERAL COMMERCIAL CONTRACTORS HAVE CONTRIBUTED TO ALPHA, INCLUDING AEROSPATIALE (FRANCE), LOCKHEED MARTIN (US), KRUNICHEV (RUSSIA) AND FOKKER SPACE (NETHERLANDS). NASA ADVERTISES ISS AS THE "LARGEST INTERNATIONAL PEACETIME LABORATORY IN HISTORY [THAT] DEMONSTRATES U.S. LEADERSHIP OVER THE GLOBAL COMMUNITY, LIGHTING THE PATHWAY FOR PEACEFUL COOPERATION BETWEEN NATIONS IN THE 21ST CENTURY." EVERY TWO YEARS, TWO SPACE SHUTTLES WILL NEED TO RAISE THE STATION TO KEEP IT IN ITS APPROPRIATE ORBIT, 300 KM ABOVE EARTH.

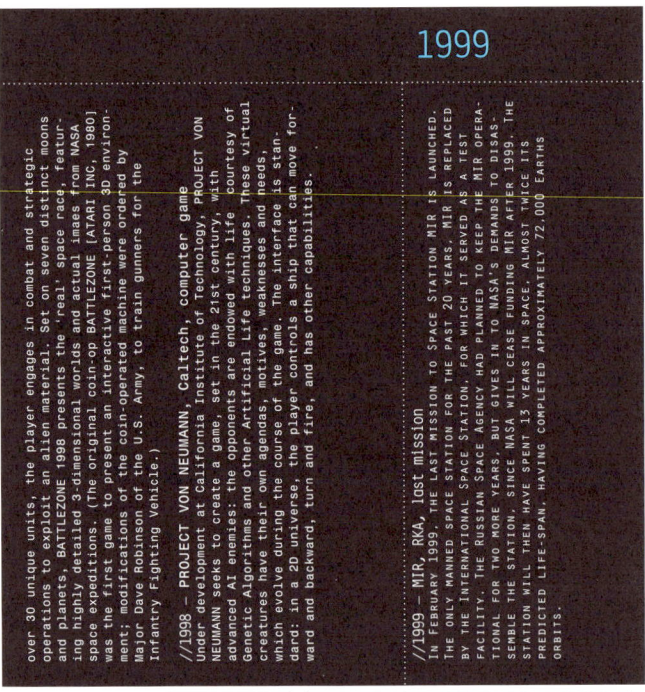
BATTLEZONE ACTION.JPG

VON NEUMANN.LOGO.GIF

CONSOLE.JPG

Dreamcast™
LOGO.GIF

//1998 – PIONEER 10 radio-signals are still in use
WITH ITS INTEL-CHIP AND RADIO-ANTENNAE STILL FUNCTIONING, PIONEER 10's REAL-TIME TRACKS PROVIDE A RADIO-BEACON TO CONFIRM STATION TRACKING, AND SERVE TO TEST RECEIVER PERFORMANCE DURING LUNAR PROSPECTOR – NASA's DISCOVERY-MISSION, AND HEIR TO PIONEER'S COMMUNICATIONS CENTER. THE SIGNALS ARE ALSO USED TO TRAIN SPACECRAFT CONTROLLERS IN STATION-TRACKING PROTOCOL AND DATA-ARCHIVING PROCEDURES AT AMES RESEARCH CENTER.

//1998 – DEEP SPACE 1, NASA, asteroid flyby
IN NOVEMBER, NASA LAUNCHES DEEP SPACE I. THE FIRST PROBE OF THE NEW MILLENNIUM PROGRAM, WHICH WILL FLY BY A NEAR-EARTH ASTEROID AS CLOSE AS 10 KM ABOVE THE SURFACE. THE SPACECRAFT IS EQUIPPED WITH IONIC PROPULSION AND OTHER CUTTING-EDGE TECHNOLOGIES, AS A REMOTE AGENT, DEEP SPACE 1 NAVIGATES THE ASTEROID BELT PARTLY AUTONOMOUSLY, AND CONTACTS MISSION CONTROL ONLY WHEN SPECIFIC PROBLEMS OCCUR. IT IS PROGRAMMED TO IGNORE INSTRUCTIONS IN THE CASE OF ERRONEOUS COMMANDS.

//1998 – SEGA releases first 128-bit game console
Expected to retail at $250, the SEGA DREAMCAST features powerful hardware – 200MHz CPU optimised for 3D performance, 16MB main memory and Microsoft's DirectX 5.2 – and also includes innovations such the VMS, a handheld memory/portable game device.

//1999 – LUNAR-A, NASDA, Lunar orbiter
IN MARCH, NASDA LAUNCHES LUNAR-A, A LUNAR ORBITER EQUIPPED WITH THREE PENETRATORS WHICH WILL BE SHOT THREE METERS DEEP INTO THE LUNAR SURFACE. WEIGHING 3 KG EACH, THEY CARRY A SEISMOMETER TO RECORD MOON-QUAKES, DEVICES TO MEASURE THE MOON'S SUBSURFACE HEAT FLOW, AND A MICROCHIP TO STORE DATA THAT WILL BE TRANSMITTED TO THE ORBITER WHEN IT COMES BACK INTO SIGHT.

//1999 – VM Labs releases PROJECT X media processor
Continuing its tactics of technology-licensing, VM Labs has created media processors capable of performing 1.5 billion programmable instructions per second (the SONY PLAYSTATION runs at 30). Taking advantage of DVD's storage capabilities, PROJECT X is capable of hosting a new level of interactive entertainment.

//42 years remaining...

1999

2000 2001 2002 2003 2004   200

06 2007 2008 2009   2010 2011 2012 2013 2014 2015 2016 2017 2018 2019 20

//52 years remaining...

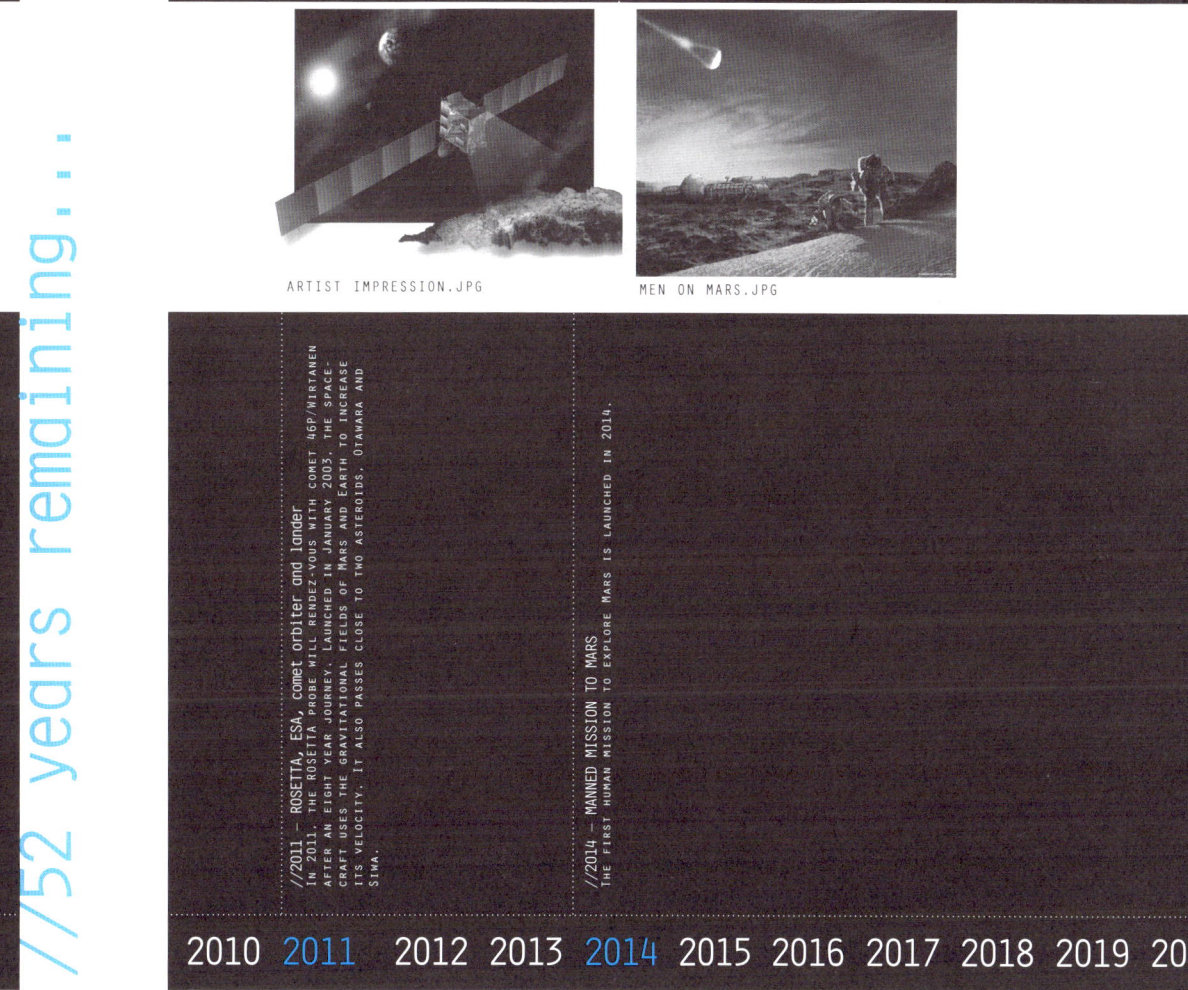

ARTIST IMPRESSION.JPG   MEN ON MARS.JPG

//2011 — ROSETTA, ESA, comet orbiter and lander
IN 2011, THE ROSETTA PROBE WILL RENDEZ-VOUS WITH COMET 46P/WIRTANEN AFTER AN EIGHT YEAR JOURNEY. LAUNCHED IN JANUARY 2003, THE SPACE-CRAFT USES THE GRAVITATIONAL FIELDS OF MARS AND EARTH TO INCREASE ITS VELOCITY. IT ALSO PASSES CLOSE TO TWO ASTEROIDS, OTAWARA AND SIWA.

//2014 — MANNED MISSION TO MARS
THE FIRST HUMAN MISSION TO EXPLORE MARS IS LAUNCHED IN 2014.

06 2007 2008 2009   2010 2011 2012 2013 2014 2015 2016 2017 2018 2019 20

KLIMT MEETS THE COIN-OPS

The 1898 Vienna Secession building is possibly the last place one would expect to find a video-game arcade. But in 1998, artist **Jason Rhoades** pitted the brash commercial art of our own fin-de-siècle against that of Vienna's rebel artists of a century ago. In *A Few Free Years: The History of the Joystick, the Button, the Knob and the Coin Slot*, 1998, Rhoades set a double row of video-game machines in this effulgent white-walled sanctuary, juxtaposing their garish hues and electronic cacophony against the delicate swirls of Gustav Klimt's *Beethoven Frieze*, painted directly beneath the ceiling. Klimt would probably have approved. As if confirming Rhoades' license to play, the Secession motto, inscribed on the building, reads "To each period, its art; to art, its liberty."

VIENNA SECESSION 1898 JASON RHOADES 1998

It was in Amsterdam that we had our first proper conversation, Pierre and myself. A mutual
Friend had introduced us in the bar at the ICA, maybe two years

Previously, but I don't think we had seen each other since, apart from that time
In Glasgow — when was that? May 1995? — when Pierre did his best to get me to see an
Exhibition of his, which was taking place somewhere in France if I
Remember correctly. I didn't make it over in the end, much as I would have liked to (I had
Recently moved to Italy so that may have had something to do with it). And so it
Ended up that we didn't meet or talk again for some time. It was nice, then, to

Be invited to take part in a conference in Amsterdam, particularly when
I learned that Pierre was to participate also. And so one day, I found myself at a table in de Balie,
Sorting out my notes, trying to make sense of my handwriting and the smudge of the barely
More legible photocopies which I had brought with me. I had been up late the previous night,
Under the deluded impression that the pressure of work might help me work, and now,
Too tired to think clearly, I clearly see Pierre's face grinning its way towards me. We
Hugged and exchanged greetings before getting some more coffee and

Talking about what we'd both been up to since we had last met. He told me about
How the show in Tours — that was it, Tours — had gone (well, it seemed) and
Explained some of the pieces which he had included there. I couldn't help
Noticing that he kept looking down at my notes as he spoke. We talked about

Jazz as he had made a piece, *Blue Monk in Progress*, which consisted of a Cage-like musical
Experiment. In this piece, Pierre attempted to play Thelonius Monk's *Blue Monk*, a feat
Remarkable for the fact that Pierre, who cannot play the piano, performed it without a score. The
Entire piece was memorised by the computer-controlled baby-grand and this new
Musical piece was played back automatically throughout the exhibition. This version was different
Yet recognisable; later, a piano teacher played the new score perfectly, Pierre's

Mistakes becoming fixed through transcription. We began talking about how errors can become
In effect, new laws, about how arbitrary decisions can have far-reaching consequences much
Later on, and for many more people. I suggested that it was something which
Lay at the heart of his own work and he looked at the notes I had made earlier and pointed
At a quotation I had taken from Sol LeWitt: 'Conceptual artists are mystics rather than
Rationalists. They leap to conclusions that logic cannot reach.' And he smiled.

Toys Were Us

PIETER BRUEGEL THE ELDER, *CHILDREN'S GAMES* KUNSTHISTORISCHES MUSEUM, VIENNA

Toys Were Us

Michiel Schwarz offers a guided tour of the games portrayed in Pieter Bruegel's famous street scene *Children's Games* — soon to be given a new spin by students in the HKU/Utrecht School of the Arts animation program.

Capturing the richness of life at play, Pieter Bruegel the Elder's painting *Children's Games* (*Kinderspelen*, 1560) shows just how much fun was to be had in the sixteenth century Flemish street: more than seventy different games, from trundling to blind-man's bluff, from skittles to walking on stilts, from the familiar to the obscure. Some games we no longer recognise, let alone play; others seem timeless, even in the Nintendo era. By contrast with today's technological culture, the specially-designed toy is conspicuous by its absence: instead, everyday objects are used for playing; broomsticks, a barrel, a string, nuts, pebbles. And the child's play of the Renaissance town had not yet entered the mechanical age. Clockwork toys did not come into being for another century or so (the first modern mechanical toy was made in 1672, when Nuremberg craftsmen were commissioned to design performing soldiers for the son of Louis XIV).

The world of play as seen by Bruegel is the world of human ingenuity and, above all, of the imagination. *Children's Games* (measuring 161 cm x 118 cm, now at the Kunsthistorisches Museum in Vienna) is probably the first detailed painting of what Johan Huizinga, another Dutchman, would describe several centuries later as *Homo Ludens* — Man as Player. In his seminal book Homo Ludens (published in 1938), Huizinga located play at the centre of human culture. In fact, in his view, "play is older than culture." Looking back at Bruegel's fascinating scene, Huizinga's reflections on play are particularly apt. "A playing child is quite literally besides himself; he almost believes that he's actually such and such a thing without, however, wholly losing consciousness of 'ordinary reality'. The child's representation is a realisation of appearance: 'imagination' in the original sense of the word." That is the perspective from which we should explore the plenitude of play in Bruegel's *Children's Games*. The more we look, the more we discover.

sources Grietje Hartman & Ellen Lens, *Hééé Jôh Kom je buiten spelen: De Spelregels bij* De kinderspelen *van Pieter Bruegel de Oude*, Bert Bakker, Amsterdam, 1976.

Johan Huizinga, *Homo Ludens — a study of the play-element in culture*. Routledge, London 1944; originally published in Dutch in 1938.

If/Then — Toys Were Us — Michiel Schwarz

The 72 games and children's play activities that can be seen in Peter Bruegel's 1560 painting *Children's Games*:

1 'Dibs' — Game of Knuckles
A game of skill with five knuckles or knuckle-shaped pebbles: throw one in the air and pick up the next one with the same hand before you make the catch.

2 Dolls Play
Let's be mother: play with your doll, dressing it, washing it, combing its hair.

3 Christening Procession
Dress up with rags as cloaks and follow the imaginary baby on its way to an imaginary church.

4 Nut Mill
Take a nut, add a stick with cardboard wings, attach a string and make it spin.

5 Blowing Soap Bubbles
Soap, water and a straw (or the stem of a pipe) is all you need for a rainbow bubble.

6 Playing with a Bird
Catch a bird and make it do whatever you want.

7 Making Rush Hats
Turn a twig and bits of rush into a cone-shaped hat.

8 Shingle Rattle
Make a little box, fill it with pebbles or seeds, fix it to a handle and shake for sound.

9 Reading Mass
Make your own altar anywhere and preach whatever you fancy.

10 Water Squirt
Fill your popgun with water and squirt away.

11 Masks Put on a mask and frighten your mates.

12 Swinging
A cord attached to a beam, and a piece of timber to sit on — all you need to make a swing.

13 Blind-man's Bluff
Catching your friend blindfold is a real skill, especially after you've been spun around a number of times.

14 Odd or Even: 'How many am I holding?'
Guess the right number of nuts or beans or marbles in your friend's hand and you win them.

15 Buttock-seat
Two pairs of crossed arms make for a fleshy seat.

16 Hobbyhorse Riding
A horse-head on a wooden stick, and off you go!

17 Pot-drum and flute
Stretch a pig skin over an earthenware pot to make music, and play the wooden flute.

18 Poop-stirring Stick a twig in the shit and stir: what fun!

19 Hoop Trundling Roll the hoop, using a hoopstick.

20 Hole of a Barrel
Call into the vessel to make hollow sounds.

21 Playing on a Pig's Bladder
Blow up the bag, then whistle and drum.

22 Seesaw on a Barrel
Rocking back and forth, who will be last to fall off?

23 Guess what's behind my back?
Your hand is a Hammer (fist), a Knife (index finger), Scissors (index and middle fingers), a Fork (three or four fingers), a Spoon (clutched hand facing up), or a Tub (two hands clutched together in a ball).

24 Play Shop
Be the shopkeeper, with make-believe merchandise and make-believe money.

25 Knife-Throwing
Choose a target on the ground and throw the knife at it. The most accurate aim wins the game.

26 Bum-thumping
The price for losing: have your buttocks banged against a beam.

27 Building Bricks
Construct a water wheel, or any other structure, out of stones and bricks.

28 Hair-pulling
Who said play was fun? Have your friends pull at your hair.

29 Beating Beetles
Hit the trunk so the beetles and insects come to the surface, then 'Wham!'

30 Holding A Pagan Loaf
Play with your bread.

31 Hat Games
Use a hat for a hood, and when the blindfolded player steps on your hat, you're game for the other hatted lot.

32 Tug of War over a Stone
A game going back to the Grecian Age: get on the horse's back and pull your enemy over the stone without falling off yourself.

33 Leap-Frog
Vault, with parted legs, over your bent-over friend and become the hurdle for the next round.

34 Run the Gauntlet
Pass the row of children, who are all trying to trip you up.

35 The Tobacco-roll
Cross your legs in crouched position, hold your left ankle with your right hand and your right ankle with your left hand, and somersault through the grass.

36 Heel-Bumming
Stand on your head, wave your legs up and down and touch your backside with your heels.

37 Tumbler
Somersault your way through the garden.

38 Horse-riding on the Fence
The fence can be your steed: spur it on and whip it up with your stick.

39 Wedding-procession
Act out a wedding procession, complete with bride (wearing a crown), a trailing skirt, and bridesmaids throwing flowers.

40 Hitting the Pot Blindfold
You're blindfold and spun around, now try to hit the pot with your stick. Three misses and you owe a forfeit.

41 Walking on Stilts
Make stilts out of hazelwood or alderwood and stand two-metres high, or make shorter ones, about half a metre above the ground.

42 Shingles and Marbles
Make a little pile with four shingles or marbles, then throw one of your shingles at the pile. A hit and you win all four; a miss and you lose four shingles.

43 Pulling the Slipper
The blindman holds a stick with a slipper attached, and hits anyone he can, while the others try to pull the slipper off. Whoever gets hit with the slipper becomes the blindman next round.

44 Sticks' Play
One player throws his little stick as close as possible to a small pot-hole in the street, while the other attempts to knock it away mid-air with his stick. The distance between stick and pothole is measured: each stick-length is a point for the opposition; 100 points and you win the game.

45 Ball in the Hole
Throw or roll your ball into one of the little holes in the ground, each hole belonging to one player. If the ball ends up in your hole, you have to throw the ball at the other players. The player who is hit most is the loser.

46 Devil with a Chord
The 'devil' on the chair and his helper are holding a cord and together try to catch one of other players (who can hit the 'devil'). If you're caught, you become the 'devil', while the former 'devil' becomes the helper, and the helper is set free.

47 Knuckle-Bones Skittles
Use the knucklebones of sheep or cows to make a row of skittles; win each of the skittles by knocking them over with your knucklebone. Other players can also lay bets on which way the skittle will fall.

48 Board-walking
Run up a sloped door or board and try to knock off the hat hanging on a stick at the top of the 'runway.'

49 Street-fight
An everyday occurrence when play gets out of hand: the battle is settled in a fisticuffs (the bucket of ice-water may help lower the heat of things).

50 Procession
March through the street with colours made out of sticks and rags for a jolly public procession.

51 Trudge
Hold on to the coat or skirt of the child in front of you and make a train, trudging through the streets.

52 Coin to Coin
Your opponent throws his coin against a wall; now try to ricochet yours against the wall so it hits his coin. If you succeed you win his coin.

53 Shoving the Balls
Hide the ball under the skirt of one of your friends: another girl has to guess where the ball has been put.

54 Follow-the-Leader
Do exactly what the leader does: hold your arms in the air, jump on a step, or whatever move the leader cares to make.

55 Horseman
Sit on your friend's shoulders and be the horseman: give orders to go right or left, gallop, run or come to a halt. But watch out: the horse may prance and throw you off.

56 The Four Sons of Ayymon and the Horse
With a broom as horse for four, try to catch your opponent running away (thereby acting out the knight's story of the Four Sons of Ayymon on their horse challenging Charlemagne in medieval times).

57 Saint John's Fire
Collect twigs, peat, wood and other fuel for a bonfire (originally for the evening of St John's, June 23).

58 Tumbling on the Bar
The bar for attaching the horses' reins can also be used for all kinds of balancing acts.

59 Balancing the Broom
Keeping the broom balanced upright is a real skill; if you can do it on your hand or finger, try balancing it on your nose.

60 Carrying the Calf
Carry someone on your back, as if carrying a calf to the shed. (This could be your penalty for losing another game.)

61 Rattle
Even the simplest rattle will get you attention.

62 Playing with a Whipping Top
Wind the cord of the whip around the spinning top, then pull — makes for one of the earliest toys (spinning tops were found in Egypt more than 3000 years ago).

63 Pinwheels' Tournament
Stick a wing on top of a stick, run, and your pinwheel will spin in the wind.

64 Climbing the Fence
If you weren't supposed to climb over it, why on earth would they have put this fence up?

65 Defending the hilltop
You're the King: push off anyone who challenges you on your 'mountain.'

66 Who sits in the Tall Tower?
Sit in your 'tower' among a circle of children, push one of them over and they all run away. The victim has to catch the next one to sit in the 'tower'.

67 Pirouette
Spin around so your skirt is raised, quickly crouch, and catch the air.

68 Playing Ball
If you don't have one of those white leather balls filled with cows' or horses' hair, you can always sew one out of a rag, filling it with saw-dust, sand, or grit.

69 Tree climbing
Climb the tree, just for fun, or for the eggs from a bird's nest (prized objects of exchange).

70 Swimming
Enjoy the fun of water play and swimming, especially with one of those pig's bladder air bags.

71 Flying a Ribbon
A ribbon on a stick: watch it fly in the wind (or make out it's a fishing rod).

72 Hanging Out the Baskets
Plaited-rush baskets can be hung on the outside of the building. (Is it a game, or mere decoration?).

Jasia Reichardt (ed.), *Play Orbit*. Studio International, London, 1969.

Simon Schama, *The Embarrassment of Riches: An interpretation of Dutch Culture in the Golden Age*. Harper Collins, New York, 1987.

THREE

In a suitably fairytale building on Amsterdam's Nieuwezijds Voorburgwal you find IJsfontein, the multimedia company famed for its beautiful children's CD-ROM game *Meesters van Macht* (*Masters of the Elements*) — a big hit, and deservedly so, because its creators paid attention not only to navigation and design, but also to the narrative and educational elements. "I was sorry to have to stop playing in order to write this review," the *NRC-Handelsblad*'s new media critic declared, when *Meesters* was published in 1998 by VNU [1]. Children learn the basic principles of natural science by exploring a big castle, assisted by several Magicians: the eponymous Masters of Light, Gravity, Coincidence, Time and Electricity. You get around not by clicking, but by grabbing things and dragging them to the right spot, figuring out what action is needed to get any further. For example, you can only make a train run if you've caught the fuel falling out of a cuckoo's nest, and the electricity only works if a battery is properly positioned.

In their spacious office, Hayo Wagenaar and Jan Willem Huisman are both wearing white shirts, blue pants and polished shoes; Hayo even has the company logo embroidered on his shirt. Along with the third partner, Sander Hassing, the IJsfontein trio graduated three years ago in interaction design from the Utrecht School of the Arts (HKU), having already begun working together during their student days. Their final thesis project *Koning Winter* (*The Winter King*) eventually developed into the *Meesters van Macht* CD-ROM, following a successful presentation at MILIA's Young Talent Pavilion. A portrait of the Winter King (precursor to the *Meesters'* Magicians) hangs framed on the office wall, a classic 'Wagenaar' recognisable by its engaging children's book illustration style.

IJsfontein's projects typically begin with discussions around a table, where ideas and words are brainstormed. Wagenaar starts sketching, designs the environments, focuses on the details and creates the visual scenarios. Huisman

FROM *MEESTERS VAN MACHT*

1 *NRC-Handelsblad* July 30 1998

When the Dutch TV station VPRO decided to get into networked games, it commissioned interaction designers IJsfontein. **Ine Poppe** meets the three magicians behind *Meesters van Macht* and the *TypoToons* TV/Internet childrens' series, launched in April 1999.

FROM *MEESTERS VAN MACHT*

keeps the overview, writes the concepts, and brings the storylines together. Hassing programs the animations and researches different ways of interacting via the mouse.

"We've known each other since puberty!" says Huisman, pointing at Wagenaar. "We started with a window-cleaning business, called *Splash*. We always wanted to be our own bosses." Asked where they think IJsfontein stands in the Dutch computer-game developers market, Wagenaar replies that "the distinctions between companies have to do with their history and their principles, for example, if they're primarily a facilities company. Our *modus operandi* is to think about the user's point of view. All our ideas are based on that."

Huisman adds, "The player is central. What follows is a simple question: how can you use the mouse creatively to increase the interaction between the user and what's on the screen?" Wagenaar explains that IJsfontein divides its work between games, education, and business in 'playful form' — by which he means that the kind of seduction used in the games context can also be deployed in business applications.

Right now, IJsfontein is designing and developing the television/internet game *TypoToons*, a project initiated by Frank Alsema, director and producer for Dutch broadcaster VPRO. Alsema is interested in working with interactive designers, and hired IJsfontein because of its game-design experience. "I saw children playing *Quake* on networks, and got interested in linking networked games with television," says Alsema. "I wanted to try combining interactivity and the use of the

2 *TypoToons*© 1998 VPRO/IJsfontein

In the first phase of *TypoToons*, children play online together, forming words which are then used to compile the basis of the TV scenario.

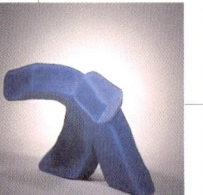 

SKETCHES FOR TYPOTOONS LETTERS, © NOB/VPRO 1998

PC with TV." And he is looking for new forms of storytelling: in *Typotoons*, children co-write the story for a television program by taking part in a multi-user Internet game.

The *TypoToons* television series consists of three phases — modules which are repeated each week:

Phase One:
Internet game

Children are introduced to the animated typographic characters known as the *TypoToons*, and their adventures, through a series of games and tasks. The first phase of the project takes place on the Web, with children playing a word-game online. Every child is assigned a letter, and together these online participants form words which are then used by a children's book author, based in the Internet studio, to compile a story forming the basis of the TV scenario. (Different authors compose each week's story.) For the three days following this first Netcast, children can help write a continuation of the story in the same way, and are also invited to submit drawings for the decor of the TV series. Every night on the web a winner is selected, so after all four evenings, there are four winners — comprising the 'Typo-Team'.

Live on VPRO's website, four nights a week, from each Sunday, 19.00-20.00, starting April 1999.

Phase Two:
TypoToon TV Animation

The story Phase One is turned into an animation, using the drawings submitted by children to create

SKETCHES FOR **TYPOTOONS** ANIMATED LETTERS
© IJSFONTEIN/VPRO 1998

THE WRITER'S ROOM, SKETCH FOR **TYPOTOONS**
© IJSFONTEIN/VPRO 1998

Children are the ideal audience for evaluating the coming hybrid of TV and Internet, because more and more of them are watching and surfing at the same time.

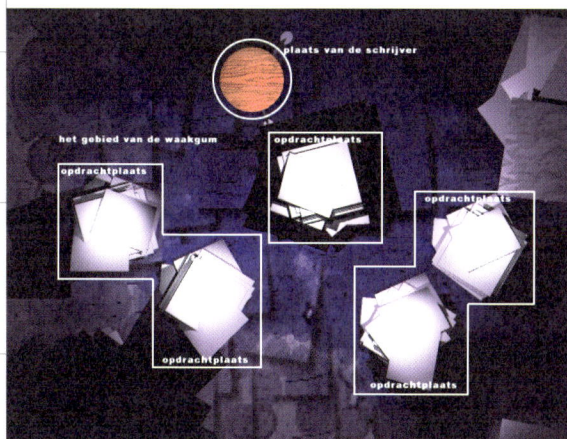

WRITER'S ROOM, PLAN VIEW, SHOWING TYPOTOONS' ACTIVITY ZONES
© IJSFONTEIN/VPRO 1998

the fairytale-like surroundings in which the *TypoToons*' adventures take place. The eight-minute animation is created by the NOB (Nederlands Omroep Bedrijf, the technical facilities for Netherlands broadcasting). The adventure ends in a cliff-hanger, challenging the TypoTeam members to come up with a happy ending.
Broadcast weekly on VPRO from 10.00-10.08 on Sundays, in the youth programming slot.

Phase Three: Television Game

Immediately after the animation, the 'interactive adventure' begins — a computer-game on television. The TypoTeam members now play against each other, practising for half a week with the *TypoToons* characters and their environment, using multimedia computers provided by VPRO, which are connected to a Silicon Graphics Onyx at NOB in Hilversum.[3] The information from the TypoTeam computers is shown live on television, rendered in high resolution and with multiple camera-angles, so VPRO viewers can actually watch what the children are doing live, at home on their PCs.

The four TypoTeam members are assigned one capital letter apiece, each of which has its own individual handicap, and they must coöperate to guess a word. The *TypoToons*' adventures are rendered in virtual space, and for the purposes of character animation, the alphabet is divided into four categories: two-legged letters (such as an 'N') are the only ones able to run faster than the eraser; 'flatfooted' ones (such as capital 'E') are slow-moving; round ones (such as 'C' or 'O') have a balance problem; and 'single-legged' letters (such as 'I') have to hop! The task of the two-legged letters is to distract the eraser so the other letters can get together and form the word that will solve the story's cliffhanger.
VistaBox interactive computer game, broadcast weekly on VPRO, 10.08-10.14, on Sundays, immediately following the animation.

And the story continues, that same evening: all children with an internet connection are now invited back to the web, to co-write the continuation of the *TypoToons*' adventure, because on Sunday nights the web phase begins again. "Simply put," says IJsfontein's Huisman, "the story is about the *TypoToons*, lively letters that — along with the children — assist the writer in composing an adventure. Together they compose the story and design the environment." Wagenaar says he's interested in the extent to which children will coöperate, and whether that can be steered by software applications. "It is an experiment in which we're trying to find out what works. It might turn out that the children can't make progress unless they help each other." Huisman explains that although a few hundred visitors can be expected to visit the Web site during the hour-long netcast, only 26 people will actually be able to take part at a time. "We've already thought of a solution to one of the technical limitations," he says. "Some children will 'drop out', as in *Musical Chairs*, so others can take their place."

Children are the ideal audience for evaluating the coming hybrid of TV and Internet, because more and more of them are watching and surfing at the same time. So *TypoToons* will be an interesting experiment in integrating different media, exploring ideas about their mutual use and influence: a combination of linear television broadcast, interactive multi-user game, and online narrative. And all this in a surrounding as attractive as *Meesters van Macht*.

---

3 *VistaBox* — the client-server technology behind *TypoToons* — has been developed by VPRO and NOB with funding from the European Union's ESPRIT Information Technology research program.

other victories

Uri Tzaig plays games with games — redefining the rules of traditional sports, such as football and basketball, and inventing new interactions, scoring systems and social dynamics on the field of play.

On the following pages, Tzaig presents his recent work in a manual made in collaboration with graphic designer Danny Goldberg.

Two soldiers playing checkers with salt and pepper shakers in a coffee bar, Tel Aviv, 1998.

A User's Guide to games by Uri Tzaig
Two-ball soccer
Two-ball basketball
Play
Trance
∞
Paint ball
Magnet ball
Moon-eye window
Buffer ball

Concept and Design: Danny Goldberg, Uri Tzaig **Photography:** Pierre Leguillon, Adi Shniderman **Technical Drawings:** Tsur Reshef

Two-Ball Soccer

Components:
Soccer field
2 teams, 11 players each
2 balls
2 referees

Rules: The game is played according to the basic rules of soccer, except for the extra ball.

Object: To score goals into the opposing team's goal.

Duration: Two 30-minute halves.

Note: In this game the player's chances of touching the ball are increased, and his/her movement is faster. He/she quickly abandons all familiar strategies, reacting to the new possibilities.

History: First played in Lod, Israel, February 1996.

Photography: One camera is placed in fixed position above one of the goals. The other goal is seen swollen in perspective. The playing field's boundaries (grid) correspond to the monitor's grid lines. The picture is remote, uninvolved.

Video Editing:

Title: *The Universal Square*

Screen Layout: A rectangular screen format as in cinema, on which the image appears in a sequence showing 30 minutes' documentation of the second half of Two Ball Soccer game. On the field, the movement continues forward (toward the goal closest to the camera) and backward (toward the goal furthest from the camera).

On the bottom part of the screen, taking up one third of its width, a line of text from *The Universal Square* (a story by Uri Tzaig) is presented. The complete text is divided equally throughout the entire film: 3 seconds for one line of English text.

The lack of immediate connection between text and image, and its presentation in a familiar format of translation/subtitles, opens up new possibilities for reading the interrelations between them, expropriating — as in the game itself — the presence of a common centre.

Note: This work can be reconstructed by translating the text into different languages (editions available in English, Hebrew, Dutch and French).

Two-Ball Basketball

Components:
Basketball court
Two teams, 5 players each
2 balls
2 referees

Rules: The game is played according to the basic rules of soccer, except for the extra ball.

Object: To score points by shooting into the opposing team's basket.

Duration: Two 20-minute halves.

Note: In this game the player's chances of touching the ball are increased, and his/her movement is faster. He/she quickly abandons all familiar strategies, reacting to the new possibilities.

History: First played in Limerick, Ireland, in April 1996.

Photography: One camera, positioned on a higher level, commands an overview. A second camera follows the action on court at eye-level.

Video Editing:

Title: *Desert*

Screen Layout: In order to translate the issue of duality, inherent in the game itself, into the elements mediating it, the video is comprised of two layers of identical materials, each tinted in a different color.

The layers are edited with a one-second delay. Two lines of text from *Desert* (a story by Uri Tzaig) appear on the screen, changing throughout the film, the English line at the center of the frame, the Hebrew line at the bottom. The rhythm of switching is kept consistent (computerized). Due to the difference in the numbers of characters per line in the respective languages, an immediate correspondence in meaning between the lines hardly ever occurs. This also undermines the familiar interrelation between translations, subtitles, picture, etc.

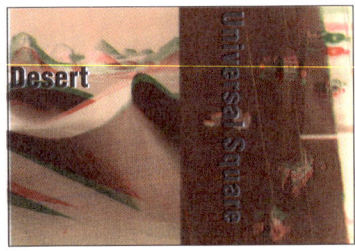

Details: Two color print

Size: 48.2 cm x 68.2 cm

Quantity: 1000 copies

History: Made for screenings held at *documenta X*, 1997, Kassel.

The poster:

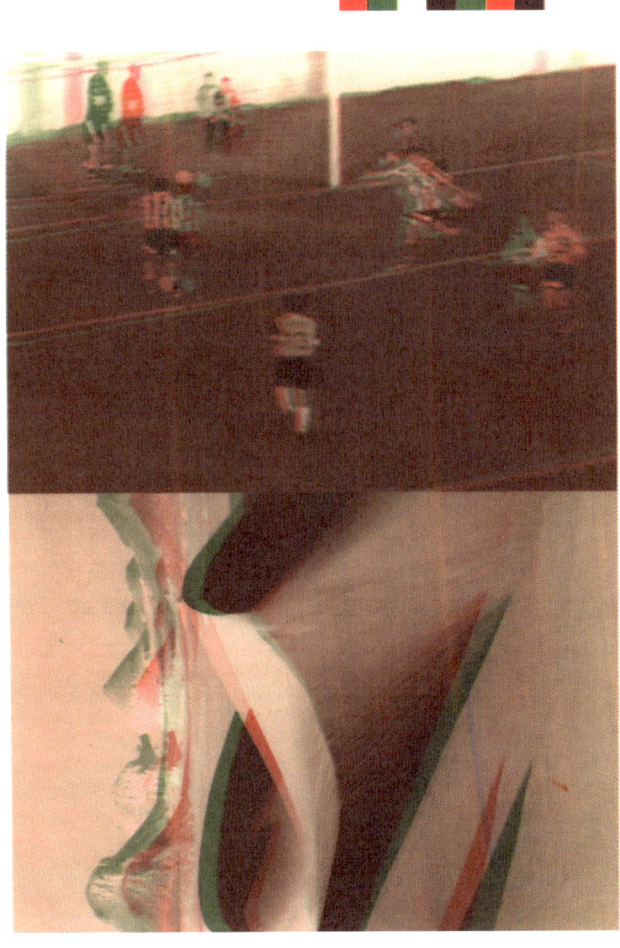

The poster for the joint presentation of the video pieces *Desert* and *The Universal Square* consists of an image of a sandy desert (on the left) and an image of a two-ball soccer game (on the right) printed in two different layers, each in a different color, with a 5 mm shift between them — like the time delay effect underlying the film *Desert*.

Play

Components:
Grass-covered playing field
(the field's boundaries defined by the camera frame)
3 players
2 balls

Rules: Each player goes on court whenever he pleases, "proposing" some kind of game through his action with the ball. The other players are invited to continue this game according to the rules defined by the first player's movements, or else to 'propose' another game.

Duration: As long as the players are interested in the game.

Note: Perfect silence must be kept in order to allow concentration, conversation without words.

History: First played in Nantes, France, July 1996.

Photography: One still camera which automatically determines its location as long as the screen area is grass-green.

Projection :

Title: *Play*

Projection: A sand-blasted glass panel (60 cm x 60 cm) is situated at the edge of a wooden table (60 cm x 160 cm x 80 cm high), on the far side of which is a video projector. The work is presented in an illuminated room. The projection thus mimics the panorama seen through a window overlooking the street.

Trance

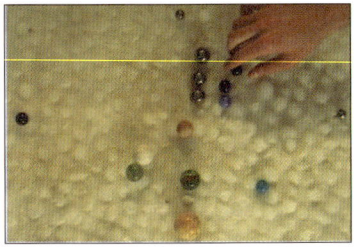

Components:
One specially-cast silicon board
(2 cm x 50 cm x 50 cm)
marbles of different sorts and sizes
(more than 20)
2 players

Rules: Each player selects 10 marbles and places them on the silicon board. The 20 selected marbles can now be used by both players. Each player in turn has to move one marble from its current place to another location on the board.

Duration: As long as the players are interested in the game.

Note: During the game the players take turns and switch strategies. Through the construction and deconstruction of shapes on the board, they expose the patterns underlying their own visual world.

History: First played in Tel Aviv, Israel, April 1998

Photography: One camera perpendicular to the surface.

Projection: Monitor.

Casting of the Game Board:

Title: *Trance*

In order to create a three-dimensional, asymmetrical, gridless board:

Prepare a clay surface, 2.5 cm x 50 cm x 50 cm, embed in it different size marbles and small gravel stones. Remove them when their shape is formed. Cast an equal quantity of silicon into the indented clay surface. The resulting board resembles a relief map or a section of cracked earth, and can also function as a reflexology foot massage carpet.

Components:
Flat court 12 m x 16 m
(proportional to a monitor screen)
2 teams, 5 players each
1 ball
Identical uniform for all players
40 round stickers (10 cm diameter each)
A mechanism that minimizes and maximizes the court area
(laser-outlining; lighting; mechanical or other elastic mechanism).

Rules: The ball has to be passed from hand to hand within the team and remain in constant motion, while preventing it from passing over to the other team.

Duration: Two 15-minute halves.

Note: During the first half of the game, the court contracts at a consistent rate until its dimensions reach 4.5 m x 6 m. During the second half, the court expands to its original dimensions. This game does not include a referee; each player is responsible for keeping score for himself/herself. The game strategy constantly changes in accordance with the changes in the space.

History: First played in Montpellier, France, June 1998.

Photography: One camera, positioned on a higher level, commands an overview. A second camera follows the action on court at eye-level.

Projection: On a white wall, in an dark room.

Video Editing:

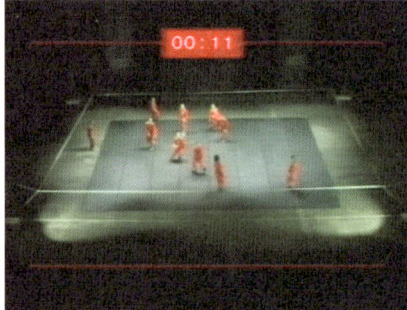 

Title:

In order to translate a game whose essence is movement in space into a medium whose essence is movement in time, the original game duration (30 minutes) is reduced to 20 minutes only. Each shot is 15 seconds long, mostly in fast-forward or slow motion.

The screen layout includes a permanent time display at its center. The video film is shown in a loop — accentuating an endless movement of constriction and release.

Players' marking and scoring system: In order to emphasize the nature of the game as a closed system, operating without the external observation of a referee or an audience, a new system of scoring is devised.

At the beginning of the game each player receives 4 round stickers to put on his/her shirt wherever he/she chooses. The player changes the location of one sticker on his uniform only when he/she is the last player to have touched the ball before it is passed to the other team. In this way, each player 'writes' and 'reads' his/her own story.

Note: No other familiar marking system may be used.

Logo Characterization:

In any characterization of the game, the logo ∞ must be used exclusively.

This logo is composed of a continuous line emphasizing the movement and rhythm, like heart beats or the operation of the lungs. The use of a closed form accentuates the aspect of infinity.

The logo must always appear in red:
process: Magenta 100% Yellow 100%
Pantone: Red Pantone 485

When used in the context of a red text, a black contour line must be added around the logo:

Paint Ball

Materials:
Pastel pigments.

Dimensions: The palm of the hand.

Mode of Preparation: Crumble the available pastels, squeeze and tighten them in the palm of your hand to form a ball.

Applications: May be used in art lessons to enhance abstract thinking, in music lessons to develop music appreciation, or in physical exercise for individuals suffering from motor problems.

Magnet Ball

Materials:
Iron ball and square magnets.

Dimensions: in any preferred size.

Preparation: Attach the magnets to the iron ball, until it becomes a magnet ball.

Applications: All kinds of metal objects, such as keys, pins, nails, etc, can be attached.

Moon-Eye Window

Materials:
Two half-translucent, half-opaque (plastic/glass) balls.

Dimensions: 80 cm in diameter.

Preparation: Roll the window-ball in any desired direction.

Applications: This window provides maximum control over the entry of light into the house from the outside.

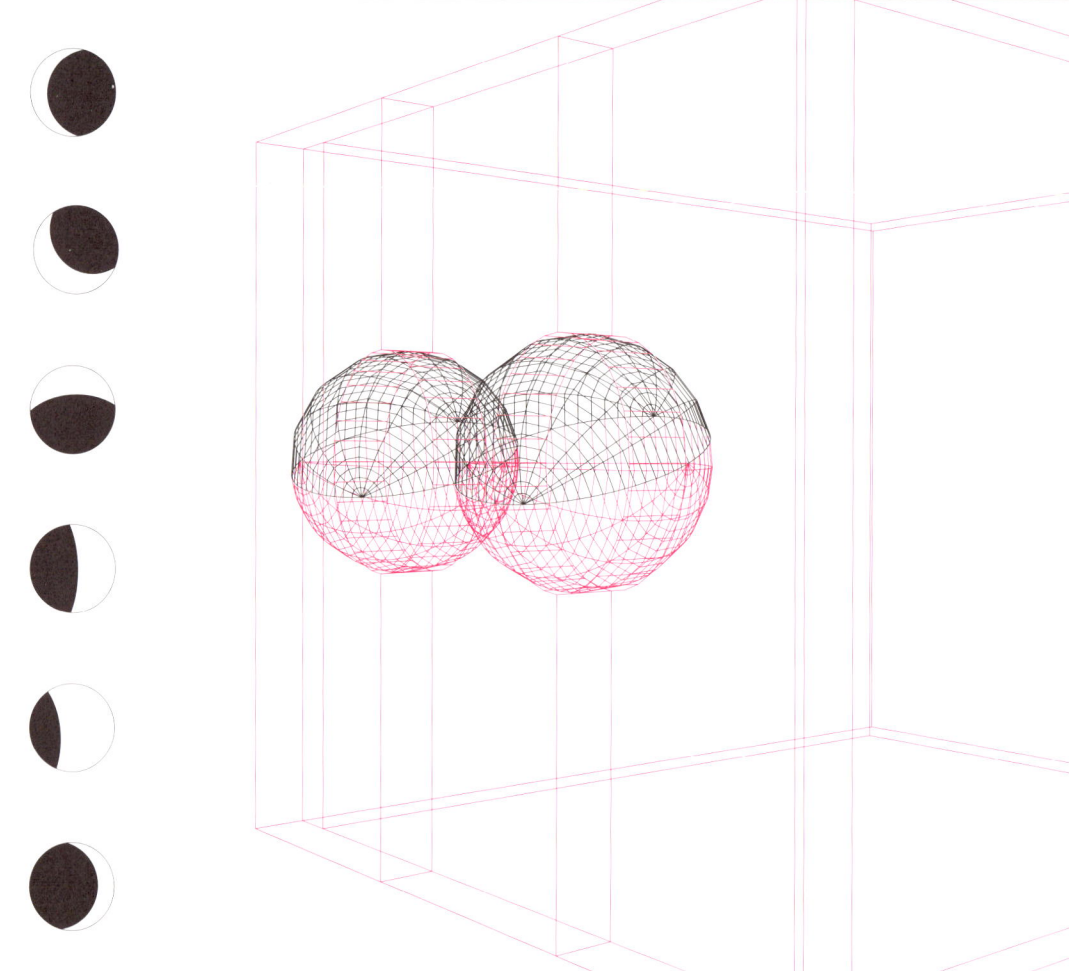

Buffer Ball

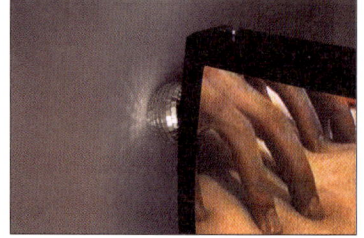

Materials:
Compass
mirror ball.

Applications: Place the compass on one piece of furniture in the room. Move that piece of furniture toward the north according to the compass arrow until it touches the wall. Place the mirror ball at the angle created between the piece of furniture and the wall.

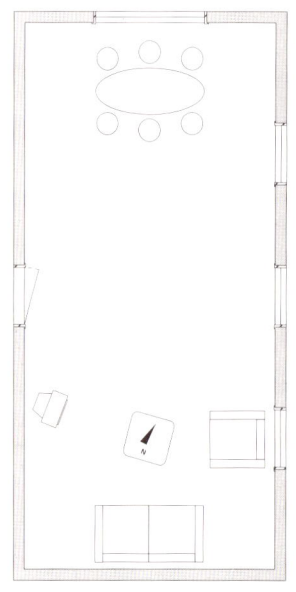 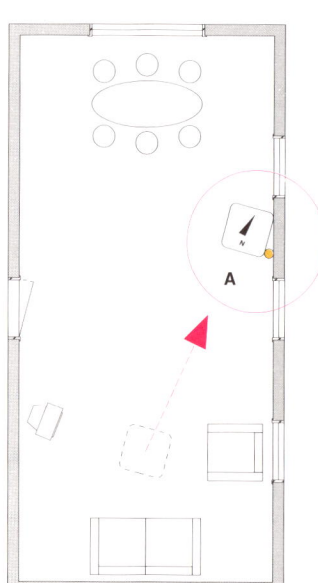 

detail A

Most of the time we play to win. Sports, casino gambling, pachinko, a game of Scrabble, global business. Players, rules a zone of engagement. What would happen if the object of the exercise was not to win but something else entirely?

Could there be a different form of game in which playing itself is the explicit aim, rather than one side vanquishing the other? **Uri Tzaig**'s work is a whole new ballgame, says **Janet Abrams**.

In their recent book, *Mastering the Infinite Game*, economists Charles Hampden-Turner and Fons Trompenaars identify two fundamentally contrasting styles of behaviour in global business, defining them as 'Finite and Infinite Games'. In the former, "who wins and who loses is the whole point of playing in the first place." [1] Aimed at conquest, this is the *modus operandi* in the West. "There is surely another source of improvement, the evolution and improvement of the Game itself," they write, alluding to the strategy of the Infinite Game that prevails in East Asian cultures. "The problem with the Darwinist metaphor is the assumption that the unit of survival is the individual, whereas in the reality of today, rather than the nineteenth century, the unit of survival is the individual-in-the-game-being-played..." [2] Pointing towards a less punitive form of economic competition, Hampden-Turner and Trompenaars explain that "with Infinite Games, losers are not so much eliminated or knocked out of the workplace, but are invited to learn from winners." [3]

Though referring to the probable exhaustion of the West's long-dominant mode of economic behaviour, these observations nevertheless find a curious resonance in the work of the Israeli artist Uri Tzaig. For several years, Tzaig has investigated the fundamental ways in which games — especially team sports — are structured, and how their mass media representation reinforces deep-rooted expectations that every game should have a singular focus, and a single winner.

Tzaig makes objects, texts, videos and installations. But primarily, he works in the medium of the spectacle: he stages live events coordinating real people (professional sports players, or dancers) in real performances of recognised team games. Then he changes the rules, subtly but consummately — not only disrupting the 'normal' game, but calling into question the entire artifice of these ritualised engagements. Whether the game is football, basketball or just a boardgame for two players, Tzaig's 'alterations' to the conventions of playing and spectating reveal the similar motivations underlying all such competitions. He raises issues of 'us versus them' that are perhaps not so surprising, given his experience growing up in a country that is virtually a permanent war-zone.

---

1 Charles Hampden-Turner and Fons Trompenaars, *Mastering the Infinite Game*, Capstone Publishing, 1997, p 30
2 *ibid*. p 33
3 *ibid*. p 34

Tzaig sets out to question the primacy of "the image at the center of the frame, and what is represented to you: the way the TV camera is always focussed on the ball." So, in 1996, he made a work that deliberately sabotaged this normative centrality. In Lod, a poor city with a mixed Arab/Israeli population, Tzaig invited the two main football teams to the stadium, hired a professional TV crew, and two famous TV football commentators (one Arabic, one Israeli, both speaking Hebrew) to cover the game. "I wanted to create a new situation for the citizens of the city, as well as for myself." Billboard posters invited the townspeople to attend for free; the TV crew conferred a certain legitimacy on the endeavor, which was quite normal except in one respect.

The difference? Tzaig gave them not one but *two* footballs to play with. Suddenly the customary angle of vision — the eyes of the TV cameras and spectators focused on a single sphere — could not be sustained. After five minutes, the coaches (who, like the Mayor of Lod, had expressed their disquiet about the artist's enterprise to begin with) told the players to stop the game and divide up into teams, to try to make it more focused. "I wanted to offer them a different kind of focus: more elliptical," says Tzaig. "The only thing that is changed is that there are two balls. You have more chances of striking a goal." The spectators were equally 'thrown' by doubling the object-of-attention: images of the crowd, normally all facing one way, show them all looking in different directions.

From football, Tzaig went on to explore the norms of rugby, arranging a match in Ireland, and a professional TV crew to cover it — again taken as a sign of his 'seriousness' by the powers that be. "I was interested in more physical engagement, because it's very dangerous to take these gestures and translate them only conceptually." But two hours before the game was to start, he was called in to the stadium manager's office, and told that Rugby Union authorities had determined that the long tradition of the game could not be tampered with. Did they think Tzaig was mocking those traditions? "Probably. It's a lot about losing control. It's less about the team and being strategic, and more about being present in time, reacting to whatever is happening at the same moment."

So instead, he staged a basketball game with two basketballs, played by 18 year olds, also held in

"For me it's very important not to direct people in a classical way, not to tell them what to do. But to create situations and to trust them that they will react in a certain way."

"We tend to think we have one enemy in front of us at a time. But actually the enemy is everywhere."

Ireland. Tzaig's video *Desert*, shown at *documenta X* (1997) in Kassel, Germany, is based on this match, and incorporates a visual echo (a delay of one second) between identical layers made in red and in green, so there are apparently four balls in play. The images are accompanied by a text by Tzaig that also appears twice, in English and Hebrew. These languages flow in opposite directions (Hebrew is read from right to left) and take up different letterspace to say the same thing, so there is a deliberate disjuncture between any two portions of the narrative appearing on screen at one time.

Whereas, for many artists, the city is the touchstone of their work, for Tzaig (who lived in Tzde Boker, in the Negev desert, for several years) "the desert is a context." Indeed, the video's title is even more loaded: the Hebrew word for desert, *midbar*, comes from the same three-letter root (*DaBaR*) as does the word for object/speech, *dibur*; the desert is also where The Text (the *Torah*) was given to the Jewish people. "It was very important for me to bring Hebrew to *documenta*," Tzaig reflects. "As I see it, the historical basis of what we call art today is Christianity, which is connected to the basis of capitalism. For people raised in that culture, it's very natural, but not for people like myself who grew up with different traditions and ideas about architecture, language, iconography and spirituality."

Tzaig works on the idea of play from many angles, including a series of projects in which the ball is the subject — reconceived in different materials and hence endowed with different properties (see his User's Guide on pages 225-236). Tzaig's *Paint Ball*, composed of crushed crayons, yields its pigments randomly, defeating any attempt to 'color in' an area within an outline. A tool for "listening to your internal reality," it also offers release from other constrictions. "When you use a pen, you work mostly from the hand, but because the *Paint Ball* is so big, you use much more shoulder-movement." The *Magnet Ball*, at first glance a ferocious-looking creature, armored and not unlike a grenade, is actually more benign: it attracts and gathers metal items encountered in its path — tracing a hypothetical journey through a ferrous pasture, as if a football could simultaneously mow the grass it rolls across. Both the *Moon Window* and the *Compass Ball* are explorations of the ball as figure, within the domestic realm.

In *Trance*, a boardgame, Tzaig throws another curve-ball: cast in silicon from the impressions of small stones, the board's surface is convex and bears no grid or marking system. What kind of a game can be played on such a board? Certainly not one of point-scoring and one-sided victory. "Mainly it's about meditation," says Tzaig, who performed this game with his assistant over a 30-minute period, with a camera tracking their moves. The 'rules' are wilfully indeterminate: in silence, each player takes turns moving a marble from any place to any other, for as long as it engages them to do so. "After a few minutes you forget which is *your* marble. You're only interested in the image. Sometimes it becomes like the stars, sometimes it creates a picture. You really feel your own aesthetic structure — because you have this tendency to create compositions."

The fixed dimensions of the playing field also come in for questioning in Tzaig's 1998 work, ∞, in which the size of the court contracts to nearly a third of its original dimensions during the first half, and then expands back during the second half. The players monitor their own 'score' within this fluctuating zone of engagement by relocating one of four circular stickers on their uniform, when they are the last to have handled the ball before surrendering it to the opposite team. These moveable discs semaphore the score as a completely arbitrary pattern on mobile bodies, as if the pixels of a dot-matrix scoreboard had somehow fallen off the Jumbotron and peppered the players.

First played in Montpellier, France, in June 1998, with ten dancers and no referee, ∞, is an exercise in improvised team-play. "For me it's very important not to direct people in a classical way, not to tell them what to do, but to create situations and trust that they will react in a certain way." Sceptics often ask, 'isn't it chaotic?' But Tzaig isn't concerned. He's content to set these aleatory contests in motion, not as part of the action, but as their progenitor on the sidelines.

"In the war zone, we tend to think we have one enemy in front of us at a time," he reflects. "But actually the enemy is everywhere. It could be the weight of your equipment, or the missiles from above. It could be that you pee from fear, and it really itches. Or it could just be the dark."

For Tzaig, the rules of engagement and linear demarcations of the ritualized battlefields of sport are mere social conventions, serving to focus the gaze on a single item of concern, perhaps as a comforting distraction from the multiple alternative points of view that might otherwise also have to be considered. The idea that there is *one* thing on which our attention should be trained is revealed as a convenient but deluded construct. In the infinite game, the outcome is no longer so straightforwardly 'winner-takes-all'.

For the past three years, a diverse group of designers and design critics has converged each Labor Day Weekend on a turn-of-the-century boat-house in the northern Adirondacks, in upstate New York. Co-founded by industrial designer **Don Carr** and *If/Then* editor **Janet Abrams**, the Long Lake Design Camp is a laboratory in which the emerging links between architecture, product design, graphics and interaction design are explored through individual presentations and campfire discussions. When the proceedings threaten to get too lofty, the participants take a quick dip in Long Lake, balance on the Bongo Board, or go for a spin on an inner-tube tethered to Don's speedboat. In September 1998, anticipating *Doors of Perception 5*, the topic of play was addressed in a conversation framed around 'Toys versus Tools'. This hypothetical distinction quickly became a roller-coaster ride through improvisation, ingenuity, gambling, doodling and the addictive power of fun. Edited and photographed by Janet Abrams.

Long Lake III
Toys vs Tools

Janet Abrams
Let's start with some questions we've used to structure the *Doors* conference. In design we tend to think of play as limited to the times and tools of childhood. Can there be playtime again for adults, other than mindless entertainment? What is the relationship between play, learning, education and media? How do you differentiate between a toy and a tool in your particular world of practice?

Gong Szeto
I started thinking about the relationship between tools and toys in conversations with Sawad Brooks, who wrote his art history dissertation on Matisse's attitude toward his drawing and painting instruments, and the range of interfaces between mind, body and surface that enable us to make marks.

There's a famous photograph of Matisse in his later years, painting on a canvas from five feet away, because he was very far-sighted, so he built a number of extensions to his paintbrushes. His painting got much looser as he got older, perhaps because of his eyesight and the behaviour of his elongated paintbrush.

Commercial tools like Adobe Photoshop and Illustrator use algorithms to simulate things we previously did with our hands — that had to be translated into the digital environment and then translated back. Which came first: the need to manipulate photography precede Photoshop, or the algorithms that came out of university image-processing labs? At i/o360, we've been rethinking some common software applications: our *Parasite* project attempts to imbue email with a more playful notion of reading and writing.[1]

In his book *The Hand*, Frank Wilson asserts that we learn much more with our hands, perceptually and cognitively, than we give credit to.[2] It's very primal to manipulate things with our hands. How much of that ability have we lost since infancy? How much has simply been displaced? Is it alive and well, but sleeping?

Janet
Malcolm, you talk specifically about hand-eye coordination in your book.[3] Would you like to pick up on this?

Malcolm McCullough
Take any object, put it slightly out of your reach and see what it seems like to you. Then put it within your reach and see if it hasn't changed somehow.

The capacity to act on things really informs our take on them. We see a lot we need not act upon. But when things are within our reach, quite often we take them up. Once you're holding something, it presents possibilities. That creates a certain continuum between work and play. Hands are playful. They don't like to do anything the same way each time. If I take ten packages to UPS, I'll write the zip code on nine of them, because I get bored, or I'll put it in a different place on each one because my hands get tired.

Musicians know best how the hand tends to grab hold of things a little bit differently each time. There's a chapter about this in *Ways Of The Hand* by the jazz musician David Sudnow, whom I cite extensively.[3]

Sigi Moeslinger
One key factor about toys is that they provide some sort of pleasure. Tools always require a certain amount of skill: some are easy to learn, like scissors, but with others, you need to reach a certain level of mastery to get pleasure from it. You know it well enough to subvert it. Subversion of a tool is often what makes it into a toy.

Janet
What makes a toy pleasuresome?

Sigi
Once you know a tool well enough that it becomes second nature to you, there's a lightness about it that opens up the realm of pleasure.

Peter Girardi
I always marvel at programmers, who have incredible mastery. Whatever problem you throw at them — even if they have to make the tool, or make it do something it doesn't want to do — they can still figure it out. Musicians and programmers are so unthreatened that essentially there *are* no problems for them any more. Or if there are, they're just that much more fun.

Malcolm
Play is an acting-out of conditions without risk in preparation for doing it for real later, *with* risk. If there's always an opportunity to 'Undo' or 'Save As', does that compromise the committed, risky nature of involvement in the art form?

Peter
I am the hugest abuser of 'Save As'. I'm always saying, "Oh, let's see... maybe I want to go back to this one," and I end up with 60 documents or so.

Janet
What do you do with them?

Peter
Throw 59 of them out.

Masamichi Udagawa
A switch in attitude is what makes something a tool or a toy. I remember as a child at primary school imagining a wooden triangle as a wing, or as a jet fighter. But when I had some rudimentary mathematics assignment, it was a tool. I don't really buy the argument that a tool is difficult and once it's mastered it becomes a toy. What about surfing? It takes a lifetime's commit-

> Take any object, put it slightly out of your reach and see what it seems like to you. Then put it within your reach and see if it hasn't changed somehow. The capacity to act on things really informs our take on them.

---

1 see Marek Kohn's article on *Parasite*, pp 70-71
2 Frank R. Wilson, *The Hand, How Its Use Shapes the Brain, Language and Human Culture*, Pantheon, New York, 1998.
3 Malcolm McCullough, *Abstracting Craft: The Practiced Digital Hand*, MIT Press 1996. See the excerpt, *Discovery in Digital Craft*, on pages 132-139.

ment to become a good surfer, and requires incredible mastery, but it has no function whatsoever. Is it a tool, or play-acting? Again, I remember from my childhood, when I got bored I flipped my tricycle upside-down, and it became an ice-cream maker.

Peter
I did the same exact thing! An ice-cream maker!

Don Carr
Separated at birth!

Masamichi
So point-of-view is everything.

Sigi
I think you're mixing up 'game' and 'play'. Surfing is more of a game.

Masamichi
Surfing is not a game. 'Game' means rules.

Andrea Moed
Can you have a game with yourself?

Masamichi
Sure, but you have to set the rules for yourself.

Don
Play is a strong motivator, especially when it comes to learning. So Play is a tool, in a sense. I am intrigued by the spectrum of very abstract tools to which young children associate meaning. A stick can be ten things and it's still a stick, as opposed to, say, transformers. There's a German toy manufacturer thirty miles from Syracuse called Habermas — because there's a good selection of hardwoods in Upstate New York — and they talk about 'play-value'. They sell to schools; they would never go after the 'Happy Meal' market. Habermas blocks have almost infinite play-value:

a child's authorship of what they can be is so open-ended.

Julie
Play is really about a lack of self-consciousness and self-absorption. That's why we admire it so much in children, though they develop self-consciousness at quite a young age. The opposite of play isn't work; it's grief, which is about total self-involvement. The contrast between work and play comes down to what is produced through those activities. Play can produce all sorts of things that last, but we think of it as an end in itself.

Bonnie Schwartz
That links to a distinction I've been making in my notes just now. I want my toys to be very simple, obvious, and to give me feedback. And I want to keep them. Whereas tools I don't necessarily want to keep; I want to buy new ones as I get better at using them, so they help mark my progress. I think the new i-Mac computer is an interesting example of something that's both a toy and a tool. You want it because it's so cute. Yet it's really a tool. Actually, I can't think of many things that straddle those two worlds so well.

Julie
How about language? Few of us speak for the sheer joy of hearing the sound of the words, though we certainly see that in children. Language is there for a purpose, for communication, but there certainly is that link. The way you move your tongue when you write has to do with the connection between tools and language.

Andrea
As a toy, language seems almost inevitably a social thing. It's difficult (although certainly possible) to make yourself laugh in writing, to hear yourself. That play with abstraction — with

what's unseen and unfelt — can only be recognized among a group.

Bonnie
Are you talking about a fantasy like *Let's play house?*

Andrea
I'm thinking about a something like simple game of *Ghost,* where you're spelling a word collaboratively, or you're describing things whose resonances only get played out when other people hear them. Whereas building something — creating a material juxtaposition of things — produces an artifact that you yourself can look at.

Lisa Waltuch
When I was working at Kodak, we installed something called 'Cyber-Mirrors' at Universal Studios in Florida, in a waiting area preceding an attraction. To us it was definitely a tool. To the people who interacted with it, it was a toy. You entered the room, which had lights and music going, and saw all these monitors, called 'makeup mirrors', that distorted your image. There were also ceiling-mounted monitors, so people could see each other's faces, all weirded out, on opposite sides of the room. The software engineers made programs that could do real-time distortion with two-way mirrors. People clumped around the monitors, individually or in groups, laughing, trying to get their image in, even videoing the feedback. There were huge crowds even when the real attraction wasn't happening. Our goal was to create a location-based entertainment with a social component — and this really did that. People were reacting to images of each other, and of strangers.

Andrea
Even if you yourself aren't playing, that witnessing is also important.

Janet Abrams is editor of *If/Then*, based at the Netherlands Design Institute, Amsterdam, and co-founder of the Long Lake Design Camp.

Don Carr is associate professor and program coordinator of the Industrial Design program at Syracuse University, and partner in Carr & Lamb Design, Syracuse. Don was a senior consultant at NCR Corporation from 1992-1995.

Peter Girardi is a founder-partner of Funny Garbage interactive design studio, New York. He was previously at the Voyager Company, where he created CD-ROMs including *MAUS, The Beat Experience, Body Voyage,* and *Painters Painting.*

Lisa
In fact there were people who didn't have enough 'clown' in them, who stood back and watched their friends playing, and just snickered to themselves. The project certainly divided active participants from the passive.

Janet
Bonnie, I was surprised that you would want to grow out of your tools. The expectation, rather, might be that you would want to grow out of your toys.

Bonnie
I like new toys too! Still, I don't regard the equipment associated with the hobbies I've had as toys, but as tools. I want to feel worthy of the next pair of skis that will help me get to the next level, or a new dressage saddle that has less padding and is closer to the horse — more beautiful, more handcrafted. So there's a progression reflected in the implement. With toys, that's less important, to me anyway.

Malcolm
That canoe over there is neither a tool nor a toy, but that paddle is. If you were a Mohawk or François Indian living up here and using the canoe out of necessity, you could be completely absorbed, unselfconscious and yet not at play if you were in a hurry to get somewhere before a storm front came through. But if you were a New Yorker visiting for the weekend, you might be at play. In either case, you would probably paddle with a variation to your strokes just for the fun of it, or to rest your muscles and dance with the water. So there's work *and* play in that paddle, because you're bodily involved. Whereas the canoe is carrying you. It is a piece of technology, to get something done. But you're not guiding it. You're guiding the paddle.

We get in a lot of trouble in the high-tech business thinking that anything that serves a purpose is a tool. The problem is that we get metaphorical confusion in interface design: things that do not actually enact or guide manually are treated as tools. The confusion of tool and medium, and of tool and process, muddies our appreciation of things that really *are* more tool-like, and makes the whole thing just seem like a computer.

Bonnie
I don't know if I agree. Most objects we interact with are tools in some way.

Malcolm
Does there have to be physical interaction to make something a tool or a toy?

Masamichi
Christianity was a tool, but it was just a certain set of rules and beliefs. So it doesn't need to be physical at all.

Andrea
I can't imagine anything with a sense of autonomy — like a city, which has such complexity and lack of predictability, because it results from so many variables — being a tool.

Malcolm
It's useful to distinguish a tool from a medium (not that there's a cut-and-dried distinction). And from a machine. And from a setting — like a studio.

Andrea
Is the distinction between things you use to act *with* and the set of external things that act *upon* you? The Canoe and the Paddle example made me think about tools and toys as empowering extensions of oneself. In some computer-driven interactive environments the aim, it seems, is to make you feel supernatural, to take your imagination two steps beyond where you would practically want it to be as a tool. A tool makes you more powerful. A toy makes you *way* more powerful. It helps you escape.

Malcolm
And neither of them does anything when you're not looking. The thing I hear most often from architects about computers is, 'Oh, it's just a tool'. Meaning, it won't do things you don't want it to do — won't even color your expression, the way a medium would.

Lisa
It won't do something *for* you. You have to have inspiration to put *into* it.

Janet
A tool is something that has been honed to accomplish a very specific task in a particular way. It narrows down the application such that you play purposefully and to great effect. Whereas a toy requires that you add to it — a good toy, anyway.

Don
Industrial designer Alexander Manu would say it's hard to beat the ball.

Bonnie
Don, you said before that play is a tool. What did you mean by that?

Don
I was thinking in terms of learning. To paraphrase a quote from Montaigne, it 'sugar-coats the cup'.

Gong
Where does the word 'instrument' fit into this? Is it a subset of 'tool'?

Malcolm
An instrument can be configured, it can be used to measure things...

Don
What about 'professional toys', like apparatus or equipment?

Julie Lasky is editor-in-chief of *Interiors* magazine, in New York. She was previously Managing Editor of *Print* magazine, New York, and held a National Arts Journalism Fellowship in 1995-1996.

Malcolm McCullough, architect and 1998-99 Fitz-Gibbon Visiting Professor at Carnegie-Mellon University in Pittsburgh, is author of *Abstracting Craft: The Practiced Digital Hand* (MIT 1996).

Sigi Moeslinger is a founding partner of Antenna Design, New York. She was previously an Interval Research Fellow at New York University's ITP program and a designer at IDEO San Francisco.

Gong
I'm really fascinated with the word 'instrument' because it's in the middle of that oscillation. Take the way a musical instrument is played. A virtuoso's relationship to their instrument isn't just that they're playing it, but they've taken it to a certain level of precision and accomplishment. Precision maps well to operations and techniques. Then I think of surgery and surgical operation. Then I'm back to surgical instruments. So there's this oscillation…

Malcolm
In the physical tradition of the tool, there is a spectrum between force and finesse. You can brute force something or you can finesse it. This is something that's often missing on a computer keyboard. You can't gradually substitute finesse for force by being more practiced at it. The learning is different. It's more a sequence or code or set of reflexes. When you're zooming in and out on Netscape, you aren't thinking that your hands have learned to do this. There is no touch to it. Your attack on the keys doesn't matter at all. It matters that you don't have to use your mind to remember those keys.

Peter
Oh, I would totally disagree. There is *total* finesse in the way one can subvert certain illustration programs. But it's not a matter of the tactile: it's about knowing the limits of a certain application, and saying, 'Well, these two motions aren't supposed to go together, but if I put them together I get this result'. That's where the finesse lies: in thinking-past what the programmers wanted the application to do. It's in the manoeuvre.

Lisa
You can also set different constraints, that allow more control of detail.

Bonnie
But wouldn't it be more fun to use those programs if there were some interesting physical interaction with those instruments?

Peter
I don't look at it that way. Right now I have my production flow to where I'm really happy with it. I know what I really like to do outside the machine, and what I really like to do on it. I've got the balance together, so I can be really productive.

Malcolm
How many people would really want force-feedback on their mouse when the cursor went over the edge of a window?

Peter
People are always asking me, 'Why don't you use the tablet? You're a drawing guy'. I hate that thing — the feeling and sensitivity of it, and its mapping of metaphors…

Bonnie
But if it felt good, you'd want to use it…

Peter
Sure. But my head is not in that place with the box, with the computer.

Gong
I think you adapt to certain nuances. I was banging on Peter's machine once, and it felt *bad*. [*LAUGHTER*] It wasn't mine. But in the end, I couldn't really quantify what it was…

Peter
When it's somebody else's machine, they have their icons laid out in a certain place and they've set the speed the windows open and the sensitivity of the mouse. It's like, 'How do you get any work done with this thing?'

Malcolm
It's like cooking in someone else's kitchen.

Gong
What is the role of improvisation in this discussion? We're often called upon to improvise when we're problem-solving, in work-mode. If you don't have the full luxury of conditions at your disposal, you navigate the in-between.

Peter
If you're improvising without knowing all the rules, aren't you just playing badly?

Bonnie
Is improvising the same as intuiting?

Gong
I don't know. I watched Itzhak Perlman performing recently. After a virtuoso hour-and-a-half of impeccable works, he did an encore. His assistant brought out this cardboard box full of sheet music, and he just dug around, pulled one out, turned it upside-down and played it.

Janet
There's a saying about the New Orleans jazz marching bands, that if a fly lands on the sheet music, they can play that too!

Gong
But why did Perlman do that? To provide relief from the strictness of the hour-and-a-half? As if to say, 'I gave you the rational part of my art. Here's the emotive part — but it's still me and I'm still using the same instrument'. The encore was almost as long as the performance, and the audience behaved in a very different way. They were relieved. There was this lightness all of a sudden, as if watching him perform in the first half was working, and the second half was play.

Bonnie Schwartz is senior editor at *I.D. Magazine* in New York. Before joining *I.D.*, she wrote for *Metropolis* and other New York-based architecture and design publications.

Gong Szeto is vice president for design at io360/RareMedium, in New York. He teaches in the interactive design program at Parson's School of Design, New York.

Masamichi Udagawa is a founding partner in Antenna Design, where he is leading the design of new trains for New York City's subway system. He previously worked at IDEO and Apple.

Andrea
He's relying upon the evanescence of what he's doing to say, 'indulge me. I'm going to play with these sounds, and it's not going to have consequence'. Or long-term consequence.

Malcolm
In that sense, we can compare improvisation to composition. Composition has a score, a specific symbolic notation manipulated according to a learned body of principles. Picture Alberti tweaking the proportions of an elevation. Composition is deliberative, and composition closes. It's often easier to ask '*When* is Design?' than '*What* is design?' The former is when you can only do one more thing. Or, as Alberti said, when there's nothing more to take away and nothing more to add. Composition is deliberative, whereas improvisation is the opposite of that in so many ways. But it has to have a structure. You're absolutely right to improvise without rules.

Bonnie
Gong and I went to the Henry Miller Library in Big Sur recently, and I was telling him about the Beat Generation writers, who really turned literature on its head, made it into something intuitive and playful but — in so doing — developed a really serious literature. You have to have a very close relationship with your discipline to be able to be intuitive about it, or maybe improvisational. I'm not sure they're equal.

Peter
Intuition gets you to where you're comfortable enough to improvise.

Janet
Maybe the problem we have as grown-ups is that we're too self-conscious to get to the point of intuition just by improvising.

Peter
You have to be vigilant and let yourself improvise. That's the biggest lesson I learned from Gary Panter, the artist.

Lisa
Intuition implies a certain knowledge base, that you've worked long enough in an arena to be able to make very educated decisions. To me, improvisation implies fantasy, going in one direction. When you mention improvisation, the first thing I think of is 'improv' theater. There is a fabulous improv group I used to go see all the time in San Francisco, six people. I know they have their own internal rules because I've seen them often enough to see the patterns emerge. Some people are just expert at improvisation, and others aren't. There's expertise in improvisation, and novice improvisation.

Julie
I think improvisation is making do with what you have, so the more you know, the better you can improvise. It also has to do with process and a degree of uncertainty about the end-product.

Gong
I've been really fixated on MacGyver recently. I used him in a slide talk recently: he's the patron saint of Web design, because there's a lot of jerry-rigging in Web design, finding loopholes and hacks and things like that. MacGyver's someone who could defuse a bomb with a paper clip and his shoelaces.

Janet
Could you tell me more about this character? Is he like Houdini?

Gong
He's from an '80s TV series, a government agent. But he's a pacifist. His whole thing is, 'I won't use a gun'. He goes on these missions and gets into these super-dangerous situations. He'd be trapped in the airport baggage room and how does he get out? He finds the stitching on a suitcase, then grabs a bunch of them and creates this amazing super-tensile rope. Then he'd say, 'Oh, there's a coat-hanger, and I happen to know the exact spacing of the wall studs', and then attach it to the conveyor belt, and all of a sudden he would rip this hole into the wall and escape! But not with bombs or guns or anything; just what he had at his disposal. It presumes this incredible insight into the nature of things.

Lisa
Like you said, he knows the spacing of the studs in the wall.

Gong
Tools are also very designed objects. The industrial designers in this room probably have more insight into tool design. But in MacGyver's case, there were no tools. He was probably subverting things, but he also looked at materials for what they were. I'm sure he wasn't thinking about the coefficient of elasticity in a paper clip at the time. But he has that deep knowledge.

Janet
Why don't we hear from our two resident product designers on this?

Don
We were talking a moment ago about getting on someone else's computer. Similarly, when you pick up your grandfather's hammer, something unfamiliar is transmitted to you. I think this speaks to the very American concept of ingenuity. I have real trouble distinguishing what is a tool and what is a toy. Beautiful tools speak of their function. It's hard to critique them as anything other than they present themselves — that is, as pure functionalism.

Lisa Waltuch is creative director for the Metropolitan Museum of Art's Web site, at Nicholson NY. She previously worked at Kodak Imagination Works and Silicon Graphics.

Andrea Moed writes on design and new media, for *Metropolis* and other publications. She entered New York University's Interactive Telecommunications Program in autumn 1998.

Janet
When you're designing a product like the ATM that we talked about earlier today, how do you know the right amount of play to build in for the user?

Don
Well, the stainless steel enclosures I designed for many years for NCR Corporation were about surviving in the urban context. Those devices look like a tank because they have to perform like a tank — let's face it! I once did an ATM for a place called Incredible Universe, which was pure toy: all about fantasy, about putting your card in and having your expectations totally changed. Any time you're on the street and you turn your back to the world and ask for money, there's instant fear. So these are the issues being played out when you design these products.

Janet
How do you alleviate that fear? Is the interface meant to be this the moment of soft, cartoon-like seduction that helps you forget you're actually in a vulnerable position?

Don
Right. But if so many people are being attacked using these machines, maybe it's wrong to put across the perception that there's gaming involved. The machine could say 'I'll give you a hundred dollars, but I could also sell you a Lotto ticket, so how would you like to play for $5 and maybe win $300?' But combining the game with the serious transaction might be giving out mixed messages.

Lisa
Silicon Gaming in Palo Alto is doing the next generation of slot machines, all video-supported. They decided to keep the handle on screen, even though it isn't needed, because people like it — it's such a convention. They tested a poker game in Las Vegas, using a hand to deal, and it's been hugely successful. Rather than having bitmapped numbers and cards come up on the screen, people love seeing this magical white-gloved hand come out and play the cards.

Malcolm
There are dangers of deadly verisimilitude, if you take it too far, though. Would they also like to have virtual parking outside before they go into the building to play the game?

Lisa
That would prolong the experience. You just want to get there and play. I think it's an issue of delight, which is a crucial component in play. Yes, you're gambling. Yes, it's a vice. Yes, you may be losing tons of money. But there is something delightful about it.

Malcolm
There is something very simian about gambling. Any time I've been around it, I always have the same feeling: 'Yeah, this is something monkeys would do'. Which is not pejorative. It's the sense that there's play. We can see ourselves playing and making fun of ourselves and being less serious than we might.

Janet
In gambling specifically?

Malcolm
In games and in the rhythms of pulling the handle, playing the cards...

Julie
Gambling is different. It's power over chance.

Lisa
Gambling is also hope. That you'll win the lottery.

Janet
It's manufactured emotion. In his book *Gargantua,* Julian Stallabrass gets into the links between computer games and gambling, and the trance-like hypnotic state they both induce — the repetitive strain, you could say, of doing a few gestures repeatedly — which is maybe where monkeys rather than humans come in.[4]

Andrea
There is great literalism to gambling. In the course of this game, you see your fortunes rise and fall quite literally in counters — something you'd have to look across your whole life to see. When you see the physical interplay arising from what you do, there is an element of delight, whether you're winning or losing. I can see why people can be addicted to gambling even if they keep losing.

Lisa
We did some research at the University of Newcastle on what compels people to keep playing and whether, if you got rewards based on winning, that could improve your performance as an incentive to continue. One person suggested that, as you got up to a certain point spread, maybe you could get a shot of oxygen which would literally enhance your performance, making you more alert or quicker with your reflexes. It was an interesting physiological possibility.

Malcolm
They say a cat can find its way around a neighborhood, but it can't see itself finding its way around a neighbourhood. (Sounds like something Wittgenstein would have said.) We can see ourselves playing, and we like that.

Janet
What is delight?

Play is really about a lack of self-consciousness and self-absorption. That's why we admire it so much in children, though they develop self-consciousness at quite a young age. The opposite of play isn't work. It's grief, which is about total self-involvement.

4 Julian Stallabrass, 'Just Gaming', in *Gargantua*, Verso, 1996, pp 84-112.

Bonnie
Isn't it the opposite of play being unselfconscious?

Malcolm
It is, now that you've mentioned it.

Bonnie
Maybe once you achieve a certain skill level, it's not play any more. One of the ways I like to play is when I don't really know how to do something. Like that Bongo Board.[5] It's fun to play with because I don't know how to do it. But if I got so good that I was a competitive Bongo Boarder, I don't know if it would be so much fun.

Malcolm
When Shakespeare was writing a play, he had a play within the play, so you would remember you were watching.

Gong
Where do professional actors fit in?

Bonnie
They're professionals, so it's their work. The difference between work and play, to me, is that you have to work but you don't have to play.

Lisa
I know a lot of photographers who refuse to take pictures unless they are paid for them. You go on vacation with them, and they won't take pictures. They say, 'Well, that's work for me'.

Andrea
There's this mythology in our culture, particularly regarding Hollywood actors. When they're interviewed, they say, 'My life is perfect: my work is play. It could never get any better than this'. It always disturbs me that the pinnacle is there's no separation.

Janet
Why does that disturb you?

Andrea
I can't imagine being happy that way! [*LAUGHTER*].

Janet
Well, we'll keep your nose to the grindstone, in that case, Ms Moed! I was going to pick up on the paradox you addressed, Malcolm. If what you're doing when you're gambling is consciously realizing that you're playing, then maybe the pleasure of it is the recollection of the time when you *just* played, without being conscious of it. In other words, childhood play. I'm talking about a time when you didn't know there was such a thing as play, and specifically the difference between play and work.

Malcolm
That fits with the definition of addiction. Looking for all the right things in all the wrong places.

Janet
Well, addiction usually has to do with something that happened to you pretty early, doesn't it?

Bonnie
But isn't it also expectation-related? Something about playing has to do with being a novice and allowing yourself to fail. Whereas in work situations, you can't do that. Isn't part of the fun of new challenges a fear of failure?

Janet
Part of the *fun*?

Malcolm
That's that risk element.

Lisa
You can define motivation by fear of failure or the happiness of success. It's a personal viewpoint, what's inside of you, what motivates you.

Don
Which is directly tied to gambling. One of my first students was an avid bicyclist. We talked about monitoring the body in physical sports, and about hitting the wall and getting the endorphin rush. Could that be not just predicted, but monitored? Could you actually wear enough sensors on your body to match your heart rate to gauge this thing, so you knew, 'if I peddle my butt off for another two minutes, I will actually hit the endorphin rush and get my reward?'

Janet
Don't you have to randomize it to increase as you get better?

Don
Sure. And we could track it. So in the end we named this piece, *Are We Having Fun Yet?*

Janet
One of the slogans we've been thinking of using for *Doors 5* T-shirts is *What made you think PLAY was fun?*

Bonnie
Uh-oh! That makes me not want to go.

Malcolm
How about *Play: It's Not What You Think*?

Janet
That's good.

Peter
Or *It's Not Just For Kids Any More*?

Malcolm
No. Just *It's Not What You Think*. This 'not-for-kids' thing, though, is something quite striking that's come out of this conversation. Your assertion, Jan — that adult play is largely a self-conscious revisitation of childhood play — resolves the contradiction I had raised.

I'd leap off the end of our picnic table and deploy the umbrella, and for a brief millisecond, I was floating. Any work or play where, for a brief second, you get to that feeling — that's what I'm always looking for.

---

5 A 1950s-1960s American toy: a spruce plank and cylinder that one attempts to balance on; skilled Bongo Boarders can move sideways, seesaw-style, across a room.

Andrea
It definitely de-idealises play to think about it that way. We tend to think about the purposefulness of play and education in reference to children, but we aren't so self-conscious about the developmental value of our own play, usually. It can be difficult.

Bonnie
You know, Jan, when I found out you guys were doing a conference on Play, I thought, "oh, what a task!" Here you are, having to graft onto this spontaneous event, the exact opposite of play: schedule, deliberation.

Janet
It's perhaps more paradoxical this year than in previous *Doors*, when the theme was something else. Even though conferences are, ideally, opportunities for spontaneous connections to be made between people, any event of this sort takes a good deal of deliberation. We're just ramping up the pressure, by making Play the topic. This year's theme emerged without much effort. It was ripe. It had an immediate richness of possibility, though in a very short time it also became quite contentious...

Bonnie
So it became work?

Janet
Yes, because it is such a capacious subject. The conference could have been called 'Learning' for a while, but there was an impetus that it should also be about games — electronic as well as non-electronic — asking what lessons from them can be applied to formal education environments.

To end, I'd like a quick round-robin of answers on the following questions: Is there a game or activity from your own childhood that you find yourself returning to in your work?

Andrea
I'm fidgeting. I fidget.

Janet
Is that a game?

Andrea
Yes: how long can you prolong the fidgeting before you have to do work?

Sigi
I still often play a version of this game, Daisy: 'He loves me, he loves me not'. But applied to other things. If something falls one way, then it means this and this. If it falls the other way, then it has another impact. I frequently use it to attribute the outcome of something that couldn't be predicted at first, or not to any extent.

Janet
Is that like tossing a coin maybe?

Sigi
Yeah, but a bit more complicated.

Malcolm
Anything with landscape memory, often involving moving symbols around on maps. Wayfinding in the forest. Bushwhack.

Julie
I have rediscovered Solitaire on the computer, and it has been the curse of my working life. I try to keep justifying it by coming up with metaphors for why this is important — what I'm learning about randomness. I mean, when I was talking about power over fate, that was personal. It's really shocking how many games of Solitaire I've played since January. It's pathetic.

Lisa
They say Clinton plays Solitaire during meetings, and the whole Cabinet will be there, and he'll be really concentrating on the cards. It drives his staff crazy, because they'll see a move that's so obvious, and they're not supposed to interrupt him. It shows his incredible focus of attention, which channels into whatever issues they're discussing. There was an article in the *New York Times* on this.

Julie
I curse the person who made this program for making the Alert sound come on whenever you reshuffle the cards.

Lisa
You can turn off the sound.

Julie
Tell me how to do it! Because when I'm on the phone, people say, 'Oh, you just got e-mail?' At the same time, I find it diverts whatever nervous energy I have, and I listen very well while I play Solitaire and I win more games.

Peter
I've always been an incessant doodler. It translates to everything. When I'm designing on the box, the best it gets is when I shut off and I'm doodling. That's when it's really play.

Janet
Is doodling different than fidgeting?

Peter
I didn't say it was. I bite my nails, too, so I get the best of both worlds!

Malcolm
You never get kipple from doodling?

Peter
It's a very fine line when doodling is kipple and when it's something you're actually going to use.

Masamichi
I have a bad habit of fantasising things.

Peter Girardi takes notes

Gong
Daydreaming?

Janet
Did you ever make things? Were there props you would...?

Masamichi
That's the bad part. I don't make things out of my fantasising. Or maybe that's a good thing.

Lisa
Matching. I don't know if you guys remember the Gr'animals.

Peter
This has become a real a pop culture festival: the Gr'animals and MacGyver together!

Lisa
Gr'animals was a brand of mix'n'match children's clothing. I used to like combining things that were similar, but now that I'm a professional, I try and go against it! As a kid, I matched and made things more.

Bonnie
I liked to play Scrabble when I was a kid, and still do. Juggling around letters to form words helps me write headlines and coverlines, helps me get used to making intuitive leaps. The words you use for Scrabble don't necessarily mean anything; they just have to give you lots of points.
   I found the playground really stressful as a child, so I think that's why I reacted to your conference the way I did. It sounds to me like a playground, where I'm going to have to go into a corral and be forced to play.

Peter
Nobody likes institutionalised fun. It sucks.

Bonnie
Yeah. And also the social aspect of the playground felt stressful to me.

Don
Growing up, we had an extremely long picnic table which I would run across at full speed with an umbrella. I'd leap off the end and deploy the umbrella, and for a brief millisecond, I was floating. Kind of like when I jumped off that rock last night. Any work or play where, for a brief second, you get to that feeling — however long you can prolong it — that's what I'm always looking for. I'm usually finding ways to get there, whatever the work is.

Bonnie
What about you, Jan?

Janet
I had a very active imaginary family when I was about four years old. They all had names, and I played with them, particularly in the garden, where I was very involved in cooking, using mud and plants. These days, I am usually 'cooking' my articles in my head while doing household activities, particularly chopping vegetables.

Bonnie
There is something very interesting about the physical connection, for you, of cooking...

Janet
It's about a focus with my hands, using tools. I used to play the piano, and I think that it's very difficult for me to get out of the verbal mode, so making something which uses the arms, the hands, the shoulders, is a way of releasing. I find yoga does this as well.

Lisa
I was a gymnast all my life, and when I'm stuck on a design problem, I'll stand on my hands or walk around a little bit. I used to think maybe it's because all the blood is rushing to my head, giving me more ideas. But I think it's just the physical act.

Janet
It's muscle memory.

Peter
Nobody uses drugs any more? [LAUGHTER] I wasn't joking, really.

Lisa
Just Spring Mountain Water and yoga and exercise!

Janet
Well, shall we repair to some play?

Bonnie
No, it's work!

When Hollywood actors are interviewed, they say, 'My life is perfect: my work is play. It could never get any better than this'. It always disturbs me that the pinnacle is there's no separation. I can't imagine being happy that way.

Finger on the Button

Ine Poppe talks to **Bas Ording**, recent graduate of Utrecht School of the Arts' interaction design programme, who has just been hand-picked by Steve Jobs to join Apple Computer's Human Interface Group.

"There are all kinds of things that irritate me when I use the computer," says Bas Ording, a rather unassuming, averagely-dressed young man. "You can see the way the screen is built up: a computer window is really just a rectangle with a series of buttons. It makes changing the image unnecessarily disruptive and looks amateurish. I find that annoying. And it doesn't feel nice."

A 1997 graduate of the Interaction Design course at the Hogeschool voor de Kunsten Utrecht (HKU), Ording, now 25, has strong opinions about the dynamics of the user interface. "It's not just about clicking a mouse, it's about details and the feel of the interface for the user. I want tactile, dynamic interaction. The tools I use are limited, but that isn't a problem. I explore and try to create an organic design. But pure graphic design isn't a priority for me. It's got to feel right." He makes a comparison: "If a chair isn't comfortable, it's useless — however cool it looks."

Three years ago, Ording went on a tour of several Silicon Valley firms with his HKU teacher, Dick Rijken.

SLIT THE TRASH CAN RECONCEIVED © BAS ORDING, 1998

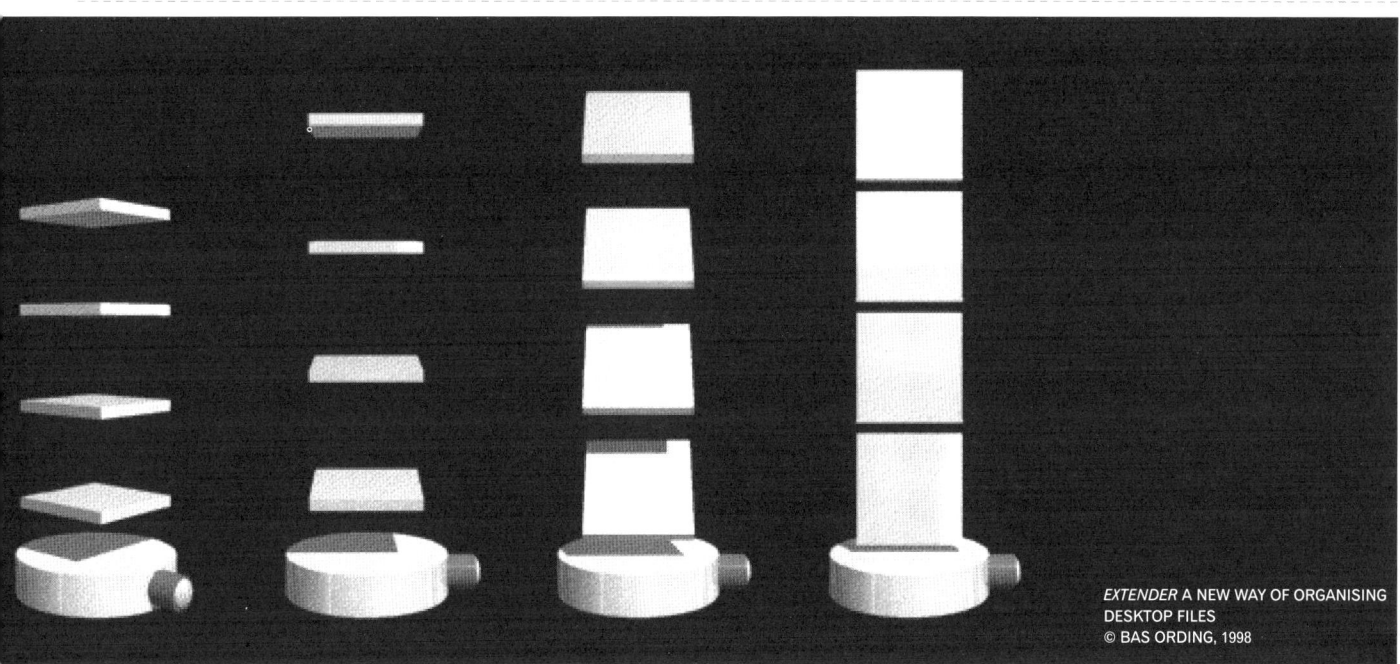

EXTENDER A NEW WAY OF ORGANISING DESKTOP FILES
© BAS ORDING, 1998

Having worked for several multi-media companies in the Netherlands (on projects such as visual database representations, shockwave games for the web, and CD-ROMs), Ording retraced his steps in the U.S. last June, visiting Adobe, MetaCreations, and Apple Computer. His CD-ROM portfolio was impressive enough to gain him interviews with Kai Krause of Meta-Creations, and Steve Jobs, Apple's CEO.

On the CD-ROM, an image scroll bar appears on the right of the screen, offering a choice of his designs.

One of Ording's ideas is a playful update of the trash can: a horizontal groove into which icons or folders may be dragged. Carved in the grey surface of the screen, and softly shadowed to give it seductive three-dimensionality, this slit recalls the incised canvases of artist Lucio Fontana (1899-1968). By touching the groove with the mouse, a string of icons shoots out like a tongue. "Jobs liked that," says Ording, with characteristic understatement.

Ording prefers buttons that have a certain tempo and a particular way of moving, giving an 'organic touch' — almost rubbery in some cases — when you click the mouse. "There are so many kinds of buttons. I started toying with the idea and experimenting with 3D programs out of curiosity, as a kind of hobby. It could all be so much more fun than it is now!"

In Ording's universe, icons float in groups and scatter when you select one, or enlarge under a moveable magnifying glass; windows fold out and get thrown backwards and forwards; text alternately conceals and reveals itself; objects can be arranged next to rather than over each other; folders spin in carousels. It was on the strength of this work that he was invited to join Apple Computer's Human Interface Group, where he started in September 1998.

"Apple focuses on quality. I like that," says Ording. "I feel a certain loyalty towards the company and want to help Apple survive. Because in the end, working with computers is about what the user feels and experiences."

GO/TO

I
Esprit Long Term Research http://www.cordis.lu/esprit/home.html
i3net http://www.i3net.org

Getting On! 1
Society for Old and New Media http://www.waag.org
KPN-Telecom http://www.kpn-telecom.nl
British Telecom http://www.bt.com
Landmark Design http://www.landmark.nl

Getting On! 2
Therefore Design http://www.therefore.co.uk
Philips Design http://www.-eu.design.philips.com

Getting On! 3
Rabobank, The Netherlands http://www.rabobank.nl
NCR Knowledge Lab http://www.knowledgelab.com
Cap Gemini http://www.capgemini.com

Demi Dubbel
http://www.waag.org/demidubbel
Producer: Caroline Nevejan; project manager: Lara Ankersmit; executive producer: Ine Poppe; programmers: Antoine van de Ven and Walter Hop; script: Leendert van Veldhuizen; educational supervision: Fons Cornelissen, Mirjam Vosmeer, Peter Dekkers, Maaike Zurcher, Ietje van Poll

Pauline Thinks It Over
Baby Think It Over, Inc http://www.btio.com

Bricks with Brains
Lego Group http://www.LEGO.com

Knowledge Maps
Dynamic Diagrams http://dynamicdiagrams.com
Perspecta http://www.perspecta.com
i/o360 Digital Design/Rare Medium http://www.raremedium.com

Anatomy Lessons
Shu Lea Cheang shulea@earthlink.net
Society for Old and New Media http://www.waag.org
Guggenheim Museum http://www.guggenheim.org
http://brandon.guggenheim.org

Strange Enough Already
San Francisco Museum of Modern Art http://www.sfmoma.org

Virtual Platform
http://www.dds.nl/~virtplat
De Balie http://www.dds.nl/~balie
Paradiso http://www.paradiso.nl
Society for Old and New Media http://www.waag.org
Netherlands Design Institute http://www.design-inst.nl
V2 Organisatie http://www.v2.nl
Montevideo/TBA http://www.montevideo.nl
STEIM http://www.xs4all.nl/~steim
Media-GN, Centre for Emergent Media http://www.media-gn.nl
Interfaculty for Image and Sound, Royal Conservatory
http://www.koncon.nl/220/BGmain.html

Finger On The Button
Bas Ording ording@apple.com

Melting Media
International Film Festival Rotterdam January 27-February 7 1999
http://www.iffrotterdam.nl

Lara Joins The Corps
Krisztina de Châtel dance group http://www.dechatel.nl
Lara and Change performed in the Netherlands October 21 1998 - January 29 1999
dechatel@xs4all.nl

CONTRIBUTORS

Paul Auster
is a poet, novelist and screenwriter, living in Brooklyn, New York. Born in Newark, he graduated from Columbia University and worked as a merchant sea man on an Esso oil tanker. He then lived in France from 1971-1974 before returning to New York to begin his writing career. Having produced mainly poetry and essays in the 1970s, he concentrated on prose in the 1980s. Among his publications are *The New York Trilogy* (1987), *In The Country of Last Things* (1988), *The Music of Chance* (1991), *Mr Vertigo* (1994), *Smoke* and *Blue in The Face* (screenplays, 1996), and *The Art of Hunger* (1998) all published by Faber and Faber.

Jeroen Barendse
<lust@lust.nl> studied graphic design at the Arnhem Institute for the Arts, and worked for a year as a freelance designer before founding the two-person design studio LUST <http://www.lust.nl> with Thomas Castro in The Hague in 1996. Dividing their time between commissioned projects and LUST projects, their work has been featured in *Emigre* and *Eye* magazines and was also included in *Do Normal*, the 1998 exhibition at San Francisco Museum of Modern Art. Since 1998, Barendse has been attending Karel Martens' Werkplaats Typografie (Typography Workplace) in Arnhem.

Pauline Bax
<pbmax@netlinq.nl> is a freelance journalist currently based in Amsterdam. She has written for various Dutch periodicals. Her recent features include a story on the video game industry for *HP/De Tijd* and a report on Internet Service Providers in Mali, Africa, for *Onze Wereld*. In 1996, she was the first foreign intern to work at *Harper's Magazine*, New York.

Pierre Bismuth
is an artist, born in Paris in 1963, now living and working in Brussels. He has had solo exhibitions at the Lisson Gallery, London, Witte de With, Rotterdam, Kunsthalle, Vienna, and The Showroom, London. His work has been in many group exhibitions including *Wish You Were Here* at De Appel 1996, Amsterdam, *French Art* at The Cartier Foundation 1997, Paris and *Speed* at The Whitechapel Gallery 1998, London.

Matilda Blyth
<Matilda.Blyth@brunel.ac.uk> has spent eight years researching the social and cultural aspects of technological change. She is currently working with BT's research laboratories, analysing the production and consumption of interactive technology for the home, and is a doctoral student at the Centre for Innovation, Culture and Technology (CRICT) at Brunel University in the UK. She undertook the initial programme research for *Doors of Perception 5: Play*.

Cathy Brickwood
<cathy@design-inst.nl> graduated in modern languages from the University of Bristol in 1989 and pursued a career in publishing (London), teaching (Cairo) and translating before taking a Master's degree in contemporary European cultural theory at the University of Southampton. She currently divides her working week between the Virtual Platform, of which she is coordinator, and the Boekman Foundation, where she is developing a European centre for cultural policy information. She writes for the Foundation's journal, *Boekmancahier*, and reviews publications for its website.

Sawad Brooks
<sawad@utensil.net> and Beth Stryker <bes@infohouse.com> presented their web-based project *DissemiNETion* September 1998 in *body mechanique* at the Wexner Center for the Arts in Columbus, Ohio. Stryker and Brooks have collaborated on several previous installation and web site projects, including *mo/nu/ment* (Channel/-ARTEC, England, 1997), *Invertigo*, with Christa Erickson (Banff Centre for the Arts, Alberta, 1997), *Radarweb* (Tokyo Atopic Site, 1996) and *Bowling Alley*, with Erickson and Shu Lea Cheang (Walker Art Center, Minneapolis, 1995). They both live and work in New York, where Brooks recently founded Utensil, a software design company <http://www.utensil.net>.

Max Bruinsma
<maxb@xs4all.nl> is editor of *Eye*, the London-based international review of graphic design. Resident in Amsterdam, he studied architecture and art history in Groningen and Amsterdam. His critical writings have featured regularly in major Dutch art and design journals and in a range of international design magazines. He has published books on graphic design in the Netherlands and collaborated on two international compilations of new media design, *Multimedia Graphics* (1996), and *Website Graphics* (1997). A guest lecturer at numerous art academies in Europe and the United States, he was for many years a music editor for VPRO, the Dutch radio and television broadcasting organisation.

Susan Delson
<sd29@is2.nyu.edu> is a writer and museum media consultant in New York City. She is a faculty member in the Museum Studies Department at New York University, and former film and video programmer at The Metropolitan Museum of Art.

Dick van Dijk
<dick@design-inst.nl> is project manager at the Netherlands Design Institute, with particular responsibility for the Connectivity programme (focusing on interactive media and the Internet). In 1998 he served as Executive Producer for *Doors of Perception 5: Play*. Until 1996, he was policy assistant at the Dutch Ministry of Economic Affairs. He graduated from Tilburg University with a degree in business economics, specializing in marketing and market research.

Rineke Dijkstra
studied photography at the Gerrit Rietveld Academie in Amsterdam from 1981 to 1986. She travelled through America, England, Poland and Belgium to produce her beach portraits (1992), candid shots of individual bathers at the water's edge. In 1996 she photographed street-children in Ghana for Unicef, and the following year her work was shown at the Museum of Modern Art as part of its *New Photography* series. Her recent video-portraits of teenagers at schools and nightclubs in England and the Netherlands — *The Buzz Club, Mystery World* — have been shown at various venues, including the Stedelijk Museum, Amsterdam.

Yuri Engelhardt
<yuri@wins.uva.nl> found during his years in medical school that he was less interested in the endless verbal information in his textbooks than in figuring out how to make the subject-matter understandable visually. In 1993, after diverse jobs in the medical field, he went back to school to study cognitive psychology and graphic design. He is currently a Ph.D. student at the University of Amsterdam, conducting research on the 'visual grammar' of information graphics. He is founder/editor of the *InfoDesign* online mailing list <InfoDesign@wins.uva.nl> and in his spare time practises rollerblading backwards.

Hannah Ford
<h.ford@vam.ac.uk> completed her M.A. in the Victoria & Albert Museum/ Royal College of Art History of Design program in 1998, after working in publishing for five years. During her postgraduate studies she began teaching at Surrey Institute of Design and Ravensbourne College of Design and Communication. She previously worked for the National Trust at 2 Willow Road, London (the former home of Modernist architect, Ernö Goldfinger), conserving 20th century objects, giving lecture tours and working as locum custodian.

Danny Goldberg
<goldberg@dds.nl> graduated from the Bezalel Academy of Fine Arts and Design in Jerusalem, with a B.A. (with honours) in graphic design, and was awarded the International Sandberg Award for excellence in typographic design, both in 1994. A senior creative director at Yarom Vardimon's design studio from 1996-97, he teaches design and typography at the Shenkar Academy of Textile Technology & Fashion and at the Bezalel Academy. Since 1994 he has specialised in typography and corporate identity for a wide variety of clients. He now lives and works in Amsterdam.

Paul Groot
is an art critic, based in Amsterdam. He publishes books and CD-ROMs, organises art shows and writes for art magazines all round the world, including *Mediamatic*, of which he is an editor. He has worked with choreographer Krizstina de Châtel on the scenario for dance performances including the 1998 production *Lara*, based on Lara Croft, heroine of the computer game *Tomb Raider*.

Peter Hall
<PeterHall@aol.com> is senior writer at *I.D. Magazine* in New York and editor of the recently-published *Tibor Kalman: Perverse Optimist* (Booth Clibborn Editions/-Princeton Architectural Press, 1998). He has previously written on subjects vaguely related to the Brandon theme, including a feature for *I.D. Magazine* about the Anatomical Travelogue, an early commercial adaptation of the National Library of Medicine's Visible Human Project; and a profile of digital designer John Maeda for *Print* magazine. He plays bass guitar in a New York 'Latin Lounge' band known as The Moonrats.

Bart Hendriks
graduated in 1997 from the Rietveld Academie, Amsterdam, and is now a student at the post-graduate Rijksacademie, where he is working on a new book of his photographs, *I Guess You're Beautiful*, due to be published in 1999.

J. C. Herz
<mischief@interport.net> is the author of *Joystick Nation*, Little Brown, US/ Abacus, UK), a pop social history of videogames and their impact on popular culture. She writes a weekly column, 'Game Theory', about digital entertainment for the *New York Times 'Circuits' Section* <http://www.nytimes.com/library/tech/reference/indexgametheory.html> and has published articles in *Rolling Stone*, *GQ*, and the *New York Observer*.

Alan Kay is Disney Fellow and Vice President of Research and Development, The Walt Disney Company. He is best known for the concepts of personal computing and for inventing the overlapping-window interface and modern object-oriented programming. A founder of Xerox PARC, Kay led one of the groups there that developed these ideas into modern workstations (and the forerunners of the Macintosh), Smalltalk, desktop publishing, the Ethernet, laser printing, and network 'client-servers'. He holds undergraduate degrees in mathematics and molecular biology from the University of Colorado, and a doctorate from the University of Utah, where he was a member of the ARPA research team that developed 3-D graphics. A Fellow of the American Academy of Arts and Sciences and the Royal Society of Arts, his honors include the ACM Software Systems Award and the J-D Warnier Prix D'Informatique. A former professional jazz guitarist, composer, and theatrical designer, he is now an amateur classical pipe organist.

J.J. King <jamie@jamie.com> is a freelance writer and academic working out of Shoreditch, London. Editor of Metamute <http://www.metamute.com> and co-reviews editor of Mute magazine, Jamie is currently completing a doctoral thesis examining the role of frontier discourse in the creation and operation of the Internet. He amuses himself by constructing febrile theories about schlock science fiction films and trying to set up an electronic music studio. Jamie is always working on his sci-fi systems novel, The Resolution.

Max Kisman <maxk@sirius.com> studied graphic design, illustration and animation at the Academy for Art and Industry in Enschede and the Gerrit Rietveld Academie in Amsterdam. In the 1980s he pioneered the use of digital technology in graphic design in posters for Amsterdam's Paradiso concert hall, and co-founded the alternative typography magazine TYP/Typografisch Papier. For many years associated with the Amsterdam graphic design collective Wild Plakken, he moved to San Francisco, in 1996. His designs for typefaces and Web sites (including for VPRO-digital and HotWired) have been published worldwide <http:www.sirius.com/~maxk>.

Marek Kohn <marek.kohn@mcr1.poptel.org.uk> studied neurobiology at Sussex University and began his journalistic career writing for The Face, moving on to magazines and newspapers such as the New Statesman and The Independent. He continues to contribute 'Technofile', a weekly feature on digital culture, to The Independent on Sunday. Kohn is the author of two books on drugs and their social meaning, Narcomania: On Heroin (Faber, 1987), and Dope Girls: The Birth of the British Drug Underground (Lawrence & Wishart, 1992). Over the past five years, he has been trying to work out new ways of writing about science for a general readership. The first book resulting from this effort was The Race Gallery: The Return of Racial Science (Cape, 1995); the second will be As We Know It: Coming to Terms with an Evolved Mind (Granta, 1999).

Sharon Lockhart is a photographer and filmmaker based in Los Angeles. Her latest film, Goshogaoka, about a Japanese girls' junior high school basketball team, was selected for the 1998 New Directors/New Films season presented by the Museum of Modern Art and the Film Society of Lincoln Center, New York, and also screened at the Rotterdam and Sundance film festivals. Her photographs have been selected for many group shows, most recently at the ICA, London, Walker Art Center, Minneapolis, Los Angeles County Museum of Art, and the Whitney Biennale 1997. A solo show of her work will open at the Museum Boymans van Beuningen in Rotterdam in December 1999.

Nico Macdonald <nico@spy.co.uk> has been helping design studios and publishing clients to use digital technology for ten years — initially in the United States, then in the UK, through his consultancy, Spy <www.spy.co.uk>. He also consults and writes on the emerging discipline of Web/interaction design. His first DataButler was a Microwriter Agenda, with its as-yet unsurpassed 'chording' keyboard. He went into overdraft to purchase an Apple Newton the day it was launched in the UK and has since been upgrading past its demise, not having found a suitable replacement. His partner uses a Palm Pilot and they have two eMates as house pets.

Noortje Marres <n.s.marres@mail1.remote.uva.nl> is studying toward an M.A. in Philosophy of Science and Technology at the University of Amsterdam, having previously studied at the New School for Social Research, New York. She is currently participating in the Debate Mapping project Geographies, a collaboration between the University of Amsterdam and the Royal College of Art, London. She writes about the public reception of globalising technologies, focusing on environmental and space technology. Her articles have appeared in Discorsi, Cimedart and Mediamatic.

Jules Marshall <jules@xs4all.nl> is a freelance writer and multimedia designer whose work on technology and culture has appeared in magazines such as Wired, Mediamatic, The Hollywood Reporter, i-D, Time Out, and the Web sites of the Netherlands Design Institute and the International Film Festival Rotterdam. He was co-organiser of the first Doors of Perception conference and editor/meta-designer of its award-winning eponymous CD-ROM. He was an electronic democracy consultant for Ponton Media Lab (Hanover, Germany) and is currently editor-in-chief of the HotGuide to Amsterdam <http://www.amstel.nl>

Malcolm McCullough <mmm3@andrew.cmu.edu> is the 1998-1999 Fitz-Gibbon visiting professor in architecture at Carnegie Mellon University, Pittsburgh. In his most recent book, Abstracting Craft: The Practiced Digital Hand (MIT Press 1996), he explored tacit knowledge in digital form-giving. Currently he is at work on a book about place perception in the digital age. Active in new media for over fifteen years, and a member of the Harvard Graduate School of Design faculty for ten years, he has served as a product manager with Autodesk and has been a visitor-in-residence at Xerox PARC.

Jeremy Millar <jeremy@photonet.org.uk> is an artist and Programme Organiser at The Photographers' Gallery, London. He has written for numerous publications and is the editor (with Steve Bode) of Airport (1997). He is co-editor, with Michiel Schwarz, of Speed - Visions of an Accelerated Age, which accompanied three exhibitions on the same theme that he curated in 1998 at the Whitechapel Art Gallery, The Photographers' Gallery London, and (with Nancy Campbell) at the Macdonald Stewart Art Centre, Ontario, Canada.

Andrea Moed <andrea@panix.com> writes about design and technology for Metropolis and other print and online publications. She has worked for Edwin Schlossberg Incorporated, and has consulted to several new media companies. Based in Brooklyn, New York, she is currently a graduate student in the Interactive Telecommunications Program at New York University.

Maureen Mooren and Daniël van der Velden <eap@geocities.com> are graphic designers. They both graduated in 1996 from the Rotterdam Academy of Art and Design. From 1996 to early 1998, Maureen worked in New York for design studios such as 2x4 and Bureau; in the same period, Daniel completed his studies at the Jan van Eyck Akademie in Maastricht. In 1998 they established a collaborative design studio in Amsterdam, working on both commissioned and self-initiated projects.

Ine Poppe <poppy@dds.nl> writes about Internet culture for the NRC-Handelsblad, <http://www.nrc.nl> <http://www.nrc.nl/W2/Lab/Netkunst/inhoud.html> and for numerous online magazines including <http://www.idg.nl>. She created the Website Women with Beards <http://www.dds.nl/%7Ebeards> and the documentary Gantenbein, about the catastrophic consequences of brain surgery <http://www.nrc.nl/W2/Nieuws/1997/10/14/Rtv/02.html>. With Christine Karman she has produced educational 3D environments <http://channels.reed-elsevier.com/ScienceRTW/ElsevierScience/docs/d8040901.htm> and she was executive producer for the educational MOO, Demi Dubbel. She is assisted in her digital work by her son Zoroaster Feigl <http://huizen.dds.nl/%7Ezoro>

David Rinella is a New York Photographer. He was assistant to fashion photographer Mark Hom for four years, and since 1997 has been working independently, for magazines including Mirabella, Glamour and Details.

Martijn Sandberg <martijnsandberg@hotmail.com> is an artist living and working in Amsterdam. He studied at the Academy of Fine Arts Utrecht and the Rijksakademie Amsterdam. His work has been exhibited in various locations in Holland and in Germany. He is currently producing metallic typographic wallpapers for a public art-piece in Amsterdam.

Ineke Schwartz <ischwa@xs4all.nl> writes about art, architecture, design and new media for de Volkskrant (The Netherlands' largest-circulation quality newspaper), Archis, Elsevier and several other magazines. She is currently editor of a non-linear (online) documentary and a new TV series DNW (The New World), both for the Dutch television company VPRO.

Michiel Schwarz <michiel@design-inst.nl> is an independent researcher and consultant on technological culture based in Amsterdam. He co-programmed Doors of Perception 4: Speed in 1996, and was a member of the programme team for Doors of *Perception 5: Play* in 1998, both organised by the Netherlands Design Institute, where he is senior advisor. Schwarz holds a Ph.D. in the sociology of technology. His books include *The Technological Culture* (edited with Rein Jansma, 1989) and *Speed - Visions of an Accelerated Age* (edited with Jeremy Millar, and co-published by the Netherlands Design Institute, 1998).

John Thackara <thack@design-inst.nl> is director of the Netherlands Design Institute in Amsterdam. An expert on design, innovation and new media, he is a consultant on design and innovation to governments, cities, associations and companies; a member of expert groups advising the European Commission; chairman of the European Design Industry Summit; and chairman of the *Doors of Perception* conferences.

Uri Tzaig <uritzaig@hotmail.com> is an artist based in Tel Aviv, Israel. He graduated in 1990 from the School of Visual Theatre in Jerusalem, with a major in theatre direction, design and playwriting. Within the last five years his work has been featured in group exhibitions at the Museum Boymans van Beuningen, the Jewish Museum, New York, Jack Tilton Gallery, New York, Venice Biennale, *documenta X*, Kassel, and the University Art Museum, Berkeley, California, among others. His recent solo projects include the video and sound installation *Tempo* at De Vleeshal, Middelburg, Holland, and a dance/video installation at Ateliers du FRAC, Montpellier, France.

Kristian Waagner <thewag@earthlink.net> is a photographer who recently moved to New York. Born in Germany, his fashion photography has appeared in magazines including German *Elle* and *Cosmopolitan*.

Alex Wilkie <a.wilkie@rca.ac.uk> is currently studying toward an M.A. in Computer Related Design at the Royal College of Art, London, having previously attended Chelsea College Art and Design. He was the video games researcher for *Doors of Perception 5: Play*. His prototype gravity-browser *Kooker* is being developed as part of the *Geographies* Debate-Mapping project, a collaboration between the University of Amsterdam and the RCA.

Femke Wolting <femke@vpro.nl> graduated from the School of Journalism in Tilburg in 1991, and in Film and Television Studies from the University of Amsterdam in 1994. She is curator of the *Exploding Cinema* section of the International Film Festival Rotterdam and a staff member at VPRO-Digital, which researches the effects of communication technology on the production, distribution and consumption of media. Femke is editor-in-chief of *Lifesavers*, the VPRO website in which innovative interactive programmes are created by a new generation of media artists.

Eric Zimmerman <eric@flat.com> is co-founder and Product Development Director at Flat Inc. <http://www.flat.com>, a New York company focusing on multiplayer games and artificial life technology. He previously worked as Senior Game Designer at R/GA Interactive where he directed the CD-ROM game *Gearheads*. An Adjunct Professor at New York University's Interactive Telecommunications Program, Eric's first boardgame will be published in January 1999 by Flesh Eating Technologies, a project of Semiotext(e) Press and Banff Center for the Arts.

EDITORIAL TEAM

Janet Abrams <jan@design-inst.nl> is editor of *If/Then*. A London-born writer and producer of events on design, new media and urbanism, she was based in the U.S. for much of the past fifteen years before joining the Netherlands Design Institute in early 1998. Recent projects include *Doors of Perception 5: Play* (programme team); *Jambalaya*, the American Institute of Graphic Arts' 1997 National Design Conference (programme director); *DIALogue* at Cooper Union, New York; and *Long Lake Design Camp* 1996-98. Writer-at-Large for *I.D. Magazine* from 1994-96, and editor of *Rethinking Design: MEDIUM* (1997), her writings have appeared in numerous publications. She holds a B.Sc. from London University, and a Ph.D. in Architectural History (1989) from Princeton University, where she was a Fulbright Scholar.

Julia van Mourik <julia@design-inst.nl> is assistant editor of *If/Then*. In her 'spare time' she is completing her M.A. degree in Publicity & Culture at the Hogeschool van Amsterdam, and writes on literature and youth culture. She co-produced the *Kunstbende*, a national arts game for teenagers, and produced/directed *Stem-in*, a documentary for NIVON Jeugd en Jongeren. She has previously worked as publicist for the film *Antonia*, for Bergen, the television, film and theater production company, in Amsterdam.

Mevis & Van Deursen <105273.2713@compuserve.com> are art directors of *If/Then*. From their studio in Amsterdam, Armand Mevis and Linda van Deursen have made catalogues for the Stedelijk Museum Amsterdam, posters for the Muziektheater and stamps for the Dutch post (KPN). Their work has been published in *Eye*, *Emigre*, *Typography Now*, *The Graphic Edge* and was selected for the 1998 *I.D. Forty*. They have been exhibited in Holland, France, Japan, Germany and the United States. They have lectured and conducted workshops at educational institutions throughout Holland, Austria, France, the UK and the United States. Both are instructors, respectively at the Jan van Eyck Akademie in Maastricht, and the Gerrit Rietveld Academie, Amsterdam.

Editor
: Janet Abrams

Assistant Editor
: Julia van Mourik

Art Direction
: Mevis & Van Deursen

Printing
: Veenman drukkers, Ede

Binding
: Boekbinderij Epping

ISBN 90-72007-52-2

© the authors and the Netherlands Design Institute, Amsterdam, 1999

http://www.ifthen.org
info@ifthen.org

Cover Photograph
: Rineke Dijkstra
Alexandra Bradley/Tomb Raider, 1998

Co-Publisher
: Netherlands Design Institute
Keizersgracht 609
1017 DS Amsterdam
The Netherlands
T +31 20 551 6500
F +31 20 620 1031
http://www.design-inst.nl

Co-Publisher
Sales and Distribution:
The Netherlands and Europe
: BIS Publishers
Nw Spiegelgracht 36
1017 DG Amsterdam
The Netherlands
T +31 20 620 5171
F +31 20 627 9251
http://www.bispublishers.nl

Distribution: North America, South America and Asia
: D.A.P. Inc. Distributed Art Publishers
155 Avenue of the Americas, 2nd Floor
10013-1507 New York N.Y., U.S.
T +1 212 627 1955
F +1 212 627 9484

Special Thanks to
All our *medewerkers* at the Netherlands Design Institute, especially John Thackara, director; Dick van Dijk, co-producer, *Getting On!* and executive producer, *Doors of Perception 5: Play*; Erna Theys, project coördinator, *Knowledge Maps* and *Getting On!*; Mariëtte Overschie for solidarity on the 'late shift'.
Nynke Venema for proofreading.
Sammy Herman for translations.
Ted Panken and Margo van Mourik for transcriptions.
Carl Goodman for computer games expertise.
Christina Lorentz for boardgames photographs.
Paul, Mark and Leo, DEPT.
Masja Ros, Caulfield & Tensing.
Department of Education, Jewish Theological Seminary, New York, for permission to publish Alan Kay's lecture.
Vicki Harris, Laurence Miller Gallery, New York.
Dagny Pennewitz, Kunstmuseum, Wolfsburg.
Jan Mot, Gallery Mot & Van den Boogaard, Brussels.
Rebekka Ladewig, Gallery Neugerriemschneider, Berlin.

Alana Cowan, Marc Hacker, Nick Hornig and Lisa Waltuch for 'holding the fort' in New York.
Don Carr and Liza Lamb for hosting the Long Lake Design Camp three years running.
Anne Burdick and Kristi van Riet for some essential introductions.
Bart Ten Rel.
Misha de Ridder.